THE SEXUAL GERRYMANDER

Women and the Economics of Power

Jocelynne A. Scutt

SPINIFEX

Spinifex Press Pty Ltd,
504 Queensberry Street,
North Melbourne, Vic. 3051
Australia

First published by Spinifex Press, 1994

Typeset in 11/14 pt Times
    by Claire Warren, Melbourne
Printed in Australia by The Law Printer
Cover illustration by Sonia Kretschmar
Cover design by The Letterbox

National Library of Australia
Cataloguing-in-Publication entry:
CIP
Scutt, Jocelynne A., 1947–
    The sexual gerrymander.

    ISBN 1 875559 16 7.

    1. Feminism. 2. Sex discrimination
    against women. I. Title.

305.42

Contents

PART I: The Herstory of History

PART II: Violence

PART III: Up from Under

Acknowledgements

I am grateful, in the publishing of *The Sexual Gerrymander*, to those many conference, workshop and public meeting organisers who requested that I give a speech or write a paper, or accepted a proposal that one be written. Making speeches and presenting papers is always a good way of meeting deadlines. Without deadlines and conference organisers, some of these speeches and essays would not have been written – or at least not as they now appear. I am also appreciative of having studied law – which enabled me to write a number of the articles in this book, and ensures that there is ever-ready material for me to research, critique, analyse and write on.

I appreciate the support of the Women's Movement and my colleagues which has enabled me to compile *The Sexual Gerrymander*. I thank Claire Warren, Janet Smith, Kerry Herbstreit, Jane Farago, Renate Klein and Susan Hawthorne for their contributions to the final presentation of the book.

My supporters and supports are too numerous to name. I thank them all.

Jocelynne A. Scutt
Melbourne, September 1993

You must know who is the object and who is the subject of a sentence in order to know if you are the object or the subject of history.

Nelida Pinon, quoted in Cheris Kramerae and Paula A. Treichler, *A Feminist Dictionary*, 1985, Pandora Press, London

Introduction

Economics is more than money and international trade deficits. Since Harriet Martineau pioneered the discipline, women have recognised this. History is more than the "heroic" feats of men climbing mountains and sailing around the globe, instituting political coups, or ordering other men into war and applauding or covering up, or refusing to acknowledge, the rape, violence and other abuse meted out to women in the name of victory. Women have long recognised the essential value of the words of "ordinary" people in recording the realities of their lives, their *real* history of the world, through diaries, letters, and (thinly or better disguised) novels and other works called "fiction". Law can be more than a record of the powerful using the rules to keep the less powerful, and the powerless, in their place. Women, who fought so long through the nineteenth century in common law countries (and who had their counterparts in other nations, and in other times) for the right to study law, then for the right to practise it, have understood the relevance of law to their lives and the way the law could be used against the exploitation by the powerful of their position.

The Sexual Gerrymander – Women and the Economics of Power is a collection of essays, articles and speeches written over some fifteen to twenty years. Often, the pieces were written because I was asked to present a paper at a conference or workshop; sometimes they were written because I determined that a particular issue should be included on a conference program. In other instances, the writing was a consequence of my research into a particular aspect of the law, or a desire to reclaim history and economics for women, and a need to ensure that the research was not lost and the reclaiming could not be overlooked.

The ideas in *The Sexual Gerrymander* have developed since my first years at school and law school, together with the firm family grounding I gained in developing an insight into equality and equal rights for women. Many of the essays draw upon my legal learning, both in Australia and abroad. Others emphasise the need for women to open up economic analysis to make sense of it and to render it useful rather than useless in remaking the world. Most begin from an acceptance that we can understand the position of women only through relearning history, and uncovering the history which has been kept from us, allowed to go out of print, or never reached the publishing house or printing press. The essays recognise that changing the world is possible only with the benefit of knowing what has gone before, what women have done and been before, and what women can be and will become.

Some people think that economics is necessarily obfuscating, that history is dull, and that law is fusty, musty and uninteresting. I am fortunate in never having held any of those views. Economics is obtuse only if the reader, activist or scholar accepts that economics is the one-dimensional discipline taught in conventional economics courses. Some economics teachers class themselves as teaching economics from a more radical perspective than others. But convention dictates their teaching, so long as they do not incorporate feminist perspectives and women's realities into their work. Patriarchal economics, from whatever stance it is taught, is enlightening only as an indicator of the way in which patriarchy informs the discipline. Feminist economics has the advantage of a dual approach: being a critique of economics of the patriarchal type, and having as its base feminist analysis of money, national economic power and domestic economies.

History is always lively, when the lives of women are understood as central to the history of the world and to the development of an historical perspective. Certainly history may be grim. The crimes committed against women in the name of religion, nationalism and so many other 'isms' (all of which are informed by patriarchal power) are not easy to read about. For women, it is difficult to come to terms with the way in which women have, through history, been used and abused. At the same time, the re-opening of history to see how women's lives are a real part of the way the world has developed – both the forward and backward steps – brings with it new insights into the present. It also enables us to appreciate properly the strengths and abilities of women of the past (and present), and to acknowledge and commemorate the great bravery and courage our mothers, grandmothers, great grandmothers and all women of the past have shown in refusing to be put down, shut up and ignored, whether literally or figuratively. Part I, "The Herstory of History", is designed to inform both as to women's history, and to the ways in which HIStory has denied the history of women. As well, it highlights the ways in which the history of women is being written back into the history of the world.

In studying law and writing about it, I have become even more attuned to the fact that the law is far from boring. Power – and too often the exploitation and manipulation of power – is at the heart of law, the legal system, and jurisprudence. Law is a most political discipline. Politics and power are never boring. Indeed, one of the most political aspects of the law is the way in which (most of) those who wield the most power within the legal system — the judiciary – are so determined to assert their neutrality, and to use for their own ends the principle of "judicial independence". The Women's Movement has been central in showing that judicial neutrality does not exist; that judges, like other human beings, harbour their own prejudices and biases and too often fail to acknowledge them; and that the law is patriarchal and political. At the same time, the Women's Movement has been a great defender of the positive aspects of the legal system, in particular its public nature: that judges are not allowed to make decisions "behind closed doors", without public scrutiny. Ironically, this great strength of the Australian legal system is too often used by some judges to support a contradictory idea. First, they say that they are open to public scrutiny, and this is what makes them publicly accountable. This, they say, means that they are more accountable than any other trade or profession. Next, they (or their supporters) assert that *negative* public criticism, or *critical* analysis, is unfair, or inimical to the legal system. Apparently public scrutiny in some judicial eyes means that only positive praise is allowed. Or that a *feminist* critique is out of bounds. Fortunately, more often, now, the public generally does not accept this limitation on judicial accountability. Part II, "Violence Against Women", shows how the law has been devised and interpreted in ways that do not protect women from violence, but rather promote physical, psychological and economic violence against women and children.

There is a real need for women to continue to demand of economics and economists, of history and historians, and of the legal system and jurisprudence, lawyers and judges, that they reorientate themselves to accept that 52 per cent of the population are women and women's concerns are vital to the making sense of any discipline, and particularly these. Economists, historians and lawyers who refuse to acknowledge this reality are living more and more in a world which, permeated with a false vision, is being recognised as a lie. The falsity of the vision is being replaced with an acknowledged truth that is centred in the real. As Part III, "Up From Under", shows, the lives of women are less and less likely to be forgotten or left out of consideration in remaking the world. Those who refuse to acknowledge this render their work more and more irrelevant, so that its value lies only in its existence as an historical record of a paternalistic past and a patriarchal present, and as a backdrop to a future which, in its recognition of the equal worth and the value of women, is feminist.

PART I

THE HERSTORY OF HISTORY

1

THE GERRYMANDER OF SEX:
Women, Men and the Politics of History

SECOND CAROLINE CHISHOLM ORATION
Chisholm Institute of Technology, Melbourne
20 October 1988

The Caroline Chisholm Oration was established in 1987 to commemorate the namesake of Chisholm Institute of Technology, a tertiary educational institution which was formed out of an amalgamation of Caulfield and Frankston Institutes. This amalgamation was a part of federal government moves to create the (now superseded) 'two-tier' system of tertiary education: universities and colleges of advanced education (CAEs). As pointed out in this essay, the choice of name was not straightforward: names of male political figures were originally advocated, and it was only after considerable debate that Caroline Chisholm's name graced the newly formed institution. This in itself underlines the importance of 'women, men and the politics of history': men are more often remembered in history. HIStory is all about men. Just as it is rare that women are remembered through 'naming' for institutions, rarely are Memorial or Commemorative Lectures named for women. Only in recent years have electorates been named after women – Goldstein (after Vida Goldstein), Cowan (after Edith Cowan), Tangey (after Dorothy Tangey).

In delivering the Second Caroline Chisholm Oration, I was concerned to show the way that women have been 'left out' and traditional forms of women's history (diaries and letters, for example) have been passed over. I was equally concerned to illustrate that women who have been 'remembered' are remembered in such a way as to deny readers of history a real picture of women as a part of history. Women like Caroline Chisholm are referred to implicitly or explicitly as the 'exceptions proving the rule'. The very fact of their being recorded in history means that they were alone in what they did, and stood above the mass of women who – so this form of history asserts – never did anything worth recording, never had views worth remembering, never engaged in action worthy of recall. In short, the few women allowed to 'get through' in history

3

confirm that women *are not historical figures.* Women *play no part in this history.*

In 1982 Dale Spender published Women of Ideas – and What Men Have Done to Them,[1] *recording the lives of women-of-herstory and the way women have been written out of history. In 1988 Portia Robinson's work,* The Women of Botany Bay[2] *recaptured for contemporary readers the real lives of convict women coming to Australia in 1788. The gerrymander of women's history in Australia is gradually being set aside. At the same time, there are backward steps. In 1990 Caroline Chisholm's portrait was removed from the $A5.00 note, to be replaced by the British monarch. Amongst a multiplicity of men's heads on notes, no Australian women appear on any Australian currency. (This, says the Mint, is to change in the future. But today is* now.*) And in 1992 Chisholm Institute was incorporated into Monash University. That institution is named for General Monash. It is ironic, indeed, that Caroline Chisholm, a woman who devoted herself to ensuring, so far as she was able, that British women should find productive lives in Australia, should have been ousted by a man whose memory is based in war.*

> **Gerrymander** (gerimæ·ndeɹ), *sb. U.S.* 1868. [f. the surname *Gerry.*] A method of arranging electoral districts so that one party will be enabled to elect more representatives than they could on a fair system. This was done in Massachusetts, in 1812, while Elbridge Gerry was Governor; hence the name.
>
> **Gerrymander** (gerimæ·ndeɹ), *v.* Also *erron.* (in England) **jerry-.** 1859. [f. the sb.] *trans.* To subject (a state, a constituency) to a gerrymander. Also *transf.* to manipulate in order to gain an unfair advantage.
>
> To g. a bench of magistrates 1893.
>
> – Oxford Dictionary

> *v.* **take (unfair) advantage,** come in (be on) the grouter; **discriminate (against),** favour, gerrymander, load the scales, rig, rob Peter to pay Paul, stack; **not play the game,** break the rules, commit a foul, hit below the belt.
>
> – Macquarie Thesaurus

In September 1988 in a federal Constitutional referendum, Australia gained the dubious honour of becoming possibly the only democratic country in the world to vote against the proposition that gerrymandered electorates are unlawful. The majority of citizens, in a majority of states, voted against the state and federal implementation of the principle "one vote, one value", or "one person, one vote". If such a basic proposition could be rejected by the majority of Australians, thereby renouncing what has

---

1. Dale Spender, *Women of Ideas – and What Men Have Done to Them*, 1982, Routledge and Kegan Paul, London.
2. Portia Robinson, *The Women of Botany Bay*, 1993, Penguin Books Australia, Ringwood.

generally been taken as a democratic heritage, what hope is there for overturning the greatest gerrymander in history, that against the 52 per cent constituency, women?

Like so many women before and after him, John Stuart Mill in 1858 clearly recognised the gerrymander of sex: a method of arranging electoral districts so that one party (of the male kind) will be enabled to elect more representatives than they could on a fair system: namely, "more" in its absolute – "all". Mill wrote to the Attorney-General of Victoria of the day, congratulating him upon the recent extension of suffrage – the right to vote in colonial elections – to all men of the colony. But, he said:

The only thing which seems wanting to make the suffrage really universal, is to get rid of the Toryism of sex, by admitting women to vote; and it will be a great test how far the bulk of your population deserve to have the suffrage themselves, their being willing or not to extend it to women.[3]

In that test, Victorians were found wanting for a further fifty years. Women were able to vote in federal elections from 1901, but did not gain the right to vote in Victorian state elections until 1908. The campaign was not without ridicule. One parliamentarian remarked during the lengthy antipodean fight for the right of women to vote and to stand for Parliament:

There is nothing so admirable as a beautiful noble woman discharging her duty in the sickroom, [but] there is another class, the raw-boned long bearded ones that I do not want to come into contact with at the ballot box or elsewhere.[4]

But the centuries long gerrymander is not limited to the vote, nor to the parliamentary seat. The sexual gerrymander extends through the public and private spheres. An overwhelming historical certainty cannot be denied: history irrefutably substantiates the *Oxford Dictionary* definition of "gerrymander": "to manipulate in order to gain an unfair advantage."

The Private World – Marriage

In the private world, with the colonisation of Australia in 1788, manipulatory foundations were laid through the application of British laws, adapted in the colonies. On betrothal a woman was obliged to acknowledge her husband-to-be as controller and owner-in-waiting of any property or income she might have: if she gave any property away prior to the marriage, the husband had a right, following the signing ceremony in the vestry, to declare the gift invalid and demand return of the property.

---

3. John Stuart Mill, *Collected Works*, Vol. XV, reprinted 1983, Routledge, London, pp. 557–558.
4. Quoted Farley Kelly, "Feminism and the Family – Brettena Smyth" in *Rebels and Radicals*, Eric Fry (ed.), 1983, Allen and Unwin, Sydney, Australia p. 137.

The laws affected women of whatever economic or social class. The washerwoman or char or shopworker had no right to her own wages, however small: her husband could at any time claim them as his. The woman-of-property did not exist in law, unless she was widowed before her husband wasted the property for his own purposes or tied it up in trusts so that she could gain no access to it, or unless her father arranged by use of equity laws to secure whatever property he had given her, so that her husband could not do with it as he wished. And in such a case, the overwhelming use of the law of trusts was to ensure that the property passed to the children: fathers of girls who became women and wives wanted to ensure that whatever property they had went to the male children. The wife generally held a life interest only, without power to sell or otherwise deal with the property.[5]

In law, at the time of anglo-Australian settlement, women were seen as dependants. The husband was owner of her father's property given to her. Her children benefitted financially from the manipulation of the law so that upon the death of her husband a woman became dependent upon her male children. The law thus created woman as subordinate, whose personhood was effectively governed first by her father when she was a child, then by her husband when she married, later by her (male) children when she was widowed. Single women were allowed to retain their own property. Although some cleverly and courageously overcame many of the constraints, it was rare that a single woman could live a fully independent life. Private worlds were impinged upon by the world of public life.

The Public World – Public Office and Paidwork

In the public world, women had no legal standing, if married, to sign contracts in their own right; to own their own incomes; to enter numerous trades and professions – medicine, law, shipping, the church; or to hold public office. Women had, nonetheless,

---

5. Maureen E. Montgomery, *Gilded Prostitution – Status, Money and Transatlantic Marriages 1870–1914*, 1989, Routledge, London, provides a number of examples where an American father attempted to secure property of his daughter independent of her husband-to-be. This was seen as "contrary to British custom". Letters and protest led the father to drop the proposed property settle-ments or the bridegroom would drop out of the ceremony. Leonard Jerome proposed to settle an annual income of £2000 on his daughter Jennie alone and a third of his fortune on his death. Lawyers stated this was "not in accordance with English custom, that is to say that the bulk of the dowry should have been settled [on the husband] Lord Randolph for life with a small amount of pin money settled on Jennie [Jerome] for her personal use. Jerome was persuaded to modify his settlement despite his reservations about making his daughter 'so entirely dependent on her husband'."

In another instance the Duke of Roxburgh, "who eventually married the heiress, allegedly broke off his discussions with William Astor over the marriage settlement for his daughter Pauline. The *New York Journal* reported that the Duke had objected to the stringency of the marriage settlement as arranged by Mr Astor. He considered this stringency offensive to his personal dignity and social position. The undisclosed reason for this stringency may well have been similar to what Leonard Jerome had had in mind, namely, that the dowry should be for the sole use of his daughter." (At pp. 96, 97.)

gained access to "mining rights" in Britain: women were given the most taxing jobs in the smallest parts of the tunnels, hauling heavy loads in sweltering conditions along-side children, until – in the name of "protection" of the fairer sex and simultaneously with the introduction of "advanced" technology which began to eliminate the worst abuses – they were excluded from employment at relatively high rates of pay. Laws passed by parliaments of men manipulated relations between the sexes and women's relations with public and private worlds, gaining an unfair advantage for the male sex.

Even where laws were seemingly neutral, those in positions of power, in private corporations and in public office, were able to apply those laws so as to exclude the constituency women from advantages, privileges and rights to which they were in human terms entitled, but by male definitions of "human" were not. Thus in 1904 in Western Australia when Edith Haynes, having completed her university legal studies, sought to be admitted to the practice of law by taking her final examinations, she was refused. She applied to the Supreme Court of Western Australia for permission. The *Legal Practitioners Act* stated all "persons" with the requisite qualifications were entitled to be admitted. Because there was no definition of "persons" in the Act, the Court held she was not one. One judge said:

I think that the right of a woman to be admitted [to practise law] is a misnomer ... The Common Law of England has never recognised the right of women to be admitted to the Bar ... It appears to me that we must bear in mind that throughout the civilised [*sic*] world, so far as we know, we have not been able to ascertain any instances under the Common Law or the United States which is based on the Common Law of England, or of any instance in England or any British-speaking Colony where the right of women to be admitted to the Bar has ever been suggested. That being so, it is said here that it should exist, because the words in the Statute are "every person". That does not appear to me to be very forcible. The counsel representing the applicant said that there were lady doctors, why not lawyers? The *Medical Act* says, "Every person, male and female, may be a doctor." Those are different words to what are used in the *Legal Practitioners Act*. I am unable to find any instances where any right has been conferred. It is not a Common Law right. It is a privilege which has been conferred by the Courts originally, and then been regulated subsequently by Statute from almost time immemorial, and which has been confined to the male sex. I agree with what has been said by my learned brothers, and I am not prepared to start making law. When the Legislature in its wisdom confers the right on women, then we shall be pleased to admit them ...[6]

All the judges stressed the enormity of any proposition that women might become barristers, which would lead inevitably to their being eligible to "sit on this bench" – to join the Court as justices. None of the three judges was prepared to make any ruling which would result in any women having the opportunity of, eventually, becoming his "brother" judge.

---

6. Justice Burnside in *In re Edith Haynes* [1904] WAR 209, 213–214.

The Gerrymander of History

This is our history. Yet history itself has been gerrymandered. A method has been used, relating to access to education, access to publishing, control of ideas, priorities in research, and the very definition of what is history, to ensure that one party will be enabled to elect more representatives to the text-books of history than they could on a fair system. History has been manipulated so that one half of the sex equation gains an unfair advantage over the other.

Back in the early part of this century, the writer, publisher, editor, Women's Liberationist and fighter for women's rights, Louisa Lawson, wrote:

I was married when I was eighteen – and what I've gone through since then! It would fill a book.[7]

In 1987 one book appeared. In *Louisa*, a biography of Louisa Lawson, at last some balance is achieved in relation to her past existence. This balance is achieved in respect of her individual self, not only in relation to her life as it has been portrayed in biographies of her son, Henry, and in his own writings. The earlier history – the gerrymandered history – of Louisa Lawson paints her, in the small acknowledgement given to her, as cold, self-centred, a trial to her genius son Henry, a falsifier of her own history and consequent falsifier of his. And the ultimate gerrymander is that she is recorded in HIStory *only* because she mothered Henry Lawson and then only because he and his biographers have sought a scapegoat for his own failings, or the failings of the society in which he grew to adulthood.

The gerrymander of history occurs when important sources of historical truth are ignored, downgraded, denigrated or denied, as occurred for so many years with oral history, and even diaries and letters. Oral history is crucial to the recollection of the lives and realities of those who cannot write, whether through not having the time, or not having the opportunity to learn. Those who have less or no access to publishing have been persuaded by the dominant culture that what they know, what they have seen and experienced, is of no consequence, is undeserving of being recorded, is lost to future generations if no one recognised the importance of recording it – in "accepted" forms. History does not traditionally acknowledge that diaries and letters were the mainstay of many women's lives, women who individually believed their observations worth recording, but who accepted simultaneously that what they were recording was of worth only to themselves, or to their family and friends. How "important" are they in HIStory?

---

7. Louisa Lawson, quoted Brian Matthews, *Louisa*, 1987, McPhee Gribble/Penguin Books Australia, Ringwood. See also Olive Lawson, *The First Voice of Australian Feminism – Excerpts from Louisa Lawson's The Dawn 1888–1895*, 1990, Simon and Schuster, Brookvale.

Even where diaries are preserved to become sources for historical research, the gerrymander ensures that certain parts only are kept, or that what is kept is sanitised for public consumption. This involves a "writing out" of history. That this writing-out occurs is revealed in Lucy Frost's researches into Australian women's history. In recording a trip from Sydney in the nineteenth century, to the Ovens River region in what became Victoria, Sarah Davenport apparently recorded:

There was a great deal of bad language among [the men above], and fighting going on one with another. We never spoke to them but armed ourselves my husband with a small axe, and I with a carving knife. I was determined to defend myself, and was in that position till daylight. At last I heard them make up a robbery for the next night, so they disappeared. I heartily thanked God for preserving us from violence.[8]

Lucy Frost's work shows that someone altered this section of the diary (and this section only) crossing out the real words of Mrs Davenport, which read:

... they was a great deal of bad language used among them and fighting one among another and they was for pulling poor me from under the dray for their own brutal purpose we never spoke to them but we armed ourselves my husband with a small axe and me with a carving knife   i felt determined to defend myself   we was in that Position till Daylight   i believe they would have assaulted me but one more humane resisted them that was one cause for thair fighting   at last i heard them make up a robbery for the next night so they dispersed at that   i hartly thanked god for preserving me from violence.

So are women's words and meanings distorted, women's reality denied, history manipulated.

This same historical gerrymander is manifest where a gloss is placed upon motivations for action, or the motives of individuals are not sought out, rather being "second guessed" by those who commit them to history as HIStory. The anglo-Australian settlement of the antipodes has been well-recorded – or, at least, "widely" recorded. The quality of the recording is questionable. In the early period, if women were mentioned at all it was as profligates – "the women convicts are worse than the men" – or commodities, as when, two years before the landing at Botany Bay, one member of the British cabinet argued a need to have sufficient women for the men at the proposed settlement. Katrina Alford, the economic historian, reports that the problem of a preponderance of males was expressed as early as 1786:

... when a proposal to procure women from the South Seas Islands was mooted, Lord Sydney argued that a numerical imbalance between the sexes was in itself a cause of "gross

---

8. Excerpted in Lucy Frost, *No Place for a Nervous Lady*, 1985, Penguin Books Australia, Ringwood, p. 14. The immediately following quotation comes from the same source.

irregularities and disorders". This view subsequently became the conventional wisdom among policy makers and commentators on early colonial life.[9]

Marriage and the production of children to create families became the ideal. This led to many women convicts being transported for far less serious offences than those for which men convicts were transported. When assisted immigration of free settlers was supported by the British government, the overwhelming theme was that "sufficient numbers" of women of a marriageable age should swell the ranks. In 1831 a system of assisted female immigration was introduced for New South Wales and Van Diemen's Land, the basis being in the authorities' eyes that this would assist in creating a stable populace.

The aim of the dominant culture was to provide for marriage fodder. For while women were encouraged to emigrate, few paid jobs were made available for them. What jobs there were, were not well paid. Thus HIStory records that women flocked to Australia to marry. Yet whatever these "historians" say about their travels, women did not necessarily come to marry. They, like some of the men, came out of a sense of adventure. They came courageously. They sought to establish themselves as independent human beings. In New South Wales, for example, Miss Eliza Walsh owned land she intended working as a farm. She sought a further grant of land from Governor Macquarie, only to meet with his refusal. Macquarie manufactured his own gerrymander for land distribution. Katrina Alford reports:

Governor Macquarie's ... refusal to grant land to women [was evidenced by his reply] to one unmarried woman applicant, Miss Eliza Walsh [where] Macquarie asserted: "I cannot comply with your request, it being contrary to the Regulations to give Grants of Land to Ladies ..." When pressed on the matter of government policy of land grants to women, Governor Macquarie acknowledged that he had not received any instructions at all, but had determined the policy himself, on the basis that women were "incapable of cultivating land".

The courage and sense of adventure in the women who came in those early days of migrant settlement is subsumed in, so as to be lost or ignored by, a HIStory which sees the male spirit of adventure in colonial settlement, the gold rushes, denuding the land of its natural vegetation, chasing away and attempting to destroy the original inhabitants as they went. Yet recognising the existing social, cultural, legal and economic restrictions upon those women, their courage should have been feted or at least acknowledged as history. For those women who did come to Australia with a vision of matrimony in an old but new land, any misapprehension that they were lacking in courage must be swept away with force: they undoubtedly were brave, too. Coming

---

9. Katrina Alford, *Production or Reproduction? An Economic History of Women in Australia 1788–1850*, 1984, Oxford University Press, Melbourne, p. 14. The immediately following quotation comes from the same source, p. 194.

alone or with families, from thousands of miles, to a land different in many respects from that with which they were familiar, is brave, and it is courageous. It is evidence of spiritedness, a desire to be creative and to build. But the historians of the dominant culture did not – do not – "play the game"; or if they do, then the name of the game is one having a certain resonance redolent of that of a governor of the North American state of Massachusetts, back in 1812.

The Politics of History

The politics are not one dimensional. The historical disadvantages under which women have laboured are real. Sometimes they have been increased by a dual gerrymander – the ethnocentric arrangement which manipulates in order that one group, male and of anglo origins, gains a dual advantage; the racially based arrangement manipulated in order that the same group gains a double or triple advantage. In addition to all this, redressing the imbalance means another level of reality has to be properly and realistically acknowledged so that the electoral districts can be rearranged. The "electoral districts" must also be *actually* rearranged, so that as a practical matter no built-in bias remains: no longer do inappropriate measures of representation, inappropriate measures of importance rule *what is*; no longer are there, as an actuality, unfair boundaries and divisions. The rearrangement so that there no longer is a gerrymander of sex can be engineered only when we can acknowledge not only the gerrymander of the external world, the world "out there", but also the gerrymander of the internal world, the gerrymander inside our heads.

To those of us who are feminist, who profess feminism and live, as far as we are able according to our own personal situation, in accordance with our feminist principles, ideals and ethos, it sometimes comes as a shock, a rude awakening, to have to acknowledge that some historians of the dominant culture have been women, adhering to the HIStory view of history. Some, the gerrymander firmly affixed in soul and intellect, have adhered even more strongly to it than have the male beneficiaries of the distorted boundaries of the external world. Some, sadly, have written histories wholly attuned to the message that importance is dictated by (male) gender, worthiness of recording or being recorded by (masculine) sex, and that history *is* a word with a male prefix. Simultaneously with this acknowledgement, it may be difficult at first to recognise that some who have attempted, fought for, achieved, a partial rearrangement of the electoral districts have been men.

Women in all the Australian colonies, and later in the states, fought hard (as did women in the United States, India, Uganda, Kenya, West Africa, Britain, Canada, New Zealand …) for the right to vote and for the right to stand for Parliament. One of the many was Brettena Smyth, who became active in the movement in the early 1890s in Victoria. She wrote and lectured on issues such as women's role – particularly in marriage, birth control, women's political rights and legal standing. As the historian Farley Kelly writes:

[Brettena Smyth] was to be found "conspicuous in blue shaded goggles" delivering a "sharply constructed address" on the need for women's suffrage on the classic ground of No Taxation without Representation. She had performed the major duties of the citizen for seventeen years, paying rates and taxes, running both business and family single-handed; and she could not see why she should be denied a voice in the government of the state ...[10]

Brettena Smyth's courage and persistence, the sheer ability to keep on, to continue to demand and to assert a right to autonomy, equal power and equal sharing of the power, is a trait that is common to women. It has had to be. Simultaneously, it is right to acknowledge that during the long years of the fight for the vote, just as during the long years of struggle that women have waged in other areas – equal pay, equal access to equally good education, the right to enter universities (and to stay there until the course is successfully completed), the right to enter various trades and professions, the right to personal space, to childcare, to abortion, to define our own sexuality – there have been men who have been able to acknowledge the justice of those demands. Some men – too few, it is true, but they are there nevertheless – have had sufficient capacity to recognise the injustice of the gerrymander. They too have worked to destroy it. Women's right to vote, as women's rights generally, would never have been achieved nor acceded to had women not been the major players in the field. Yet neither would it have been won had some men not been able to step outside their patriarchal conditioning, outside their HIStory, to accept the justice of the claim and to vote, in male-populated parliaments, for legislation acknowledging women's right to vote and women's right to stand for, and to sit in, parliament.

The reasoning has sometimes been for short-term personal or political gain. But it is also true that for some, acknowledgement of injustice to women has been the motivating force. If we do not acknowledge this – that HIStory can be rewritten as history by both women *and* men – then the politics of history has won out and the goal we are seeking can never be achieved. As the United States historian Gerda Lerner has said:

I begin with the conviction, shared by most feminist thinkers, that patriarchy as a system is historical; it has a beginning in history. If that is so, it can be ended by historical process. If patriarchy were "natural", that is, based on biological determinism, then to change it would mean to change nature. One might argue that changing nature is precisely what civilization has done, but that so far most of the benefits of that domination over nature which men call "progress" has accrued to the male of the species. Why and how this happened are historical questions, regardless of how one explains the causes of female subordination.[11]

If, as Gerda Lerner says, patriarchy is historical, we have a right to demand that men change and that they work toward altering the electoral boundaries so that women are

---

10. Farley Kelly, note 4, p. 136.
11. Gerda Lerner, *The Creation of Patriarchy*, 1986, Oxford University Press, Oxford, p.6. The immediately following quotation comes from the same source, p. 230.

able to participate equally in both the private and the public worlds. That right is increased by the sheer force of the reality – that some women's voices and demands have been truly heard, with significance, in some parts of the dominant culture. If, as others believe, patriarchy is "natural", then the fact that some men have listened to women's demands and acknowledged them shows that human nature (as in patriarchy) can be changed. The gerrymander is not immutable.

Toward the Historical Reality of Humanity as Whole

Some people may say there is no gerrymander, that history is apolitical. In so doing, they point to women who have been recognised in HIStory. But who are these women? It is difficult to deny the existence of Elizabeth I: after all, to ignore her would leave an unbridgeable gap in the records; Henry VIII or James I's reign would have to be falsely lengthened; and what explanation could be given for the turmoil which preceded Elizabeth I onto the throne and the significance of that mercantile period? The writing out would be too obvious. Another is Truganini, a third Florence Nightingale and a fourth Caroline Chisholm. It would be difficult to leave them out. And anyway, in their acknowledgement, it is easy for history as politics to deal with each of them so as not to upset the generalised view of history as the history of men.

Both Florence Nightingale and Elizabeth I survive in HIStory because of the difficulty of ignoring the latter in a succession of sovereigns; and, for the former, in the problem of dealing with the reality of the military in the Crimean War being served by the ministrations of a team of nursing professionals. Caroline Chisholm is unable to be passed over by the pens of the dominant culture, because she was a very public figure in a small colonial community; she made her mark also in the Colonial Office of Britain; and HIStory needs its (few) heroines as the exceptions proving the rule. Similarly, Truganini has been allowed to remain in HIStory because it would be difficult to keep her out: she was a strong, intelligent figure in a community where Black Australians had been psychologically and physically oppressed.

But HIStory deals with each of the women so as to negate, as far as possible, their *connection* with other women. It is as if these women do not belong to the group "women". Their membership of the constituency women is denied. Rather, they are depicted as "different" from other women, extraordinary, exceptional so justifying the rule. Question marks are placed over the sexuality of Elizabeth I and Florence Nightingale. Neither of them was "'really' a woman"; each of them was "as good as" or "thought like" a man. Truganini's recognition by the dominant culture allowed a great lie to be perpetrated, the lie that all persons of Aboriginal descent had been eliminated from Tasmania, so that there were no Aborigines left. She was the "last" Tasmanian according to this version of history, a palpable lie. As for Caroline Chisholm, she has been allowed to grace the $5.00 note, as no other woman has featured on Australian currency (apart from a royal symbol). Her appearance was permitted because she is associated in the minds (and words) of the historians of the dominant culture as concerning herself with matters of appropriate moment to a woman – namely marriage, and good marriages for her charges, the young women she organised to be brought out from England, Ireland, Scotland and Wales.

Nonetheless we would fall into error if we ignored these women *because* of the way each has been portrayed historically. As Gerda Lerner further says:

... men have built a conceptual error of vast proportion into all of their thought [by making the term "man" subsume "woman"]. By taking the half for the whole, they have not only missed the essence of whatever they are describing, but they have distorted it in such a fashion that they cannot see it correctly. As long as men believed the earth to be flat, they could not understand its reality, its function, and its actual relationship to other bodies in the universe. As long as men believe their experiences, their viewpoint, and their ideas represent all of human experience and all of human thought, they are not only unable to define correctly in the abstract, but they are unable to describe reality accurately.

Gerda Lerner is right. At the same time, where women have been recognised, it would be foolish of us to believe them thereby inevitably to be tainted by HIStory. Does a feminist vision of the world mean that we must repudiate the history now written of Louisa Lawson, in the biography *Louisa*, because it was written by Brian Matthews rather than Briony? The *sex* of an historian is not always a clear indicator of political position. Matthews does enable Louisa Lawson to speak to present-day readers in a way that was previously denied to her in HIStory. Her politics and political action are, after decades of denial or HIStorical ignorance, brought into the open. Of Louisa and her writing in *The Dawn*, the feminist journal of which she was editor, publisher, printer, job-(wo)man ..., Brian Matthews says:

... the general spirit of *The Dawn* philosophy [was] to seek to help women live a better but simpler life, to rescue them from dependencies of all kinds ... The impulse behind [*The Dawn*] is a recognition of the virtues of communication. Quite apart from its information exchange columns, *The Dawn* carries frequent exhortations to women to communicate with each other, to use every opportunity to do so.

The idea of women as helpers and supporters of each other – the notion that they might be brought to recognise their collective capacities and that this would be used for the betterment of other women – extended, as far as Louisa was concerned, well beyond the [information] exchange columns. "Is there a place in our town," she asks in the January 1889 editorial, "in which any homeless woman could shelter? And have we taken pains to have its location, and purpose, so well advertised that no one could fail to know of it?"[12]

He goes on to write:

As in [the] May [issue] of [1890] ...: women's shelters again, and the plight of battered women: "We could quickly fill the largest building in Sydney with women and children who

---

12. Brian Matthews, note 7, p. 176. The immediately following quotation comes from the same source.

now, for the sake of food and shelter, but more for the sake of what is called their 'good name', are bearing blows, insults, servitude and degradation."

Feminist history which, after all, is about the history of humanity as a whole, humanity as human, humanity as woman *and* man, has a threefold role:
- to acknowledge to ourselves the voices of women, the history of women that always has been "there", that has been recorded, that exists, if only we open our eyes to it and see it as legitimate, as history in the real sense;
- to recapture the women who have been recognised in HIStory and to ensure that their contribution and their essence in history is recorded so that they are "living" persons rather than icons or targets in a sideshow;
- to reconstruct history as a coherent whole, where significant human concerns at myriad levels are recognised as central to historic reality and fundamental to what is recorded.

It is untrue that there is no history of women, although HIStory has bypassed us. The first role of feminist history is to recognise, as Lerner says:

Women's literary voices, successfully marginalised and trivialised by the dominant male establishment, nevertheless *survived*. The voices of anonymous women were present as a steady undercurrent in the oral tradition, in folk song and nursery rhymes, tales of powerful witches and good fairies. In stitchery, embroidery, and quilting women's artistic creativity expressed an alternate vision. In letters, diaries, prayers, and song the symbol-making force of women's creativity pulsed and persisted.

How did women manage to survive ...?[13]

The second role is that played out by a reassessment of the few women who have been granted a niche, however niggardly, in HIStory – the Caroline Chisholms, Louisa Lawsons, Elizabeth Macarthurs, the few other women who have been "allowed" to feature in HIStory, but whom history has still not seen in their true humanity, or at least apart from the gloss of patriarchy. This is currently occurring with Caroline Chisholm. The selection of her name as "right" for Chisholm Institute: what boundless debate must have taken place during proposals for naming the amalgamation between Caulfield Institute and Frankston, and the new college thereby created. And when the proposal eventually went forward, it was taken by a woman – the head of the Amalgamation Committee, Norma Ford, solicitor from Traralgon – to the Minister of Education at the time who was not, as in 1988, a woman (the Hon. Joan Kirner, MLC), but a man (the Hon. Alan Hunt, MLC). The introduction of the Caroline Chisholm Memorial Lecture is a recognition of her both as a woman remembered in traditional history books, and as a woman whose real history has yet to be written. Her courage must have been boundless. Growing up in a culture which told her women were dependent, helpless, wont to swooning on cue, Caroline Chisholm simultaneously

---

13. Gerda Lerner, note 11, p. 230.

lived in a world where women worked in heavy labouring jobs down mines, slaving over washing elbow deep in water and soap, plagued by genuine health problems including malnutrition which too often led to premature death. The women of her world were so often frustrated and limited by the boundaries set on their everyday actions and denial to them of human rights of accomplishment, engagement in public life, achievement and a sense of their own worth. Yet she forged forth between London and the Australian colonies, trusting and believing in the resilience and courage of the young women whom she ferried out to new lives. Was her "real" object to ensure that men in the colonies were provided with wives? Was it truly to "stitch up" marriages for young women whom she thought would otherwise "go off the rails" and disgrace themselves, England and her? Or was the impetus behind her endless energy and real enthusiasm for work a desire that women, her sisters, should not be sentenced to lives of predictability in the "old country"? I believe, standing here today in 1988, that she wanted with her whole heart to give young women, other women, a chance – a chance to participate in a new history where they played a central role, rather than a subsidiary or marginal one as she had been forced to do until breaking out.

And the third task – reconstructing history as wholeness. This involves ensuring that the first two steps – acknowledging the history of women as "there"; recapturing women from HIStory – are combined and joined with a critical reassessment of the world stage and the places of women and men on it. We must trust our own sense of the world and what is important in it. At the same time, we must critically assess the principles, the history, the order created within the world as it is. This is not to claim that all history yet written is wrong, unhelpful, to be despised or ignored; it is not to assert that if it is not written by a woman we won't read it, won't consider it. It is to say that we must learn to recognise, acknowledge and make use of what is there.

Women must also learn to recognise, acknowledge and make use of the knowledge that women for so many years have participated in the process ending in our own subordination. We have internalised the message of the dominant ethos, a message that denies our history as HIStory and that equates HIStory with the story of the world. The endeavour is to develop in ourselves a real intellectual courage:

... the courage to stand alone, the courage to reach farther than our grasp, the courage to risk failure. Perhaps the greatest challenge to thinking women is the challenge to move from the desire for s ⸍ty and approval to the most "unfeminine" quality of all – that of intellectual arrogance, the supreme hubris which asserts to itself the right to reorder the world.[14]

A reordering of the world is coming. Slowly but surely the electoral districts are being reordered, so that no longer will the dominant group be in a position to elect more representatives of humanity to the historical record; no longer will the dominant group be enabled to manipulate law, society, culture, economics to gain an unfair advantage.

---

14. Gerda Lerner, note 11, p. 228.

No longer will there be loaded scales, rigging, robbing Peter to pay Paul, stacking, making the rules then breaking them. Women – and some men – are engaged in the task of recording *all* voices, which has a long history. And as the women work on, changing the boundaries, eradicating the gerrymander, I have no doubt that Caroline Chisholm is somewhere, right now, cheering us on. And I am further sure, with the utmost certainty, that the cheers are not polite hurrahs. Rather, they are firm, clear, proud, loud, urgent and unmistakable bellows. Whatever side of the gerrymandered fence, no one of us has a right to ignore them.

2

FAIR SHARES OF OUR HERITAGE:
Women, Men and the Socialist Ideal

INAUGURAL PEGGY MARTIN MEMORIAL LECTURE
Heidelberg Town Hall, Victoria
12 October 1986

Peggy Martin died in 1986. She had long been active in the Australian Labor Party on a local and state level, and most recently in the federal seat of Jika Jika. Her life, and her party political and union activism, provided such a strong illustration of the way in which women were active in the public sphere in the 1950s and well before, that it seemed important to me to take this as the theme of the inaugural lecture honouring her. The lies of the dominant culture are too often accepted as truth, denying the political work of women in the past. It is vital to keep reiterating the truth of women's lives, so that eventually that truth will be recognised.

Subsequent to the lecture, on 13 March 1993, the Prime Minister of Australia, the Hon. Paul Keating, acknowledged the vital role women played in the re-election on that day of the Labor Government. In the course of his victory speech, he made a particular point of thanking the women of Australia. This was the first time, in Australia's political history, that a prime minister had recognised by a direct "thank you" the power of women and the women's vote in dictating the outcome of a government election.

The Australian Labor Party elected women to parliamentary leadership positions for the first time in the 1990s – beginning with the Hon. Rosemary Follett who became Chief Minister in the Australian Capital Territory (ACT) government, then the Hon. Carmen Lawrence and the Hon. Joan Kirner as Premiers of Western Australia and Victoria respectively. Nonetheless, women remain unrepresented in the major political parties, both in administrative and parliamentary positions. Following in the tradition of women's activism which was a significant part of Peggy Martin's life, the Status of Women Policy Committee of the Victorian branch of the ALP presented a paper at the June 1993 State Conference, recommending that a broadly representative working group should be established within the Party to develop recommendations leading to greater levels of participation of women. Women have been stalwart members of

Australian political parties from the time of their inception. It can be no surprise that women's demands for political representation are growing more insistent. Australian women rightly demand that thanks be translated into significant and substantial political and governmental action.

> The Labor movement can only be great ... by the united efforts of all those who believe in it, of individuals, who are not in it to get out of it something personal, but in it because it is a great political party designed to bring to all the community a fair share of the things the world is capable of giving them.
>
> Ben Chifley, *Things Worth Fighting For.*[1]

In the eulogy delivered at the funeral of Peggy Martin early in 1986, the Hon. Brian Howe, MHR, acknowledged Peggy Martin as in the Labor Party not to get something personal out of it, but in the ALP because of its ethos and ideology. Striving to create a reality where all the community shares fairly in what the world is capable of giving was crucial to her. She was, said Brian Howe, a person in the mould of those individuals of whom Ben Chifley, once Australian Labor Party Prime Minister and leader, was speaking:

Not in the sense only that she gave her all to the Labor Party, but rather in the sense that she gave everything which was in her to fighting for the benefit of her fellow human beings.[2]

For those of us who believe in and fight for the socialist ideal, Peggy Martin's life is a guide to where that ideal stands in the labour movement and the Australian Labor Party. Born in Melbourne in 1922, Peg Martin was a member of the League of Young Democrats from the age of 16 to 20 years. She joined the Coburg branch of the Australian Labor Party in 1958, holding virtually every position in the local electorate in federal, state and municipal committees from 1958 to 1970, including the presidency of the Wills Electorate Campaign Committee for many years. She worked for the federal branch of the Liquor Trades Union and for the Moulders Union. Peg Martin was a member of the Trades Hall Council Equal Pay Committee from approximately 1958 to the mid 1960s. She was executive member of the Women's Central Organising Committee of the Victorian Branch of the ALP. She worked for the Italian Union paper, *Il Progresso*, and the trade union paper, *Scope*, for about 10 years.

In the 1950s, a time when (we have been told), women returned in force to the home-ground, producing children to the exclusion of all outside activities, it is appropriate to ask why Peg Martin, married to Felix, mother of Paul, Felicity and Peter, should have

---

1. Quoted David Stephens, "Political Theory – History and the Australian Labor Governments 1941–1949", 1974, MA Thesis, Monash University, p. 382, footnotes section. In the footnotes, square brackets [...] indicate new material added for this edition.
2. Brian Howe, "Vale Peggy Martin" (1986) *Labor Star* 8.

been leading an apparently double life. Or is the better question to ask, why is our history – the history of women, the history of activism in Australia, the history of socialism, the history of the Australian Labor Party – distorted through the lack, in official writings, of recognition of the work, the presence, the very existence of women like Peg Martin.

In Australia today, real efforts are being made to recapture the lives of women, lives which have been written out of official history, or simply ignored by the pundits. Yet sadly some feminist historians have fallen into the trap of accepting the 1950s as the dark ages of women, a time of total absence of women from the political scene, the public world. This deception has been practised so that too many of us accept that feminism "began" in the late 1960s and early 1970s. That if it didn't begin then, that was the time of the "second wave" of feminism. That women had lain supine, dormant since the early part of this century, until a second awakening in the decade of the seventies.

The dominant ideology has persuaded us that women's efforts to gain a foothold in policy making in political parties, to ensure women's voices should be heard beyond the private sphere, run in cycles. This ideology paints the efforts of women as subject to rises and falls, to pits and troughs, to peaks and shallows. It discounts the consistent and continuing efforts of women – alongside some men – in the cause of women's rights. It also bypasses a recognition of socialism as encompassing not just equal rights and distribution of wealth amongst and between men, but equal rights and distribution of wealth amongst and between all persons – women and men.

There is an equally damning and distorted vision of women's efforts as solely directed at making the tea. In "Labor Women: Political Housekeepers or Politicians?" the feminist political historian Robin Joyce, seeing through the fallacy of the dominant view, writes:

One myth which has been particularly damaging to women involved in party political activity is that perpetuated in relation to women's past role in the parties. The main discussion has centred on the Australian Labor Party which has been seen as particularly male dominated, and the effect which this has had on women members' role. It has been described as a housekeeping role which limited women to the areas traditionally described as women's work: tea-making, fund-raising and supporting male activists.[3]

Joyce continues:

Although it is true that a number of women undertook these tasks, it is also true that some women were active in areas which have been seen as exclusively male. That this occurred in the labour movement as early as the beginning of this century demands thorough scrutiny of the myth [and] a complete reassessment of women's past political experience, a justification for discarding the myth and [finding] new approaches to old problems.

---

3. Robin Joyce, "Labor Women – Political Housekeepers or Politicians?" in *Australian Women and the Political System*, Marian Simms, editor, 1966, Longman Cheshire, Melbourne. The immediately following quotation comes from the same source.

The fallacy of assuming that the women of the past contributed only through cookery has been repeated up through the 1940s and 1950s. Yet Peg Martin's efforts make clear the mistake. She was a principal in organising catering for ALP conferences. On one occasion, a dinner was arranged by the ALP to be held at Richmond Town Hall. Over 600 people paid for tickets and were poised to attend. "Who's doing the catering?" came the cry on the morning of the planned event. No one had thought to arrange for the food! Peg Martin and three union officials went out to buy, and Peg Brown, Peg McNolty and Peg Martin arranged the smorgasbord dinner. (Peg Martin and Peg McNolty were known within the Party as "the two Pegs". On this day, together with Peg Brown, they became "the three Pegs".) At the end of the evening, when everyone had been well fed and entertained, these workers sat upstairs on the floor spread with tablecloths (chairs and tables had by that time, late into the early morning hours, been removed), and drank in celebration.

Simultaneously with saving such an event with catering and culinary skills – "making the sandwiches", and no doubt the punch on this occasion – Peg Martin was active as a delegate to ALP conferences, and active as a unionist. That role – as political activist in the traditional sense (seen by some, wrongly, as exclusively male) – was not made less significant by reason of her catering activities.

The truth is that women have always played a firm role in feminist-socialist development and feminist-socialist thought, on their own terms, or at least fighting for their own terms against less enlightened views of the meaning of socialism. In the early days of the ALP, from the 1890s and onward, women were active in recruiting members, holding conferences and formulating resolutions for action. They were not solely involved in making cups of tea, scones and sandwiches. In the various states, women fought for the right to vote and did so through feminist organisations as well as though political parties. A foremother of the women of the 1950s, and of ourselves, involved in the campaign for the vote and other feminist campaigns in the ALP, was the Western Australian activist, Jean Beadle. In 1909 she said:

We are enthroned in the hearts of men; that is why men use us and pay us half the wages, but we don't want to be enthroned in men's hearts under these conditions.[4]

Jean Beadle was special in the sense that she was outspoken about the rights of women. Like Peg Martin, she was active in a high profile way, within the ALP movement and the union movement. However, like Peg Martin, she was not alone in doing this, in that many women fought alongside her and lobbied on the issues which were her and their concerns. Nor was she alone, because many women backed her on those political

---

4. Quoted Robin R. Joyce, "Feminism – An Early Tradition Amongst Western Australian Labor Women" in *All Her Labors – Working It Out*, Vol. 1, Women and Labour Conference Collective, 1984, Hale and Iremonger, Sydney, p. 148.

and industrial issues – which took the time and energies of Peg Martin and other women activists in the 1950s, 1960s and 1970s, and which continue as prime concerns of the women of today.

It is sometimes wrongly said that women were granted the vote without a fight, throughout Australia. In Victoria the right of women to vote in state elections was not conceded until 1908, and this after much lobbying against – and numerous derogatory remarks about – individual women who demanded their rights, their entitlements to equal political participation and decision-making, and claimed these rights and entitlements for all women. It is further suggested that after gaining the vote women simply went home, giving up fighting for anything more. Again the myth that pursues the women of the 1950s: home they supposedly went, to the fireside, the public sphere forgotten. This was far from the truth. The women did their fireside chores (as well as those their husbands should rightly have done) but retained a firm foothold in the public world:

Many activists realised that the vote was not a panacea for all women's problems. In the following years they established themselves as politically influential pressure groups committed to a general feminist position. Some of the women were radical feminists who attempted to change the low status of women rather than concentrate on the need for amelioration of the consequences of injustice. They attempted to raise the status of female roles in economic terms rather than in myth-making, and sought participation in the roles which were the exclusive property of men.[5]

Labor Women began organising at the turn of the century and before. In 1912 a women's conference was held, for the first time, by Labor Women, which became an organisation in its own right within the Western Australian branch of the ALP. A similar approach was adopted in other states. A Labor Women's organisation was established in New South Wales, and one in Queensland. Other states took a different route, with women forming policy committees rather than their own organisation within the ALP. In Western Australia, the Labor Women's organisation went further than in any other state, creating women-only branches alongside mixed branches. Thus women at that time were involved in the same debates we hear and participate in today – of separatism versus assimilation or mainstreaming; whether women have particular ideas and views demanding separate representation; about whether, on the contrary, women are "the same" as men and should gain recognition through the same channels as men.

The concerns of Labor Women in the early part of this century have a familiar ring. Resolutions from the Labor Women's conference of 1912 included:

1. That this first Labor Women's conference urges upon the government to promote legislation that will remove sex disability and grant to women full citizenship, thereby permitting [women]

---

5. Robin R. Joyce, note 3, p. 7.

to nominate as candidates for the Legislative Council and Assembly, Municipal Councils, Road Boards, Licensing Benches, etc.

2. Also, since women find it a great hardship and injustice that [women] should have to plead before men only, and since it is so evident that the interests of women suffer from the want of comprehension of prejudice of the male jury, this conference of women urges upon the government the need in all cases where women and children are concerned that [women] shall be eligible therefore.

3. This conference of Labor Women is of opinion that women magistrates shall be appointed to deal with (all) cases concerning women and children, and that conference further urges that in all government offices (state and federal) men and women shall receive equal pay for equal work.

4. That this conference of Labor Women affirms the desirability of admission of women to Parliament, and considers that when elected they shall be regarded as being eligible to accept and fill any positions open to members of the opposite sex.[6]

The contemporary flavour of these demands meshes with the realisation that the demands of women today have moved on. This movement forward is a direct result of the achievements of women early this century and before, and of the women in the 1940s, 1950s and 1960s.

Taking the first resolution, the aim was "to remove sex disability". Today, the demand goes further, to affirmative action, supporting legislation and policies taking into account past discrimination and actively working towards eliminating or overcoming it. With resolution 2, women were concerned to sit as jurors on cases involving women and children. Women have now won the appropriate right – to sit on all juries, whatever the age or sex of the defendant. Taking the third resolution, women demanded the right to sit as magistrates on cases involving women and children. Today, we demand the right – but are only slowly winning it – to sit as judges and magistrates on all cases. Finally, resolution 4 saw the need for women to gain the right to enter Parliament and, once there, to participate at all levels equally with men. Women of today are demanding that equal opportunity and affirmative action policies be implemented to ensure that women stand for winnable seats, rather than the (mostly) unwinnable or swinging seats for which they have run in the past, if at all. Women have achieved the right, now, to hold office as Speaker of the House of Representatives and President of the Legislative Council.[7]

Women's struggle to win these goals did not arise out of the dead ashes of a past Women's Movement. The present-day fight is founded directly upon a live and vigorous tradition of the work of women throughout this century and before. But within Australia generally, and in the ALP, there is a lack of recognition of women's efforts, and a desire to downgrade or deny women's role in shaping reforms which

---

6. Quoted Robin R. Joyce, note 3, p. 7.

7. The Hon. Joan Child, MHR, took up the position of Speaker in federal Parliament, and the Hon. Anne Levy, MLC, that of President of the South Australian Upper House, in 1986. Once women were entitled to take seats in Parliament no *law* prevented women from holding any parliamentary post. But law and practice need not be – and in this case were not – synonymous.

have given greater substance to the cause of socialism. This arises out of an inability, on the part of some (male) members of the socialist movement, to embrace fully the socialist ideal of fair shares for all.

As former Labor Prime Minister Gough Whitlam points out in *The Whitlam Government 1972–1975*:

For most of Australia's history, women have lived without visible social power. They have been excluded from almost all levels of government, most forms of corporate management and virtually all modes of trade union activity. The momentous decisions of war and peace, of finance and technology, as well as the everyday decisions which affect how all people live, have been made by a minority of individuals who happen to be born white and male.[8]

But he adds:

The dilemma is that women have actively sought representation and social power and have actively fought to have women's issues seriously discussed within all the significant forums of national debate. Yet over the decades success at either of these endeavours has been at best only sporadic.

Whitlam pinpoints the problem: it is not that women have not been active; that women went home, refused to participate, or attempt to participate, in political and trade union activism, and feminist separatist activism. Rather, the so-called "waves of feminism", the "retreat of the fifties" arises out of a lack of external recognition of women's efforts, women's work. It arises out of a refusal of public institutions to recognise women's role as significant in the scheme of things, both in the private sphere and the public world of paidwork and officialdom. Sadly, it arises too from the refusal of those in power to overcome institutionalised prejudice, to overthrow their own socialised acceptance of women as non-existent in the public world, and recognise women's achievements and brave political stands as real.

The ALP has at various intervals been driven to acknowledge – or chosen to ignore – "the woman problem". (Women, of course, know that this problem is wrongly named: for women [and the world], it's "the man problem".) The woman question was relevant to the National Committee of Enquiry established in the ALP after the 1977 federal election. The 1979 *Report of the National Committee of Enquiry to the National Executive* of the ALP stated that the ALP's "blue collar, male, Anglo-Irish image increasingly handicaps its ability to appeal to emerging forces in contemporary Australia". (It could have added that the image conceals the reality of women working within the party, with the same energy and commitment, though rarely – most times never – the same rewards.) That report stressed the need to improve the representation of women within the party, to improve the party's performance among female voters:

---

8. Gough Whitlam, *The Whitlam Government 1972–1975*, 1985, Penguin Books Australia, Ringwood. The immediately following quotation comes from the same source.

The reasons for the relative weakness of female support for the ALP are complex, and they are not peculiar to Australia, since the greater conservatism of women voters has been observed almost everywhere. In the long run, the move by women from a predominantly domestic role is likely to reduce the difference between male and female voters. For the immediate future, however, positive action is imperative, if only for electoral purposes. In this sense, there is an obvious connection between lack of female involvement in ALP affairs and lack of electoral support.[9]

But the women have always been there, in the party. Maybe 30 or 33 per cent, not 50 per cent, but the women are not the problem. The problem arises out of the limited meaning given to the socialist ideal, the narrowing of that ideal to male concerns, or world concerns seen through male eyes, from the viewpoint of the masculine ethos. Today the major party professing socialism, the Australian Labor Party, prides itself on closing the "gender gap": the gap between women and men voting for the Labor Party. It prides itself on gaining more votes from women than does the conservative side of politics. Yet it is important to understand why this change has come about, and what the fundamental reasons were for the failure of more women to vote socialist in the past. Any swing of women's votes to Labor will not continue nor be sustained unless the reason for it is recognised and followed through. Women are not easily fooled, and if their legitimate expectations are not met, can withdraw their votes just as easily as they can bestow them.

Women have a particularly strong sense of "fairness" and "injustice", a sense basic to the socialist ideal. In the past, women were socialised into distancing themselves from personal injustices – unfairness directed against themselves as individuals – and developing a strong commitment to fairness derived through the way their husbands and families were treated by the community, by social mores. There have always been women ready to fight for the rights of the whole of humanity, not just on behalf of men. These women have fought against injustices meted out to women themselves, fighting for women as human. These women have seen the fallacy of accepting that women's role is to stand by and accept that any "rights" she might have come not to her as a person, but as a by-product of the fact that she is a member of a family, or one of a couple, the male partner of which really has the rights. These women have not traditionally been in the majority. Now, through the unremitting efforts of women such as Peg Martin, whose motto was "I don't have to *ask* to be equal; I *am* equal", that these women will become numerically significant is a real possibility. The demands of women for economic equality with men, for redistribution of power and resources amongst women and men as individuals who may simultaneously be part of a couple or family unit, and who are part of the general community, will have to be met. This is the great change in the political equation.

---

9. Australian Labor Party, Federal Branch, *Report of the National Committee of Enquiry to the Executive*, 1979, ALP National Secretariat, Canberra.

But this change will not be effected without a sincere recognition amongst men that women's demands are legitimate. As well, men must acknowledge that without the fulfilment of women's demands, the socialist ideal will never come to fruition. It is not just a problem of public sphere recognition of women and women's rights. It is a problem of private sphere acknowledgment, too. The issue is not limited to Australia, nor to Australian male chauvinism. In Sweden, where a concept of socialism as including equal rights of and for women as well as for men is ostensibly accepted, Christina Anderson (the executive secretary of one of the women's organisations within a major political party) has said:

We have trouble with our men, although the younger ones are better than the older ones. But people in political life have arranged their own lives in a conservative way, and it is difficult to talk to them because we are challenging their private lives.[10]

It is far more comfortable for men to believe that the status quo is the way the world should be, because it is more favourable to their short-term interests; longer-term interests will not be met without upheaval which may cause short-term distress for them. For the proponents of socialism and the seekers after the woman's vote, it should also be remembered that it is far more comfortable for women to believe that they can find security and economic support through marriage rather than fighting in a hostile "male" world of paidwork, particularly alongside men who are unhappy about women taking non-traditional roles. It is also easy for those who are dependent upon male paidworkers (though there are fewer and fewer in this category) to believe that women should not enter the paid workforce after marriage and should leave, when they marry, to provide jobs for men. A spurious tradition is being reasserted by conservative forces calling for a return to a false past of husband, wife, several children, cat, dog and (today) television set, the mother being full-time in the home. Yet there is no way women can in reality be "sent back to the home" – to which the majority have never really been confined, anyway, being forced throughout the nineteenth and twentieth centuries by economic circumstances to bring some income, however small, however sporadic, into the household. Women's participation is as vital to the operation of the economy as it ever was.

But if socialism does not follow through on its present day promise of equal rights for women and men and the proposed opportunities and realities going with that egalitarianism, then the voices of conservatism will make more and more sense to women who work in degrading conditions in factories or offices, who have to bear daily the (sexual) harassment of the boss or fellow workers, or both. Who wouldn't want to give up that eight-hour day in the factory or chicken shed, for what might seem like relative bliss at home? Even if the home is inhabited by a husband who is

---

10. Quoted Hilda Scott, *Sweden's Right to be Human – Sex-Role Equality, The Goal and the Reality,* 1982, Allison and Busby, London.

abusive or worse, the husband has to be put up with only for the time he is at home, and the times he is abusive – if he is. If she is in paidwork under inhuman conditions, her whole day is divided between the harassing supervisor and the possibly abusive husband, or other likely detrimental conditions at home.

It is important to expose the anti-woman nature of conservative philosophy. It is most important to reveal socialism in its positive light, but the negative nature of conservatism must also be made clear, so that a true assessment can be made of the possible place of women in the political and social structure. This is not difficult. The lack of concern for women in conservative policies and the abject indifference of those policies to the realities of current socio-economic structures and the place of women is patent. A professor of the Centre of Policy Studies at Monash University uses the tourist industry as a paradigm for the creation of an economy where growth is the answer, and "benefits" accrue. Michael Porter says:

Within the tourism sector one finds that where restaurants and other tourist ventures have managed to free themselves of market constraints such as penalty rates, they have proven able to expand quite considerably. A common example is Chinese restaurants – employing family labour. Other examples include fast food chains which are able to expand so long as they are able to employ labour at competitive rates. Rather than employ almost no labour on weekends because of penalty rates, such restaurants and fast food outlets, to the extent they can internalise employment arrangements through family and equity arrangements or avoid penalty structures, can thereby continue to offer full service at the most profitable time – for example, weekends and nights. As a result of this differential capacity to avoid regulation we have seen the small restaurant prosper.[11]

But who prospers? Who benefits? Within the family organisation, research shows that the major income is controlled by the husband and father (where one exists). Research into financial arrangements amongst families shows that where a man's wages or salary increases, this increase is not passed on to the person organising the homeground – the wife and mother. Rather, her housekeeping remains set at the level arrived at prior to the raise. Housekeeping money does not keep pace with the consumer price index (CPI), despite wage and salary rises. Thus it is false to assert that within family businesses "the whole family" prospers, as the proponent of conservatism tells us. As well, the right of employees to decline to work long hours for little pay should not be removed simply because a worker is employed in a family business or is a member of that family. It is wrong to say that within family businesses prosperity and benefits are equally or equitably divided amongst members. Promoting "prosperity" for one member of a family against the better interests of other members ought not to stand the scrutiny of a society adhering, at base, to egalitarianism and to a fair return for a fair

---

11. Michael Porter, "The Labour of Liberalisation" in *Poor Nation of the Pacific – Australia's Future?* 1985, Jocelynne A. Scutt (ed.), Allen and Unwin, Sydney. A critical analysis of this position is contained in Victorian Parliamentary Legal and Constitutional Committee, *Report on the Subordinate Legislation (Deregulation) Bill 1983*, 1985, Government Printer, Melbourne.

day's work. "Benefit" should not be promoted as overriding the regressive nature of "arrangements" avoiding legislative standards which are set on the basis of preventing exploitation. Exploitation should be outlawed equally in "family businesses" as in businesses where workers have no blood ties.[12]

Numerous problems arise within a sterile conservative debate that ignores women's very existence, or considers women will be satisfied if only "their men" are prospering. Yet the attitude of the conservatives to women has parallels apparently crossing party and ideological lines. The idea that "family business" prospers because the head of the family makes more money has too often had its place in the ideals of some professing to be socialist. We have accepted as good socialist philosophy the famed *Harvester* judgment of Henry Bournes Higgins in 1907, the foundation of the "family wage". Yet feminists have come to protest about the lack of recognition given to women's existence as independent beings, with a right to financial self-sufficiency, which is evident in that judgment. Justice Higgins established a basic wage for an unskilled adult male labourer keeping a wife and children. In 1912 in the *Fruit Pickers' case* he affirmed that women doing "men's work" (fruitpicking) should receive identical wages as men, but women working at "women's work" (millinery) should not. In 1919 in the *Clothing Trades case*, Higgins subsequently determined that the female wage should be 54 per cent of the male basic wage. He referred in passing to an earlier judgment, by Jethro Brown of South Australia, in the *Printing Trades case*. In that case, Justice Brown maintained:

... the comparative inefficiency of women in a large number of occupations may be attributed to a physiological constitution which involves periods of relative inefficiency ... In many industries the value of the employee is largely dependent upon an ability to cope with periods of exceptional stress. This ability in men as distinguished from women is not affected by the physiological condition just referred to ... In the case of women, their occupation (beyond the domestic sphere) is, in most cases, transitory ... It is not that women are not intelligent, individual women have again and again in various branches proved their worth. It is not that women are physically weak, individually they may be stronger than individual men and, at any rate physical strength is no longer the greatest factor in industry. Women are inferiors in the industrial world because they have not decided (except individually) that they desire to be otherwise, or at least that they desire to pay in training the price of efficiency.[13]

Jethro Brown also deplored the "serious menace" to Australia of "the growing sterility of the population". He was not referring to any lack of ability on the part of men. Rather, he was referring to the deplorable fact, as he saw it, that, "... so many women would rather work in factories at low wages than assist in domestic service", leading to

---

12. On distribution of wealth and income in families, see Meredith Edwards, *Report on Income Distribution in Families*, 1982, National Women's Advisory Council, Canberra; Jocelynne A. Scutt and Di Graham, *For Richer, For Poorer – Money, Marriage and Property Rights*, 1984, Penguin Books Australia, Ringwood.
13. *Printing Trades Case* (1918) SAIR 31, pp. 42–43.

women lacking a desire to enter into motherhood as quickly as he would have wished. "What would happen", he asked:

if the wage for women in factories were doubled ... Woman's true apprenticeship for her future career is to be found, not in the workshop or the salesroom, but in some form of training or apprenticeship directly related to wifehood and motherhood.

Henry Bournes Higgins apparently shared something of that view, in that in the *Harvester case* one of the items he took into account as relevant in assessing the male basic wage was a component for domestic help. There was no component for domestic help in the female basic wage: to women fell the task of doing their own chores, presumably so they might develop a liking for that form of activity and gracefully retire from the paid workforce.

To be critical of the *Harvester* judgment is not to repudiate the achievement against "the bosses" that it represents. (Though what a greater achievement against them would it have been, had women been seen as rightful recipients of the same basic wage as the men!) Nor is it to join other critics of Henry Bournes Higgins. But one of the major problems facing women (and those few men) fighting for women's participation and autonomy, is that a myth of women's dependence has been founded in law. It has been founded in many areas of law apart from the industrial sphere, and other judges are responsible for that. Yet it cannot be ignored that in the industrial sphere women's dependency has had far-reaching effects on women's rights. The dependency myth has succeeded in establishing women who work – hard – in the home, for no monetary reward, as "dependants". For a woman who cleans, cooks, washes, vacuums; plays the efficient and charming hostess to business colleagues, family friends, trade unionist mates; uses her energies and resourcefulness in building up a family business or farm; cares lovingly and effectively for the children – often on a twenty-four hour basis, alone; psychologically supports and ministers to her spouse, the idea that she is a "dependant" must be taken as a wry jest.

In the private realm, this myth of dependency underpins assessments of women's contribution as less than that made by men, particularly to marital assets. As men are accepted as independent beings, it follows naturally that in traditional thought they are assumed to do all the work on their own; build up the business alone; work the farm without wifely assistance; contribute all the business acumen (which women are seen as lacking – falsely); survive in the world of paidwork – the factory, the shop, the market place – through their own efforts, alone. This ignores two realities: first, the reality that women work hard at home, and often work equally hard in the paid work-force; further, that men give little assistance at home, mostly expending their energies in the paid workforce alone. And secondly, the reality that men do not "do it alone" – do not possess business acumen or political nous in isolation from discussions about business and politics with their wives; nor work in industry in isolation from the psychological support, comfort and care received daily on the home ground, that makes their masculine life in the paid workforce easier to organise and sustain.

The myth of the dependent woman operates not only against the rightful interests of those few women exerting their energies full-time in the home. It operates also against the interests of women engaging in part-time paidwork, and setting themselves up in businesses into which they put a deal of their energies, whilst simultaneously maintaining marriage and family.[14]

For women in part-time employment, the dependency myth ensures that part-time work is seen as trivial, of little moment (rather than the hard work it really is, with inadequate return), and thus not worth assessing in real wage terms, or as a contribution to the marital economy.

For women engaging in full-time paid employment, it is not seriously recognised that they are required to carry out two full-time jobs – in the home, and in the paid workplace. Judicial determinations distributing assets on marital breakdown show that a husband is, in legal interpretation, entitled to have his effort seen as exceptional when he engages in business alone, failing to make an equal (or any) contribution to the home and family life through housework, homecare or childcare. In most cases the husband does minimal amounts (if anything) in this regard. With women working full-time at building up a career or business, the myth of dependency makes it almost inevitable that in assessing contribution to marital assets, or estimating worth in the paidwork world, the assessor will be looking for the "brains" behind the woman. How could one of those delicate, dependent creatures known as "a woman" possibly build up a business all alone, from her own skills, energies, acumen, vigour? How could a woman working in a "women's profession" possibly be working as hard, and require as much money for it, as a man working in a "man's profession" who *needs* a full wage? Faced with a dissonant view of womankind when confronted by a real-life woman who exhibits skills usually attributed solely (though wrongly) to men, and who is *really* (in the law's eyes) a "dependant", little wonder that courts are unable to place a realistic measure on her contribution to the marriage. Similarly, in industrial arbitration and wages policy, small wonder that it is difficult for women to gain a real recognition of their work's worth.

In trade unions, as in the Australian Labor Party, women have fought strongly for recognition both of their own skills and for the rights of women generally, and continue to carry on that battle. The fight within the trade union movement, by women, for the passage of and updating of the *Working Women's Charter*[15] had its forerunner in demands of women at the turn of the century for equal pay, through the 1920s, 1930s and 1940s. It had its origins in the campaigns during the 1950s, by the Peg Martins, the women teachers and others, during those dark years of the 1950s

---

14. See for example the analysis of *Mallett v. Mallett* (1984) 56 CLR 605, in Jocelynne A. Scutt and Di Graham, *For Richer, For Poorer – Money, Marriage and Property Rights*, 1984, Penguin Books Australia, Ringwood.
15. The *Working Women's Charter* was devised in the 1970s by a group of union-based and union-concerned women in Melbourne, and gained support from women around Australia. It did not originate with the Australian Council of Trade Unions (ACTU).

when, we are cajoled into accepting, women were silently contemplating the family hearth. As we know, those in control were not, and are not, usually receptive to such demands. What receptiveness there is too often relegates the talents of women in the unions, and concerns relating to all women workers, to the lower reaches of the paid-work agenda. The Australian Industrial Relations Commission compounded the problem during the 1983 *National Wage case*. The Women's Electoral Lobby asked the Commission to establish a panel to deal with work value cases relating to "women's professions" and "women's trades" on a systematic basis. The response was that this was impossible; that the economy could not bear the recognition of women's work as of equal value to men's and worthy to be paid at equal rates. The Commission endorsed the long-standing view that women should continue to work equally hard as men, but continue to forebear from achieving equal pay. The Commission effectively acknowledged that women must continue to be robbed by their bosses of 25 cents or 35 cents in the dollar, in the name of keeping the economy afloat.[16]

But whatever the Commission says, if trade unions adopted a consistent and continuous policy of bringing work value cases on women's trades and professions before the Commission, demanding that they be heard, the pattern and practice of economic deprivation for women would have to be remedied. At minimum, such a campaign would succeed in exposing at the highest industrial level the anomalous position of women workers who consistently throughout this century have been categorised within the industrial relations system as second class citizens, to be paid second class wages.

For socialism to come into its own, indeed to survive, feminism must be seen to be, and accepted fully as, a fundamental tenet. Most important is to map out positive policies and strategies for implementation. If there are positive socialist policies and strategies in the offing (which, being truly socialist, incorporate feminist principles and concerns) then the rights and demands of women will be properly addressed. The principle of fair shares for all will be on its way to fulfilment. To ensure that this be so, the Australian Labor Party must recognise more fully women's demands. Otherwise the party professing to be socialist will be exposed to women's rightful anger. And trade unions must reorientate themselves to the socialist demands of the women's electorate: demands for equal recognition of women's rights to fair pay for "women's work", whether done in so-called traditional women's fields, or in non-traditional areas. Trade unions otherwise open themselves to attacks not only from conservative forces, but from angry women (rightly) railing at generalised ignorance of women's rights in the paid workplace, and a lack of political will on the part of authorities to follow through the implementation of those rights.

---

16. For a discussion of the case, see Jocelynne A. Scutt, *Growing Up Feminist – A New Generation of Australian Women*, 1985, Angus and Robertson, Sydney. [For post-1986 developments and further comment, see Jocelynne A. Scutt, *Women and the Law – Commentary and Materials*, 1990, Law Book Co., Sydney. Extracts from the 1983 and 1988 *National Wage Cases* appear together with analysis of these and the *Equal Pay Cases*.]

The debate on superannuation illustrates this dilemma well. It is not sufficient to classify superannuation for all paidworkers as a socialist demand, as covering the entire paid workforce, without simultaneously recognising that it will continue to be those with low-paid, part-time, casual or broken working lives and jobs who end with less superannuation benefits at the close of their paid workforce life. The feminist-socialist demand is for a recognition of co-contribution to superannuation and rightful benefits accruing to the co-contributing spouse. Trade unions must not only demand extension of superannuation to all paid workers. They must ensure that the way schemes operate – the rationale upon which superannuation accrual comes about – recognises the nature of the contribution made to build up of superannuation, and the benefits which a direct contributor gains from the efforts of a partner outside the paid-work relationship. Also to be recognised is the benefit of both parties – direct (monetary) contributor and co-contributor (contributor in kind) – foregone through the setting aside of income into the superannuation scheme, or the deferment of employer benefits to a later date. The onus is on trade unions to determine the nature of superannuation and contribution, and the egalitarian operation of the schemes, or to establish such egalitarian operation, if the drive toward recognising superannuation as a socialist measure (aimed at redistribution of wealth) is to be accepted in its entirety.[17]

Sometimes those professing to be socialist lament that women members or women's organisations appear to be opposed to a particular measure, or that measures women work toward implementing are "not socialist" (as defined by men). The issue here is too often of the making of these "socialists" themselves, through their failure to acknowledge sexism and discrimination existing within the present system and hindering the road towards the socialist ideal. One such instance arose in the early 1970s with probate laws and their eventual abolition. Another has arisen more recently, regarding property rights of de facto spouses on breakup of the relationship. If a socialist proposal in the private sphere had been accepted before those debates arose, or during discussion of the issues, there would have been no need for differences to arise between socialists and feminists, differences weakening the socialist cause.

In the 1970s, women recognised the discrimination inherent in probate laws operating between spouses. Because all property was classed as belonging to the husband in a marriage, upon his death his surviving spouse was forced to wait for long periods to have the estate admitted to probate and administration wound up. This affected not only those with substantial holdings. Relatively modest estates were also caught up, particularly with rising inflation. (Take, for example, the case of the war-grants home purchased in the name of the ex-serviceman only.) During this time, after the husband's death, the wife had no access to any finance or property which was in her husband's name. Most property was in the husband's name, although it gradually became the practice for women to be advised to have their names added to the title of

---

17. See generally *Submission of the Women's Electoral Lobby on Superannuation*, 1982, WEL Sydney. (Drafted by Family Law Action Group under convenorship of Di Graham.)

the family home. (If a house is owned in joint names, on the death of one, the ownership of the whole transfers automatically to the survivor.) The idea of joint ownership meant that where a woman survived her husband, she would at least be securely housed whilst waiting for probate – though she might have difficulty with paying the mortgage. Certainly the smallest estates were not subject to probate. Yet this does not mean that the plight of women in the survivor situation should be ignored. Women's groups lobbied to abolish probate between husbands and wives, purely on the ground of sex discrimination. Simultaneously, capitalist forces were lobbying for abolition of probate on capitalist grounds. In the upshot, beginning in 1976, the law was changed federally and in the various states, so that probate was abolished between spouses. But the Queensland and Tasmanian governments abolished probate between parents and children as well. The move was replicated in the other states and federally, too. This is an obviously non-socialist policy.[18]

The abolition of probate between spouses is also non-socialist. Yet it would have been unnecessary had a socialist-feminist proposal been accepted and implemented: namely that of recognising husbands and wives as owning in equal shares any property built up during the course of the marriage. On the death of one of the parties, under such a system of equal rights to marital assets, the survivor would own intact 50 per cent of the assets (his or her share). Probate could then be levied against the 50 per cent share of the non-surviving spouse. The surviving wife would, like the surviving husband, have immediate access to the 50 per cent share of the property rightfully hers or his. After probate, the remainder of the deceased's share would pass in accordance with the deceased's wishes. The demand that probate be paid on estates of certain value would be met. So, had there been a will to implement the ideal – that women's and men's efforts in contributing to marital property are equal, as are women's and men's efforts in contributing to the outside economy – the abolition of probate laws as sex-discriminatory would not have been necessary. Socialists have, sadly, been slow to recognise the need to extend their egalitarian ideas into the realm of marriage. In the case of probate abolition, this ignorance led to an apparent conjunction between feminist demands and those of capitalists. But this seeming conjunction had no common basis in ideological aim. The force of capitalists was nonetheless added to by the force of women fighting for recognition of their rights not to be discriminated against in probate law.

In New South Wales, laws now cover property rights of those living in de facto relationships; a similar proposal passed the Victorian legislature in 1986. The legislation provides that if the parties to a de facto relationship have lived together for a particular period – say two years – then the surviving spouse, or aggrieved spouse in a

---

18. Di Graham of the Probate Action Group, WEL Sydney, led this campaign. On the campaign, see Di Graham, "Through Life in Pursuit of Equality" in *Different Lives – Reflections on the Women's Movement and Visions of its Future*, 1987, Jocelynne A. Scutt (ed.), Penguin Books Australia, Ringwood, pp. 178–187.

separation, can bring an action in the (state) Supreme Court for a share of the property accumulated during the course of the relationship. The spouse argues that her (it usually is her) efforts as childcarer, husbandcarer, housecarer contributed to the accumulation of property. She can then be awarded a share of the property on the basis of that contribution. (This effects rights similar to those accruing to married parties under the *Family Law Act* 1975, which operates federally.) But what if the man has previously been married and has built up assets in that marriage, together with his former wife, yet property settlement with that former wife has not yet been finalised. What if the settlement has been finalised, but (as is too often the case) the husband retains a greater share of the assets – a share incorporating a portion which rightly should have gone to his former spouse? If under these circumstances the de facto wife brings an action in the Supreme Court, her action will be related to the totality of the property, some of which really belongs to the former wife. (That is, part is attributable to the efforts of that wife in care of children, husband, house, and likely monetary contribution, whether direct or indirect.) Yet again, if the feminist-socialist proposal of equal rights to marital assets – socialist or egalitarian marriage – were recognised, this problem would not arise. Feminists would not have to agitate against the form of the new de facto property laws on the grounds that this pits woman against woman, in that whilst recognising one woman's rights (de facto spouse), it ignores the rights of another (legal wife).[19]

There is little point in introducing policies or legislation without regard to the feminist content of that policy or legislation. There is less point in railing against the women who are obliged to lobby against measures which ALP governments wish to implement, if those measures have not been thought through for all their implications and effects on women, for all their implications in accordance with socialist-feminist ideals.

Questions of superannuation and equal rights to marital assets illustrate another problem with current socialist debate. Socialism does not begin in the paid workplace and end at the cottage door or garden gate. Socialism is not a recipe for the outside world, whilst the world of the home continues in its medieval way, a hangover from the manorial system. Nonetheless where social change is being argued for, it is the home ground, or aspects of men's and women's personal lives, that are used to counter demands for equal rights. As has too starkly been pointed out in 1983 by Lisa Peattie and Martin Rein:

Every movement for social reform comes up, sooner or later, against the barrier of the natural: that which cannot be changed because it is in the order of things, outside the span of intervention ... We may argue about the circumstances under which it is appropriate for women

---

19. On equal rights to marital assets, see Scutt and Graham, *For Richer, For Poorer*, 1984, note 12; also *Submission to the Australian Government and the Australian Law Reform Commission on Equal Rights to Marital Assets*, WEL Sydney (drafted by WEL Family Law Action Group under convenorship of Di Graham).

to work, and the kinds of employment they may appropriately enter, and we may argue about the proper allocation of rights and responsibilities between husband and wife in the family, but most people consider it is only natural that the man should be both the main breadwinner and the family head because women naturally are best adapted to rearing children, and men are able to earn better in the world of work outside.[20]

Current policies too readily shirk the task of confronting exploitation on the home front, however brave they may be about addressing it in the depersonalised work world outside. Efforts are afoot, with equal opportunity, science and maths programmes in schools, to ensure that girls and women develop skills in the public as well as the private sector. Men and boys continue to see the public sphere as their sole arena for full participation.

Yet the boy and man problem is so much less expensive to correct: having men and boys learn how to participate in the home life of cooking, cleaning and childcare, costs nothing in money terms. Just as girls and women have learned these skills on the home-ground during their growing years, boys and men can learn them, with reinforcement from school surrounds. It is far more expensive (though equally fundamental) to ensure that girls participate equally in mathematics and science classes, gain equal access to computers, equal attention from teachers and career guides. It is far more expensive (though vital) to ensure that all teachers become skilled in non-sexist teaching, and that employers become attuned to the talents and skills of young women. Far more expensive (though essential) to embark upon re-education for employers in terms of equal opportunity programming and of procedures to deal with – and hopefully eliminate – sexual harassment in education institutions and on the job. Fundamentally important, though relatively expensive, too, are equal opportunity recruitment and promotion and affirmative action training programmes, to ensure that women and men, boys and girls, are equally well trained, equally skilled and have equal experience. It is only then that they may compete equally for positions.

The expense involved in ensuring that girls are able to gain access to interesting careers in the public world of paid employment is essential: it means that girls and women develop their intellectual and other abilities, and make good use of those skills; it means that knowledge and skills are increased throughout Australia and the world. It means that more opportunities are created for the development of positive technology, of better ways of working. All members of society would be working together to ensure that the political economy works to its optimum capacity. Yet the lack of expense involved in ensuring that boys gain access to participatory skills in the private world of the home and community is equally worthwhile. Is there a lack of will involved where boys, men and the private world of the home is concerned?

---

20. Lisa Peattie and Martin Rein, *Women's Claims – A Study in Political Economy*, 1983, Oxford University Press, London, p. 1.

The domestic economy – the world of the home – suffers because women are participating (as they have a right to do) in paidwork and public effort, in combination with unpaidwork and care of the homeground, while men have less readily recognised the need to combine paid and public work with unpaid, private work and caring in the home. The efforts undertaken by girls and women in the paidwork world must be matched by efforts of boys and men in the unpaid world of the home. Efforts in the public world must be integrated with efforts in the private world. Each will boost and assist the other.

An economic debate exists which goes well beyond that reaching the daily financial pages or public recognition. Economics is still seen in limited terms. Economic well-being should be measured not just at the level of the dollar, the balance of trade, or the size of the deficit, but as to human economy: human needs, the pursuit of happiness, comfort, leisure, and hard, satisfying work outside and inside the home.

Conclusion

We are faced with a world where women's concerns are, as always, at risk, even with Labor governments in power. The opposition to women's rights is based on the notion that the economy cannot afford to recognise on equal terms women's paidwork efforts; nor can it recognise, vis-a-vis men, women's efforts in the unpaid world of the home. A danger of malaise also rises: charges are levelled that women have what we want. There is affirmative action legislation and sex discrimination legislation at federal level. All Labor states have implemented equal opportunity or anti-discrimination legislation. Federal offices of human rights, equal opportunity, or women's information services exist in Queensland and Tasmania, where state governments have been inadequate in recognising human rights for women – their governments being wedded to conservative ideologies. Laws have been amended to eliminate the most obvious injustices of sexism and discrimination. The implication is that we should (again) shut up, pack our bags and retreat to silence. Or simply cease to speak so loudly, so that it becomes easier for our voices to be ignored.

In *Modern Capitalism and Revolution*, Paul Carden has said:

Meaningful action is whatever increases the confidence, the autonomy, the initiative, the participation, the solidarity, the equalitarian tendencies and the self-activity of the masses, and decreases their apathy, their cynicism, their differentiation through hierarchy, their alienation, their reliance on others to do things for them and the degree to which they can therefore be manipulated by others – even by those acting allegedly on their behalf.[21]

---

21. Paul Carden, *Modern Capitalism and Revolution*, 1974, London, quoted Dennis Altman, *Rehearsals for Change – Politics and Culture in Australia*, 1980, Fontana Books, Sydney, p. 150. [Note that the incoming Labor government in Queensland passed anti-discrimination legislation in 1991.]

For women, these words have real meaning. For women like Peg Martin, efforts over their lifetime have ensured that women have engaged in meaningful action. The lesson we have to learn is that we have made strides. We must recognise real wins. The passage of affirmative action legislation, the distribution of jobs under job creation programmes so that women gained an equal footing in that allocation, the increase of women members of Parliament, the establishment of rape crisis centres, women's health centres, refuges and shelters, and all the other advances which demand recognition, have been won by women, by women's action. (With participation by some men, sometimes, in Parliament, the executive government and labour organisations.)

But for the action of women, governments would never have taken up and run with those issues. To keep ourselves going, and to continue the work of the women before us, the Peg Martins of this world, we have to acknowledge the advances that they and we have brought about. Once an oppressed or deprived group has achieved recognition, however inadequate, this stirs the group to further effort. Once the group has gained some aims, however few, this prods the group toward further advances. Understandably, the demands and advances of the oppressed and deprived are often depicted as "selfish". Ironically, those who should be supportive not uncommonly see them in this light, too. Ironically, those who regard themselves as fighting for the rights of the downtrodden sometimes see the goals and gains of those who are disadvantaged as detrimental to the "real" cause. But, together with the demands of their oppressed compatriots, the demands of the disadvantaged majority, women, *are* the real cause.

As Ben Chifley said, the real cause is socialism. The real cause is to ensure that fair shares of the things the world is capable of giving are dealt around, amongst us all. It is only when women gain fair shares in Australia, that socialism can truly come into its own. As Peg Martin said, "I don't have to ask to be equal. I am equal." Women aren't asking any more. Knowing we are equal, we're demanding a recognition of that equality, demanding our incorporation into the true equation of fair shares.

IN PRAISE OF DISSENT:
Power, Politics and the Democratic Ideal

FOURTH MAURICE BLACKBURN MEMORIAL LECTURE,
Coburg, Victoria
5 April 1990

Doris Blackburn was an activist and federal parliamentarian who worked for many years in tandem with her husband, Maurice. Upon his death in 1984 the Blackburn family home in Louisville Avenue, Coburg, passed under a bequest to the Coburg Council. It was sold and the monies invested to provide an income of which 50 per cent would be used to purchase books and newspapers on subjects including the history and cultures of the people of the world, 25 per cent to encourage children to use the Coburg Library, and the remaining 25 per cent to stage a lecture from the fields of sociology, history and cultures of the various peoples of the world.[1]

Because so much of their work was done together, and each saw the other as a central support in their lives, I wanted to honour that partnership and each of them in the Fourth Memorial Lecture.

An issue of prime concern to Doris Blackburn was the provision of multifaceted childcare – creches and playgrounds, free kindergartens, nurseries and pre-schools. Three years after this lecture was delivered, the funding of kindergartens was under threat from the Victorian Liberal government, with funding cuts of over 20 per cent and fee increases projected. Parents, teachers and the community were demonstrating, writing letters-to-the-editor, distributing petitions, holding rallies and signifying in other ways their dissent. The March federal election had seen childcare again elevated to a prime position in policy speeches, with the ALP offering a new Home Childcare Allowance of up to $60 per fortnight for women caring for their own children full-time at home, and a 30 per cent cash rebate for work-related childcare

---

1. See further, Ron Lang, "Vote of Thanks" in *Maurice Blackburn – Seventh Memorial Lecture*, 1993, Council of the City of Coburg, p. 15. In the footnotes, square brackets [...] indicate new material added for this edition.

expenses (in respect of women requiring childcare when engaged in paid employment). These promises were implemented through the August 1993 Budget.

Doris Blackburn and Maurice Blackburn were strong supporters of Aboriginal Land Rights. Two years after the lecture, in June 1992, the High Court of Australia delivered its judgment in the Mabo *case: for the first time, an Australian court recognised the legal existence of "native title". Thus the false notion that Australia was* terra nullius *upon European settlement or invasion was put to rest. No longer is the lie to be perpetuated in Australian jurisprudence that Australia was uninhabited in 1778 when convicts and soldiers arrived to set up a convict colony; or that the inhabitants were "barbarians" and incapable of being taken into account in determining property rights; or that the Aboriginal people had no concept of attachment to land which could indicate rights in the land; or that the Aboriginal people had no system of law through which land could be "owned". Apart from this, the High Court decision is strongly conservative, in that it sees "native title" as applicable only to those Aborigines or Torres Strait Islanders who have maintained, and can prove, a close and continuing relationship with the land. The decision effectively gives imprimature to the disruption many Aboriginal people suffered as a consequence of British colonialism, which pushed them out of their country. Colonisation has meant it is difficult for the vast majority of Aboriginal people to establish Land Rights in accordance with the* Mabo *dictate. Ironically, governments who have interfered most with the rights of Aboriginal people will have fewer* Mabo *claims to settle. Nonetheless conservative governments lashed out against the High Court and the decision and, more importantly, against the indigenous Australian people. Public figures gained airtime expressing views which were little different from those contained in earlier court judgments denying Land Rights to Aboriginal people.*

Doris Blackburn and Maurice Blackburn would no doubt be elated by the overthrow of the terra nullius *doctrine, but saddened by the failure of some to welcome the breakthrough. They might also regret the narrowness of the decision.Certainly they would remain optimistic (in consultation with their compatriots in the Aboriginal Land Rights Movement) at possibilities for positive implementation of the decision and the potential for the Australian people – Aboriginal and non-Aboriginal – to go beyond it.*

Back in 1955 Gordon Bryant, later the Minister for Aboriginal Affairs in the Whitlam Labor government, was campaigning for the seat of Wills in Victoria:

The seat of Wills was being hotly contested, and one of the people who took part in my campaign was Doris Blackburn. She had previously been an Independent Member for the electorate and was a redoubtable political figure. One night I was at a meeting of the Coburg Citizens' Committee where I met Ian Kelly, a senior librarian, who told me about a meeting at the Assembly Hall the following Tuesday night on the matter of the Aborigines. He said it was organised by some of the people who supported me in the election campaign and suggested I come. So I went along to the Assembly Hall. The meeting was underway and on the platform was Doris Blackburn, Charles Duguid [who had come over from Adelaide and was well-known for his experiences in the Warburton Ranges], Doug Nichols, Bill Grayden [member of the Western Australian Parliament], and perhaps one or two other people. I sat at the back of the hall and listened, and later went up to the front to say hello to some of the speakers.[2]

This was one of the important causes for which Doris Blackburn worked. She was instrumental in the establishment and growth of the Aboriginal Advancement League (AAL). Doris Blackburn had contacts with church groups and trade unions in other states, so that the organisation, begun in Victoria, spread throughout Australia.

Earlier, from 1946 to 1949, Doris Blackburn spent some three years in federal Parliament, sitting in the House of Representatives. Some decades before, Maurice Blackburn, her husband, had sat as a Member of the Victorian state Parliament, for Essendon. He lost the seat in 1917, but was re-elected in 1925. He represented the electors of Coburg and Brunswick in the federal Parliament from 1934 to 1943.

Whether regarded as individuals – which each most assuredly was – or as a couple – which they formed in a belief and understanding that it was possible to live independent though intertwined lives – Doris Blackburn and Maurice Blackburn represent in full-blown worth the embodiment of dissent which is rightfully praised.

Having known "both poverty and hardship", as well as the modest though relatively comfortable supports of parliamentary life, Doris Blackburn and Maurice Blackburn were well-placed to recognise the need for dissent from the dominant ethos. They were positioned also to support the democratic notion that power ought not to be differentially distributed so to deprive the disadvantaged, and that politics lies at the bottom of disadvantage, deprivation, and strivings for equality and democracy.

Doris Blackburn and Maurice Blackburn recognised that political action must be taken to eradicate discrimination. Equally they acknowledged that, although the politics of the Parliament is vital to democratic egalitarianism, political action goes beyond this, to everyday life at home and in the streets.

Dissent on the Streets

From the time of colonisation of Australia, Kooris, Murris, Nungas, Yamagees, Nyungas, Bardis and their fellow Aboriginal people have fought back against the destruction of their culture and the blighting of their lives. Some non-Aboriginal Australians have always lobbied alongside them. In the twentieth century Doris Blackburn and Maurice Blackburn joined those in dissent against this deprivation.

In 1958 goals set by one strong Aboriginal lobby were that there should be:

---

2. Quoted Faith Bandler, *Turning the Tide – A Personal History of the Federal Council for the Advancement of Aborigines and Torres Strait Islanders*, 1989, Aboriginal Studies Press, Canberra, pp. 10–11.

- repeal of all legislation, federal and state, which discriminates against Aborigines;
- amendment of the Commonwealth Constitution to give the Commonwealth power to legislate for Aborigines as with all other citizens;
- immediate plans for improved housing for all Aborigines throughout Australia;
- equal pay for equal work for all Aborigines, and the same industrial protection as other Australians;
- special facilities for education and training for Aboriginal children unable to attend schools through distance or economic [disadvantage];
- educational and vocational facilities to allow Aboriginal youths and adults to attain an equal standard of living;
- absolute retention of all remaining native reserves, with native communal or individual ownership.[3]

In 1967 the Australian federal government assumed responsibility for Aboriginal affairs, which had previously been left to the individual states. Although the Aboriginal rights referendum was (rarely, for Australia) passed with significant majorities in all states (and none below 80 per cent), those who began and followed through with the campaign for this referendum were seen, at the outset, as in dissent.

Not only did that dissent eventually bring with it success in the referendum, it brought other changes, in accordance with the original demands of the Aboriginal rights lobby. In 1974 the *Racial Discrimination Act*, having been introduced by (former) Attorney-General, Senator Lionel Murphy, was passed by the federal Labor government. In 1982 the High Court of Australia upheld the law as constitutional in *Koowarta v. Bjelke-Petersen*. Mr Koowarta and others of his Murri group sought to purchase a pastoral property in northern Queensland leased from the Crown. This was not a question of any acquisition of land under Aboriginal Land Rights legislation. Rather, it was a question of whether Mr Koowarta and his confreres had the same rights as other citizens of Australia, namely to purchase land in accordance with general laws of real property. The Queensland government refused permission on the basis that it was government policy not to permit acquisition of large areas of land by Aboriginal groups. Mr Koowarta claimed this refusal was discriminatory under the *Racial Discrimination Act*. The Queensland government challenged the Commonwealth's right to enact such legislation. The majority view of the High Court (Justices Stephen, Mason, Murphy and Brennan) was that the law was valid, under the foreign affairs power. Justice Murphy said:

For years, almost daily, Australian Governments, by Ministers in Parliament and elsewhere, and by other representatives in the United Nations and other international agencies, have condemned violations of human rights in other countries. Likewise, complaints are made by others of Australia's violations of human rights, especially of discrimination against Aborigines. A considerable literature exists on the subject of racial discrimination against

---

3. Faith Bandler, note 2, p. 13.

Aborigines ... Australia's history since the British entry in 1788 to a land peopled by Aborigines has been one of racism and racial discrimination which persists strongly. The subsequent entry of non-British migrants in great numbers has meant that the racism and discrimination extends well beyond the Aborigines. The Executive Government's concern with racial discrimination in Australia is related, perhaps inextricably, to its concern with racial discrimination elsewhere. In the practical realm of international politics it would be futile for Australia to criticise racial discrimination or other human rights' violations in other countries if it were to tolerate such discrimination within Australia. The Australian people can reasonably expect other peoples to take measures to eliminate racial discrimination in their countries only if Australia does likewise ...[4]

In the 1960s the (then) Commonwealth Conciliation and Arbitration Commission determined that equal pay should be adopted as a principle for the wages of Aboriginal workers, to be implemented over a period of years. Later, Land Rights legislation was enacted in South Australia, federally (covering in particular the Northern Territory), New South Wales and Victoria. The Northern Territory government attempted to evade the federal Act by declaring the town limits of Darwin to be square miles into the hinterland, so that claims could not be made for land within miles of the 'city'. This attempt was unsuccessful.[5]

The Whitlam Labor government in the early 1970s set aside funds for the housing of Aboriginal people. Programmes in the Northern Territory have met with particular success. The Tangentyere Council gained financial support through the Whitlam programme. Its brief is particularly to build housing for town camp dwellers, and to incorporate landscaping into town camps and surrounds. Tangentyere employs architects who work in close consultation with residents and town camp housing associations to design houses suitable for the climate and needs of the people. It also undertakes "local government" tasks such as garbage collection, repair and maintenance of sewers, building of internal roads, fences and landscaping. The Council's work is central to the health and well-being of town campers.[6]

---

4. Lionel K. Murphy, Justice of the High Court of Australia, in *Koowarta v. Bjelke-Petersen and Ors; State of Queensland v. Commonwealth of Australia* (1982) 153 CLR 168, 239–240.

5. The relevant provision (s. 50(1)) of the *Aboriginal Land Rights (Northern Territory) Act* 1976 describes land which may be the subject of an application to the Aboriginal Land Commissioner (at that time John Toohey, QC) as that "(i) which is not currently held for an estate in fee simple; (ii) which is not set apart for or dedicated to a public purpose under any statute; (iii) which is not the subject of a deed of grant held in escrow by a Land Council; (iv) which is not in a 'Town' ... ; and (v) in which any estates or interests are not held by the Crown, are all held by, or on behalf of, persons who are members of the Aboriginal race of Australia".

6. The author is privileged to have spoken with a number of persons from Tangentyere Council and in their company visited with the Council and town camps in Alice Springs, to learn about Tangentyere's activities. She is indebted in this regard to, amongst others, Geoff Shaw, Manager of Tangentyere; Bob Durnan, Assistant Manager; Wenten Rabuntja, sometime President of Tangentyere; Eli Rabuntja, President of Tangentyere; Margaret Mary Turner, Alcohol Awareness Worker; Doug Abbot, Alcohol Counsellor and former Community Officer; Jane Dillon, Architect; Michael Savage, Architect; Di Holdaway, Executive Officer; Pam Ditton, Solicitor.

In Alice Springs the Yiparinya school provides education for Aboriginal children, classes being taught and curricula developed in Luritja, Western Arrente and Eastern Arrente. Teacher training of Aboriginal people is undertaken by Yiparinya school and childcare is provided. Tangentyere Council designed the school and office space. The Northern Territory government refused to register the school, but this decision was challenged through the courts. Eventually the government registered the school in the ordinary way.[7]

Other educational and vocational facilities were provided for, out of dissent and lobbying of Black and white Australians, often working together, many times Black Australians fighting alone. Tranby College in New South Wales and a college in Alice Springs for youths and adults are examples of the results of dissent and agitation. In Tennant Creek the Ninkannunyu School Council proposed to establish an independent school, the Ninkannunyu School. In 1990 the Council launched an appeal against refusal of funding. Broad educational requirements are being met in various ways, through the establishment of CAAMA (the Central Australian Aboriginal Media Association), JAMIS (the Joint Aboriginal Management and Information Service) – which operated for some years – and Imparja, the Aboriginal television station which operates throughout the Northern Territory and into surrounding parts of Australia.

Yet despite the work of the dissenters and agitators, the lobbyists and "rabble rousers", and their successes, the position of Aboriginal people in Australia remains shameful to all of us who profited from our privileged position as a consequence of displacement of Aboriginal people by white colonists and their followers. Of Alice Springs it has been said, by way of example, that the Aboriginal children dwelling in the town camps suffer a high rate of infection. Diarrhoeal disease; skin lesion infections, including scabies; chronic eye disease including trachoma and other forms of conjunctivitis; meningitis; ear infections; upper respiratory tract infections; hepatitis and pneumonia are common complaints. A high rate of infective disease and alcohol-related disease and trauma is suffered by adult town campers. Common are chronic non-communicable diseases, caused by alcohol and petrol sniffing in particular. So, too, are liver, gut and nervous system problems, cardio-vascular disease, diabetes and high blood pressure. Many Aboriginal people die at a young age through heart disease resulting in strokes.[8]

In July 1985 a study carried out by Congress (the Central Australian Aboriginal Congress, medical service for Central Australian Aborigines) found sub-standard

---

7. See *Rabuntja v. Minister for Education* (1983) 19 NTR 5.
8. The author is indebted to Dr Rob Moodie, formerly of the Central Australian Aboriginal Congress and presently with the Victorian Department of Health, for this information and various studies relating to Aboriginal health, and relevant United Nations' World Health Organisation standards. [The 1990s also saw AIDS being recognised as an increasing problem, and positive campaigns, under the control of Aboriginal people, introduced. See for example, Gracelyn Smallwood, "Demanding More Than a Great Vocabulary" in *Breaking Through – Women, Work and Careers*, 1992, Jocelynne A. Scutt, (ed.), Artemis Publishing, Melbourne, pp. 71–80; also community advertisements on Imparja television.]

conditions relating to poor health. Charles Creek, Mount Nancy, Little Sisters, Karnte and Larapinta camps were surveyed. Of the 85 people in the study, 45 per cent had no functioning shower and in one camp, Karnte, there were no houses. For all those camps without showers, the rate of trachoma was 65.2 per cent; for those with showers, the rate was 23 per cent. For those without showers, the rate of infected ears was 47.4 per cent, whilst it was 23 per cent for those with showers. At Karnte, with no houses and one shower only, the rates of infections were 78 per cent and 58 per cent, as contrasted to the average for those with showers at 23 per cent and 10.6 per cent.[9]

The dominant ethos in 1950s and 1960s Australia was one of complacency, giving rise to the coining of the term, by the political scientist Donald Horne, "the lucky country". Those who did not recognise their luck and be still, but rather spoke out against material and intellectual complacency, were regarded generally as ungrateful, a dissatisfied lot. Speaking out was seen, almost, as treachery. Speaking out in the name of Aboriginal rights was even less esteemed by those in power.

Yet there were always those who spoke out nonetheless, and whose voices grew louder as discouragement doubled. Gordon Bryant again:

I think I got myself a reputation of being a bit of a nut in the Caucus because I kept talking about [the Aboriginal Advancement League] … In the Labor Party there were statesmen like Dr Evatt and Arthur Calwell, but they were not activists. Most members of Parliament were pretty good spokesmen who turned up at meetings which someone else had organised. I'd been a school teacher in Victoria where one didn't have many resources. Everything I had ever done was difficult. Now I suddenly found myself as a member of the federal Parliament with telephones I could use, and telegrams I could send without hesitation throughout Australia. I had an office, a secretary, a duplicator, and a chance to con people into doing things. For the Aboriginal movement I became what you might call a runner for the show.[10]

As Gordon Bryant writes, the role of dissenter is not easy. But it is enhanced by access to facilities that can legitimately be used against anti-democratic tendencies, and for the promotion of egalitarian democracy.

Just as Doris Blackburn fought alongside Australian Aborigines and non-Aboriginal Australians alike, women and men have continued to dissent against the notion that a 60,000-year-old culture should be destroyed or not lamented, and left without effort to recapture and regain its worth.

Around Australia, Koori, Murri, Yamagee, Nunga, Nyunga, Bardi and other Aboriginal women's voices are joined by the voices of Aboriginal men, non-Aboriginal women and men in the continuing demand for Aboriginal rights – human rights and citizenship rights, which are seen as inextricably bound up in Land Rights.

---

9. Central Australian Aboriginal Congress, *Supplementary Submission to the Trachoma and Eye Health Review Committee*, Congress, Alice Springs, NT; see also E. J. Beck, *The Enigma of Aboriginal Health*, 1985, Institute of Aboriginal Studies, Canberra. See also note 7 above.
10. Quoted Faith Bandler, note 2, p. 11.

From the time of colonisation, Aboriginal Australians protested against the taking of the land from them. Those voices continue to speak out.

In the 1980s, Lilla Watson, the Murri activist and scholar, reflected upon her childhood in a Queensland country town, where she grew up in the 1950s and 1960s:

I was born in spring in 1940, given my mother's name "Lilla". My grandmother died before we met, but I know her through my mother. As a small child I grew up secure in my family; I knew my father, I knew my mother, I knew my sisters and brothers. It wasn't until I began school that I was brought to a rude awakening. There was a black world and a white world. In the black world I was safe; in the white world I was unsafe.[11]

Lilla Watson describes life for her family:

Once, my middle brother was invited by a white boy in his class to a birthday party. When he came home and told us, we were excited for him. It was the very first time any of us had been invited to a birthday party. Mum washed his best shirt, pressed his best serge (short) pants, and sent him off all shining clean. Years later my brother told us that when he turned up at the party he wasn't allowed in the door: the child's mother had come to the door, and seeing who it was demanded, "What do you want?" When he said he had come for the birthday party she sent her child out to say to my brother, "Sorry but you can't come to the party because you're black". That same brother was made to stand up in front of his class and empty his pockets whenever any money or a rubber or pencil was reported missing ...

I remember mum taking my two older sisters down to the local dances. She and I would stand on the verandah, looking through the doorway at my sisters dancing inside. They never danced with men; only with each other; except there was one fellow who they danced with occasionally and he was considered an outcast because he had been born out of wedlock. But he was the only man I ever saw them dance with in that small country town, and of course they were the only black people who ever went to those dances.

The dominance of any one group inevitably gives rise to dissent. Without a dominant caste, there can be nothing against which to protest. Dominance and dissent go hand in hand, or one behind the other, just as a striving for the democratic ideal is an inevitable outcome of autocracy and authoritarianism.

But even for those who join the dissenters, acknowledging their allegiance in practical terms, or their membership of the dissenting group through birth or other circumstance, the dominant ideology operates to divide. Activist, Pat Eatock, living variously in Sydney, Canberra and places between, writes:

In 1971 I was a suburban housewife, the mother of five children. The youngest, then seven years old, was severely retarded and epileptic. Then I became pregnant again.

---

11. Lilla Watson, "Sister, Black is the Colour of My Soul", in *Different Lives – Reflections on the Women's Movement and Visions of its Future*, Jocelynne A. Scutt (ed.), 1987, Penguin Books Australia, Ringwood, p. 44. The immediately following quotation comes from the same source, pp. 44, 47–48.

In those days, one could get a legal abortion only on grounds that the pregnancy presented a danger to the physical or mental health of the mother. Unaware that I would have qualified for a termination on medical grounds, and having lived the previous seven years on the brink of a total breakdown, I signed myself into a mental institution. I did not have an abortion. I was told that I was "too sane". I had not come in dripping blood. They suggested I "have her adopted". This decision, made by others, was the beginning of my conscious desire for real control of my life ...

[Some five years later] I saw the grand finale [of the International Year of the Woman] in the Women and Politics Conference ... I was an official rapporteur on the "campaigning" session of the conference ... Tolerance – if not complete forgiveness – was extended to me for my political consciousness of my working-classness and femaleness, as well as my Aboriginality. But then a sister started a rumour that I was not Aboriginal at all. This charge was not made easier by originating from a sister-by-blood (my biological sister) in a futile attempt to retain her Queensland country town eminence as a member of the Junior Chamber of Commerce and president of the local Parents and Citizens Association. (Years later my mother accused me of "destroying" my sister's life by "coming out" as an Aborigine: my sister was forced to retreat into the anonymity of Brisbane's suburbia!) Fortunately, all but a few die-hards accepted the truth when confronted with it ...[12]

But dissent brings with it comradeship, sisterhood, sorority, fraternity. It can begin in a small way, an almost unknowing (though known) refusal to obey, to conform, to deflate oneself, to submerge. An everyday rebellion:

Back to Australia and [the] Women and Labour Conference in May 1978 ... Women came out of their factories and offices, their carrels and consciousness raising groups, out of their homes to share experience and research. The usual distress was voiced about the middle-classness of the [Women's Movement]. One woman halted the breast-beating. A factory worker, she said middle-class women working during war years had radically affected all women workers. The middle-class women had refused to follow the rules – like going to the toilet in scheduled breaks only. "We'll go when we want to," they said, and did. She said: "We suddenly realised the foreman wasn't god. He could be defied. We had a right to go to the loo. We learned he couldn't stop us. In other things too. Your 'middle-class women' taught us that. Defiance. Action."[13]

Dissent on the streets brings change. Born in Lima, Peru in 1952 of Uruguayan/Cuban parents, Patricia Boero came to Australia having lived in Santa Domingo and in Montevideo. As she writes, such dissent culminates in personal change, underlining the feminist notion "the personal is political":

[Living in Australia] I was no longer paranoid about participating in political activities, meetings, and rallies, wearing my ponchos and badges oblivious to the cameras of the ASIO men lining George Street as we marched by [in the 1970s]. Some of those marches were for International Women's Day ...[14]

---

12. Pat Eatock, "There's a Snake in my Caravan", in *Different Lives*, note 11, pp. 22, 28.
13. Jocelynne A. Scutt, "Good for Women", in *Different Lives*, note 11, pp. 228–229.
14. Patricia Boero, "The Double Burden – A Woman and a Wog", in *Different Lives*, note 11, p. 63.

The goals fought for by Doris Blackburn and Maurice Blackburn through their dissentient position, against dominance in the public space of one group over another, are not yet wholly achieved. Indeed, battles against the assumed superiority of the economically, socially and politically advantaged over others continue unabated. Dissenters continue to stand out and stand up for the right of all to practical equality, and to democracy not only as a process, but in substance.

Dissent on the Homeground

Throughout her life, Doris Blackburn saw as central to the achievement of a true democracy the need for egalitarian changes on the homeground. The historian Carolyn Rasmussen writes of her:

A belief in the positive power of education was central to all her ideas and activities; she saw in it the best hope for change. Her support for progressive schools, kindergartens, playgrounds and creches rested on a deep conviction that each individual ought to be given the power and opportunity to develop potential fully – "a child when born [is] the expression of a good idea and when given the opportunity for self expression [will] grow into a good citizen. Education [is] not a matter of putting something into a mould, but the freeing of an idea".[15]

Leading individually and jointly active lives, for Maurice Blackburn and Doris Blackburn to care for and educate a family required additional household assistance. Doris Blackburn particularly was attuned to the need for help on the homeground if a parent were to participate free of mind and spirit in the outside world. To this end Doris Blackburn lobbied and organised for the provision of creches and playgrounds; she played a leading role in the Free Kindergarten Movement. At times, her disappointment at the lack of attention paid by governments and private industry to these needs was evident in her writings:

Position and power still belong to men in our particular level of civilisation. Even when women have earned these positions they are filled by men. There are capable women in minor positions today who should be authoritative in the execution of our social services, in the planning of a better system of education and in the direction of matters concerning the health of the people and the peace of the world. Women do not have access to the public purse. The National housekeeping is not for them. Let them, it seems, be grateful for the pin money they receive for a few struggling nurseries and pre-school enterprises.[16]

And in 1952:

... it may do [women] good to learn something of government and departmental methods. When they had nothing they could get no assistance for the care of their children. When they

---

15. Carolyn Rasmussen, "Doris Blackburn MHR – Radical Representative", in *Double Time – Women in Victoria – 150 Years*, Marilyn Lake and Farley Kelly (eds.), 1985, Penguin Books Australia, Ringwood, p. 357.
16. Quoted Carolyn Rasmussen, note 15, pp. 359–360.

have built a good Kindergarten and it is completely free of debt owing to their own efforts it will be taken away from them ...[17]

Childcare has provided a focus of dissent in public and private, in the past and today. That it should have featured prominently in the campaigns of both major parties in the 1990 federal election is not a quirk of fate, a rudderless happening. It is publicly expressed dissension, and persistent public and private lobbying, which have elevated childcare and parental responsibilities to the agendas of political parties.

Building on the work of women before them, women have continued the protest against inadequate recognition of children's needs and the needs of childcarers. This protest is being voiced through public demonstrations on the streets. It is being heard in National Wage cases before the Australian Industrial Relations Tribunal, and in logs for wage demands of paid family daycare workers and waged childcare centre workers. It is registered in demands for placing a high priority on public funding for childcare places and the building of capital works, for the establishment of more childcare centres. It is also heard in protests directed at the biased nature of the income taxation system, which refuses to acknowledge the direct link between childcare expenses and the gaining of income.[18]

Women have highlighted, and continue to highlight, tax discrimination. Conflicts arise in the application of income taxation laws, which are read to refuse deductibility or rebatability to expenditure on childcare, although a parent is unable to participate in paidwork without it. In 1977 in *Ballesty's case* Mr Ballesty, a professional footballer, was allowed, as a deductible expense, the use of his private motor vehicle to travel to football games. His argument was that he was required to arrive at the game calm and in a peaceful frame of mind, so that he could earn the requisite income – his payments for games of football. In 1983 in *Martin's case* Ms Martin put before the courts an apparently similar argument: that she was required to arrive at her place of paid employment calm and of peaceful frame of mind, so that she could earn the requisite income. Being a single parent, her calm and peaceful mind were predicated upon her being able to place her child in a comfortable, secure and stimulating childcare centre, for which she was required to pay fees. Despite *Ballesty's case*, Ms Martin's argument was given short shrift: it was rejected.[19]

---

17. Quoted Carolyn Rasmussen, note 15, p. 362.
18. In the 1983 *National Wage case* the Women's Electoral Lobby, Union of Australian Women and National Council of Women intervened. In addition to other matters relating to equal pay, the Women's Electoral Lobby submission substantially dealt with the question of childcare as central to women's right to engage in paid employment and to benefit from Australian Conciliation and Arbitration Commission determinations as to equal pay (1969), "equal pay for work of equal value" (1972), a minimum wage for women (1974) and maternity leave (1979). The Commission's response to this was that it was not a matter with which the Commission could deal – that is, childcare is not (sic) an industrial matter. [See discussion of the case and approach, Jocelynne A. Scutt, *Women and the Law*, 1990, Law Book Co., Sydney, pp. 93–99.]
19. See *Federal Commissioner of Taxation v. Ballesty* (1977) 7 ATR 411; *Martin v. Federal Commissioner of Taxation* (1983) 14 ATR 383. [Also discussion in Jocelynne A. Scutt, note 18, pp. 353–363.]

Yet women have refused to accept this conundrum. Arguing in accordance with the requirements of section 51(1) of the *Income Tax Act* 1936 that childcare expenses are necessarily incurred in gaining or producing assessable income, and that where they are so expended they are not classifiable under the Act as "private or domestic", women have appeared before Taxation Boards of Review, the Administrative Appeals Tribunal, Supreme Courts, the Federal Court and the High Court. In accordance with the true tradition of dissenters, the arguments put have been sound in substance, and ingenious in their presentation. In 1982 Ms Smith argued it was an "implied term" of her contract of employment that she make "satisfactory childcare arrangements".[20] Her case was lost. Ms Johnston put to the Board of Review that "the cost of childcare incurred for the purpose of earning income by people who have full-time responsibility for the care of children cannot be regarded as a cost incurred by choice".[21] The Board rejected her claim. Ms Douglas resorted to the *Community Welfare Services Act* (Victoria) 1970 provision that every person who neglects to provide adequate and proper food, nursing, clothing, medical aid or lodging for any child in his or her care or custody, or causes or procures such child to be so neglected, without reasonable cause, is guilty of an offence and liable to a penalty of $1000 or imprisonment for twelve months. She made submissions that:

- she had a statutory duty of care for her child;
- her financial and domestic situation were such that she had to enter paidwork in order to provide that care;
- she had to incur child-minding expenses to work in paid employment;
- therefore, the expenses incurred to have her child properly minded were inextricably bound up with her employment, and so were properly deductible under section 51(1) of the *Income Tax Act*.[22]

Her claim was rejected. In *Jayatilake's case*, a different approach was taken. A parallel was drawn with travel expense cases, and expenses associated with higher education. Ms Jayatilake was engaged in full-time paid employment, a condition of which was that she engage in studies to improve her skills in computer science and accountancy, in order to gain higher duties and higher income. She enrolled in various courses, claiming expenses in respect of those courses. Expenses included photocopying, books, travel to the higher educational institution, stamps for that part of the course conducted by correspondence, gas and electricity for heating and lighting in her home study, and childcare expenses whilst the child was being professionally cared for, when she attended formal lectures and computer courses. The Commissioner accepted as legitimate expenses of higher education all apart from childcare expenses. This was despite *Hyde's case*, in which the Federal Court of Australia held that childcare is not to be treated as a generic expense, never deductible. In *Hyde's case* Justice French said

---

20. Case P65 (1982) 82 ATC 312.
21. *K. J. Johnston v. Federal Commissioner of Taxation* (Case P70) (1982) 82 ATC 335.
22. *Douglas v. Federal Commissioner of Taxation* (Case R48) (1984) 84 ATC 384, 385–386.

that there are cases where these expenses are relevant to the gaining of assessable income, and are not in such cases "private" or "domestic". Just as travel expenses can be private or domestic, or can be business expenses, so too with childcare. Ms Jayatilake has appealed.[23]

As Doris Blackburn once said:

We must have an ideal and think for ourselves instead of permitting governments [and courts] to do our planning and thinking. We can have no progress if we cannot think.[24]

The notion of dissent is one directly associated with the capacity to think for oneself. It is not one of mindless objection, directionless obstruction, contradiction for the sake of it, contrariness for itself. It is for the dissenter to require governments to plan in accordance with democratic thought, democratic demands. Progress is premised on thinking which directs dissent and pushes the parameters.

Conclusion

Doris Blackburn argued:

The most important matter is education through which means alone definite progress has been made in the world, and which must be greatly improved and intensified. It must be desired by the people, and must not be purely a means of supplying children with a vocation, but must concentrate on teaching the idea of service to the community.

But wanting education is not enough. The dominant culture that dictates the educational quality and educational access must accede to the demands of the dissenters to change, to accommodate, to truly embrace the ideal of education as accessible and encouraging to all, not the few or the already advantaged. As Pat Eatock reflects:

As a child I had been fascinated by the distant white gleam of buildings at the University of Queensland at St Lucia. I gradually realised that working-class kids don't go to university. At least not unless you were a "real brain". High School didn't enter my thinking because in my day, you didn't enter high school until you were thirteen or fourteen. I left school at fourteen, beginning a "career" in factory process work. Years later I realised how lucky I was to be in school at all. Until 1948 (the year I was ten), any principal could refuse to accept an aboriginal child into his school.[25]

---

23. *Jayatilake v. Federal Commissioner of Taxation*, unreported Administrative Claims Tribunal. [The taxpayers' appeal to the Federal Court was heard by Justice Beaumont, *Jayatilake v. FCT* (1990) 2 ATC 4776. The Full Court appeal was heard by Justices Sweeney, Jenkinson and Hill, *Jayatilake v. FCT* (1991) ATC 4516. In 1991 the High Court, constituted by Justices Dawson, Toohey and McHugh, refused leave to appeal, *Jayatilake v. FCT* (1991) 39 *Weekly Tax Bull.* [634] 391.]
24. Quoted Carolyn Rasmussen, note 15, p. 357. The quotation at the start of the Conclusion comes from the same source, p. 358.
25. Pat Eatock, "There's a Snake in My Caravan" in *Different Lives*, note 11, pp.24–25.

Lilla Watson writes:

When
I think
of my childhood
it's
like
a bad dream
filled with nightmares
but
I never screamed
it's frozen inside
locked up
in me
hidden
deep down
where
white folks
can't see ...

I actually went to school wanting to learn, wanting to get to know other kids and to be part of everything at school.[26]

She goes on:

I
can remember
when I
went to school
how
I'd approach
the gate
to my awaited fate
how my head
felt tight
like being squeezed
in a vice
with hate
and always, always
I was late
dragging my feet
in the dust
head bowed low
trying to think
of some excuse
to allow me

---

26. Lilla Watson, note 11, p. 46. The immediately following quotation comes from the same source, pp. 46–47.

> to go home
> to try
> to escape
> the misery
> and hate
> How I hated
> this thing
> "schooling"
> they said
> "education's the thing"
> I'd sit at my desk
> and not learn a thing
> and wish to hell
> it had never
> begun ...

Maurice Blackburn was expelled twice from the Australian Labor Party (ALP): first in 1935 for refusing to dissociate himself from the Movement Against War and Fascism. Readmitted in 1937, he was expelled for the second time in the 1940s, standing as an independent for his previously held Labor seat, suffering defeat, then dying in 1944. Doris Blackburn won the same seat two years later. Doris Blackburn and Maurice Blackburn stood out consistently against conscription, against war, and against fascism. They stood together in dissent.

Some may believe it important not to dissent to the extent of being at odds with a political organisation which is itself founded in dissent against the dominant culture. This may be to be at odds with a political party (such as the ALP) which dissents against the promotion and support of inegalitarianism and anti-democratic principles. It may be to be in dissent against a political party which is itself in dissent against social structures based on an elitism centred in corporate power and material wealth. Others may identify with a need to dissent, even where that places the dissenter at odds with those who belong to a political party the aim of which is to nurture egalitarian ideals and strive for redistribution of wealth and power.

The thinkers upon whom Doris Blackburn relies for progress may take varying positions on this question. Indeed, they are more likely than not to do so. The ultimate answer must be that it is by dissent based in the caring imagination that the abuse of power, exploitation of the powerless, and the very existence of the exploitative powerful and dominated powerless will be ended.

In 1982 the High Court of Australia heard an appeal by Mr Neal, an Australian Aborigine living on a reserve in Queensland, against a sentence of six months imprisonment imposed by the Queensland Court of Criminal Appeal. Mr Neal, together with a number of fellow residents of the reserve, engaged in a protest against the running of the reserve. Amongst other causes of dissatisfaction, putrid meat was being sold through the only store on the reserve, run by the (white) overseer. Overcome with frustration, Mr Neal approached the overseer and spoke with him through the flywire door of his house; Mr Neal concluded the conversation by spitting at him, the spittle hitting the wire of the door rather than the man behind it. He was initially sentenced by a Queensland magistrate to two months imprisonment with hard labour. The magistrate made a series of remarks about the offence which, said Justice Murphy of the High Court, showed that he had put himself in opposition to the political stance of Mr Neal, that conditions need changing on the reserves. Although the reserve director told Mr Neal he should "go through the channels" if he desired change, the magistrate told Mr Neal it was wrong to seek to change anything. The Court of Criminal Appeal did not dis-approve or comment on these remarks. The magistrate, said Justice Murphy, took into account political views and actions in sentencing Mr Neal:

[The magistrate's] remarks were not only patronising and insulting; they also made clear that anyone who agitated for change, "in any shape or form" in the Aboriginal communities, would be under a disadvantage in that Magistrate's Court. In its supervision of the criminal justice system of the state, the Court of Criminal Appeal has a duty to see that racism is not allowed to operate within the judicial system. It should have disapproved of the unjudicial manner in which the magistrate dealt with sentence.[27]

Justice Murphy concluded:

That Mr Neal was an "agitator" or stirrer in the magistrate's view obviously contributed to the severe penalty. If he is an agitator he is in good company. Many of the great religious and political figures of history have been agitators, and human progress owes much to the efforts of these and many who are unknown. As Wilde aptly pointed out in *The Soul of Man Under Socialism*, "Agitators are a set of interfering meddling people, who come down to some perfectly contented class of the community and sow the seeds of discontent amongst them. That is the reason why agitators are so absolutely necessary. Without them, in our incomplete state, there would be no advance towards civilisation." Mr Neal is entitled to be an agitator.

These words require constant reiteration, as do the actions of those who are in dissent. Without the agitators, there would be no advance towards civilisation. Without dissent, power remains a quality owned by the powerful; democracy in its true sense remains incapable of achievement. In a political world, whether in private or in public, dissent is essential to any advance toward a democratic ideal where power is possessed in equal shares, and is used not to destroy or stultify, not to impede or rule over, but to advance collectively. The Maurice Blackburn Memorial Lecture enables us to reflect annually upon the value of dissent and the courage of those who continue to stand out against conformity. In reflecting upon the work of Doris Blackburn and Maurice Blackburn and upon their sentiments, we are enabled to move further along the way they chose. To dissent at the right time, in the right place, and in right measure is to support the democratic ideal. The choice of time, place and measure can be determined only by the dissenter. But it is upon those in dissent that democracy depends.

---

27. Lionel K. Murphy, Justice of the High Court of Australia, in *Neal v. The Queen* (1982) 149 CLR 305, 316. The immediately following quotation comes from the same source, pp. 316–317.

4

RECONSTRUCTING THE AUSTRALIAN ETHOS:
Women, Men and Values in Australian Society

KEYNOTE SPEECH, UNIVERSITY OF WESTERN AUSTRALIA SUMMER SCHOOL
Perth, Western Australia.
13 January 1986

As a Western Australian living in the eastern states, I had often noticed the newspaper advertisements announcing the University of Western Australia Summer School, which is held in Perth early in each new year. Although the Summer School had invited women as speakers in some previous years, a woman had never been invited to present the keynote speech. As Irene Greenwood writes in "Chronicle of Change",[1] in 1974 Elizabeth Reid (then adviser to the Prime Minister, Gough Whitlam) was a speaker, and "took up the theme of women's role; one sadly neglected at official levels". In 1983, Irene Greenwood adds, "the Summer School moved backwards: the topic was 'The Nation is People'. Not one woman participated as invited speaker." In 1986 a decision was made that this lack should be rectified. The theme was "Australia: Values and Visions", which provided an opportunity to dissect and reject the insularity of the notion that the "real" Aussie is macho and male. I was also determined to confront the tyranny of "the first": the first woman sea captain, the first woman deep-sea diver, the first woman dictator, the first woman man-in-the-moon. This mode of highlighting women does much to cover up *what women have achieved at the same time as purporting to celebrate women's achievements. Dr Maureen Smith, Director of the University Extension which organises the Summer School, and I laughed at the irony that I had berated this tendency in my keynote speech, when she had wished proudly to announce that the Summer School had at last invited its first woman keynote speaker.*

---

1. Irene Greenwood, "Chronicle of Change" in *As a Woman – Writing Women's Lives*, 1992, Jocelynne A. Scutt (ed.), Artemis Publishing, Melbourne, pp. 107–120 at p. 117. In the footnotes, square brackets [...] indicate new material added for this edition.

The year was a good one. Of the ten Summer School speakers, five were women. Dr Barbara Thiering (School of Divinity, Sydney University), Pat O'Shane (then Secretary of the New South Wales Ministry of Aboriginal Affairs), Wendy McCarthy (General Manager, Marketing and Communications, Australian Bicentennial Authority, and Deputy Chairperson, Australian Broadcasting Corporation [ABC]) and Professor Carla Fasano (Professor of Education, University of Wollongong) completed the list.

———————

On the first day of term I set to work, with several willing helpers, shovelling out bucketsful of sand. Then I attacked the floor, desks and windows with masses of soap and water.

In those days the teacher was given an extra allowance of two shillings and sixpence a week for cleaning the school buildings every day ...

– Jean Clark, a teacher at Ninda West, Victoria 1939[2]

My father was a country school-teacher ... Dad thought girls should stay home and help their mothers. God knows she could have done with it. Mother believed in making sacrifices for education and she stood up for me. I was mad on science and at High School I got ten subjects in Intermediate and six in Leaving – all leading to Science, and won a "free place" at the University. I would have lived on turnips and in rags if I could have added even a little to our knowledge. But now mother ruled that they could not afford to keep me ...

– Thelma Fry, died 1985[3]

I was always very interested in politics ... In Cranbourne they were starting a branch of a political party ... They tried to get me to join ... They sat there talking about these men on sustenance, how they were leaning on their shovels. Now ... I knew how much they paid their workers. A man would go there at six o'clock in the morning, work till about eleven o'clock, go back at one o'clock and work till six o'clock, and he got a pound a week! So I stood up like this, and I said, "Fancy you ladies talking like this about those poor men who are working on sustenance!"... I said, "You pay a man a pound a week for all those hours. I'm in the wrong place!" And I walked out.

– Lillian, arrived Australia March 1928[4]

My husband became qualified, too, but only men could get permanency. And what was really shocking was that I did the same job as he did but got very much less money ... And they used to call me to interpret nearly every day, not only for my own language but for any Slavonic language and also Italian and German. I was not paid anything especially for that and, of course, you were expected to get your

———————

2. "Rust" in *Equal to the Occasion*, Errol Broome, Helen Gibson, Dorothy Richards, Shirley Thomas and Jean Turnely (eds.), 1985, Cole Publications, Hawthorn, p. 105.
3. "People" in *Equal to the Occasion*, p. 66.
4. "Lillian" in *The Immigrants*, Wendy Lowenstein and Moragh Loh (eds.), 1977, Penguin Books Australia, Ringwood, pp. 52–53.

ordinary quota of work done as usual. They didn't consider interpreting as a professional job, they took it as something anybody can do. Cleaners, anybody, would be required to interpret. I know about a Greek lady who comforted a child in her own language while she was visiting a hospital, and the doctor said to her, "Oh, you are very good at this. How about taking a job as a cleaner so you can interpret for us."

– Gordana, arrived in Australia 1952[5]

Introduction

From the time of white settlement in Australia, assessments have been made of the essential character of "Australia" and "Australians". In her classic work, *Damned Whores and God's Police*, Anne Summers discerns two major themes. The one, she writes:

… was the evolving of the Australian Man of the Bush, that brash, rugged, sardonic individual (despite his dependence on his mates) who has been the hero of countless sagas from Clancy of the Overflow, through Ned Kelly to the various characters who inhabit the pages of Steele Rudd, Joseph Furphy and Henry Lawson. He might be a swaggie, a stockman or even a city larrikin; later he was a member of the AIF, an urban worker or an itinerant rural wanderer, but he always possessed at least some of those characteristics, which a swarm of men and writers detected in themselves or in the males they observed and which they were anxious to transpose into a living legend. Probably more written words have been devoted to creating, and then to analysing and extolling, this composite Australian male than to any other single facet of Australian life.[6]

The second theme, setting itself up "in opposition to the crude nationalism of the first", was that of "the pristine intellectual, again always male, who was revulsed by the barbarism of colonial, especially rural or small-town colonial mores." Summers continues:

His cultural affinities were invariably with England although he was strongly drawn to the physical immediacy of the Australian continent, a land which fascinated him and gripped his imagination while it stultified his intellect, and as a result he suffered from what Martin Boyd had labelled "geographic schizophrenia" and was destined to wander relentlessly between the two countries, a spiritual exile in search of an ineluctable and remote fulfilment.

In *The Australian Legend*, historian Russel Ward, writing in 1958, is true to the earlier myth-making. He purports not to present a history of Australia or Australians, "or even primarily an explanation of what most Australians are like and how they came to be that way." His aim, he states, is to "try to trace and explain the development of the Australian self-image – of the often romanticized and exaggerated stereotypes in men's minds of what the *typical*, not the *average* Australian likes (or in some cases

---

5. "Gordana" in *The Immigrants*, note 4, p. 86.
6. Anne Summers, *Damned Whores and God's Police – The Colonization of Women in Australia*, 1975, Penguin Books Australia, Ringwood, pp. 36–37. The immediately following quotation comes from the same source, p. 37.

*dis*likes) to believe he is like." Ward's use of the masculine pronoun is, apparently, intentional. The myth outlined by Ward is that:

... the "typical Australian" is a practical man, rough and ready in his manners and quick to decry any appearance of affectation in others. He is a great improviser, ever willing "to have a go" at anything, but willing too to be content with a task done in a way that is "near enough". Though capable of great exertion in an emergency, he normally feels no impulse to work hard without good cause. He swears hard and consistently, gambles heavily and often, and drinks deeply on occasions. Though he is "the world's best confidence man", he is usually taciturn rather than talkative, one who endures stoically rather than one who acts busily. He is a "hard case", sceptical about the value of religion and of intellectual and cultural pursuits generally. He believes that Jack is not only as good as his master but, at least in principle, probably a good deal better, and so he is a great "knocker" of eminent people unless, as in the case of his sporting heroes, they are distinguished by physical prowess. He is a fiercely independent person who hates officiousness and authority, especially when these qualities are embodied in military officers and policemen. Yet he is very hospitable and, above all, will stick to his mates through thick and thin, even if he thinks they may be in the wrong. No epithet in his vocabulary is more completely damning than "scab", unless it is "pimp" used in its peculiarly Australasian slang meaning of "informer". He tends to be a rolling stone, highly suspect if he should chance to gather much moss.[7]

Although women are mentioned on odd occasions in Ward's exposition, there is no acknowledgement or even suspicion that women come within the profile of the "typical Australian". Nor indeed is there any recognition that the characteristics of the "typical Australian" equate with those of the women of the country, or that those characteristics are distinguishable from the women. It is the occasional mention of women which makes it clear that women are simply outside the myth. Ward seems not to consider that women might have a part to play in the creation of the myth and, more importantly, in the reality of Australia and Australians – nor indeed does he seem to be interested in the question.

To look at "what is" (rather than accepting Ward's blinkered vision), evidence is readily available that some of the characteristics of the "mythical Australian" are the reality of the Australian woman, or are at least as real for some Australian women as for some Australian men. "He is a fiercely independent person who hates officiousness or authority, especially when these qualities are embodied in military officers and policemen," writes Ward. In 1878 Ellen Kelly was convicted by Judge Redmond Barry of "aiding and abetting the attempted murder of a local policeman and sentenced to three years gaol with hard labour". The occasion was that of the attempted arrest of her son Ned, in an altercation which finally led to his capture and death.[8] That her son was

---

7. Russel Ward, *The Australian Legend*, Oxford University Press, Melbourne, pp. 1–2. The preceding quotation is taken from the foreword to the second edition, published in 1965, pp. vi–ix, 1956, pp. 1–2.
8. Marilyn Lake, "The Trials of Ellen Kelly" in *Double Time – Women in Victoria – 150 Years*, Marilyn Lake and Farley Kelly (eds.), 1985, Penguin Books Australia, Ringwood, p. 86.

involved does not detract from the "fierce independence" displayed by Ellen Kelly and her "hatred of officiousness and authority". And the example is not isolated. Throughout Australia's history there have been women who have stood out against abuses by officialdom and the misuse of authority. Queen Aggie, daughter of Jim and Sarah Crowe, born near the Edwards River in New South Wales some twenty-two miles north of Swan Hill in the mid-Murray region, was once "questioned about the loss of a fowl noticed after [she had visited] ... a nearby station to collect her tobacco allowance." She replied, "Ah well, Mr. Laird, you [have taken] my country, I [take] your fowl".[9]

Ward writes that the "typical Australian" is "a great improviser, ever willing 'to have a go' at anything ..." Women were often left alone in bush shanties, huts, tents and camps; often they worked side by side with the men of the family. Threatened by bushfires, Louisa Meredith of Port Sorrell, Van Diemen's Land wrote in the 1840s:

I began to count up our carpets and blankets, intending to have them all soaked in the brook, and laid over the roof to prevent its becoming ignited by the falling flakes, and I had our small stock of gunpowder ready to bury in the garden, under the camp oven, if the danger increased.[10]

Travelling from Goolwa along the South Australian coast in the 1850s, Lucy Jones wrote in her diary, "I helped dig a small waterhole yesterday, chopped down several trees and wood, so you can imagine what nice hands I have for piano!"[11]

That there might have been a positive correlation between women's talents, abilities, prowess and the character depicted as typically Australian has not been a subject concerning the majority of historians whose works have been published or, being published, have been remembered. Although it is said that the "typical (male) Australian" outlined by Ward is by no means the average Australian of today and never was the average Australian, the few times women are mentioned gives an even more stereotypical or cardboard cut-out vision of Australia and Australians. Women, when observed, traditionally are seen as harlots, whores, drunkards. The typical Australian male of Ward's thesis appears to live a life of isolation from women. Yet suddenly, with no explanation of how women arrived, where they lived, their daily lives – women are simply there – at least for a word, a sentence or two, or at the most, a paragraph. Readers learn there were no women on the goldfields – only to be told a short time later that the children on the fields took the bad language of their (male) elders, and became capital at swearing. Unless the obvious is accepted – that some women inhabited the goldfields – there is a less believable proposition to be accepted, and one that goes against what is generally accepted to be the male ethos of the time –

9. Jan Penney, "Queen Aggie – The Last of Her Tribe" in *Double Time*, 1985, note 8, p. 101.
10. Louisa Meredith, *My Home in Tasmania*, 1840, pp. 213–214; extract in *Colonial Ladies*, Maggie Weidenhofer (compiler/ed.), 1985, Currey O'Neil, South Yarra, p. 71.
11. Excerpted in Lucy Frost (compiler and ed.), *No Place for a Nervous Lady – Voices from the Australian Bush*, 1984, Penguin Books Australia, Ringwood, p. 236.

that the goldfields were the centre of a new family formation, namely single-parent, father-headed households!

Indirectly readers learn that women (and children) were expected to starve alongside their husbands and fathers, when living in the traditional household:

... the outback offered something nearly approaching absolute economic security, albeit at what was, from a middle-class point of view, a relatively low level. Gargantuan quantities of mutton, damper and tea, and sufficient rough slop clothing, were always available to a competent workman unencumbered by wife and children.[12]

Shepherds and handymen are depicted as bachelors, every one. But then follows the anecdote of Jack, the shepherd and handyman, who:

... for many months remained at work, held back from the rush by the tongue of his wife who feared that the sly grog sellers on the field would immediately receive any gold he might find. In the end he left, fell in with three old mates from New South Wales, and rapidly dug £200 worth of gold. With this he took his wife and two bush-bred daughters to Melbourne ...

Earlier the tale has been that the bush harbours no women – despite the statistical evidence Ward quotes to the contrary, showing that in the areas around the towns, in 1841 and 1851 in New South Wales, males were only slightly above 50 per cent; in 1851 in the squatting districts, 30 per cent of the population was female; and in the same period women comprised some 44 per cent of the population in country areas outside the immediate city area of Sydney. Percentages in other colonies were similar – and Black Australian women also were a part of the population.

This overlooking of women, or recognising women only as a charge upon the male worker or an encumbrance upon the courageous, adventure-seeking "true" Australian continues. A programme broadcast on the national airwaves in December 1985, and titled "Definitions of Australia and Being Australian", talked of the embodiment of the typical Australian in the 1950s and 1960s as Chips Rafferty. This, mouthed the pundits, had passed in the 1980s to the Mel Gibson image of *Gallipoli* – the contemporary Australian film of the Anzacs. The picture of the typical Australian put before Australian Broadcasting Corporation (ABC) listeners remained the "tall, lean, bronze digger looking off into the distance with squinting blue eyes". Although the programme recognised that this is an untrue picture – recall all those of us who are short, beer bellied and Norm-be-in-it-like, emphasised an ABC male speaker (no female speakers appeared to be participating) – there was no acknowledgement that for 51 per cent of the Australian population the myth was neither a myth nor a reality having any close approximation to ourselves, or having any possible approximation.[13]

---

12. Russel Ward, *The Australian Legend*, note 7, p. 76. The immediately following quotation comes from the same source, p. 54.
13. Monday, 23 December 1985, ABC second network (Radio National).

And the myth quickly brushes over other realities such as the ethnic mix of Australia from the very early days: apart from the Irish, English, Scots and a few Welsh immigrating, whether freely or by compulsion, Chinese settled in Australia in the early nineteenth century. But despite their contribution to the culture on the goldfields and elsewhere, they were painted as in Australia – not of it. A steady flow of women and men from many other countries, over long periods, has brought with them their values and characteristics. And what of our Aboriginal heritage in social, cultural and hereditary terms? The dominant image of the male anglo-Australian distorts Australian reality, presenting a false ethos to the world and, equally importantly, to ourselves. This is damaging to all Australians, women and men; white and Black; of recent, ancient or far less ancient ethnic origin; non-English speaking, or with English as a first (and often only) language. It is damaging because not only are many crucial elements left out, but those which are left in can be distorted. They inevitably will be distorted, because they do not represent the true picture. As well, the exclusion of some characteristics and the inflation of those included can create a sometimes misdirected, though legitimate, antagonism from those whose attributes have been excluded.

Values and Value Systems

That the relevance of values, and their very nature, is affected by the group having power to define relevance and values, is easily illustrated by reference to questions of violence, anger, justice, humour, courage, caring and power.

Values: Violence

White settlement in Australia brought with it violence legitimated by authority having little regard to human suffering. It brought also the ethos of the intrepid explorer desiring to conquer the land, followed by those taking as given that they should exploit the natural resources of the land, without reference to other factors, other values. Edward Kynaston, in *Book of the Bush*, points out:

Once the initial settlement was established at Botany Bay the occupation of the land followed with remarkable rapidity. Free settlers and ex-convicts followed the typical pattern of exploitation and development of a new country, still in innocent ignorance of the destruction they were causing and the damage they would leave to subsequent generations ... The result was that the early graziers overloaded the seemingly abundant land with sheep, and the native grasses hitherto only lightly grazed by the native marsupials quickly declined. The process of erosion began, followed by tunnelling, and finally the bare, crumbling, ugly characteristic gullies came out like sores on the land. That was how it was in central Victoria. Elsewhere destruction of a slightly different sort was in the making. Once natural cover was reduced and essentially poor soils compacted and became unable to absorb rain water, which instead ran ruinously, eroding over its surface, producing the extensive gully erosion that is widespread throughout eastern Australia.[14]

---

14. Edward Kynaston, *Book of the Bush*, 1977, Penguin Books Australia, Ringwood, p. 31. The immediately following quotation comes from the same source.

What is telling about the image of the Australian riding roughshod over the country-side, ignorant of the needs of the bush and the ecological balance, is the equivocation expressed toward this form of violence to the land. Thus Kynaston, although obviously deploring the exploitation occurring during those early years, goes on to mix his metaphors and adjectives in a contradictory stance of adulation and horror:

The farmer-explorers swarm across the empty map of the east, busy as bush flies round a carcass, a legion of indomitable, indefatigable, curious, optimistic men. They are aggressively intent on finding their fortunes somewhere in the huge, rich quietness of the desert landscape that they were already beginning to call "the bush". Soon their names are too numerous to record comfortably and only a few of the more outstanding are left to fix themselves, alongside their exploits, in the memory.

As Kynaston recognises, it was not always ignorance which led the early Australians to act in this way.

Violence against humanity was played out on a three-tier stage – against the convicts, by their gaolers; against the Aborigines, by the white colonial invasion; and against women. Women were vulnerable to violence from the authorities, their masters, mates or husbands; from "friends" or acquaintances; and from strangers. Violence against women is either ignored by the dominant culture, or depicted as a "crime worse than death". The occasional rape trial stands out, like the notorious Mt Renny case in New South Wales where, in 1885, 16 men faced charges of pack rape, 12 being committed for trial, nine being convicted and all those being sentenced to death. After community lobbying for and against execution of the penalty, four were ultimately hanged, the remainder escaping that fate. This caused such controversy that the maximum penalty of death was never again used for that crime.[15] But this was altogether unusual – most often, rape was not prosecuted and rarely did it come to the attention of authorities. Women's fears and reality have been written out of the Australian ethos.

The casual way in which this writing out takes place is illustrated in the diary written by Sarah Davenport in recording a trip from Sydney to the Ovens River region in what became Victoria. The sanitised version of her diary had Sarah Davenport writing as if the danger presented to her and her husband was sex-neutral; as if the two of them were equally affected, the threatened violence unrelated to one of the two of them being female.[16] When in the 1980s Lucy Frost sought out the original manuscript, she found that someone "had gone through this section (and only this section) of the diary with a blue pencil" eliminating the words by which Mrs Davenport made her specific vulnerability *as a woman* crystal clear: she was in danger of being raped; she

---

15. See Anne Summers, "Hidden from History – Women Victims of Crime", in *Women and Crime*, S. K. Mukherjee and Jocelynne A. Scutt, (eds.), 1981, Allen and Unwin, Sydney, pp. 26–28; for a popularised account, see James Holledge, "Four Hanged for Rape – A Brutal Crime and Punishment Equally Shocking" *Sunday Telegraph* 6 October 1885, p. 62.
16. The example of Sarah Davenport's diary, excerpted in *No Place for a Nervous Lady*, note 11, p. 14 is more fully described at p. 9, Chapter 1 of this volume.

and her husband armed themselves to prevent the violence from happening to *her*.

While the full reality of violence of strangers against women needs to be acknowledged, it is the violence against women by husbands or mates which is the most pervasive, but most overlooked. That criminal assault at home and other forms of domestic violence, have, from the beginnings of white settlement of Australia, been understated deliberately, is not for the want of women speaking out. Martha Clendinning, living in Victoria at the time of the Eureka Stockade in the mid-nineteenth century, told of an incident "involving the butcher's wife, who visited [her] tent for a gossip and a drink and who was beaten and kicked by her husband till the blood streamed from her face". At the same time, Thomas Ford, a pig farmer living in the Ballarat district, was reported as being convicted "of burning his wife's clothes and threatening to take her life". He was fined £50 and sentenced to three months imprisonment, although he must have been released early, or had the conviction set aside, for less than two months after the date of conviction he was charged with assaulting Ellen Kelly, who lived on a neighbouring property.[17] In a letter dated 23 December 1849 Penelope Selby, living in the Port Fairy district in Victoria writes:

Courtships are always very short in this country seen one week and married the next. Another peculiarity of this country is that men, gentle and simple, are rather fond of beating their wives – a gentleman residing in Belfast killed his the other day. He had not been married six months.

This aspect of the "real Australian ethos" is no less prevalent today. Just as during the nineteenth century women fought to have the problem of violence against women in marriage recognised, women in the twentieth century fight for the right of women not to be beaten or raped by their husbands. During the nineteenth century, Rose Scott recognised that battering and abuse, including rape, occurred in family homes; Louisa Lawson advocated more simple divorce laws to enable women to escape from violent men, and published informative articles in her feminist newspaper, *The Dawn*, to stir women to support divorce law reform. Today, women lobby for the recognition of violence in the home as criminal. Under the laws as existing, the beating, bashing and abuse of a woman by her husband is unlawful, but feminists demand that the law be put into effect.[18]

Despite historical and contemporary reality, the vision of the characteristic Australian fails to record this theme, unless in "jest", or as an acceptable way for a man to keep a

---

17. The Martha Clendinning example is given by Louis Asher, "Martha Clendinning – A Woman's Life on the Goldfields" in *Double Time*, note 3, p. 57. The Thomas Ford example is given by Marilyn Lake, "The Trials of Ellen Kelly", in *Double Time*, note 8, p. 88. The Penelope Selby example is extracted in *No Place for a Nervous Lady*, note 11, p. 181.
18. See Hilary Golder, *Divorce in Nineteenth Century New South Wales*, 1985, New South Wales University Press, Kensington, p. 228; Jocelynne A. Scutt, *Even in the Best of Homes – Violence in the Family*, 1983, Penguin Books Australia, Ringwood; Terese Rod, "Marital Murder" in *Violence in the Family*, 1980, Jocelynne A. Scutt (ed.), Australian Institute of Criminology, Canberra, p. 95.

wife under control. And the sorrow directly for women (and indirectly for men), is that the masculine ethic of domination, brute strength, aggression – such as that which Kynaston half-admiringly speaks of as underlying the exploitation of the land – is just that ethic giving foundation to criminal assault at home. Its depiction as the Australian ethic also ignores another reality – those Australian men who are capable of gentleness and the recognition of women's right to autonomy, and who put that capability into practice. Sadly, the distortion of our Australian background – the way in which the existence of women has been ignored – seems to have given credence to a view that Australian men are not and never will be a gentle race, and are not able to create genuine, gentle relationships with women. Ignoring the violence on one level, and tolerating it on another, conceals both the extent of violence against women and those relationships developed between Australian women and men in which violence is not a theme.

Values: Anger

Where anger is acknowledged as a part of Australia's history, it is linked with violence done to men in an oppressed position. Australia's convict heritage again supplies the background. Bushrangers – often convicts escaping harsh conditions imposed by the authorities or their masters, or others considering themselves wrongly treated under the class system – were reported as declaiming angrily as they went to the gallows. William Webber, a confederate of Jack Donahoe, was given the choice of being sent to Norfolk Island if he revealed information about other crimes committed; otherwise he would be hanged. Russel Ward reports his angry reply, "No ... I would rather be hanged than go [to Norfolk Island]. Don't trouble yourself about me; leave me to my fate." Webber was "hanged at the appointed time next day".[19]

A second bushranger, Hall, said from the dock when sentenced to death:

I've been all over the country in my time without taking the life of anyone. I've been baited like a bulldog and I'm only sorry now I didn't shoot every bloody tyrant in New South Wales.

Outside the courtroom he added:

I've never had anything to say against the prisoners, but I've got a grudge against every bloody swell in the country. I'll go to the gallows and die as comfortable as a biddy, and be glad of the chance.

The anger of women is spoken of little, yet anger is there. Just as men in the past protested angrily against abuse by those in positions of power, women rebelled against exploitative masters. Rather than viewing their reaction as anger, however, the

---

19 Russel Ward, note 7, p. 148. The two immediately following quotations come from the same source, pp.148–149.

authorities depicted it as "incorrigibility", or labelled the women as possessing "bad habits", being "lazy" or "depraved".

Women's anger is also trivialised, rather than accepted as brave outrage against injustice or oppressive behaviour, or the abuse of power. Thus in the nineteenth century, women in Australia were angered at being prevented from training at universities, or entering various trades or professions. They took action, but through judicial manipulation of language were denied the right. In South Australia Mary Cecil Kitson applied to the Supreme Court in 1920 for admission to practice as a public notary. She was already admitted to practise law, because the South Australian Parliament had passed the *Female Law Practitioners Act* in 1911 stating women could be so admitted. The *Public Notaries Act* had not been so amended. It said that any "person" with certain qualifications was entitled to be admitted to the office of notary. The Supreme Court refused entry to Mary Kitson. The basis of the decision was that the court had never had such an approach before, and it was irrelevant that women were entitled to become lawyers or doctors (because those laws had been amended to include women). The Act said any "person", and it was clear to the court that women were *not* persons.[20] Earlier, in the United States, Canada, various Australian states, England and other countries with a legal system deriving from the British, similar decisions were made. As in Australia, women were refused the right to attend university, gain admission to practise law, enter the medical profession, stand for Parliament and local government, and vote in municipal and state elections. In *Bebb's case* an English court considered that a married women is not a person, because upon marriage a woman and her husband become "one", and that one "is the husband". It then went on to look at the problem of single women, saying:

... it is true that difficulty does not apply to single women, but every woman can be married at some time in her life, and it would be a serious inconvenience if, in the middle of her articles, or in the middle of conducting a piece of litigation, a woman was suddenly to be disqualified ... by reason of her marriage.[21]

In 1982 the Australian Broadcasting Commission (ABC) reported upon the case of a law lecturer at an Australian university where:

... about one third of the students were female, but [he] insisted on referring to the entire class as "gentlemen". Halfway through the semester his students got a bit fed up with this, particularly the females, of course, and they persuaded the male students to stay from one of his lectures. When the lecturer walked into the lecture hall and looked around and noted that there were no

---

20. *In re Kitson* (1920) SALR 230; see further Albie Sachs and Joan Hoff Wilson, *Sexism and the Law – A Study of Male Beliefs and Judicial Bias*, 1978, Martin Robertson, Oxford; Jocelynne A. Scutt, *Growing Up Feminist – The New Generation of Australian Women*, 1985, Angus and Robertson, Sydney, pp. 6–8, 38–42. [See also Jocelynne A. Scutt, *Women and the Law – Commentary and Materials*, 1990, Law Book Co., Sydney, particularly Chapter 1, "Women in Law", pp. 2–21.]
21. *Bebb v. Law Society* [1914] Ch. 286, at 299.

males present, only females, he said, "Well, seeing there's nobody here we'll finish early," and in fact lectured for only 15 minutes before leaving.[22]

The anger experienced in such circumstances is legitimate and demands recognition. It reacts against a less pleasant side of the Australian ethos, one which does not equate with the traditional view of Australians as egalitarian, unless egalitarianism is defined as including some and not others. The value system which underpins this behaviour cannot be changed until it is acknowledged as a part of the dominant Australian ethos, and the angry response as legitimate and real.

Values: Justice

Equivocal beliefs exist in the Australian psyche in the case of justice. Accepted wisdom has it that the law treats people neutrally: the rich and the poor have a right to sleep under bridges; the rich and the poor have a right to dine at the Ritz. Traditionally women, like men, have grown up with this view of the world firmly entrenched – although some come to recognise that sleeping under bridges brings with it the possibility of being classified a vagrant, and dining at the Ritz means having the money to pay the bill – or hopefully escaping legal action, when without the funds, by contracting to wash the dishes instead. And some Australians grow up learning that "justice" does not apply to them.

Simultaneously with the view of Australia as a "just" society, individuals and groups have agitated strongly for the extension to themselves of the rights they perceive others to have. (Thus, the story of Queen Aggie, who considered it a fair answer to the charge that she had taken a neighbour's chicken – "You've taken my land, I've taken your chicken.") The history of agitation in Australia in the name of justice is not inconsequential. Aborigines, Torres Strait and Pacific Islanders, and some non-Aboriginal Australians have a long, proud tradition of fighting against racial intolerance and for equal rights irrespective of race, ethnic origin and other characteristics used by some as a means of discrimination and deprivation of rights. From before the turn of the century women's organisations lobbied for equal pay for work of equal value; for representation of women on governmental boards and committees; for access to good quality health services. Equal opportunities for women are championed by the National Council of Women, the Union of Australian Women, the United Associations of Women, the Karakatta Club, the League of Women Voters and various suffrage organisations now and in the past.[23] "Equal opportunities" demands included full citizenship for

---

22. Alicia Lee, 'If you do not say that you are a woman you are taken to be a man," in "'He-Man' Language – How Sexism is Reflected and Perpetuated by Words", in *Coming Out! Women's Voices, Women's Lives*, Julie Rigg and Julie Copeland (eds.), 1985, Nelson/ABC, Melbourne, p. 121.
23. See for example, item 327. National Council of Women. Records. Acc. No. 1389A/1–23, in *Women in Australia – An Annotated Guide to Records*, vol. 1 Tasmania, West Australia and South Australia, 1977, AGPS, Canberra. (Edited for the National Research Programme by Kay Daniels, Mary Murnane and Anne Picot.)

women (meaning the right to stand for various public offices, including Parliament and local government; the right to vote in all public elections and so on); appointment of women as full Justices of the Peace, and "women representatives on all Government boards, Royal Commissions and Select Committees". On 20 January 1926 the National Council of Women of Western Australia requested that in "the appointment of the new Physicians and Surgeons on the Perth Public Hospital there should always be equal consideration given to women, especially in the matter of gynaecological and surgical work."[24] The early established women's organisations "took a keen interest in current legislation and several deputations in the 1920s waited on the government requesting amendments to the *Divorce Act*, the *State Children Act* and the *Factories Act*". Today, those same organisations, or others in their tradition such as the Women's Electoral Lobby (WEL), Australian Federation of Business and Professional Women (AFBPW), and Women's Liberation, lobby for legislation relevant to justice for women and other "out" groups, or review legislation in Bill form. The *Family Law Act* 1975 and various state and federal *Affirmative Action*, *Sex Discrimination*, *Anti-Discrimination* or *Equal Opportunity Acts* are readily available examples.

Councils of Action for Equal Pay were established early this century, and worked from at least the 1930s for equal pay for work of equal value. In Victoria in 1984 the Campaign of Action for Equal Pay was re-formed to intervene in the *Nurses case*, a case before the Australian Conciliation and Arbitration Commission for equal pay for work done in the main by women which has comparable worth with work done in the main by men.[25]

In addition to collective action, women have fought individually for access to jobs on equal footing with men. The first person appointed to the newly created position of Assistant Chief Inspector of the Education Department was a man, Leslie Wrigley. He had earlier been appointed, simultaneously with a woman, Julia Flynn, to a lower-ranked post. He left the position in 1928 to become principal of the Teachers College and Professor of Education. His job was advertised at the salary range for a man. Julia Flynn protested; she said she wanted to apply. She was eventually appointed to the position of Assistant Chief Inspector at four-fifths of the salary set when Leslie Wrigley occupied it.

Next the Chief Inspector's job was advertised, stating unequivocally that men only need apply:

While the government vacillated, women's organisations protested at the restriction of the Chief Inspector's job to men. In particular they were concerned that Julia Flynn, "whose qualifications were recognised as unsurpassed", would be debarred even from competing for the position. The National Council of Women speculated on a "conspiracy" to keep women

---

24. National Council of Women, resolution 24 May 1921, note 23.
25. See Carol O'Donnell and Nerolie Golder, "A Comparative Analysis of Equal Pay in the United States, Britain and Australia" (1986) 3 *Aust. Fem. Studies* 59. [See Jocelynne A. Scutt, *Women and the Law*, note 21, pp. 101, 107-108; and 82-138 generally.]

from the "top of the tree" and called for a united effort to "beam down the obstacles placed by those who evidently fear women's capability". The advertisement represented not a conspiracy but the decision of Martin Hansen, the new Director of Education, who in defence of the exclusive terms of the advertisement asserted that he knew the job because he had done it and "a woman could not do the work".[26]

Judith Biddington notes that the Director "expressed concern at the embarrassment Julia Flynn must be feeling as a result of the public agitation". He then "suggested that the matter be dropped". It was not. The *Australian Women's Mirror* "voiced outrage at both the inequality of pay in the teaching profession and the possibility that Julia Flynn had been barred from the position because she was a woman".

In the upshot, direction was given that the job should be advertised so that women as well as men could apply. Julia Flynn applied. A man whom she had beaten for the position was appointed. She appealed and her appeal was upheld. However, her probationary appointment was not made permanent. The other man was appointed in her place, and she resumed the position of Assistant in 1928. When in 1936 he resigned to move upward, she was appointed to the Chief Inspector's position "without fuss".

And in the so-called non-traditional fields, in Victoria by 1918 Alice Anderson had established her own garage and hire-car service in Kew. She bought more cars, employed young women to be drivers and mechanics for the service, and in 1919 "... the business expanded when she built a large brick garage and 'Miss Anderson's Motor Service' was advertised". Alice Anderson patented a "Get Out and Get Under Trolley" for ease of access under cars when needing to do repairs.[27] Earlier, Ivy Rudd had noted sexist assumptions in the motor industry, and wrote:

It was a lovely May morning in 1911 when I took my test for a driving licence. I wore a formal frock and hat... I was driven up to the Old Melbourne Gaol. A policeman took over there, and sat next to me. He was very nice to me, although he gave me a fright when he yelled out to a hansom cab driver who was on the wrong side of the road.

I drove around the Russell Street block, not far.

When we came to fill in the licence form, the policeman had to strike out every time there was a "his" and write in "her".[28]

In 1916 Alice Anderson had suffered "many refusals" before she found a mechanic who would take her on for a six-month "apprenticeship". In 1982 Emel Corley, an eighteen-year-old living in Brisbane, wrote of her experience in gaining qualifications from a local college:

26. Judith Biddington, "Julia Flynn – Teacher at the Top" in *Double Time*, note 8, p. 322. The quotations in the next paragraph come from the same source.
27. "Alice Anderson – Garage Proprietor", in *Double Time*, p. 308.
28. Ivy Rudd, "Licence" in *Equal to the Occasion*, Errol Broome, Helen Gibson, Dorothy Richards, Shirley Thomas and Jean Turnely (eds.), 1985, Cole Publications, Hawthorn, pp. 60–61.

... I discovered the college had an affirmative action system of selection; ten per cent of positions were reserved for women, and ten per cent for black Australians, ten per cent for the disabled, and the other seventy per cent for boys. This is a well-kept secret. I was the only woman who applied to the course, out of 750 applicants (which was probably because I was the only woman in Brisbane who knew the course was available to us) so I got in straight away.

... Finishing the course, I came second in my class. At graduation I was ignored by the principal and teachers: they commented only on how well the boys had performed.

I went overseas. When I returned to Brisbane I found an apprenticeship as a motor mechanic, but not without trouble. Prospective employers could not ignore my good results, but neither could they ignore my sex. It took me six months to find an employer who was prepared to employ a woman.[29]

Even where the Australian propensity to strike against unjust work conditions is referred to, there is little or no mention in traditional works of women's agitation against unjust work conditions, nor of some men's agitation, on "justice for the sexes" grounds, against unequal conditions of work for women. Indeed, it is often said that women in Australia distance themselves from strike action and are unable to be organised into joining trade unions, nor to join voluntarily. This is contrary to a strong ethic within Australian society: many women have taken strike action, as with the Bryant and May strikes in the match factories against low pay in the early part of this century; last century women established the Tailoresses and Laundresses Unions; and although numbers of women unionists in Australia have traditionally been smaller than those of men unionists, women have nonetheless founded and joined additional unions.[30] In recent years the numbers of women joining trade unions have been proportionately larger than those of men. Why should history be distorted to write out of the working class the aspirations and efforts of women?

In view of the long tradition that women have in Australia for fighting for the extension of the concept of justice to include equal rights of the sexes, it is odd that this receives no mention in traditional accounts of the Australian ethos. It is detrimental to Australia's concept of values that this should be so, for cutting out acknowledgement of this battle excludes aspects of courage from our understanding of the real Australia and Australian, just as much as it covers up the inequities and injustices inherent in the dominant ethos. It also excludes from consideration those few men who have recognised the indignities piled upon Australian women, and eliminates that egalitarian section of the population, however small it might be, from inclusion in the recognised Australian system of values.

---

29. Emel Corley, in *Growing Up Feminist*, note 21, pp. 59, 60.
30. Jennifer Feeney, "Match Girls – Strikers at Bryant and May" in *Double Time*, note 8, p. 261; Edna Ryan, *Two-Thirds of a Man*, 1984, Hale and Iremonger, Sydney; Robin Joyce, "Labor Women – Political Housekeepers or Politicians?" in *Australian Women and the Political System*, Marian Simms (ed.), 1984, Longman Cheshire, Melbourne.

Values: Humour

Humour is another part of being Australian about which our society seems ambivalent. There is a tendency to assert that Australia has inherited its "Cockney humour" from "good old England". Alternatively, our humour is seen as self-directed – Australians are notorious for "taking the mickey" out of themselves. There is a healthy streak of irreverence in Australian humour, but it is rarely recognised in analyses of the "typical Australian" that our multicultural background has added to the Australian capacity for laughter. Australians of ethnic origins other than anglo-Australian have their humour too. It is a part of the real ethos.

Ting, arriving in Australia from China in 1950, recalls an incident some ten to fifteen years after his arrival:

I live in Malvern and go to the Green Man in High Street. More or less that's my hiding place. I go there most every night and make a lot of friends there. One time I remember, one stupid one in the Green Man, during the Vietnam War, it's very hot time. He just pointing a finger at me saying, "Hey you, Chinaman! Hey you! When all your Chinamen coming over?" What he means actually, is the communists might come over. I just answer him coolly and I say, "What you talking about? I'm in here already!" And the whole bloody Green Man roar like mad, because he yell out so loud and I yell out so loud and the people catch the joke and they all laugh.[31]

A second strand of humour often missed is women's laughter; on the contrary, it is often forcefully said that feminists in particular have no sense of humour. No doubt this misunderstanding arises from the different perspective which may be brought to humorous (or otherwise) situations. As has been said, "Only 'humourless' feminists suggest that popular strip cartoons like Andy Capp, in which Andy regularly punches his wife, are not all that funny."[32]

Anecdotes of the past may be humorous today, though why should the butt of the "jokes" have been blamed at the time for failing to smile. In an 1893 case, the New South Wales Supreme Court denied the personhood of a woman exercising the right to vote in local council elections, by comparing her with a dead man or a dog. One judge

---

31. "Ting" in *The Immigrants*, note 4, p. 78.
32. Christine Dann, *Up From Under – Women and Liberation in New Zealand 1970–1985*, 1985, Allen and Unwin, Wellington, p. 130. An illustration of this "lack of humour" appeared in the *Canberra Times*, 22 December 1982, p. 2:

    Sir,

    I would like to voice my absolute disgust at the above cartoon published in the Sunday edition of the *Canberra Times* (15 December).

    Domestic violence is not funny and neither is it a fit subject for humour. To the people (mainly women) out there who are incarcerated in a living hell this is an absolutely brilliant way of perpetuating a vicious cycle. Make it something you joke about; dismiss it as ludicrous. After all it's a great exercise. Life. Be in it – indeed!

    Rhian Williams, Canberra.

said that if a dead man's name appeared on the voting roll he had no right to vote; similarly if a woman, despite being well and truly alive, asserted the right to vote because her name appeared on the roll, she had no such right. The other judge rhetorically asked (simply assuming a respectfully negative answer), "Suppose a Newfoundland dog's name is inserted on the electoral roll, would you contend that he would be an elector?"[33] On reflection, at the time that would have been no joke for either side: it was meant seriously by the judges, and the women took it seriously: they fought on for some ten years to achieve the right to vote in all public elections.

Women's sense of humour is often of the wry kind. The response to an Education Memorandum dated 1 July 1908, from the Inspector General of Schools to the Western Australian Minister for Education, illustrates this well. On 23 June 1908, a letter in the *Kalgoorlie Miner* objected to the employment as teachers of married women, on the basis of their already being supported by husbands on wages of £5 or more a week. They are, thundered the correspondent, "a disgrace to wifehood and motherhood", relinquishing as they do "the care of their little children to servants or indifferent relations". The Inspector General (no doubt a married man) pointed out in reply:

While women in this category might be employed it is not true that they are keeping out others: "Married women are only employed when other teachers cannot be obtained ..."[34]

The wry smile with which we greet these words no doubt is partly due to their blatancy. Hopefully no one would be foolish enough to emulate it in Australia today, whatever their opinion, particularly if engaged in the hiring of employees.

And what of the Director of Goode, Durrant and Co., who was unwilling to co-operate with the Royal Commission of Inquiry into Costs of Necessary Life in Western Australia? Questioned on aspects concerning the Boot Trade, Price of Butter, Apparel, and Manchester Goods, was he or was he not serious in declaring he had no need to co-operate "because he regarded female apparel (unlike that of men) not as part of the necessaries of life" but "largely for the purposes of personal adornment".[35]

Sometimes, those who consider themselves superior, or profess to do so, open themselves to smiles from the vantage point below. To the charge that feminists have no sense of humour and that there is no women's humour to enhance the Australian ethos, the following responses are sufficient answer:

---

33. Per Justice Foster in *Ex parte Ogden* (1903) 16 NSWLR 86, p. 88. In the same case, Justice Windeyer made the remark about a dead man.
34. Item 251, Education Department. Complaint about the employment of married women teachers. 2895/1908, in *Women in Australia*, note 23, p. 79.
35. Item 370, *Report of the Royal Commission of Inquiry into costs of the necessaries of life in Western Australia. Concerning the boot trade, the price of butter, apparel, and manchester goods together with minutes of evidence and appendices*, Perth, 1911, extracted in *Women in Australia*, note 23, p. 116.

Item One: Editorial, *Farrago*, 1929

The observant law student can hardly view with equanimity the rapid deterioration of the University owing to the increasing number of women students. Man is by nature a student; woman never was and has no appreciation of its intrinsic aims. The function of woman has always been to attract. University women are vamps in disguise – some very well disguised.

The Regiment replied:

To the Editors of *Farrago*

Dear Sirs,

The Second Trumpet blast against this Monstrous Regiment of Women does not come as a bolt from the blue; it has been heralded by sundry ominous reverberations; in fact, the atmosphere has been fraught with meaning for years...

This modern Knox has, I conclude, Napoleonic admiration for the harem of the East, since he declares that the sole function of women is to attract (presumably men). If this is so, I retaliate by expressing man's function in like terms, solely as to his relationship with the female sex – that is, to be attracted; and in comparison, the feminine role offers considerably more scope. I sometimes anticipate that men will be ousted from the forefront of society, ... their place to be taken by women after the manner of the organisation of the hive, where the males are but useless drones tolerated only until they have fulfilled their sexual function, and then expelled from the hive. It is an interesting conjecture!

But to return to coarse facts – such as the undesirable juvenility of women students ... Are there no evidences of ... juvenility among male students?

Lastly, if academic honours mean anything, how to account for cases where the "lesser man" has wrested them from bewildered and incensed members of the superior order of beings?

Margaret Kemp.[36]

Item Two: "Puck's Girdle" *Sydney Morning Herald* 12 January 1910

Frenchmen have hit upon a unique method of boycotting women from the professions usually held sacred to men. The woman lawyer is fairly firmly established in Paris, but her confreres do not mean her to remain so, for the junior members of the Bar have entered into a solemn league not to propose marriage to any other sex. The movement has been joined by other professional men who are afraid of female competition, and seems to be formed in all seriousness. Apparently it has not occurred to these gentlemen that women who are capable of entering the learned professions would hardly be likely to listen to proposals of marriage from men who so openly confess their weakness and inefficiency.[37]

Values: Courage

Courage and valour have had a real place in Australian history, although sometimes less often talked of or written about. Perhaps the traditional Australian view of simply doing the job, or carrying out the grand deed, without expecting thanks or demanding recognition has impeded too vocal a recognition of sheer Australian courage. One field

---

36. Margaret Kemp, "Overcharged Balloon" in *Equal to the Occasion*, note 28, pp. 117–118.
37. Quoted Jocelynne A. Scutt, *Growing Up Feminist*, note 21, p. 71.

wherein the notion of valour has, however, held full sway is wartime, with stereo-typically described "heroic feats" of war.

It is sad that the so-called typical Australian view of courage should be so closely allied with the madness that characterises war. Disappointing also that debate about the nature of courage and heroism has been stifled in too many instances, as though criticism of war will somehow negate the bravery of those Australians who simply went because they were ordered to do so, and struggled silently in inhumane circumstances. In Australia, the heroic image, seen by some to promote Australia's recognition as an independent country, must be questioned. The Anzac story, told and retold with the same basic theme by generation upon generation, sets limits upon the way Australians look at the courage of their fellows.

The courage which should rate mention is that of the everyday settler in the early days, coping with an unfamiliar country, fear of bushfires, starvation, floods. Even where this form of courage is acknowledged, the courage of women tends to be for-gotten, often because the picture describes the women settlers as making their way to Australia to fulfil the "maiden's dream" of marriage. Certainly that picture is as false as the picture of the "typical Australian" hero.[38] Yet even if it were true that women travelled thousands of miles to Australia to find their knight in shining armour and to settle down, why should this mean they were not brave, their lives were not sparked with courage? Constance Ellis is not unusual when she writes in her diary, when living near Charleville in Queensland in 1892:

We decided to put up our tent on the spot we had picked out for our house, a beautiful level space right up on the bank of the river ... Tom selected trees that would make uprights and other parts of the frame of our house-to-be. These he cut and stripped off their bark. Then we started – for I took one end of the cross-cut saw and we felled bigger trees to be split up into slabs for our walls ...

So time marched on, and the morning of May 24 dawned fair and sunny. We determined to do roofing on that day ... It was just after sundown when the last sheet was put in place. Then Tom got two long and fairly heavy saplings. He fixed a rope near each end of one, lifted it on to the roof, put a narrow sheet over the joining at the ridge, then while I hung on to the ends of the rope he slid the tied saplings over, then tied the ends to another long sapling – thus making a weight that would keep the bark flat on each side of the ridge ...

As soon as the meal was over I had to throw my bombshell. He would have to fetch Mrs Jones the nurse, who had arranged to look after me and my nearest neighbour Mrs Kean, who lived at the Rabbit proof hut, four miles away. Of course hubby was horrified to think that I had been doing all that hard work all day, but he knew that the roof wouldn't have been on without my help ... So he set off to walk ... Very soon he returned with a rough sort of a woman, but who appeared capable and good natured. I had gone to bed and things were becoming decidedly lively. She had a look at me and remarked cheerfully – "You'll be a good deal worse

---

38. See Charlotte J. Macdonald, "Ellen Silk and Her Sisters – Female Emigration to the New World" in *Men's Power, Women's Resistance – The Sexual Dynamics of History*, London Feminist History Group (eds.), 1983, Pluto Press, London, p. 66. [See also Jocelynne A. Scutt (ed.), *No Fear of Flying – Women at Home and Abroad*, 1993, Artemis Publishing, Melbourne.]

before you're better" – and went and sat by the fire with Tom. She started to tell him what they both seemed to think a most amusing yarn ... At last I called for her to come as the baby had arrived. "Wait on," she said. "I must finish the yarn" – which she did. Then she came and took the baby, saying it was just twenty past ten, and she would have to go back home soon. She and Tom went on talking and I called out "Is it a he or a she, Mrs Holmes[*sic*]?"[39]

Constance Ellis' circumstances being described as "traditional" carries too far the idea that women's "traditional role" of wife and mother is unchanging, unchangeable, and always consistent. Yet her courage and that of women in traditional circumstances is matched by that of women in less well-recognised roles. Dorothea Lock, a school teacher with the Western Australian Education Department in the 1930s, taught at a small country school in Mia Noon. In July 1934 she wrote to the Department saying that the school had been closed on two days:

... she boarded six miles from the school and had become lost walking there during a violent gale: "I do not walk daily to my school, but am given a lift by some of my pupils in a car. It is only necessary for me to walk on very wet days, as these children do not attend on such days."[40]

And even if the courage of women and men in the early days of white settlement is acknowledged, it is rarely that we recognise like valour in the circumstances of Australians more recently arrived. Soriya Suong left the country of her birth, Cambodia, on 7 January 1981. She "vividly remembers her first impressions of Melbourne":

Maribyrnong Hostel was like a paradise – brick houses, proper beds and sheets again after seven years, enough food. Then I realised that my nearest relatives were thousands of miles away. I was alone.[41]

She continues:

The eighteen months until my mother arrived were among the worst times I've ever had, especially the first six months. Of course the Pol Pot period was the worst but at least everyone had terrible conditions then. And in the camps you thought only of surviving and getting to a third country. Here I was alone. I was continually asked to help Cambodians who couldn't speak English. In Cambodia women had always walked behind and now I had to walk in front – for everyone – and I was only twenty ...

And what simple, unstated courage is concealed in the bald statement of Maria Margaretha, born in 1931 in the town of Bregenz in Austria, who grew up there, then after marriage migrated to Australia in 1956:

---

39. Constance Ellis, "A Bombshell" in *Colonial Ladies*, note 10, pp. 88–89.
40. See item 253, Education Department, Mia Moon. Attendance. 2579/26, excerpted in *Women in Australia*, note 23, p. 88.
41. Moragh Loh, "Soriya Suong" in *Double Time*, note 8, p. 457. The immediately following quotation comes from the same source, p. 458.

I loved Austria and never had any intentions to leave. I'm very proud of the country, of my parents and my family, and it really hurt to leave my mother and father. But I simply followed my husband.[42]

Whatever one's attitude toward marriage, or the ancient idea that a woman should follow her husband, the circumstances surrounding the emigration make the courage no less.

The courage of Black Australians in the face of white settlement demands recognition in the Australian ethos. Nothing can detract from the fortitude with which Murri, Nyunga, Nunga, Yamagee, Bardi, Koori and all Aboriginal, Torres Strait and Pacific Islander women, men and children faced and presently face the destruction of their own culture and the accretion of European culture that denies, or sets itself as superior to, their own. In many respects, for many Aborigines and Islanders, non-Aboriginal culture is inconsistent with their own way of living. The failure of the dominant ethos to acknowledge the strength and complexity of Aboriginal and Islander society meant Black Australian children were taken from their families and fostered out with white families. British society had a similar derogatory view of the lower socio-economic categories of Europeans: young children were sometimes brought from England and Scotland under settlement schemes which ignored the existence of parents or other relatives in their home country, transporting them willy-nilly into a new country, without the familiarity of another family member. Brothers and sisters were separated, although sometimes, at least, they were left together. So too with Aboriginal families. In both cases, a similar ideology underlay the actions of those who removed the children – sometimes a pious belief that the parent or parents were uncaring, unable to educate the children and "saviours" of the children must step in; sometimes a judgmental spirit. At least the British children came into a not unfamiliar culture. For the Aboriginal children, it was loss of family and cultural ties. Nonetheless, all were brave.

The courageous ability to simply keep living, to keep on, not to give in, is often ignored even when the pain under which Australians have laboured is explicit. Lilla Watson, growing up in Queensland in the 1940s to 1960s relates:

I did most of my growing up in a small country town. One vivid memory is of going to school one morning when the whole school was buzzing with talk about how a family had been forced to move from their house into living in a disused dairy shed. The white children said it was dreadful that the family had to live in such terrible conditions. I couldn't understand why they thought a disused dairy was a terrible place. We lived in a bag hut with a dirt floor and scraps of iron bark from trees straightened out by my dad for a roof. The dairy was a well constructed building with good solid walls and concrete floor. No one had offered us a dairy to live in.[43]

---

42. "Maria Margaretha" in *The Immigrants*, note 4, p. 88.
43. Lilla Watson, "Sister, Black is the Colour of My Soul" in Jocelynne A. Scutt (ed.), *Different Lives – Reflections on the Women's Movement and Visions of Its Future*, 1987, Penguin Books Australia, Ringwood, p. 46.

Values: Caring

As Russel Ward says, the "typical Australian" is "rough and ready in his manners". Many analyses assert that Australians are rare to show affection – unless it is the oft talked-about, oft-lauded, great Australian "mateship". Yet the traditional concept of mateship excludes 52 per cent of Australians; women are not subjects in the "mateship" system; the values of "mateship" do not extend to them. Stereotypical views of the meaning of mateship often project the idea that if women are included, mateship walks out the window. Its very essence is of men together, men without women. It is almost as if men cannot be "bosom buddies", great friends, true companions, unless women are banished from the scene.

Certainly "mateship" comes in for criticism from men as well as women. Jim emigrated from England to Australia. In 1924, when he was about 16, he worked in cattle stations in Western Queensland, in the Gulf Country and the Northern Territory. Working as a stockman, "offsider" for a horse breaker, working with a party of fossickers, doing "anything that was going", of mateship he says:

You read about mateship in the bush. You find it between navy gangs and hoboes, and other knockabouts, but not much between sedentary station workers. If you put six or seven men together under rotten conditions with no mental relaxation at all, they blow up. Some don't like the Irish. Some think that Scots are mean. They fight about nothing. And you see some bloody frightful fights. A bushman will kill his mate fifty times as often as an industrial worker.

According to the old hands there was a technique for killing your mate in the territory. You might be out in the bush together away from the station. Firearms are always available and, if you were a careful sort, you'd shoot him in the guts where you could dig the bullet out, then you'd get hold of a native spear, which was never hard to come by, and you rammed the spear into the wound. Then you clubbed him, because an aborigine couldn't kill any big game with a spear. The animal had to be killed, finished off, with a nulla nulla, so you'd ram the spear into the wound, then you'd beat the cove's head in. It was simple. People wouldn't ask too many questions. The copper would probably come out and shoot two or three aborigines and justice would appear to have been done![44]

More recently, Helen Hughes, professor of economics at the Australian National University and 1985 Boyer Lecturer for the Australian Broadcasting Corporation, said:

Mateship has exacerbated the self-interest inherent in business, trade unions and other lobbies, leading to sharp confrontations and fragmenting Australian social and political life.[45]

Putting to one side for a moment these criticisms of the old Australian standby (that is, apparently, a standby, so long as one is male and tolerable), what of expressions of caring in Australian society where women are concerned? Women's caring is less mentioned by the pundits pronouncing upon the Australian character. However, where

---

44. "Jim" in *The Immigrants*, note 4, p. 28.
45. Cited in "Sayings of 1985" in *Sydney Morning Herald*, 28 December 1985, p. 10.

it does rate a line, for women the concept of caring is seen as bound up in an ability to do household chores (mainly) and childcare. The housewife role of cooking, cleaning, dusting, sweeping, washing the dishes and the clothes, making the beds, is depicted traditionally in Australia as a labour of love for woman and wife. Yet what is important about this picture is its falsity. If the great Australian mateship myth is open to criticism, the myth of the ever-loving housewife is equally ready for demolition. Indeed, what is extraordinary about the ethos is that the actual activity is not the most crucial part of the myth; central to the myth of labouring for love in cleaning up is the character of the person doing the chores – namely that she must be female. That is, if the picture is to be believed.

The reality of housework and other such chores is not, traditionally, that women always did them: numerous accounts appear in early tales of Australian white settlement to convey the opposite. Men did these chores, as did women; men washed clothes, cooked damper, cleaned up. Sometimes, they did it with women. To assert that the only reason men undertook such work was that women were not readily available, is incorrect. Of the family washing in Western Australia, Charlotte Bussell writes in 1842:

John and I were in secret excessively pleased at [Mrs Dawson's] refusal [to do the washing for the household]; we both thought it an immense expense to enter into for one large household though as all the ladies had such a dread of the wash tub we would not raise our voices against Charley making the application ...

John and I were the first to make the starch. I soaked in the white clothes the day before which made them more easy to get clean when we began to rub the next morning – being young beginners we did not get thro' our work that day so quickly as we do now, but we managed most comfortably considering it was the first time – now we begin in the morning and get it all finished and on the lines by dinner time, our dresses changed and seated at dinner as though nothing of the kind had been going on – the next day all our clothes are in our drawers again and looking much better washed than they ever were ...[46]

Russel Ward in *The Australian Legend* cites many examples of bushmen and miners cooking their damper, making meals out of kangaroo, other native animals and birds. On one occasion he writes of anglo-Australians in the Van Diemen's Land settlement "teaching Aboriginal women to make damper"![47]

It is in the realm of caring that stereotypical attitudes play a fundamental part in shaping present day attitudes and behaviours. Thus, where men do the work the implication arises that it is not "love" or "caring" which underlies it; rather, the work simply must be done, so is done. Where women do the work, the implication is that "love" or "caring" motivates it; that the work *is* love or caring. The difference is illustrated clearly in an excerpt from Mrs W. J. Williams' diary written at Kongwak in

---

46. Charlotte Bussell, "The Washtub" in *Colonial Ladies*, note 10, pp. 98–99.
47. Russel Ward, *The Australian Legend*, note 7.

South Gippsland, Victoria around 1886. She says:

... my husband pointed to what appeared to be some galvanised iron on top of a pile of logs and said, 'There is your home'. At first I could not speak, and my eyes filled with tears. That one spot of iron, in the midst of a sea of logs and stumps, looked so desolate that my heart failed me for a moment ...[48]

Mrs Williams and her husband get on with the job, however – or is it that Mrs Williams gets on with the caring, whilst Mr Williams gets on with the job (although both do identical tasks, both participate equally in making the home)? She continues:

As the logs did not touch each other in places, there was plenty of ventilation, and the wind blew our hair about during the night. Next day we cut strips of tree and ferns and put them in the crevices on the inside, and at night we started to line the rooms with hessian and paper. We got on very well with the hessian, but it was not so with the paper. Before we could get the second piece ready the first was blown on to the floor, so we had to stop and get more ferns, and pack them in well from the outside. That done, we had no further trouble, and our cabin began to look comfortable. The next work was to make some furniture out of a few pine boards and blackwood logs. The latter required a lot of chopping and planing to get it to the size required. We made a sofa, cot and two easy chairs, which, when covered with cretonne, looked very nice and comfortable. All this kind of work had to be done at night.

What is extraordinary about the way values like caring are depicted traditionally in Australian life is that the nature of the concept appears to change according to who is doing what – in particular, which sex is doing what. One could almost guarantee that if women were garbage collectors, the job would be classed as a "caring profession"; or if women dominated petrol pumping, the oil-change industry would be redefined as labouring for love.

And where a task or an involvement is difficult to classify as anything other than caring, whatever the gender of the party doing the activity, Australian memory, Australian stereotypes concentrate to eliminate the activity where it is done by men. Thus, it is untrue that men have not involved themselves in childcare – in the caring of and for children. It would be wrong to exaggerate the amount of time men have traditionally spent with children. Yet it would be equally wrong to deny that some men, some of the time, and a few men, most of the time, have sincerely engaged in the caring for children. In *The Changing Role of Fathers* sociologist Graham Russell points out that ideas of men becoming more involved in childcare than in the past are not borne out to any great degree by the reality: about one per cent of men share childcare equally with women, when living in traditional relationships. Even that one per cent is not static – the men who have participated equally in childcare need not continue to do so for long periods of time. Russell's research shows that men might

---

48. Mrs W. J. Williams, "There is Your Home" in *Colonial Ladies*, note 10, pp. 67–68. The immediately following quotation comes from the same source.

participate equally whilst on leave from university jobs or the like, but revert to a less participatory role when leave is up.[49] However, examples are available now – as in the past – of men who do engage in such caring. What must be questioned is why this facet of Australian society has been written out – so that it appears that *no* men *ever* engage in caring for children, as (equally erroneously) *all* women appear to, *ever* and *forever*.

The problem with "caring" as depicted in traditional views of the Australian ethos is that the real strengths existing within our society where caring is in question are passed over. The caring that is observed – that of women – is too frequently trivialised or made mundane, ordinary, of little essential importance. The way to recover the reality of caring is not to laud the activities of women, painting them as invariably "from the heart" when those tasks are mundane, ordinary, everyday and simply have to be done. Rather it is to acknowledge the real strengths of women in developing the capacity for caring, and the capacity of Australians generally – be they women or men – to develop caring attitudes and behaviours. For unless the caring qualities present in both women and men are acknowledged, women who are caring will continue to be obliged to labour in the name of love, when those for whom they are labouring should rightly be developing their own skills in the world of the home. As Vic Seidler has pointed out in "Fear and Intimacy":

[Men] feel the support of partners is owed to them so that they can successfully compete against other men. This is what makes men react so impulsively and aggressively when they are told that they aren't giving enough in relationships. As men, we expect our partners to do the emotional work in supporting us at work, but we resent it if demands are made on us to respond more openly in our emotional relationships...

We learn to despise our own needs as a sign of weakness and to fear any forms of dependency, especially ones we cannot control. [Even] if we ask very little from our partners, we do expect them to do our emotional work for us. But since we are largely unaware of these needs, we rarely appreciate others for doing this. This becomes another part of invisible female domestic labour.[50]

Conclusion: Regaining an Australian Ethos

We need to regain for ourselves a more realistic picture of Australia and the inherited value system which will inevitably form the basis for our future values (whether by agreement and confirmation of those values, or re-evaluation and repudiation). To do this, we need to determine why memory blocks occur, why mental blackouts prevent the reality from being preserved, and why distortions have been introduced to produce an inaccurate picture. We need also to understand how these memory blocks or mental

---

49. Graham Russell, *The Changing Role of Fathers?* 1983, University of Queensland Press, Brisbane.
50. Vic Seidler, "Fear and Intimacy" in *The Sexuality of Men*, Andy Metcalf and Martin Humphries (eds.), 1985, Pluto Press, London, pp. 157–158.

blackouts come about. What is the process by which certain values become accepted as *the* values; how are particular perspectives "agreed" upon as *the* value perspectives? And how are voices crowded out, stifled, stopped, the more so when those voices seek to protest against their exclusion and against their perspective being eradicated.

The 1960s and 1970s in Australia saw pronounced activity by women, Aborigines (women and men), and those women and men of non-anglo-Australian background, in bringing their views and values into the public arena. The period is depicted as one of enthusiasm and promise. In the Women's Movement there was an all-pervading sense of its "never having been done before". The "out" groups became militant about their rights and wrongs. They began demanding access to institutions of power – government, Parliament, the bureaucracy. (The private sector was generally left alone.) Simultaneously they fought outside those forums. Sometimes, groups, organisations or individuals took both approaches – demanding the right to work through existing institutions whilst decrying those institutions and refusing to acknowledge their legitimacy. Some groups took the wholly institution-directed approach – though this was less common. Others refused to co-operate with present structures, adopting a separatist approach.

Newspaper headlines began to record "firsts". When I attended law school at the University of Western Australia in the latter half of the 1960s, stories were published about the "first" woman studying in the engineering faculty. In 1975 Elizabeth Reid was appointed adviser to the Prime Minister, to be billed as the "first ever" appointment. Women fought for the passage of anti-discrimination, sex discrimination and equal opportunity legislation, holding meetings that went on late into the night, writing submissions for childcare centres and funding of women's refuges, health centres and rape crisis centres. They believed it had never been done before. The emphasis was on the demand for women's rights, recognition of women's equality with men, and the right of women to have autonomy over their bodies and their lives. Never before, they thought, had women been so bold and brave.

Nungas, Kooris, Murris, Nyungas, Yamagee, Bardi and other Aborigines organised around the demand for Land Rights, setting up the Aboriginal Embassy on the lawns in front of Parliament House in Canberra. Lilla Watson of Queensland recalls the drama of those years:

I didn't want to go on scrubbing floors, cooking, cleaning, and when Aboriginal study grants became available in the early 1960s I went back to school to educate myself to play a better part for the Black movement.

While I was studying for matriculation in 1972, the Aboriginal Embassy in Canberra was brought down by the McMahon Liberal government. The day it happened my sister, my brothers, my cousins and myself saw it on the 6 o'clock television news. We cried. By 7 o'clock we had collected enough petrol money to take us to Canberra. There were five – my brother Len, our cousin Tiga and his then wife Laurel, and a friend Donna, and myself. We stopped at the Newcastle airforce base to speak with my brother Charlie who was then a member of the force, to learn he had gone on a one-man strike in protest at the government's action. His superior officers didn't know how to handle the situation, so when he said he was leaving the base to carry his protest to Canberra, I think they were glad to see him go. The Embassy was part of our history.[51]

Women and men recently arrived from other countries organised in setting up ethnic communities, councils and ethnic women's advisory councils, as well as gaining government grants or other (often piecemeal) support. Ethnic Radio 2EA in Sydney began when a group of ethnic activists began meeting at the home of Al Grassby, then Minister for Ethnic Affairs. Reporting on its success, Franca Arena, now Member of the Legislative Council of New South Wales, says:

The station was launched in June 1975. I was a volunteer producer and announcer of the Italian-language programmes. We broadcast in seven languages. (Today, 2EA broadcasts in 52 languages in Sydney and 47 in Melbourne.)

We were all thrilled to take part in the existing project. But I look back in anger sometimes at our struggle to set up a station with no equipment and hardly any facilities. The underlying philosophy seemed to be that we have to prove ourselves to be "good little ethnics", deserving a radio station of our own – and that after surveys showing that in Sydney and Melbourne two million people could not be contacted because of language difficulties. It was difficult, demanding work. I had to buy my tape recorder, tapes, everything necessary to produce a good programme promoting responses from the community.

We were inundated with letters, most from migrant women or their children, who wrote: "Mother loves the programme, she loves to understand what is happening in the community, she feels so cut off by her lack of English," or "My parents' language is spoken on the radio!" All this reinforced my feeling that there was a lot of work to do in ethnic communities.[52]

The achievements of those years have been celebrated as renewing Australia and developing a new ethos to include the "out" groups – or at least make a good start on it. Other reactions or assessments are less optimistic or favourable.

One of the most important features of the period was the notion that it was somehow all "new" and that the "newness" made it better. The truth is, that it was new for that period, but in all eras of Australian history since white settlement such groups had agitated for those same rights to freedom, equality, autonomy, self-definition. In 1975, when the federal government made funding available for various International Women's Year Projects, women without formal training, but with skills developed out of their own experience, and women historians, researchers, health professionals, sociologists, were funded for the writing of Australian women's history. Two volumes of an *Annotated Guide to Records on Women in Australia* were produced; a volume of historical records relating to women's health, and Carol Ambrus' biography of women artists, were two further projects completed in this time. Many more women began writing books to recapture the history of the real lives of Australian women.

---

51. Lilla Watson, note 43, p. 50.
52. Franca Arena, "No More Crumbs" in *Different Lives*, note 43.

The evidence produced is overwhelming, just as evidence is available that from the first days of anglo-Australian settlement Aborigines fought hard for Land Rights. Throughout the 200 years of Australia's anglo-Australian history, demands for the right to equality, the right to autonomy, the right to economic freedom, have been made by women individually and collectively, by Aborigines and Islanders individually and collectively, and by recently arrived Australians. Women's demands have been made on a theoretical level, through the writing of our own histories, autobiographies, biographies, novels, poetry, plays, music, painting, the setting-up of women's own businesses, purchasing of land, requests for grants of land from governors during the colonial period. The "firsts" we learned about via the newspapers were not "firsts" at all. A woman studied engineering in the late 1920s or early 1930s at the University of Western Australia, and the woman attending whilst I was at university was following a sister's footsteps. Women were appointed to advise government during the second world war, and probably before.

The lesson available for the learning is crucial to the development of a strong ethos which is truly Australian and which rightly credits women with achievements, at the same time as recognising the value of ordinary lives. It is not only the dominant culture which covers up women's participation in private and public life. Groups which are oppressed are cut off from their history by the refusal to publish sources, the destruction of sources which have been published, or the loss or mislaying of the sources; their classification in places not readily accessible; the denigration of important sources of history, like oral history; and by the groups' own failure to hold on to that history as important. For women and other such groups this severance from history occurs too because we are socialised into disbelieving our own knowledge of ourselves, the truth about our own and our sisters' realities.[53] Not only does the dominant group impose a version of the world through exercising their power to portray events. The dominated group is thrust into a disbelief of their own reality and an acceptance of the false vision.

---

53. This is clearly illustrated in the case of Aboriginal women in South Australia. In her article "Seeing Women in the Landscape", Faye Gale writes: "In spite of the constant attempts by Pitjantjatjara women to be involved in the Pitjantjatjara Land Rights negotiations, the whole process was decided between Aboriginal males and non-Aboriginal males in the form of lawyers, anthropologists, public servants and politicians. Pitjantjatjara women protested at their exclusion. They hired buses to bring them to Adelaide when their male relatives came south for negotiations so as to ensure that they were not entirely neglected. But the premier and his various advisors talked only with the men. The press, along with everyone else, largely ignored the presence of the women so that few outsiders even realised that the women were there, let alone knew how they felt.

   "Other Aboriginal women saw this public image being put forward. It was, after all, well advertised with frequent photographs in the daily press of the 'all-male' team. The Adnjamathanha women of the Flinders Ranges assumed therefore that in Pitjantjatjara country the men were in control and that women had little influence. But in the Flinders area the women knew this was not true. Theirs was a
   cont. next page

I began by saying that women's character had been omitted from the myth-making about Australia and Australians, just as it had been left out of the accounts of Australian reality. The tragedy is that it is all there, written down and lodged in archives and in living women's own lives. Those women knew that what they were writing was important for posterity – that is, that we should know it – even when being "told" by the dominant ethic in Australian society that Black and white women's activities were not important, were not the stuff of which history is made. Black men have run the same road as have men of more recent ethnic origin. Our responsibility is to acknowledge the existence of that history rather than to believe that what women do now is so much better and so much stronger because it's not been done before.

The notion that a woman is more important because she is the first to do something, in fact detracts from rather than adds to the feat. In the process of supposedly elevating one woman, it denigrates women as a group – the apparent way to gain recognition is to do something that no woman has ever been believed to be capable of doing before. It also denigrates the woman herself, suggesting that the only relevant aspect of the job she has taken on, or the feat she has performed, is that no other woman has ever done it before. This denies the woman's own strengths as an individual who has chosen to take on a different role, or do a difficult task, painting her as a momentary first "X", notable only for a picture in the paper – until the next so-called first happens along. What is also astonishing about this approach is that it can make a mundane task carried out every day by men appear to be mysterious, extraordinary – *just because* "no woman has ever done it before".

Underlying this problem is the concept of power. Those who are in positions of power are able to define the world. They define the "typical Australian" and determine the underpinnings of the Australian ethos. However, to think that this answers it all is to consider the problem from too narrow a perspective. Even those who hold no such positions are not totally bereft of power. The power that is overlooked by both women and men is the resilience, the staying power, the commitment of women and other disadvantaged groups to creating a new society. Women especially must remember that it has all happened before, and build upon that.

It is often said that feminists are men-haters, and that this underlies feminist strivings for a re-ordering of values. But it is the very quality of caring which women have for the creation of a society recognising the positive dimensions of women's and men's

---

53. *cont. from previous page*
society where women have strong positions of power and where women, as well as men, worked for Land Rights. When the Southern Lands Council was established, the women of the Adnjamathanha group were reluctant for their people to join. The women felt that the inclusion of Pitjantjatjara people, whose male domination had been clearly publicised, would lead to a demise of their own status."

Faye Gale, "Seeing Women in the Landscape – Alternative Views of the World Around Us" in *Women, Social Science and Public Policy*, Jacqueline Goodnow and Carole Pateman (eds.), 1985, Allen and Unwin, Sydney, p. 56, citing Jane Jacobs, "Aboriginal Land Rights in Port Augusta", 1983, MA thesis, Department of Geography, University of Adelaide.

contributions that has kept women in there, despite the violence, and ignorance of the violence, against women. Despite the misinterpretation of women's anger, and the anger meted out against women when we protest our own oppression and that of our sisters – despite the mockery of justice in the system in which we live – women continue to persist. The persistence remains within a world where the meaning of courage has been distorted and debased, and the simple, painful courage of the supposedly weak has been ignored. Despite the trivialisation of the meaning of caring and the failure too often of men to care, or to be sufficiently brave to show they care; despite the pervasiveness of a "humour" directed against the powerless – women in all groups, migrants, the poor, and Aborigines collectively; and a failure to recognise that the so-called humourless feminist is so because her humour is not like that, women keep on. That keeping on is aimed at changing the nature of power, so that it is not to be exercised over others, but means a personal autonomy that can be used objectively to benefit, not betray, others.

It is only when power is reconstructed in theory and in practice, and the reality is of women and men working collectively to benefit all, not betray, that the significance of our Australian past will be realised. It is only when we have reconstructed the Australian ethos by integrating the ignored realities, that the caring and courageous Australian values – of which we all, deep down, have a vision – can come into their own. And it is all there, waiting for us to open our eyes.

PART II

VIOLENCE

5

THE DOMESTIC PARADIGM:
Violence, Nurturance and Stereotyping of the Sexes

PAPER PRESENTED TO THE INTERNATIONAL CONGRESS
ON ALCOHOL, OTHER DRUGS AND THE FAMILY
Sydney, New South Wales
27–30 November 1988

In 1970 I enrolled in the Master of Laws degree at the University of Sydney. For the thesis requirement, I wrote a study of women and crime, looking at theories of women and criminality, women and sentencing, and women in prison. It was in the course of this research that I first became really aware of the way the law operates differentially between women and men, where self-defence and provocation arise in cases of unlawful killing. Going through law school in the 1960s and graduating LLB in 1969 from the University of Western Australia, I was aware-but-not-aware of the sexism built into the law: "sexism" hadn't been coined as a word, then. But the anti-woman bias of the law was evident, particularly where rape was in issue. It was here that women became the focus, whereas women were invisible in most of the remainder of the course. The murmuring and general unrest that grew to a crescendo at the first session in criminal law where rape was included in the lecture was evidence of a recognition amongst the students that there was something "special" or "untoward" about this field. Ribald laughter was heard in the common room before each criminal law period when the subject was sexual violence against women (another expression not yet coined). Sniggering comments sometimes became loud shouts and outbursts of laughter, the purpose of which was to enquire (rhetorically) what a particular woman would do if she were asked a question in the fateful session commencing on the next hour. (The law school at the University of Western Australia was no different, I am sure, in this regard from any law school anywhere, at the time.)

It took moving to the other side of the country, and looking at women as criminals, to bring me to a fully conscious awareness of the discrimination built in to the criminal law, as it deals with violence against women.

I wrote "The Domestic Paradigm" almost twenty years after this. The Women's Movement had been particularly successful in emphasising the truth: that violence against women, by strangers, is less frequent than violence against women by "lovers", husbands and other "close" family friends or relations. This was a major feat, bringing as it has a shift in perceptions and understandings of violence against women, and a recognition that the problem should be analysed and dealt with differently than was so in the past. At the same time, I was conscious of a need to ensure that violence on the street not be overlooked, all the while wanting to make certain that the attention of authorities and those concerned to take positive steps against the brutality which is so injurious to humanity not once more be diverted from the problem of criminal assault at home.

Reading Robyn Holden's research into violence against nurses, the underlying essence of violence against women crystallised for me. The way women are stereotyped as all comforting, all succouring nurturers, or as depraved sexual beings wholly driven by their sexuality or "womanness" was, it seemed to me, fundamental to the infliction on women of pain, injury and violence. The notion that women – and men – rightly occupy particular roles, and that being a woman means being "sexual" or "nurturant" is basic to criminal assault at home and other forms of domestic violence, and aggression against women on the street. That women are obliged to conform to a paradigm of domesticity, and that women, men and children should conform to the paradigm of domesticity appeared to underlie the problem of violence against women. Women as domestic nurturers of men. Women as sexual objects for men. Men's violence is directed against woman-as-domestic-nurturer, woman-as-sexual-being.

Violence by men against women is centred in the very fact that women are women: the violence is directed against our womanness, our sex and our sexuality. Men may be, according to official statistics, more likely to suffer violence from other men. Yet because she is a woman, *every woman knows that* because *she is a woman, she runs the risk of violence. The risk lies in being a woman.*

I had written many articles and books, and published Even in the Best of Homes – Violence in the Family, *before this paper was written. But it encapsulates my thinking on violence against women in all its forms, bringing together much of my work on criminal assault at home and other forms of domestic violence, and rape, sexual harassment and womanslaughter.*

Margaret Atwood writes that when she asked a male friend why men felt threatened by women, he replied ..., "They are afraid women will laugh at them." When she asked a group of women why women felt threatened by men, they said, "We're afraid of being killed."

– Carolyn Moulton[1]

---

1. "Editorial", (1982) *Fireweed – A Feminist Quarterly* 14 (Fall), pp. 5–7. In the footnotes, square brackets [...] indicate new material added for this edition.

[Legislative reform] can never solve the problem of domestic violence, it can merely provide an ambulance at the bottom of the cliff. As a society we need to be educated away from our present social conditioning as to what is appropriate male behaviour.

– Vivienne H. Ullrich[2]

In 1985 Robyn Holden of the Australian Nurses Federation (ANF) conducted research into violence against nurses in hospitals.[3] She found a level of violence that should raise concern, not only amongst nursing professionals and hospital authorities, but for police, courts and law-makers. But the matter cannot rest there. It is important for all concerned about violence against women, and violence in society as a whole, to note, absorb, and utilise this information fruitfully in addressing the need to end not only criminal assault at home (crime in the family, "domestic violence", or "family violence"), but all violence against women and children, whether in the home or outside it.

Some may believe criminal assaults against nursing staff in hospitals is unrelated to criminal assault at home. They are wrong. The dynamic revealed in the research is crucial to understanding violence against women generally, and violence against women and children in the home in particular. The findings were that nurses were likely to be assaulted in various departments and wards, whilst on duty. There was no preponderance of attacks being carried out in the casualty department; they were not limited to the emergency services. Most often, a nurse who was assisting the patient was attacked by hitting, kicking, slapping, or other acts of aggression. Violent words frequently accompanied the attacks. If police were called, their invariable response was, "There's nothing we can do. It's a civil matter." They would say the nurse had to take independent action against the aggressor if she wished to gain redress through the courts.

Violence Against Women at Home and on the Street

The response that "it's a civil matter" and "we can do nothing" sounds familiar to those who have researched criminal assault at home, or have been victims or survivors of these acts of aggression. Studies in Australia (as elsewhere) show this as a frequent, possibly the most frequent, response of police to women assaulted at home by their husbands:

I thought the police should help, but was told no help was available in domestic matters. They said you don't have a problem, sort it out yourselves. They came every time [I called] except the last time and I was always told that if it was all that bad I'd find money somehow and leave. Do not bother us again, they said. Their attitude toward me was firm and patronising. Their

---

2. "Equal but not Equal – A Feminist Perspective on Family Law", (1986) 9 (1) *Women's Studies International Forum* pp. 41–48.
3. Robyn Holden, "Aggression Against Nurses" (1985) 15 (No. 3) *Australian Nurses Journal* (September) 44; see also Jack C. Horn, "The Hostage Ward" (1985) *Psychology Today* (July) 9; James Turner, *Violence in the Medical Care Setting – A Survival Guide*, 1984, Aspen Systems Corp., Colorado.

attitude to my husband was friendly and co-operative, laughing even. *They said it was a civil matter, not a criminal matter for them.*[4]

But the resonance does not end there. Patients attacking nurses in their caring role were male. Nurses being attacked were, in the main, female. This mirrors the family setting: almost invariably, the attacker is male, the attacked female. Although both male and female children may be victims of physical and sexual abuse, in the main where sexual abuse is concerned, the aggressor is male. With physical abuse of children, research shows male parents exceeding female parents in the most serious form of this abuse also (although the discrepancies do not appear to be as pronounced as they are with sexual molestation).

The parallels between aggression, by patients against nurses in hospitals, and attacks against wives in the home, are surely significant. Just as domestic violence crosses class, ethnic and racial lines, so, too, does hospital violence. There appears to be no link between aggression meted out on nurses and class, ethnicity or race. Just as women play the nurturing and caring role in the home and are beaten by those they care for and nurture – their husbands – so nurses play the nurturing and caring role in the hospital and are beaten by those they care for and nurture – their patients.

But it is not just in hospital and the home that "women's role" is central to the violence inflicted upon women. It is fashionable today to depict prostitutes as playing a much-needed psychotherapeutic role, attending to the "sexual needs" of men. The role is portrayed as one of caring and nurturance, enabling men to gratify their sexual urges and to "talk out" some of their sexual concerns with the women whose sexual services they seek. Prostitutes are greatly at risk of violence from their clients, just as wives are greatly at risk of violence from their husbands. Husband and client will inevitably, in some cases at least, be the same person.

Women who are raped also fit the stereotyped female role, in the eyes of the rapist. Some victims or survivors of rape have reported the offender as seeing himself as a lover:

He sat on the bed next to me and started talking quietly. Things like "I love you ... I would do anything in the world for you ... Oh, what's your name again? ... I always pay my way, I work forty hours a week."[5]

---

4. See Jocelynne A. Scutt, *Even in the Best of Homes – Violence in the Family*, 1983, Penguin Books Australia, Ringwood, Chapter 9, "The Police", pp. 216–241; see also AWARE and SAWL, *Men, Women and Violence*, 1988, AWARE and SAWL, Singapore; Suzanne E. Hatty (ed.) National Conference on Domestic Violence, Vols. 1 & 2, 1986, Australian Institute of Criminology, Canberrra; Jocelynne A. Scutt (ed.), *Violence in the Family*, 1980, Australian Institute of Criminology, Canberra; Jocelynne A. Scutt, "Women and the Police" in *Police in Our Society*, 1988, Butterworths, Sydney.
5. See John M. McDonald, *Rape – Offenders and Their Victims*, 1975, Charles C. Thomas, Springfield, p. 6.

Sometimes the offender expresses a desire to have a continuing relationship with the woman he rapes. Some women report receiving marriage proposals from their rapist.[6]

If the rapist does not see the women in quite this way, it is certain he imbues her with attributes by which our society identifies women as women. These are characteristics of sexuality and sexual usefulness. Thus rapists have, in research interviews, made remarks such as those reported by Diana E. H. Russell:

I wanted a piece of ass. So I went into this apartment building. I ... tried a door ... and it was open and I just went in. It was a fantastic stroke of luck. By fate the only person there was a young girl ... in there alone. I just commenced to rape her.[7]

It may be asserted that such statements bear little or no resemblance to a woman's role in the home and to the way men view wives. But this assertion is wrong. In a national study of rape in the home women made comments such as:

... he always demanded sex and I was abused if I didn't comply.[8]

My husband always wanted sex after beating me up. He would bash me up, then demand sex. I used to be so upset after being bashed up I couldn't stop him. He got more angry when I just lay there and I had to pretend to like it. When I didn't he got madder and madder until he was wild and maniacal. Then other times he got angry and said I was a faker and would never be a real woman. He blamed me for not being good in bed and said I was like an iceblock so he had to punch me around. He said other women were not like me and he never even knew why he got married.

I put up with bashings, black eyes, cut lip, made to do sex acts that now fifteen years later make me feel sick ... He used to force me into the bedroom all the time and make me have sex. In general I was led to believe that's how men treat women and that it's not rape if you're married. But he made me do other things too that I can't write about even now and it wasn't the actual intercourse I object to, it was the degrading sex acts.

For me, "making love" (as they say) was always like that – short, sharp, brutal and all his way. He did not recognise me as a human being with sexual and other rights. He knew I didn't want to have intercourse when I was saying "no". He is a strict Lutheran and believes in total obedience from a wife. He would not recognise my right to object.

In this study, the sole man who said he was a victim of unwanted sexual imposition by his wife said of laws making rape in marriage a crime:

I don't think the law should get involved in the sex life of married people. In fact when you get married the wife consents to irrevocable conjugal rights. A man works and supports the family

---

6. See Diana E. H. Russell, *The Politics of Rape – The Victim's Perspective*, 1975, Stein and Day, Cal., pp. 243, 245–246, 251–252; also note, "The Victim in a Forcible Rape Case – A Feminist View" (1973) 11 *American Journal of Criminal Law* p. 335; Jocelynne A. Scutt (ed.), *Rape Law Reform*, 1980, Australian Institute of Criminology, Canberra.
7. See Diana E. H. Russell, note 6. The immediately following quotation comes from the same source.
8. See Jocelynne A. Scutt, note 4, Chapter 6, "Marital Rape", pp. 141–173. The three immediately following quotations are from the same source.

– a wife has a right to expect that. Therefore in exchange a man has the right to expect her to make sexual intercourse available to him. If a stranger does it – it is a crime against both husband and wife (that is, if a stranger stole a man's pay packet, likewise it would be a crime against both husband and wife).[9]

In some cases, the role of wife is paralleled with that of the prostitute:

He marched me off to the bedroom and forced me to have sex with him. Then when it was over he pushed me out of bed and told me to go and finish doing the dishes. He was raving and calling me names, and kept calling out from the bedroom things like slut and whore.

The wife/whore role is combined similarly in another area of male violence against women, which further draws parallel with violence against women at home: that of sexual harassment in the educational institution or at work. The conditions enabling this form of imposition to arise and survive, in spheres where intellect and industry are ostensibly the aims of the institutions, are illustrated concisely in arguments put forward in the United States case of *Diaz v. Pan American World Airlines Inc.* Caring and nurturance and other aspects of the stereotypical female role were argued by Pan Am to be essential to the job of flight attendant, so that it would be impossible to enable men to train and work as attendants in aeroplanes. Passengers, it was said, would "subconsciously resent a male flight attendant. [In] psychological terms ... most airline passengers ... prefer to be served by female stewardesses":

The environment creates three typical passenger emotional states with which the air carrier must deal: first and most important, a sense of apprehension; second, a sense of boredom; and third, a feeling of excitement ... [F]emale stewardesses ... would be better able to deal with each of these psychological states. [The expert witness for Pan Am] concluded that there are sound psychological reasons for the general preferences of airline passengers for female flight attendants.[10]

These views seem to confirm the idea that women-on-the-job are there not simply to fulfil needs unrelated to sexual characteristics or identity; rather, the sexuality and womanliness of women is indispensable to the task of stewardessing in the air. This gave rise to media comment on the case, that what airlines should not be doing is "running brothels in the skies".[11]

Pan Am's policy of employing women only as flight attendants and its rationale that the (female) sex of the worker was crucial to the job in itself bolstered the notion that sex and sexuality are intimately related to inflight services. An observer ought not to

---

9. See Jocelynne A. Scutt, note 4. The immediately following quotation comes from the same source.
10. *Diaz v. Pan American Airlines* 311 F. Supp. 559 FD Fla (1970), reversed 442 F 2d 385.
11. See general discussion in Karen de Crow, *Sexist Justice – How Legal Sexism Affects You*, 1975, Random House, Inc., New York, Chapter 5; Jocelynne A. Scutt, "The Economics of Sex – Women in Service" (1979) 51 (No. 1) *Australian Quarterly*, pp. 32–46. [Published as Chapter 12 of this volume.]

be surprised if women working as flight attendants were then at risk of being seen, by male passengers, as there to service stereotypical male "needs". Indeed, linking inflight services with the female body seems to promote ideas of woman-as-sex-object and the right of men passengers to possess one. "Fly me," trumpeted an advertisement for one airline.

Even if the company simultaneously promotes a "look but don't touch" ideology, this does nothing to remove the concept of woman-as-nurturer/woman-as-whore which is embedded in the airline's practice. There is effectively a two-way reinforcement of the concept: passengers, says the airline (meaning men), want a woman to serve (or "service") them: this provides nurturance and promotes the passengers' views of themselves as powerful, in control, titillated and *with a right* to be titillated; we, say the passengers (men) are powerful people (men) and deserve to be served by others (women) who will do – or at least give an appearance of being ready to do – our every bidding.

When the passengers (men) take up the airline's (unstated) offer and exercise power and control resulting from the "excitement" generated by the womanliness of the (female) flight attendants, their actions and approaches are generally lacking in discernment. Whether thousands of feet above the earth's surface, in a doctor's surgery, in the plush surrounds of a company executive's boardroom, on the factory floor, or in the television studio, men committing acts of sexual harassment on the job typically lack inventiveness. The acts and sexual statements or allusions run well-worn paths. It is typical to find complaints by women sexually harassed to be of such a kind as that the aggressor:

Made comments to the woman such as "You've got a nice backside". "Do you like sex?", "I'd like to get on top of you" and "I'd like to have sex with you."[12]

Placed his hand under the woman's uniform and touched her inner thigh, whilst filling in the consultation book one night.

Pulled down the zip on the front of the woman's uniform past bra level and then pulled it up again after telling her that it was too low.

Told her she should take up the hem of her uniform as she had beautiful legs and should show them off.

Grabbed her suddenly by the arm from behind while she was in the kitchen.

Told the woman she was beautiful and that he loved her.

Put his face against hers and said, "I love to feel my lips on your skin."

Required by his words, actions, or direct force to place her hand on his penis or other parts of his body.

---

12. This and the seven immediately following quotations are from *Hall & Ors v. Sheiban* (1988) EOC 92–224; see also *O'Callaghan v. Loder* (1984) EOC 92–021; EOC 92–022; EOC 92–023.

In *Aldridge v. Booth* the harassment was imposed by the employer on the employee whilst she worked in the rear of the shop, "The Tasty Morsel" cakeshop. The exploitative violence inflicted by Mr Booth on Ms Aldridge included sexual intercourse without consent – known, in criminal law, as sexual assault or rape. The parallel with rape in marriage is unmistakable. The report of the case states:

[The applicant] says that the first act of intercourse occurred after trading on Saturday, 27 April 1985. On that occasion, Miss Aldridge said that, after the shop had closed on the Saturday, she was icing a cake and Mr Booth came behind her and was trying to kiss her. "… he started mucking around and I started to push him away saying, 'Leave me alone'. And I ended up falling on the floor, and he got on top of me, and got his penis out of his shorts, and I said, 'OK, OK, I'll do it with you then.'"[13]

If the woman resists sexual harassment or, after complying with demands, does her best to avoid the employer or co-worker whilst remaining at work for economic and other reasons (career opportunities, fears of being unable to get another job, fears of leaving the job without a reference, and so on), the employer or co-worker resorts to other forms of force, threats, and on many occasions the sack. This again mirrors the actions of men whose violence and rape in marriage is resisted or, having been "complied" with, is subsequently avoided or sought to be avoided. Women who resist sexual harassment at work frequently find that the violence escalates. They find this escalation, too, where they "obeyed" the husband, or went along with his opinion and desires at first, or for years and years, then seek to assert their own identity.

Marital murder and murder of women outside the home also have their parallels. It is unusual for a woman to be killed by murder or manslaughter in any circumstances other than those where the fact that the woman is a woman is central to the killing. The killing of women usually occurs where the woman has been a frequent victim of violence meted out upon her in the home by her husband; it occurs also where women have been attacked and raped by a stranger or strangers. The underlying issue of sexuality and the demand for nurturance and caring, and aggression directed at women for those very qualities, or the utilisation of women in sexually aggressive ways, with the aggression resulting in death for the woman, is unmistakable. And the popular mind – and sometimes the judicial mind – actually links the killing with "love", in at least some cases. It is not unusual to find banner headlines based on judicial pronouncements of "tragic" "deaths" of women at the hands of their husbands and "lovers". The notion seems to be: "I loved [*sic*] her so much I killed her." The deaths are downgraded from intentional killing (murder) to manslaughter on the basis of too much love (rather than too little) "dictating" the event.[14]

Some may deny that the dynamic underlying the murder of women outside the home

---

13. *Aldridge v. Booth* (1988) EOC 92–222.
14. See further, Jocelynne A. Scutt, note 4, chapter 7, "Marital Murder", pp. 175–197.

parallels the murder of women inside it. Indeed, when woman-killing on the streets occurs, every effort is made to depict the killer (or killers) as sub-human, psychotic. Thus the history of the search for Peter Sutcliffe, who killed a series of women in England in the 1980s, was that of the authorities misguidedly searching (and searching vainly) for an aberrant figure, a man who would stand out from the rest of (male) humanity. In the end he, like the majority of woman-killers, was an "ordinary, every-day man", a man married and living the exemplary life of the suburbs.

Although police and media may search endlessly for the psychopath, women often have a more realistic view. Jane Caputi in *The Age of Sex Crime* writes:

[D]uring the siege of the "Yorkshire Ripper" one group of citizens did ignore the myth and sought the killer in the most familiar of men ... While the police were seeking a man apart, women were turning in their husbands and brothers. In nearly every case of highly publicized serial sexual murder, a similar phenomenon occurs. Paralleling the scores of men who "confess" to the crimes, are the many women who come to the police, expressing hesitant but grave doubts about the men with whom they are intimately involved. [In one (in)famous case – that of Ted Bundy in the USA, the man's] girlfriend of six years had reported her misgivings about him to the Seattle police ... One factor stands out: this woman lived in constant fear and suspicion with a man she simultaneously "loved" for a number of years, always vacillating between romance and terror.[15]

A male researcher echoes the truth about violence against women:

It is difficult to believe that such widespread violence is the responsibility of a small lunatic fringe of psychotic men. That sexual violence is so pervasive supports the view that the locus of violence against women rests squarely in the middle of what our culture defines as "normal" interactions between women and men.[16]

Some people may also deny that the killing of women outside the home is complementary to the killing of women inside the home, or the violence of other sorts against women at home, because the women killed outside the home are not representative of homebound women, housewives, or wives and mothers generally. This is, of course, far from the truth. It is commonplace to read, where a series of women is raped and killed outside the home, that those women were prostitutes or "loose" women (as if the crimes were any less when women working as prostitutes are the victims). In the Sutcliffe case in England, law enforcement authorities helped promulgate this view. The Acting Police Chief Constable issued a statement to the killer four years after the first "sex murder" in West Yorkshire:

---

15. Jane Caputi, *The Age of Sex Crime*, 1988, The Women's Press, London.
16. Allan Griswold Johnson, "The Prevalence of Rape in the United States" (1980) 6 (No. 1) *Signs – Jrn of Women in Culture and Soc.* (Autumn) 145; also Diana E. H. Russell and Nancy Howell, "The Prevalence of Rape in the United States Revisited" (1983) 8 (No. 4) *Signs – Jrn of Women in Culture and Soc.* (Summer) 688.

He has made it clear that he hates prostitutes. Many people do. We, as a police force, will continue to arrest prostitutes. But the Ripper is now killing innocent girls. That indicates [his] mental state and that [he] is in urgent need of medical attention. [He] has made [his] point. [He should] give [himself] up before another innocent woman dies.[17]

In a case in 1979 in the United States:

The victims were universally described as runaways, prostitutes or drug addicts who "deserved" to die because of how they lived. The distorted portrayal of the girls and women could be expected in a city notorious for its racism, but there was a particular sexist turn, because the victims were not only Black, but female.

The irony is that prostitutes are wives and mothers too; like "innocent girls", they are somebody's daughter; they, just as much as non-prostitute wives and mothers (like all women) should be recognised as human beings with a right not to be raped or killed, or raped and killed.

Where sexual violence against children is in question, again there are parallels with women's general position in society; the issues of caring and nurturance, and sexuality and sex role, are crucial to the infliction of violence and abuse, whether on girls or boys. In *Family Violence in Australia*, Carol O'Donnell and Jan Craney write:

The taboo on incest in our society is so strong not because incest is "unnatural" but because, given the structure of the family, it is only too natural. Things that are unlikely to occur do not need such powerful efforts at social prevention. Families are supposed to be close, warm, loving and physical. The parents are supposed to have sex with each other and not with anybody else – especially their children. The basic contradiction at the centre of the family is the concurrent social demand for closeness and prohibition on sex. Not only this, the family is the place where sex roles are learned, and in our society, males are supposed to be "manly", aggressive and in control, whereas females are valued primarily if they are attractive and charming, and prepared to be willing pupils ... [W]hat researchers describe as the incestuous family is in fact usually indistinguishable from the normal family, except perhaps that the sex roles of all its members have become somewhat exaggerated ... [The] central problem is not incest, but power. Incest is an expression of power in many cases – the power of men to control women, and the power of adults to control children.[18]

Women talking of their experiences as children say:

After my mother died he started doing stuff to me and he said it was alright and that it happens in everyone's family like that and it was just fathers teaching their daughters about life. I didn't like it but I just thought I had to.[19]

---

17. Quoted Jane Caputi, note 15. The immediately following quotation is from the same source.
18. Carol O'Donnell and Jan Craney, "Incest and the Reproduction of the Patriarchal Family" in *Family Violence in Australia*, 1982, Longman Cheshire, Melbourne, p. 155.
19. Quoted Jocelynne A. Scutt, 1983, note 4, Chapter 4, "Child Sexual Molestation", pp. 66–95. The following quotations are from the same source.

It went on for years but happened only occasionally throughout that period. He didn't go any further than touching our genitals. He kept coming in to say good night putting his hands under the bed clothes. Once he tried to put his finger into my genitals but I moved so he couldn't.

He started on me with touching my privates, but I wouldn't let him and fought back. He was touching my other sisters and I told them I wouldn't let him do it. A couple of times he said he would "put it into me" like he was doing to them. It never happened but not for want of trying. I held myself very stiffly. He tried about six times then he stopped and went back to them. I just wouldn't let him, but it wasn't easy.

The children are told, "daddy likes this", or that they, "… should be nice to daddy", or, "daddy won't love them anymore if they do not 'do it'", or, "let him 'do it'". (Women sexually harassed on the job are told, "I thought you were going to be nice to me" or, "don't you want to do right by me?")

Violence, Nurturance, Caring and Socialisation

This is the reality of violence against women, at home or on the streets, in the workplace or in educational institutions. Yet family violence – including criminal assault at home, marital rape, sexual molestation and assault of children by a family member or "friend", and physical assault of children at home – has in the past been ignored. Alternatively, it has been variously attributed to alcohol, provocation by the victim of the violence and abuse, economic disadvantage, cultural imperatives, insanity, psychological imbalance (mostly of the victim of the abuse, less often of the attacker or abuser), conditioning, social deprivation, socialisation, stresses and strains of modern family life, failure to give proper recognition to traditional family values, family structure, "the family" itself.

Alcohol may be associated with some family violence in a direct way, but alcohol does not *cause* family violence. Critical analysis of studies alleging a link between domestic violence and alcohol shows the "relationship" is meaningless. In a comprehensive review of the literature and a survey of agencies dealing with spouse assault in Canada, Joanna Downey and Jane Howell acknowledge that the extent and nature of the association between alcohol use and family violence varies widely amongst studies and agencies:

Little distinction is made in the findings between pathological drinking (alcoholism) and episodic drinking associated with violence … [Furthermore] some studies … indicate that drunkenness is not always followed by violent behaviour … and violence may occur without any alcohol being consumed.[20]

---

20. Joanne Downey and Jane Howell, *Wife Battering – A Review and Preliminary Enquiry into Local Incidents, Needs and Resources*, 1976, Social Policy and Research Department, United Way of Greater Vancouver and the Non-Medical Use of Drugs Directorate, National Department of Health and Welfare, Vancouver, at p. 56.

Australian studies confirm that marriage to a teetotaller, or being born into a teetotaller family, does not protect a woman (or a child) from domestic abuse. Nor does violence against women outside the home or sexual abuse of children in parks, streets and other non-domestic venues have any unremitting or necessary or sufficient link with drinking or alcohol abuse. Alcohol may certainly exacerbate violence and abuse, or provide an "excuse" for the infliction of violence upon women and children, whether at home or elsewhere, but it is not at the root of that violence. (Is it significant that alcohol is rarely put forward as a reason or excuse for sexual harassment at work or in educational institutions – apart from the Christmas party syndrome.)[21]

Nevertheless it is instructive to look at the way alcohol is regarded in our society, and its relationship to socialisation. Today, alcohol is clearly associated in the public mind with sporting events accepted as crucial to the identification of masculinity: football in particular, as well as horse-racing. In advertisements, alcohol is invariably associated with sophistication, man-seducing-beautiful-woman, beautiful women being compliant and sexually available. It is also associated with "manly" sports in advertisements and a certain egalitarianess (at least for men): the idea that even if a man is a beer-bellied swiller, he can "get" the most gorgeous girl on the block. Alcohol is associated with masculinity at two levels: the full-on typical Australian male – the beer-drinking, football-playing, betting man; and with the male pursuit of the ever-willing female. Either he can identify with the "ocker Aussie" who gets his beer, and his woman, or with the upmarket sophisticate with his wine or spirits – and his woman. In the advertisements, women are invariably depicted in the clinging sex-object role; or caring, cheering on the sidelines, urging the Aussie male on. (This fits with the wife-mother role, standing on the edges of the football field in the cold, cheering on the winners or comforting the losers.)

Alcohol does not *cause* violence against women. At the same time, preventing alcohol abuse and speaking out against the portrayal of men and women in the selling of alcohol is important to bring about the cessation of violence against women and children in the home and out of it. Ending violence against women is likely to affect positively, also, the goal of prevention of alcohol abuse, just as is so for drug abuse (although here, the dynamic appears to be different).

Sometimes drug abuse is linked with violence against women in the family. However, the violence is associated not with illicit drugs, but with "legal" drugs prescribed by medical practitioners. And the aggressors are not the drug-takers. Rather, the victims or survivors of criminal assault at home are prescribed drugs such as Mogadon, Librium, Valium and other panaceas to "soften the blows": women attending at doctors' surgeries

---

21. See studies cited and analysed in Jocelynne A. Scutt, 1983, note 4, Chapter 5, "Spouse Assault", pp. 96–140; also Jocelynne A. Scutt, "The Alcoholic Imperative – A Sexist Rationalisation of Rape and Domestic Violence" (1981) 7 (No. 1) *Hecate* 88; [Published in this volume, Chapter 7.]

are, as the health writer Diana Wyndham has written, given pills to keep the doctors out of the women's misery.[22]

The social deprivation revealed in the realities of violence against women and children in and outside the home is not the classic social deprivation of tradition – the lower socio-economic strata struggling against social and economic odds to survive in a world where materialism is daily growing stronger as the acceptable ethos. The social deprivation crucial to the infliction of violence upon women and children in our society is that experienced in a male-dominated culture where male socialisation is dependent upon attitudes and behaviours glorifying dominance and male superiority, with the subjugation of women and of the qualities of nurturance and caring.

Violence in the home is the form of violence to which human beings in most cultures are most likely to be exposed. A woman is most likely to be hit, beaten, bashed, raped, abused by her husband, "lover" or boy"friend" in the bedroom of the matrimonial household. Children – girls and boys – are most likely to be hit, thrashed, or beaten at home. Children – girls and less often boys – are more frequently sexually abused in the family home than in the park or on the street. It also remains true that where women kill, the most common victim is a member of her family, frequently the husband or de facto husband, the women being victim to his violence over many years. Men suffer violence, in the main, outside the family setting. But it is in the family setting that they mainly inflict their violence.

When men suffer violence, there is little comparison between the dynamic (at least in its external manifestations, in terms of relationship between the party inflicting the violence and he upon whom it is inflicted) and the domestic setting. Yet when women suffer violence outside the home, the setting is mostly akin to the domestic paradigm: male against female, with qualities attaching to the violent "interaction" or "relation-ship" that mirror or reflect domestic abuse. This fact – that for women, the nurturing role or the "female role" is the very basis of the violence to which women are subjected, whether at home or on the street, or working or living or operating in other institutions (for example, hospitals) – all too readily can be seen as the key to family violence and to societal violence as a whole.

The social roots of violence lie in the domestic paradigm. Why should it be that (some) men feel themselves compelled to exaggerate the stereotypical male role by resorting to violence against women, and sexual abuse and exploitation of women and children? (Children are even more vulnerable than women and are used, at least where sexual violence and abuse are in question, as substitute women; they are exploited sexually as women are exploited.) Why is it that (some) men turn their violence, aggression and abuse on the woman who represents, in reality and stereotype, the nurturing mother-figure or the sex-object? Why is it that (some) men turn their sexual

---

22. Diana Wyndham, "My Doctor Gives Me Pills to Put Him out of My Misery", paper presented to the Pan Pacific International Conference on Drugs and Alcohol, Canberra, ACT, 1979; see also Jocelynne A. Scutt, 1983, note 4, Chapter 5, "Spouse Assault", pp. 96–140.

violence, aggression and abuse on that women, or upon the child who represents a substitute female figure?

Biological determinists, sociobiologists and others who applaud male and female role stereotyping claim that women's and men's biological differences (small though they are), dictate women's and men's whole existence. They claim that men are "naturally" more aggressive than women, that the dominant male role is "natural" and that, because the sexes are "complementary", women are "naturally" less aggressive than men, that the nurturant and caring role of women is "natural". At the same time these polemicists insist that parents, schools and all others working with children ensure that social and educational demands are placed upon boy children to "live up to" the so-called male ideal, and on girl children to endorse in their everyday living the so-called female ideal. The irony is clear: if these states were "natural", if the stereotype of male and female were reality because of our biology, the strong socialisation of women into being WOMEN and men into being MEN would not be necessary.

Not all men beat their wives, rape, bash or abuse them. Not all men engage in sexual exploitation of their own or others' children. Some men have developed caring and nurturance as positive qualities. That this is true immediately denies the biological determinist, sociobiologist and "traditionalist" arguments: biology is not destiny. (Nor is anatomy.) Even if it were true that men are naturally more aggressive than women, and that women are biologically programmed to be caring and nurturing whilst men are not, all the more reason to alter our patterns of socialisation and education. All the more cause to train boys and men to be less aggressive and to be nurturing, rather than to embrace patterns of socialisation and education which deliberately set out to make boys MEN and girls WOMEN.

Confronting the truth, that women are most likely to suffer violence at the hands of those to whom they administer in accordance with the "traditional" female role, or those who see their women victims as reflecting the female stereotype, may mean that the solution lies in women abandoning this role. But it more likely means that men are the problem, and that the stereotypical dominant male role, and male attitudes and actions toward those who fill "women's role" are what require abandonment.

Unless the demands of the male stereotype are abandoned, and the adulation which appears daily in the media and in the world at large of male aggression (whether it be in the illegitimate world of crime or the legitimate worlds of sport and business) ceases, violence against women and children at home and in the world at large will continue. And with its continuance, the men who inflict the violence and those men who support them in that violence by failing to reorientate their own lives to nurturance and caring, will continue to damage, and even to destroy, those qualities of nurturance and caring which alone, in the end, can grant them absolution.

6

IN SUPPORT OF DOMESTIC VIOLENCE:
The Legal Basis

PRESENTED TO SAANZ CONFERENCE
Canberra
September 1979.

In 1974 I read Erin Pizzey's Scream Quietly or the Neighbours Will Hear, *her exposé of violence against women on the homeground. From May 1973 to August 1974 I had spent 15 months in the United States, primarily at the University of Michigan, studying constitutional law, discrimination law and labour law. At the time, Michigan's rape laws were undergoing review. Under the guidance of Professor Virginia Blomer Nordby, students at the University of Michigan had a direct input to the reframing of rape into sexual assault. The marital rape exclusion – protecting husbands from prosecution for rape of the women whom they had married – was an aspect of the law which was causing a problem: those who were supportive of women's rights had no doubt the exemption should go; conservatives had other ideas.*

I had looked at Australian and United Kingdom cases on marital rape some years before, so followed this through by writing an analysis for Professor Nordby's review. This 1974 re-look at rape in marriage law stimulated my concern about violence in marriage. Rape outside marriage had already begun to develop as a focus of my research work. Erin Pizzey's book precipitated me into wider areas of criminal assault at home and the lack of resources for women and girls, victims and survivors.

"In Support of Domestic Violence: the Legal Basis" was written when I was a criminologist with the Australian Institute of Criminology in Canberra. The title is deliberately provocative. It reflects my conscious acknowledgement of the way the legal system not only through its practice, but in the actual framing of the laws, gives its support to violence in the family. Indicative of the community's ambivalence about criminal assault at home, several (women) participants in the SAANZ conference timidly asked me whether I was "in favour" of the law's stand. This was the more bemusing in that I had already been outspoken about domestic violence, and this was

not the first conference paper I had presented on the subject. I had thought that my stand was so clear that no one could be in any doubt about the intended irony of the title of this paper. Yet apparently the notion that women should simply "put up with it", that "man's home is his castle", and the police should not intervene – "it's a private matter" – was so firmly entrenched that sociologists and others could still believe that even a feminist might publicly support the law's condonation (and, effectively, encouragement) of criminal assault at home and other forms of domestic violence. At least the queries from these participants were "timid", indicating some awareness that there might be an irony implicit in the phrasing.

The paper was rejected for publication by a well-known United States journal on victims of crime and "victimology" (a concept with a high potential for anti-woman views). I heard later that the problem was the "eclectic" nature of the article. The purpose of the paper was, of course, to point out that the condonation, through the application and letter of the law, of violence in the family is universal – at least in the western world; and that it has foundations far back in the history of "civilisation". I had discovered this through my work in Australia, the United States, the United Kingdom and Germany, and my research into Canadian and New Zealand law. Perhaps it might not be surprising that countries with a legal system deriving from Britain – the common law system – should subscribe to antediluvian notions of woman-as-property, children-as-chattels. Yet the West German system has quite distinct and separate origins – and it, too, harboured the same anti-woman, man-as-head-of-household, his authority not to be questioned, legislation and application of laws.

Today, I'd probably be even tougher and much more direct were I to write this article for publication. The passive voice would feature far less, if at all. "Domestic violence" and "violence in the family" rarely feature in my vocabulary now. "Criminal assault at home", "woman bashing", "domestic terrorism", "womanslaughter" and "woman battering as attempted murder" have replaced the neutral terms which deny or dilute the anti-woman reality of violence against women. The change was not long in coming: "criminal assault at home" came into the language after a great discussion-session with Dawn Rowan in Adelaide, South Australia in the very early 1980s.[1] By 1980 I had written a paper titled "The Police and Woman Bashing". Although some of the laws have changed which in 1979 supported and condoned violence against women –marital rape is now unlawful throughout Australia, for example – the essence of the article could still be replicated by reference to laws still existing, and even to the new laws, particularly those relating to so-called non-molestation orders or Family Court injunctions.[2] No doubt Victimology *would still (and even more resoundingly!) reject it.*

---

1. Of her work in the field Dawn Rowan writes "Beware, Oh Take Care" in *Breaking Through – Women, Work and Careers*, Jocelynne A. Scutt (ed.), 1992, Artemis Publishing, Melbourne, p. 139. In the footnotes, square brackets [...] indicate new material added for this edition.
2. See for example, Jocelynne A. Scutt, "Criminal Assault at Home – Policy Directions and Implications for the Future" in Robyn Batten, Wendy Weekes and John Wilson (eds.), *Issues Facing Australian Families – Human Services Respond*, 1992, Longman Cheshire, Melbourne, p. 183.

Possibly no other institution has enjoyed the universal admiration and obeisance that has been heaped upon the family. As has been said:

The family is, and always has been, the most intimate and one of the most important of human groups ... it can be said to be universal, existing in all known human societies.[3]

The potential breakdown of the family unit by way of "easy" divorce laws, the movement of women out of the kitchen and into the workforce, disobedience to and disrespect for parents by children has been deplored.

Yet underlying this mystification of the family is an often unacknowledged reality: violence and the abuse of power exist within the confines of the unit and may be provoked by the very structure of that unit. Domestic violence finds its support in economic, political and legal structures backing the family.[4]

An analysis of laws designed to deal with crime in the family illustrates that rather than being concerned to halt domestic violence, laws are framed to preserve the unit despite it. This is evidenced by a four-fold approach of laws to violence in the family:

- legal backing is given to violence committed upon wives and children, in that some laws countenance that violence, providing no recourse to prosecution against the attacker husband or father;
- some laws are created especially to cover the instance of an attack by a family member upon another family member – such as laws prohibiting acts of incest – however due to their very "specialness" such laws are applied only in rare cases;
- sometimes laws exist to cover the case of violence in the family – just as these same laws cover the occurrence of violence outside the unit – but in practice these laws are not applied to the family situation: a socio-legal decision is made not to apply the law;
- legal backing is given to family violence in that sometimes special courts are set up to deal with crimes committed within the family, thus setting them apart from crimes committed between strangers, and endorsing the view that domestic violence is "different".

---

3. See David G. Gil, *Beyond the Jungle*, 1979, Schenkman Publishing Co., Cambridge, at Chapter 6, "Societal Violence and Violence in the Family" (also published in *Family Violence*, 1978, Butterworths, Toronto).

4. See for example David G. Gil, R. Emerson Dobash and Russell P. Dobash, *With Friends Like These Who Needs Enemies – Institutional Supports for the Patriarchy and Violence Against Women*, 1978, Paper presented at the IX World Congress of Sociology, Uppsala, Sweden; R. P. Dobash and R. Emerson Dobash, *The Importance of Historical and Contemporary Contexts in Understanding Marital Violence*, 1976, Paper presented at the annual meeting of the American Sociological Association, New York; R. Emerson Dobash, *The Negotiation of Daily Life and the "Provocation" of Violence – A Patriarchal Concept in Support of the Wife Beater*, 1978, Paper presented at the IX World Congress of Sociology, Uppsala, Sweden; Jocelynne A. Scutt, "Spouse Assault – Closing the Door on Criminal Acts" (1979) *ALJ* 724.

Domestic Violence as "No Crime"

In the past, children and wives were held in law to be possessions of the husband/father. Thus, acts of violence committed against them by the husband/father were not punishable by the criminal law. The head of the family was set up as "lawful ruler" of the domestic unit. In Roman law, for children it was considered:

The justice of a master or a father is a different thing from that of a citizen, for a son or slave is property, and there can be no injustice to one's own property.[5]

As for wives, in eighteenth-century England and North America, *Blackstone's Commentaries*, the legal "bible", pronounced:

... by marriage the husband and wife are one person in law, that is, the very being or legal existence of the wife is suspended during marriage, or at least is incorporated or consolidated into that of her husband; under whose wing, protection and care she performs everything ...[6]

Specifically as to assault of a wife by her husband, the law originally held that "beating" was within the lawful rights of a husband. In the 1840 case *In re Cochrane* the court stated that a husband has "by law power and dominion over his wife". This entitled him to keep her by force "within the bounds of duty", in addition to giving him the right to beat her "... but not in a cruel or violent manner."[7] In *Cloborn's case* the wife complained that her husband had spat in her face, whirled her about, called her a "damned whore" and given her a box on the ear. The court at first instance granted her alimony and costs. The husband appealed against the making of the orders, contending he had a right to chastise his wife in such a manner. The appeal court held that spitting in the face was an actionable wrong (at least where the victim was not a wife), but considered the husband should not be penalised, as justification for his actions would oust the penalty.[8]

Court rulings on "beating rights" were not always consistent. In 1795 it was said that a husband had no right to beat his wife, but only to "admonish her" and to confine her to his house:

Lord Kenyon, C.J. declared and all the rest agreed that where the wife will make an undue use of her liberty either by squandering any of her husband's estate or going into lewd company, it is lawful for the husband in order to preserve his honour and estate to lay such a wife under restraint.[9]

---

5. Bertrand Russell, *History of Western Philosophy*, 1969, Allen and Unwin, London, at p. 186; and see generally Mary van Stolk, "Child Abuse and Canadian Law" (1978) *Crime and Justice* 275.
6. *Blackstone's Commentaries* 1770, 4th edn, Bk I, C. 15, p. 442; Bk II, c. 29, p. 433.
7. *In re Cochrane* (1840) 8 Dowl 630. See also *Lord Leigh's Case* (1674) 3 Keble 433 (26 Car. II) Case No. 37 in BR; *R. v. Leggat* (1852) 18 QB 781; and discussion Jocelynne A. Scutt (1979) note 4.
8. *Cloborn's Case* (1629) Hetl. 149. See general discussion of the principles of this and like cases Atkin, *The Law of Husband and Wife*, 4th edn, London, p. 27 ff.
9. *R. v. Lister* (1795) 1 Stra. 478.

Today it is considered that a husband has no right to assault his wife – and may in law be prosecuted for such an act. It is further held that a husband may no longer kidnap nor imprison his wife.[10] Nonetheless, it continues to be contended that no man may be prosecuted for the rape of his wife, if he (rather than a man assisted by him) does the act.[11] This idea is based upon the pronouncement of Sir Mathew Hale in the eighteenth century, that a husband:

… cannot be guilty of a rape committed by himself upon his lawful wife, for by their mutual matrimonial consent and contract the wife hath given up herself in this kind unto her husband, which she cannot retract.[12]

Thus the less than rational position is reached whereby a husband may be prosecuted for all acts of assault leading up to the act of sexual penetration, but cannot be prosecuted for the culmination of those assaults – the act which, had the woman not been his wife, would have been classed as "rape".[13]

For children, the usual rules of assault do not apply. Assault is defined in the Queensland *Criminal Code* in accordance with general law:

A person who strikes, touches, or moves or otherwise applies force of any kind to the person of another, either directly or indirectly, without his [*sic*] consent … or who by any bodily act or gesture attempts or threatens to apply force of any kind to the person of another without his consent, under such circumstances that the person making the attempt or threat has actually or apparently a present ability to effect his purpose, is said to assault that other person, and the act is called an assault.[14]

---

10. *Miller v. DPP* (1954) 38 Cr. App. R. 1; *R. v. Jackson* [1891] 1 QB 671; *R. v. Reid* [1973] 1 QB 299. See discussion Jocelynne A. Scutt, "Consent in Rape – The Problem of the Marriage Contract" (1977) 3 *Mon. Law Review* 255.

11. At common law a husband may be prosecuted for rape as a principal where he assists another person to rape his wife: *Audley* (1631) 3 State Tr. 402. [In all Australian states and some USA jurisdictions rape in marriage has now been classed through legislation as criminal. This change commenced in 1974 in Michigan (where a husband and wife were living separately and apart, a husband could be prosecuted for rape); in 1976 in South Australia (where a complicated provision meant that if particular circumstances were found to exist, a husband still living with his wife could be prosecuted for rape (this is referred to in this chapter), and in 1981 in New South Wales where no distinction was left in the law, so that a husband could be prosecuted for raping his wife in the same way as a man could be prosecuted for raping a woman stranger. Until 1992 when the English House of Lords held rape in marriage to be a crime, British law continued to assert that a man could not be guilty of the rape of his wife. See Jocelynne A. Scutt, note 10; Jocelynne A. Scutt, *Even in the Best of Homes – Violence in the Family*, 1983, Penguin Books Australia, Ringwood, Chapter 6, "Marital Rape" and *Even in the Best of Homes*, 1990, Penguin Books Australia, Ringwood, Chapter 13, "The Politics of Violence".]

12. *Hale's Pleas of the Crown*, 1778, Vol. 1, p. 629.

13. For a refutation of the assertion that the common law remains in this state, and an argument for the proposition that prosecutorial action can be taken against a husband for the rape of his wife, see Jocelynne A. Scutt note 10; also Comment, "Rape and Battery Between Husband and Wife" (1954) 6 *Stanford Law Review* 719 (which adopts the traditional view, but points to anomolies arising out of the United Kingdom position); also Susan Maidment, "Rape Between Spouses – A Case for Reform" (1978) 8 *Family Law* 87.

14. Queensland *Criminal Code* (1897).

A child may lawfully be the subject of what amounts to an assault where it is carried out by a parent, in the name of "domestic discipline" or "lawful correction". Thus, parents are entitled to inflict "moderate and reasonable" physical chastisement upon their children:

It is lawful for a parent or a person in the place of a parent, ... to use, by way of correction, towards a child ... under his care such force as is reasonable under the circumstances.[15]

Discipline must be "reasonable", "moderate", administered with a "proper" instrument, and in the case of female children must not be applied in "an indecent manner". A parent may be prosecuted where the chastisement exceeds the standard of "reasonableness" as seen by the courts to apply. Thus correction or discipline will be unlawful:

If it be administered for the gratification of passion or rage or if it be immoderate or excessive in its nature or degree, or if it be protracted beyond the child's powers of endurance or with an instrument unfitted for the purpose and calculated to produce danger to life and limb ...[16]

Yet this hardly affords to a child the protection that is extended to victims of assault who are not in the same family relationship. Two points demand attention: one, a parent has a lawful right to assault his children; secondly, standards of "reasonableness" or "unlawfulness" as enunciated by the courts in the case of children assaulted by their parents are unsatisfactory. As has been noted, "for what it is worth", the courts have affirmed that a father exceeds the bounds of his authority where he coerces his child by pointing a loaded firearm at him.[17] In 1959 in *White v. Weller ex parte White* "hard slaps on the face", blows to the back by way of a fist, pushes and slaps about the shoulders were not considered to be "unreasonable" discipline, although a medical practitioner estimated to the court that the injuries might "make the boy quite uncomfortable up to a week".[18]

Where proposals are put forward to eliminate this lack of protection in criminal law, the response all too predictably is that the family "must be supported". Where the law

---

15. s. 280 Queensland *Criminal Code* (1897); s. 257 Western Australian *Criminal Code* (1900). See further Colin Howard, *Australian Criminal Law* 2nd edn, 1970, Law Book Co., Sydney, pp. 153–154; J. C. Smith and Brian Hogan, *Criminal Law*, 3rd edn, 1973, Butterworths, pp. 289–290; also *Smith v. O'Byrne* (1894) QCR 252; *R. v. Terry* [1955] VLR 114.

16. *Byrne v. Hebden* [1913] QSR 233; *R. v. Griffin* (1869) 11 Cox CC 402; *R. v. Miles* (1862) 6 The Jurist 243; *R. v. Connor* (1836) 7 Car. & P. 438; *R. v. Hopley* (1866) F. & F. 202. See also R. Watson and H. Purnell, *Criminal Law in New South Wales* 1970, Law Book Co., Sydney, pp. 96–97, *Hopley* (1860) 2 F. & F. 202, at p. 206 per Cockburn, C. J.

17. Colin Howard, note 15, at p. 154; *Hamilton* (1891) 12 LR (NSW) (L.) 111.

18. *White v. Weller ex parte White* [1959] Qd R. 192, p. 194. The reports states that there was "an area of bruising over the left scapular region about three inches to four inches in extent, with some area of skin abrasion over this area. There was also some bruising over the upper left arm region ... The boy says that [the shoulder and arm were] pretty stiff on Friday but the soreness and stiffness had gone on Saturday."

seeks to move into the domestic arena to protect children from abusive parents, the right of parents to "control their offspring" is invoked. Child abuse reporting laws are resisted on grounds that they invade the privacy of the domestic situation. That the right of a child not to be assaulted outweighs any alleged right of a parent to privacy in the home is often accorded very little attention.[19]

Similarly with marital rape. In South Australia when the 1976 amendment to the *Criminal Law Consolidation Act* was proposed to eliminate immunity for a husband in the case of wife-rape, it was said that such a law would "undermine the family and contribute more to the breakdown of marriages". Another reaction was to call the proposal "divisive, an attack on the family, and a ridiculous piece of legislation".[20] This, despite the fact that being raped in marriage could, in the mildest of terms, be described as "divisive", and that "ridiculous" is hardly an epithet to be applied to legislation designed to guard against an attack on a wife.

The parliamentary debate in the United Kingdom on a similar proposal (also in 1976) displayed the same protective attitude toward "the family", rather than supporting the victim of the crime. "There were some women," it was said, "... so unscrupulous that if encouraged by legal backing ... might be prepared to commit perjury and do everything necessary to convict their husbands of rape with the objective of breaking up a marriage and getting rid of an unwelcome and unloved partner."[21] That a petition for divorce would "get rid" of an unwanted partner with more certainty than would invocation of the criminal law, was ignored. "If the law were so framed so that there could be rape during cohabitation," stated a second Member of Parliament, "there might be many cases going to the Crown Court where a husband would be open to the most serious of penalties." The implication is that there are many husbands who rape their wives – and they should be allowed to continue to do so, without the possibility of suffering any "serious penalty".

Thus the law on its face condones family violence. In an effort to preserve the family as an institution, it fails to provide protection against certain acts. In 1840 it was considered that "for the sake of both" it was necessary to "protect the wife from the danger of unrestrained intercourse with the world by enforcing cohabitation and a common residence" (in circumstances where force and violence by the husband in

---

19. It was notable during the debate on the introduction of child abuse reporting laws in New South Wales that this attitude constantly found its way into media reports. See also comments noting (with disapprobation) this attitude in WEL Sydney IYC Action Group, *Issues Paper – Children's Rights*, 1978, mimeo, WEL Sydney, Surry Hills. A speech by Senator Wriedt in March 1979 canvassed the problem of lack of children's rights in the area of disciplinary assault: Commonwealth Parliamentary Debates, *Senate Daily Hansard*, Thursday, 29 March 1979, pp. 1174–1178.

20. National Council of Women, reported *National Times* 27 September 1976–2 October 1976; cited Peter Sallman, "Rape in Marriage" (1977) *Legal Service Bulletin* 202, p. 203; South Australian Women's Council of the Liberal Party, reported *National Times* 27 September 1976–2 October 1976; cited Peter Sallman, "Rape in Marriage" (1977) *Legal Service Bulletin* 202, p. 203.

21. Reported *The Times* 22 May 1976, p. 6. See also further discussion as to the United Kingdom and South Australian debates in Jocelynne A. Scutt, note 10, pp. 275–277.

doing so were upheld by the court).[22] Similar sentiments can be found today in debates concerning proposals to eliminate the right of a parent to assault offspring and the right of a husband to rape his wife.

Possibly as an acknowledgement of the lack of protection for family members in the case of attack within the domestic circle, some jurisdictions have passed special laws purportedly to afford such protection. Thus provisions are contained in the New South Wales *Crimes Act* 1900 that refer to assault of a wife. Section 60 provides:

Where any husband has been convicted of any assault [occasioning actual bodily harm], or of any aggravated assault, specially so found by the jury, upon his wife, the Judge, if satisfied that her future safety is in peril, may add to the sentence a declaration that she shall no longer be bound to cohabit with her husband.

Every such declaration shall have the effect, in all respects, of a decree of judicial separation on the ground of cruelty.[23]

Yet rather than being notable for any protection afforded to a wife, this section simply confirms the lamentable situation of the party to the marriage who is not at the same time "head of household". The provision acknowledges that a woman who is married is "bound" to cohabit with her husband. Further, it has been held that if the assault were followed by what would amount to rape if the wife was a stranger, it would not come within the section by reason of that act. If the assault were followed by "indecency", this would not elevate it into the category of an "aggravated" assault. "Abusive words" are not relevant as "aggravation".[24]

The standard of abuse required by law to be suffered by a spouse for an application for judicial separation or divorce on grounds of cruelty was high. Thus there was no cruelty or justification for leaving a husband where he was "aggressive and domineering and ... selfish; ... on several occasions ... was drunk, and on one occasion was so drunk that he became violent and threatened to shoot his brother-in-law".[25] If this is the type of assessment made by a judge in the matrimonial jurisdiction of the court, it is hardly likely that a judge exercising criminal jurisdiction would be less restrictive in calculating "aggravation", or whether a wife's safety was in "peril".

It is comparatively rarely that prosecutions of husbands who have assaulted their wives are brought under the *Crimes Act*; in most instances the wife is required to take out a summons in the Magistrates' Court. Thus provisions such as section 60 of the *Crimes Act* serve no real purpose – apart from enabling legislators, judges and those

---

22. *In re Cochrane* (1840) 8 Dowl. 630, per Coleridge, J., p. 636.
23. Note that "cruelty" in matrimonial law has been basically ousted with passage of the *Family Law Act* (Cth) 1975, where in relation to *divorce* fault is no longer relevant, the sole ground being breakdown of the marriage. [See also Jocelynne A. Scutt, "Murphy and Women's Rights" in *Lionel Murphy – A Radical Judge*, 1987, McCulloch-Macmillan, Carlton, pp. 149–152.]
24. *Munday v. Maiden* (1873) 33 LT 377 and see also section 494 *Crimes Act* (NSW) 1900; *R. v. Baker* (1883) 47 JP 666; *Ex parte Little* (1874) 12 SCR (NSW) 323.
25. *R. v. Oregan; ex parte Oregan* [1957] CLR 323, 327. See also J. Scutt, note 10.

members of the public who are not wives to believe complacently that abused wives do not exist, or where they do, the abusers are being prosecuted.[26]

In the case of sexual assault of children by parents or other relatives, courts are similarly inadequate. Laws exist, but are they effective? Inserted into the *Crimes Act 1900* (NSW) in 1924, section 78A provides:

Whosoever, being a male, has carnal knowledge of his mother, sister, daughter or grand-daughter, or being a female of or above the age of sixteen years, with her consent permits her to have carnal knowledge of her (whether in any such case the relationship is of half or full blood, or is not traced through lawful wedlock) shall be liable to penal servitude for seven years.[27]

Attempted incest is punishable under section 78B with a maximum penalty of two years' imprisonment.

For any male victim of incest[28] and any female victim under the age of sixteen years (or the relevant age of consent) these provisions are wholly superfluous. That is, "carnal knowledge" or attempts at this committed upon such individuals are prosecutable under the regular provisions of the Act that deal with those crimes.

Thus, where a father had or attempted to have sexual intercourse with his daughter of, say, fifteen years, he could be prosecuted under section 63 of the *Crimes Act* (or equivalent legislation in other jurisdictions):

Whosoever commits the crime of rape shall be liable to penal servitude for life.

---

26. See for example New South Wales Bureau of Crime Statistics and Research, *Report No. 5, Series 2, Domestic Assaults*, 1975, Bureau of Crime Statistics and Research Department of Attorney General, Sydney, Australia; paper presented by Detective Sergeant K. S. Morgan at a Seminar for Women's Centres, 20–21 April, 1978 (conducted by the NSW Women's Co-ordination Unit), p. 6; *Select Committee on Violence in Marriage*, Minutes of Evidence – Wednesday, 11 June 1975 (Session 1975–1975), 1975, HMSO; Scutt note 4; Erin Pizzey, *Scream Quietly or the Neighbours will Hear*, 1974, Penguin, Harmondsworth. [Commencing in 1981, all Australian jurisdictions commenced to introduce "new" laws providing that a victim and survivor of criminal assault at home could apply for a non-molestation order or its equivalent. The effectiveness of these provisions ·and this process is doubted by many women, particularly those who have used or attempted to use the procedure, and by women working in women's refuges. For a critique, see Jocelynne A. Scutt, note 2 and note 11; Community Council on Violence, *Report*, 1992, Victorian Government, Melbourne.]
27. Comparable provisions exist in other states and are discussed in Royal Commission on Human Relationships, *Final Report*, 1977, Vol. 5, Part VII, sec. 17, AGPS, Canberra, pp. 222–226. [Note that the provisions of the New South Wales *Crimes Act* have been extensively renumbered and recast following reforms to rape laws in 1981 and 1989.]
28. Males over the age of sixteen would come within buggery provisions, which have no recourse to the issue of consent, the issue in these provisions being to enforce a particular standard of morality rather than to protect persons who are victims of unwanted acts. [Note that since the decriminalisation of homosexual acts, in all jurisdictions (apart from Tasmania) this would apply only up to the age limit set on consent to male-male buggery – generally 18 or 21 years.]

The consent of the woman, if obtained by threats or terror, shall be no defence to a charge under this section.[29]

or under section 65:

Whosoever attempts to commit, or assaults any female with intent to commit, the crime of rape, shall be liable to penal servitude for fourteen years.

If there was any implication that the daughter consented freely to the act (and in the light of the power relationship this is objectively unlikely), a prosecution could be launched under the various provisions relating to carnal knowledge, where consent is irrelevant by reason of the youth of the victim. If the daughter were any age and did not consent to the act, the father would be liable under sections 63 and 65 of the Act.[30]

It is difficult to see that incest provisions serve any purpose in protecting young children from sexual abuse by relatives. Indeed, very few cases of incest are brought before the criminal courts. Of those that are, the offence is rarely related to one isolated act, although (generally) isolated acts only are charged. For example, in South Australia, between 1950 and 1973 only eighty cases of incest were recorded by way of criminal proceedings.[31] Evidence now coming to light in Australia shows that many more instances must have occurred over that period. As for length of time of the sexual abuse, Herbert Maisch's work shows incestuous relationships as lasting for more than one year, in seventy-one per cent of the cases studied, before action was taken by authorities.[32]

If a stranger molests a child, every effort is made on the part of the authorities to seek out the culprit and to prosecute under appropriate provisions. Where the person molesting the child happens to be a parent or close relative, however, the attitude of

---

29. In states where homosexual acts are decriminalised the position is equivalent (although "age of consent" may differ) to that relating to young women. [Note that the New South Wales *Crimes Act* rape provisions have been extensively amended, first in 1981 and again in 1989. A major report reviewing rape laws around Australia has been written by the author for the National Council on Violence Against Women, which is located in the Office of the Status of Women, Department of Prime Minister and Cabinet. At the time of writing, the report was not published.]

30. See Royal Commission on Human Relationships, *Final Report* Vol. 5, at pp. 208–220; also note 27. [Regarding s. 63 and s. 65 Crimes Act (NSW) 1900: since 1976 in South Australia and the 1980s in the other states, rape laws have been revised and broadened. It remains true that these provisions are adequate to cover the field addressed in incest laws. On rape laws and reform see Barbara Toner, *The Facts of Rape*, 1977, Arrow Books, London; Jocelynne A. Scutt (ed.) *Rape Law Reform*, 1980, Australian Institute of Criminology, Canberra; Jocelynne A. Scutt, "Sexual Assault and the Australian Criminal Justice System" in Duncan Chappell and Paul Wilson (eds.), *The Australian Criminal Justice System – The Mid 1980s*, 1986, Butterworths, Sydney. This remains true under the new provisions, introduced in 1981 and 1989.]

31. See also Herbert Maisch, *Incest*, 1973, Andre Deutsch, London, at pp. 102–104. [See further research undertaken by the Sydney Rape Crisis Centre during 1978–1979; research undertaken by the Western Australian group, Women Against Rape (WAR) during 1978, reported in Jocelynne A. Scutt, note 11.]

32. Herbert Maisch, note 31. [This would be considered by many people working in the field to be a conservative estimate today.]

those with the responsibility for putting the law into effect expresses itself in a different manner.[33] In many instances every effort is made to "keep the family together", despite the occurrence of sexual exploitation amounting to criminal acts. Often the child who is the victim will be removed, so that "disruption of the family unit" by way of the sexual relationship will be discontinued. Disruption of the child's life, and the need to properly counter this, is ignored.

Once again, rather than providing a means whereby crime within the family may be dealt with in the same way as crimes of a similar nature outside the unit, incest laws lie on the statute books, rarely used. Ostensibly, these laws prohibit incest and provide for denunciation where the act is committed. Unfortunately, because incest is an act that on the surface, at least, our society deplores, the creation of special laws opens the way to socio-legal dissonance: the law clearly states that the act is prohibited; few prosecutions are brought; ergo incest is a rarity, and the family unit – without which incest could never occur – can remain intact.[34]

Finally, the special case of murder of a family member illustrates the problem. Some United States' jurisdictions have explicitly written into the law that the killing of a wife by her husband, where he has discovered her in the act of adultery, will not be unlawful. The act will come within the bounds of the "heat of passion" doctrine, where a person is "... so rendered subject to passion or loss of control as to be led to use ... violence with fatal results, ... and [in fact acted] under the stress of such provocation".[35]

In Australia, provocation may result in a verdict of manslaughter on a prosecution for murder. Provocation in law consists of three main elements:

[T]he act of provocation, the loss of self-control, both actual and reasonable, and the retaliation proportionate to the provocation. The defence cannot require the issue to be left to the jury unless there has been produced a credible narrative of events suggesting the presence of these three elements ... provocation in law means something more than a provocative incident. That is only one of the constituent elements.[36]

In *Attorney-General for Ceylon v. Perrera* the English Privy Council held that the defence of provocation could arise where a person intends to kill or inflict grievous bodily harm (which in the normal course would render the killing murder), but the intention to do so "arises from sudden passion involving loss of self-control by reason of provocation". The court lighted upon the paradigm situation:

---

33. See discussion in Jocelynne A. Scutt, "Sexism in Psychology – The Corroboration Rule in Rape" (1979) *Hecate*. [Published this volume, as Chapter 8.]

34. [Today there is a much greater acknowledgement of the occurrence of child sexual abuse within the family. However, it remains true that many in authority and many in the general community do not wish to accept the reality of this abuse. See Jocelynne A. Scutt, *Women and the Law*, 1990, Law Book Co., Sydney, pp. 294–305, 484–486.]

35. *Attorney-General of Ceylon v. Perrera* [1953] AC 200; also *Russell on Crime*, Neville J. Turner (ed.), 10th edn, vol. 1, pp. 574–577.

36. Colin Howard, note 14, p. 88; *Russell on Crime*, note 35, pp. 574–575. [See also *Zecevic v. DPP (Vic.)* (1987) 162 CLR 645 for the current law and Jocelynne A. Scutt, note 34, pp. 414–421, 459–465 for an analysis of provocation and self-defence laws and their operation.]

An illustration is to be found in the case of a man finding his wife in the act of adultery who kills her ... and the law has always regarded that, although an intentional act, as amounting only to manslaughter by reason of provocation received, although no doubt the accused intended to cause death or grievous bodily harm.[37]

In *Homes v. DPP* the English House of Lords held, significantly, that in no case *apart from that of finding one's spouse in the act of adultery* would the doctrine of provocation apply if the defendant had actually formed an intention to kill.[38] Subsequently this limitation upon the plea in mitigation was effectively overruled so that other acts of provocation may come within the doctrine of "blind passion". Nonetheless it is significant that courts have held that the concept of finding a wife in adultery as amounting to provocation does not extend to the finding of a fiancee or a cohabitor in the act.

Once again the law has made out a special case. The origin of the law no doubt lies in the concept of wife as property and supports the idea that the family is to be maintained by way of powers residing in the husband: if his wife erred, the threat of death (with a lesser penalty to the husband) was real. Certainly Howard, although pointing out in *Australian Criminal Law* that there appears to be no case of a wife finding her husband in adultery and killing him in passion, states "no reason suggests itself why a wife should not be just as annoyed by adultery as her husband".[39] But the law may not regard her crime in kind. In the seventeenth century, husband and wife in legal language were termed "baron" and "femme". The husband was to the wife as a king to a citizen. If the citizen killed the king it was treason. If a wife killed her husband it was petit treason, more serious than murder and far more serious than manslaughter.[40]

This bears out the assertion that law traditionally has created a milieu in which family members are virtually powerless unless playing the role of husband, who gains dual support through the laws. First, the laws support him in his efforts – even where they involve violence against family members – to keep the family intact. Secondly laws act harshly against any member who has the temerity to question his authority.

---

37. *Attorney-General of Ceylon v. Perrera* [1953] AC 200, pp. 205–206.
38. *Homes v. DPP* [1946] AC 588; *Palmer* 1913 2 KB 29 (CCA); *Greening* [1913] 3 KB 846 (CCA) (obiter); but cf. *Larkin* [1943] 1 KB 174, [1943] 1 All ER 217. Note that this position may be changing: *Leyden* [1962] Tas. SR 1, which simply confirms the idea that cohabitation is more acceptable – and now cohabitees may become subject to those controls relating to married persons.
39. Colin Howard, note 14, p. 88, note 77. On "wife as property", this concept has roots far in the past. For a useful commentary, see J. Thorsten Sellin, *Slavery and the Penal System*, 1976, Elsevier, New York, p. 32:

    The disciplinary power of the head of a household was unlimited and of no concern to the tribal state. If his wife misbehaved sexually, he could cut off her hair, strip her naked, and flog her through the village in the presence of kinsmen. We are told that a woman so treated would find it difficult to get another husband. As for slaves, their masters could deal with them at will. They could be flogged, fettered, put to hard labor, or even killed ...

40. Commentary by Edward Christian (ed.) 12th edn, *Blackstone's Commentaries*, Vol. 4, 1793, p. 204.

Domestic Violence Ignored

Although laws exist by which domestic violence may be prosecuted, those laws are ineffective due to lack of enforcement. This is particularly evident for spouse assault. Thus although a man may be prosecuted for assaulting his wife, such prosecutions rarely take place. Incontrovertible evidence has been produced in the United States, in Canada, the United Kingdom and many other European countries to show that the police response to domestic violence is not comparable with their response to violence by strangers. In Australia, the research confirms a like pattern.[41]

A study of 184 cases of domestic assault coming before Chamber Magistrates in New South Wales was carried out in 1975 by the New South Wales Bureau of Crime Statistics and Research. Of these, the victim had, in 52 cases, been "severely injured" in the alleged attack by their spouse. In more than 75 per cent of the cases the victim stated she had been punched repeatedly, primarily about the head, breasts and shoulders. The majority of assaults were by kicking, punching, pulling of hair, slapping, twisting of arms, throwing the woman bodily against the furniture. One woman was dragged through the street by the hair. Although weapons were involved in only ten per cent of the attacks, referring to these the Bureau stated:

In most cases where the weapons were actually applied in the alleged assault, the attacker appeared to have seized the nearest available object in the heat of the moment. Household objects such as an ashtray, a hair brush, a chair leg, a wooden stool, a saucepan, a shoe, a burning match, a garden hose, a leather dog leash and even the kitchen sink figured in assaults involving blunt instruments ... One woman had a knife held to her throat and another was poked in the stomach with a chef's knife.[42]

In view of the severity of the assaults, the issue is why the victims had come before the Magistrates Court, bringing the action themselves, rather than by police prosecution of the offenders. Section 547 of the *Crimes Act* 1900 (NSW) provides that where it can be proved to the satisfaction of the Chamber Magistrate that apprehension of violence by a spouse is reasonable, then the defendant (husband) will be "bound over" – required to keep the peace and will be restrained from harassing or attacking the complainant. The person who is the complainant is the person who fears attack – in this case, the wife. Binding over to keep the peace is not a punishment, but a measure taken to prevent the danger that is apprehended by the potential victim. Police are reported as stating that they advise women victims of domestic violence to take this approach, either because (they assert) the police have "no power" to deal with the matter, or because the morning after the attack the women often declines to give evidence where the husband has

---

41. See sources at note 26; Michigan Governor's Commission into Domestic Assault, *Report*, 1979, Michigan, USA; Emerson Dobash and R. P. Dobash, note 4. The writer is currently undertaking a research study which supports these findings. [Subsequently published in various articles and reports, and see also Scutt, note 2.]
42. See note 26.

been prosecuted – and thus the prosecution has no chance of success.[43]

Neither contention is persuasive. Although the police have a discretion not to prosecute and in exercise of this power some criminal acts are not generally prosecuted by police, police are under a general duty to protect life and limb. Further, section 7A of the *Police Regulation Act* 1899 (NSW) provides:

(1) It is, and shall be deemed always to have been, the duty of a member of the police force to protect persons from injury or death and property from damage, whether the persons are, or the property is, endangered by the criminal law or otherwise.[44]

One of the traditional ways in which police exercise their duty of protection is by arresting and charging individuals causing or who have caused injury by criminal acts. Many of the women in the New South Wales Bureau of Crime Statistics study seem undoubtedly to qualify under provisions of the *Crimes Act* dealing with assaults of a relatively serious nature: assault with wounding, attempting to choke or strangle and the like.[45] Further, although a victim may be reluctant to give evidence, her "change of mind" cannot negate the fact that a crime has occurred. Evidence from medical practitioners, neighbours, onlookers, the law enforcement officers themselves where they were on the scene, would support any prosecution.

Problems in the failure of the police to apply the laws lie in the concept of the family as we know it. Supporting the idea that within the privacy of one's home, spouse assault is acceptable, or not susceptible to the operation of the criminal law, are statements such as that made in a mid 1970s debate in the United Kingdom Parliament:

It must cause the police considerable embarrassment to see a woman being beaten and have to say ... "We are sorry we cannot do anything about it. It is a matter between you and your husband ..." The law places the police in an invidious position.[46]

As it is not true that an assault is a "matter between the victim and her husband", but is a criminal act known to the law, the party in "an invidious position" is the wife who is

---

43. See note 26; also studies carried out by the Royal Commission on Human Relationships, *Final Report*, Vol. 4, 1977, AGPS, Canberra; R. Parnas, "Prosecutorial and Judicial Handling of Family Violence" (1973) 9 *Crim. Law Bulletin* 333; R. Parnas, "The Police Response to Domestic Disturbance" (1967) *Wis. Law Review* 945; R. Parnas, "Judicial Response to Intra-Family Violence" (1970) 54 *Minn. Law Rev.* 585. See also sources cited at note 38.

44. The common law position is referred to in *Ex parte Blackburne* [1972] 1 All ER; also E. Campbell and H. Whitmore, *Freedom in Australia*, 1967, Law Book Co., Sydney, pp. 30ff. [The binding over provisions are an old version of the "new" non-molestation or apprehended violence provisions that have been introduced into all Australian jurisdictions, commencing with South Australia and New South Wales in the early 1980s. Further on these "new" provisions see Jocelynne A. Scutt, note 2, particularly Chapter 13, "The Politics of Violence".]

45. For example, sections 33, 34, 35, 59, 61 *Crimes Act* (NSW) 1900.

46. *Hansard*. House of Commons, 1975–1976, Vol. 905, Col. 864; see also S. McCabe, "Unfinished Business – Violence in Marriage and Violence in the Family" (1977) 17 *Brit. Jrn. Criminology* 280.

not granted the protection of the law.

Yet it is not the police alone who internalise family standards operating to prevent the application of the law. Social workers are reported as adopting the view that wife-bashing is not criminal. Laws are negated by the romanticism attaching to family life, "... it can't really be bad, she's his wife"; "she knew what he was when she married him, she must fancy a bit of bashing around"; "... she must like it rough"; "... it's his inarticulate way of demonstrating his love for her." Doctors, counsellors, priests mouth the same platitudes. Husbands are reported as adhering to the belief that "I can do what I like to her. She's my wife".[47]

Sadly, wives too have been led to believe that being assaulted by their husbands is "a private matter". In the first national victimisation survey conducted by the Australian Bureau of Statistics, covering 18,694 persons throughout Australia during 1975, women were more likely than men to state that they did not report an assault to the police "because it was a private matter". Whereas men "were markedly more likely" than women to fail to report assault because "the victim would handle the situation himself" (17.1 per cent as opposed to 1.9 per cent), women were "far more likely" than men to omit reporting assault to the police because "they thought it was private not criminal" (24.4 per cent as opposed to 4.3 per cent).[48]

Generalised myths and desires as to the manner in which family life should be structured also militate against assault in the domestic sphere being dealt with by the criminal law. "Woman's place is in the home" is apparently accepted generally as true: a recent survey in the United Kingdom, some four years after the passage of the *Equal Employment Act* in 1975, found a majority of males in favour of their wives remaining at home rather than being in paid employment. The role of woman as the caring and rearing parent, taking on the duties of childcare full-time, remains predominant. The media continues to deplore the presence of married women in the workforce. An airline company has allegedly declined to employ a woman, Deborah Wardley, as a pilot in the belief that her intention to have children at an unspecified time in the future will interrupt her career – although presumably male pilots have fathered and will continue to father children.[49]

As a result of these attitudes, in combination with the reality that it is most often the wife who is confined to home to care for children and who has no continuing

---

47. See generally Erin Pizzey, note 26; Joanna Downey and Jane Howell, *Wife Battering – A Review*, 1976, United Way Social Policy and Research, USA. Cited R. and R. E. Dobash, "Wife Beating – Still a Common Form of Violence" (1977) 9 *Social Work Today* 4; see also G. Carsenat-Jones, *Behind Closed Doors – The Tragedy of a Battered Wife* (unpublished paper).

48. David Biles and John Braithwaite, "Crime Victims and the Police" (1979) *Australian Psychology*.

49. See for example "Debby gives up on flying high" *Sun-Herald* 22 April 1979, p. 7; "Baby for pilot 'less important'" *Australian* 25 April 1979, p. 3; "Ansett panel told to reject women pilot" *Sydney Morning Herald* 25 April 1979, p. 2. [See further Jocelynne A. Scutt, note 34. Deborah Lawrie/ Wardley won her case against Ansett. See Elaine McKenna and Deborah Wardley, *Letting Fly*, 1992, Allen and Unwin, Sydney.]

independent income with no possibility of gaining one through a career, it is difficult for any woman to escape the situation which leads to abuse. If she were to have recourse to the law, and her husband to be prosecuted and punished – possibly by placement in prison – the result is loss of "the breadwinner" and dependence upon inadequate social security benefits. When the husband is released, he will once more descend upon her – and the abuse begin again, possibly more violently. If she wishes to take out a complaint against her husband under section 547 of the *Crimes Act*, she has to find a babysitter for the children or struggle to court with them on public transport. If she wishes to have him removed from the home in order to prevent the violence from continuing, the court is reluctant except on the clearest evidence of necessity, to preclude the husband by way of injunction from residence in his own home: "a man's home is his castle".[50]

Family life and the role of the husband as "king of the castle" have prevented laws being designed for the protection of subordinate members of the family against abuse. This conception of the family has led in some instances to the framing of special laws that are no more than paper edicts against violence and exploitation, or confirm the right of control of family members. So too the family structure militates against the elimination of domestic violence in the failure of laws to be applied in practice.

Domestic Violence in Special Venue

Some jurisdictions have sought to contain "family problems" by placing their adjudication within the confines of a specially constituted court. In New York, the Family Court deals with domestic assaults, treating them as civil issues rather than matters for a criminal court. The family violence policy decided upon by the New York Supreme Court is that it should generally not intervene in such cases, for in the *Family Court Act*, "... the legislature sought to avoid penal sanctions in well-defined situations where intra-familial or intra-household assault had occurred ..."[51]

Similarly in Washington DC and Philadelphia, provision is made for settlement of domestic disputes outside criminal courts, by way of counselling and like methods.

---

50. In Sydney it has been reported that night-courts have not been successful, as was hoped, in serving persons who could not come during the daylight hours. Certainly it should be no surprise that babysitters are difficult to find at cheap rates at any time of the day – or night. [As earlier noted, section 547 of the New South Wales *Crimes Act* and its equivalents in other states has been replaced or supplemented by "new" injunction, non-molestation or intervention order, or apprehended violence, procedures. It is problematic whether this has improved the position for women. There remains a strong view, particularly amongst more conservative magistrates, that a man should not be removed from "his" home, nor precluded from coming near "his own" property. At the same time some magistrates are more ready to accept the realities of violence against women and women's real fear of their husbands' violence. It is not, however, *changes to the law* that have effected this change; rather, it is changes to the magistracy and the educative effect of the Women's Movement in highlighting the abuses meted out against women at home.]

51. R. Parnas, note 43. The immediately following information is from the same source.

The Bureau of Family Relations in California acts as investigator in family matters, specifying alternative methods to the criminal justice process.

What philosophy is being put into practice in the hiving off of matrimonial violence into a special venue? It places aggressors in a position warranting special consideration because they are related, by marriage, to their victims. "Problems" are passed over to counsellors for assistance. Yet as the British researcher, Erin Pizzey confirmed in her research:

As social workers mostly deal with problem families they have come to accept that violence amongst their clients is the norm. They will produce arguments to prove that an uneducated man who beats his wife is showing an inarticulate form of love for her ... Too many [social workers] accept that beatings are a part of life and urge women to put up with them.[52]

Just as society outside the "special venue" recalls and supports traditional beliefs about the family structure, so within that venue traditional beliefs exist. Field and Field in carrying out a study of police and judicial responses to marital violence in Washington DC (under a family court system) found little difference between the two groups. During 1967 only 16 per cent of all cases surveyed involving assaults in the family resulted in arrest and adjudication. Wherever a family-based assault was considered sufficiently serious to be dealt with by way of criminal dispositions, *all* were charged as misdemeanours; none was proceeded with as a felony. The conclusion was:

The poles of enforcement are the rigorous prosecution of the person accused of assaulting a stranger and the non-prosecution of the one who assaults a marital partner.[53]

Because the family unit is supported outside the family law courts by lack of laws, special laws or failure to extend laws that protect against violence, those supports are inevitably reflected in these courts. The very setting up of a special venue reinforces the idea that the family is "special", and confirms the belief that the unit per se deserves special treatment – whatever the true nature of activities occurring within it.

These attitudes are endemic in our society, permeating all institutions. Thus the *Family Law Act* 1975 by section 43(b) provides that the Family Court must exercise its jurisdiction having regard to, inter alia, "the need to give widest possible protection and assistance to the family as the natural and fundamental group unit of society ..." These words echo the statement in the United Nations' *Universal Declaration of Human Rights* article 16 (3):

The family is the natural and fundamental group unit of society and is entitled to protection by society and the State.

---

52. Erin Pizzey, note 26.
53. The Field and Field study is cited in R. Emerson Dobash and Russell P. Dobash, *With Friends Like These – Who Needs Enemies – Institutional Supports for the Patriarchy and Violence Against Women* note 4; the quotation appears pp. 30–31.

Yet clearly, any swift perusal of anthropological writings soon disabuses the reader of such a notion: the nuclear family as it exists today is a relatively modern phenomenon.[54] Despite its alleged "naturalness", crimes of violence occur within it. These crimes will not disappear merely by way of legislative exhortation, judicial pronouncement, or international edict.

Conclusion

Laws relating to the family illustrate the conflict between mysticism adhering to the family unit and the reality of that unit. Some laws on their face refuse to recognise violence as it occurs within the family: they provide no recourse to the legal process to deal with acts which, outside the family unit, would be crimes. Some laws create special rules for crimes occurring within the family; they thereby negate or mitigate the criminal element of violent acts. Sometimes, although laws exist acknowledging the occurrence of crimes within the family, these laws are not put into effect by the authorities. Thus in practice, laws are obliterated by romanticism attaching to family life. Sometimes a special forum is set up for dealing with family violence. This serves to reinforce the idea that the traditional family unit must be preserved, whatever the cost to the less powerful members of that unit.

Those seeking to preserve the family unit fail to recognise that preservation depends upon sometimes overt, sometimes surreptitious acknowledgement of greater rights existing in one of the parties – the "leader", "ruler", or husband/father. This identity exerts a "right" to order relations within the family. Because he has the right, the father must be given the power to fulfil that right – and so the law backs him. Because the wishes of family members will at times differ from the wishes of the prime mover, and because the latter has legal, economic and political backing, violence and the use of force are an inevitable outcome. Inevitably, the mystical family disappears to be replaced by the reality – a unit that depends, for its existence, on the unequal sharing of power.

---

54. See for example F. Engels, *The Origin of the Family*, 1848; J. Ekelaar, *Family Security and Family Breakdown*, 1971, Routledge and Kegan Paul, London.

7

THE ALCOHOLIC IMPERATIVE:
A Sexist Rationalisation for Rape and Domestic Violence

Published in (1981) 7 (No. 1) *Hecate* 88.

The Women and Labour conferences began at Macquarie University, in Sydney, in 1978.[1] The second conference was held at Melbourne University in 1980, and it was for this conference that "The Alcoholic Imperative" was written. The paper must have hit a nerve, as this stands out to me as a time when the response from participants in the conference was overwhelming: women are always more exacting audiences, and when there is clapping and hooting and hollering, a woman delivering a paper knows she's got through in a very real way. That is how it was for "The Alcoholic Imperative".

Since its writing, presentation and publication, I have had no cause to modify my view that alcohol is used as a prime excuse for violence against women. At the same time, it's easy to recognise that a drunk in charge of a gun or a knife can be dangerous, particularly to women. Yet women are equally at risk from a man who is stone, cold sober wielding a gun or a knife. Or fists.

In the 1980s the Victorian Transport Commission commenced running television and cinema advertisements advising against drinking and driving. Just as the Quit campaign has had a profound effect on the level of smoking and the numbers of smokers, it seems that the "Drink, Drive, You're a Bloody Idiot" campaign has affected the level of road accidents. For criminal assault at home, however, it would make little sense to confine an advertising campaign to admonishments requiring that a man not

---

1. See Elizabeth Windshuttle (ed.), *Women, Class and History*, 1980, Fontana Books, Sydney; Margaret Bevege, Margaret James, and Carmel Shute (eds.), *Worth Her Salt*, 1982, Hale and Iremonger, Sydney; Women and Labour Collective (eds.), *All Her Labours – Working It Out* and *All Her Labours – Embroidering the Framework*, vols 1 and 2, 1985, Hale and Iremonger, Sydney; Sue Bellamy, "Freedom from Unreal Loyalties" in *Different Lives – Reflections on the Women's Movement and Visions of Its Future*, 1987, Jocelynne A. Scutt (ed.), Penguin Books Australia, Ringwood, pp. 188–199; Jocelynne A. Scutt, "Good for Women" in *Different Lives*, pp. 216–235. In the footnotes, square brackets [...] indicate new material added for this edition.

drink and bash his wife, or not drink and go home. As is clear from the evidence, there would have to be an equal number of advertisements proclaiming: "Don't go home sober," or "Don't stay sober and bash your wife". "Don't be a drunk and bash your wife" would have to be matched by: "Don't be a teetotaller and bash your wife."

Nonetheless at the Second National Conference on Violence, held by the Australian Institute of Criminology in Canberra in June 1993, several of the speakers reasserted a causative link between alcohol and woman bashing. "Listen to the victims of violence," was the admonition.[2]

As we know, the entire rationale of the Women's Movement and work on violence against women is that victims and survivors must be listened to. This is where the research and women's activism in the refuge movement and rape crisis centre movement has been based. This is where the centres against sexual assault find their centring. Feminist analysis is anchored in the lives and voices of women bashed, beaten, raped and abused. And, too often, in their deaths.

The point of listening is twofold – it incorporates the notion that the listener must hear. When a large proportion of women, as victims and survivors, say no alcohol was involved in the violence, we need to listen and to see that this is equally relevant to any assessment of the "role" alcohol is said to play by researchers. We need to understand the dynamic of violence against women without being diverted by an easy way out – that the cause is the demon drink. And as pointed out in "The Alcoholic Imperative", it is nonsense to say that the "main reason" women give for their partner's violence is "excessive drinking", then in support to quote a woman saying that her husband "takes it out" on her when he's broke and can't get enough to drink. In the words of the woman, lack of alcohol rather than its presence dictates this man's violence.

As "The Domestic Paradigm"[3] argues, it is the promotion of alcohol as a "manly" means of obtaining or possessing a woman that adds to an acculturated view that women are possessions and, ultimately, "she's my wife and I can do what I like with her". This affects men who drink, and men who don't. It affects the way women and men regard women.

As an analysis of studies purporting to show a link between alcohol and violence against women reveals, what is necessary is an advertising campaign demanding: "Don't bash your wife". "Criminal assault at home is just that – a crime." The message needs to go out loud and clear to all wife bashers, not just to men who drink.

---

2. *Papers from the Second National Conference on Violence Against Women*, 1993, Australian Institute of Criminology, Canberra. See, particularly, papers by Patricia Easteal and Sandra Eggar.
3. Chapter 5, this volume.

He drank about two gallons of beer before the attack outside the disco ... The pregnancy of [his] wife may have been "one of the reasons for his committing the offence".

News of the World, 25 January 1976

In July 1979, Justice Jones said that the "imprudent behaviour of many young women did not excuse offences committed on them, but lessened the moral culpability of the offender". He said there were "too many young women hitching lifts and accepting rides with cars full of young men" they did not know. They fraternised and drank with men they did not know, in bars, and did their best to bring disaster on themselves. "These foolish young women should behave with more dignity and show some elementary prudence."

Statements by Justice Jones published by
Australian Women Against Rape Newsletter, Perth, 1979

One of the commonest types of incidence amongst co-habiting couples described by the Chamber Magistrate involved the man arriving home late affected by alcohol. An argument with the complainant ensued which rapidly erupted into physical violence. In a typical example, the husband came home at 10.30 pm from the hotel and demanded his dinner. It was not ready, and when his wife refused to prepare it, he slapped her on the face and punched her about the shoulders and chest.

Department of Attorney-General and of Justice,
NSW Bureau of Crime Statistics and Research[4]

The question arises as to whether our [*sic*] battered wives provoke their consorts to violent attack or whether they simply pick out more violent men to marry or whether both these factors operate ... The sequence of events would be:
(i)   Marry or cohabit with a violent man.
(ii) Object to his drinking (particularly to his increasing drinking) because of poor relationship with a heavy drinking and violent father.
(iii) Get battered and leave him.

John Price and Jean Armstrong, "Battered Wives:
A Controlled Study of Predisposition"[5]

Introduction

In common parlance, in anecdote and in research studies, alcohol and domestic violence are linked. Similarly with rape and other sexual offences, alcohol is said to lie at the base of many – if not all – of these criminal events. Two apparently contradictory approaches are taken. The first begins from the premise that rape and domestic violence are "unnatural" events caused by intoxication: "If he were not drunk at the time, he wouldn't have done it/it wouldn't have happened." The second commences with the premise that rape and domestic violence are "natural" occurrences within a

---

4. *Statistical Report, No. 5, Series 2, Domestic Assaults,* 1975, p. 7.
5. *ANZ Jrn. Psychiatry* (1978) vol. 12, no. 43, p. 46.

given set of circumstances: thus with domestic violence, the beating of a woman by her husband is understandable where she has provoked him ("driven to drink") – how else could he act, given the frustration to which he has been subjected? With rape, no man can be blamed (goes the theory) for following his "natural" urges when a woman drinks with him in bars, joining him for a "night cap" – "obviously she wanted it/what else could she expect?"

Although the explanation of marital and sexual violence as being "unnatural" and caused by drink, and that of their being "natural" and caused by drink are on the surface directly opposed, common ground can quickly be found. Both approaches tend to absolve the aggressor from responsibility for criminal (and damaging) acts; both absolve society from enquiring as to whether "normal" (that is, without the influence of alcohol) relations between women and men involve violence.

Domestic Violence and Alcohol: The Aggressor

The desire to link domestic violence with alcohol is of ancient vintage. In the eighteenth century, Fromageau's *Dictionnaire des cas de conscience* cites instances of drunken domestic violence, including that of Basin, who "has a habit of demanding his rights of Louise his wife when he is drunk", so that "if Basin is so drunk that he has lost the use of reason, Louise is not obliged to render him the conjugal due".[6] Similarly in England during the seventeenth century "a prominent feature of homicide" at Sussex and Herts assizes was "the prevalence of domestic violence", frequently seen as involving alcohol:

At least 13 per cent of the deaths investigated at assizes involved the killing of one member of a family by, or with the connivance of another ... On the evidence of assize indictments, wives were the victims in almost three-quarters of the instances of marital killing. Husbands, several of whom were adjudged insane, apparently favoured blunt instruments or direct physical violence as a means of eliminating family members ...[7]

At quarter sessions during the same period, drink was allegedly at the bottom of much domestic strife:

Family quarrels, even when they did not reach the level of violence, could cause problems within the local community ... A source of sudden violence was personal aggressiveness springing sometimes from drink, sometimes from personal whims or eccentricities ... Drink and personal aggressiveness had a part to play, even without actual violence, in disturbing the peace ...[8]

---

6. G. Fromageau, *Dictionnaire des cas de conscience*, 1733, Paris, cols. 1197–9 and 1201; cited Jean-Louis Landrin, *Families in Former Times – Kinship, Household and Sexuality*, Trns. Richard Southern, 1979, Cambridge University Press, Cambridge, p. 220.
7. J. S. Cockburn, "The Nature and Incidence of Crime in England 1559–1625 – A Preliminary Survey" in *Crime in England 1550–1800*, J. S. Cockburn (ed.), 1977, Princeton University Press, Princeton, p. 57.
8. T. C. Curtis, "Quarter Sessions Appearances and Their Background – A Seventeenth-Century Regional Study" in *Crime in England 1550–1800*, note 7, p. 137.

John Stuart Mill spoke out strongly against husband brutality and its links with alcohol, and in 1878 the *Matrimonial Causes Act* (UK) was passed, providing that a woman was legally entitled to bring a complaint against her husband's violence, proving he had committed an aggravated assault upon her, so that she would no longer be obliged by law to live with him. This Act came into being after Frances Power Cobbe's campaign against drink and "wife torture".[9]

One of the most publicised battles against alcohol, arising largely out of a perceived link between drunkenness and spouse assault, was that waged by the United States' temperance campaigners for the passing of an Amendment to the *Constitution*, outlawing the production and sale of alcohol. The passage of the Amendment did not result in the cessation of alcohol production and sale, nor in the cessation of drunkenness; nor did wife-beating cease. Had the desired effect of the Amendment come about, however, and alcohol-drinking stopped, there is serious doubt whether the hoped-for secondary effect – that of elimination of domestic violence – would have been achieved.

Studies undertaken to substantiate alcohol intake as a causal factor in domestic violence begin with a premise that the link exists. Evidence is then slanted to bolster this belief. A connection is made between aggression, violence and their "triggering factor", alcohol: without the presence of alcohol in the assailant, aggression would not be experienced; or without alcohol, aggression would not be expressed in violent acts directed against a spouse. The stand taken is that aggression and violence are unusual or abnormal and that domestic violence is accordingly unusual or abnormal.

In a comprehensive review of literature on alcohol and domestic violence, a Canadian study concluded "that alcohol does play a significant role in the battered wife syndrome" and that there is "a definite association between alcohol use and family violence".[10] Yet when the findings are dissected, the "relationship" of alcohol to violence in the family becomes a meaningless standard; and there is no way in which the studies reviewed can in any way bolster the idea that alcohol "causes" domestic violence.

The reviewers themselves acknowledge that "the extent and nature of [the alleged association between alcohol use and family violence] varies widely amongst studies and agencies". They further go on to outline defects in the studies:

9. See O. R. McGregor, *Divorce in England – A Centenary Study*, 1957, Heinemann, London, pp. 22–23; also note John Eekelaar, *Family Law and Social Policy*, 1978, Weidenfeld and Nicholson, London, pp. 19 and 72–73.

10. Joanne Downey and Jane Howell, *Wife Battering – A Review and Preliminary Enquiry into Local Incidence, Needs and Resources*, 1976, Social Policy and Research Department, United Way of Greater Vancouver and the Non-Medical Use of Drugs Directorate, National Department of Health and Welfare, Vancouver, Chapter 6, "Alcohol and Wife Battering", p. 49ff. The four immediately following quotations come from the same source, pp. 54–55.

Little distinction is made in the findings between pathological drinking (alcoholism) and episodic drinking associated with violence ... [Furthermore] some studies ... indicate that drunkenness is not always followed by violent behaviour in some cultures. Moreover it was found that in many families drunkenness may occur without the precipitating violence, and violence may occur without any alcohol being consumed.[11]

Responses to the question, "In approximately what proportion of [domestic violence cases] was the use or abuse of alcohol a reason for agency contact?" varied wildly:

In my experience as a counsellor the battered wife is not an infrequent client and in the majority of cases it is an alcohol related problem.

No data supplied.

Most definitely upwards of 90 per cent of our cases indicate the abuse of alcohol by the husband to be a major factor in leading to or causing the abuse of the wife. There are a few cases where alcohol is used but said not to be a factor, and only the very rare case where no alcohol is used.

No indication of what constitutes "abuse" of alcohol: would this mean that the husband is an alcoholic? That he drinks each night at the pub and each night returns to beat his wife? That he drinks each Friday at the pub and returns to beat his wife? That he drinks regularly, but not every time he drinks does he beat his wife; that it takes ten beers to add up to "abuse" and it is only when he has drunk ten that he assaults his wife? When he has drunk nine glasses, he refrains ... ?

Other agencies replying to the questionnaire in the Canadian study were less dogmatic:

Although alcohol is often present, I feel it is a mistake to focus on it as a reason. Alcohol is certainly used as an excuse ("I didn't know what I was doing"), but another would almost certainly be found if alcohol were not available. Alcohol is often symptomatic of marriage breakdown rather than the cause of it.

Alcohol abuse and assaultive behaviour are both forms of anti-social behaviour. We do not need another study explaining why men beat their wives and particularly one with a pre-judgment that it may be "because they drink".

In Australia, similarly, research has concentrated upon the alleged involvement of alcohol in violence in the family. A study by the New South Wales Bureau of Crime, Statistics and Research in 1974 showed that, according to the victims of the attacks, almost 60 per cent of the aggressors "had been drinking" prior to the assault. Yet in one-third of the cases, there was no consumption of alcohol by either party recently prior to the attack: thus in many cases drink can in no way be said to "cause" or be

---

11. Note 10, p. 54.

related to the violence – what then is the cause in those cases?[12] Similarly, it was stated by the Royal Commission on Human Relationships that "drinking was a frequent factor in domestic violence," although the Report goes on quite rightly to point out that it is "difficult to decide to what extent alcohol is a cause of stress or response to it".[13] In a study by the Elsie Refuge in New South Wales, "excessive drinking" was said to be the "main reason" women gave for their partner's violence. One of the remarks said to bolster this statement shows clearly it is lack of drink rather than over indulgence that led to the assaultive acts:

I don't know. He just seems to get the shits with himself when he can't get enough to drink – when he's broke he'll take it out on me ...

In the Canadian study by Downey and Howell, the conclusions of the review of research seeking to link alcohol with domestic violence illustrate all too clearly the programmed response to the problem of spouse assault. In assessing the results of the control questionnaire, the writers acknowledge that most of the figures given "are estimates only" and further that it is "difficult to determine their accuracy". One agency response "reports only 10 per cent alcohol involvement"; some agencies responded with 0 per cent alcohol involvement; one agency "estimates a rate of 100 per cent". Downey and Howell further accept the subjective nature of responses to such questionnaires. Rather naively they state, "It is possible that there is, to varying degrees, a belief that men who beat their wives must have been drinking," and that few "wish to believe that sober, civilized men engage in this kind of behaviour". They point out that there is no clarity as to the nature of any "association between alcohol and violence", that the person drinking – whether it was the offender alone, the victim alone, or both offender and victim – is frequently unspecified; that no details are available as to the extent of use of alcohol in family violence situations: was there simply "drinking"; was there "intoxication"; was drinking "episodic"; was it "pathological drinking"? Yet despite these uncertainties, which should make any cautious reader hesitate and any serious researcher falter, they finally state that "alcohol abuse plays a definite role in wife-beating".[14]

The dangers inherent in the superficiality of such an analysis are clear. If it is "the demon drink" that lies at the root of violence in the home, demands for a socio-legal and governmental response are limited:

---

12. Department of the Attorney-General and of Justice, NSW Bureau of Crime Statistics and Research, *Statistical Report, No. 5, Series 2, Domestic Assaults*, 1975, pp. 6–7.
13. Royal Commission on Human Relationships, *Final Report*, Vol. 4, Part V, "The Family", p. 140. The Elsie Refuge study is by Christine Gibbenson, *Domestic Violence*, Royal Commission Research Report, No. 11, 1977, unpublished, p. 88; cited Royal Commission on Human Relationships, Volume 4, note 13, pp. 140–141.
14. Joanne Downey and Jane Howell, note 10, pp. 55–56.

I. Preventing the Use of Alcohol – the use of alcohol should be banned; import duties on alcohol should be raised; prices of alcohol produced within Australia should be increased so that alcohol is outside the reach of most (all?) citizens; criminal penalties against drunkenness per se should be increased and enforced with vigour.[15]

Acknowledging that these proposals are incapable of being introduced, then if the violence–alcohol link is accepted, it must also be accepted that family violence will continue, leaving only one line of recourse:

II. Mopping up After the Violence – monies should be spent on assisting the inevitable victims of alcohol induced domestic violence, and more refuges for beaten women should be funded; monies should be spent on treating alcoholism, and more alcohol treatment units in hospitals (for abusive men) should be funded.

The "alcohol causes domestic violence" route offers little hope for eliminating the problem of spouse assault: and what must be asked is why researchers persist in adhering to a doctrine for which there are no adequate, properly controlled studies to grant it a secure foundation. The answer is not difficult to discover:

The "closeness" of the threat of disordered family relations to *any* family, and the personal experience of the "reality" of domestic conflict within the unit where security is perhaps most sought, are particularly communicable. "Violence" in itself is of course a particularly disturbing topic with its undertones of irrationality and uncontrollability. The battered wife and her children may be the object of pity … The unseen husband, on the other hand, can be ascribed a "deviant" label as either a criminal or as mentally unbalanced and thus relatively easily "neutralized" without a major challenge to the "taken for granted" world.[16]

Classifying a wife-beater "an alcoholic" or "drunken lout" enables society effectively to ignore a more disturbing reality: that built into our present social structures are patterns of male-female relationships that countenance domestic violence as a normal occurrence. That is, male-female relationships are premised upon the notion that men should be aggressive-dominant, women should be passive-submissive. "Masculinity", to which all men should aspire, encompasses controlled (and sometimes, "legitimately", uncontrolled) aggression. "Femininity", to which all women must aspire, encompasses passivity and inaction. Where a passive-submissive individual "interacts" with one

---

15. Domestic violence is not limited to – nor even shown to be more prevalent in – the lower socio-economic strata. Therefore if the "alcohol at base" argument is given credence, the price of alcohol would have to be such as to lift it out of the buying ability of all! (For the classlessness of domestic violence, see Royal Commission on Human Relationships, note 13.) [For more recent material, see Jocelynne A. Scutt, *Even in the Best of Homes – Violence in the Family*, 1983, Penguin Books Australia, Ringwood.]

16. Nick Miller, *Battered Spouses*, Occasional Papers on Social Administration, No. 57, 1975, Willmer Bros, Birkenhead, p. 51.

who is aggressive-dominant, the inevitable outcome – with or without the presence of alcohol – is violence; where the two parties interact within the family unit, the potential for violence will exist to the extent that the parties have been socially programmed to fulfil their socially dictated roles.[17]

Domestic Violence and Alcohol: The Victim

A second method of relating alcohol and domestic violence is to explain the behaviour in terms of the victim's relationship to alcohol. Some domestic violence studies take the view that women who are susceptible to domestic violence, who "provoke" violence, or who have a desire to live out a pattern incorporating violence as a way of life, marry alcoholics in order to fulfil this need; that they deliberately provoke arguments over the husband-assailant's drinking, so that he inevitably lashes out; or that they promote drinking in the husband-assailant to fulfil a need to be beaten. Here, the abuser's acts are seen as a "normal" response to provocation or aggravation; it is the wife who takes on the "abnormal" role and the responsibility for the violence.

A classic Australian study promoting the idea that women victims are responsible for being beaten is that conducted by Price and Armstrong in 1978. Taking the approach that "traditionally, it takes two to make a quarrel [*sic*]", the authors sought to examine systematically "the suggestion ... that the wife may in some way contribute towards the violence to which she is subjected ..." The study was designed "to examine in some detail the possibility that wives who are battered are in some way predisposed to be treated in this way ..."[18]

In a controlled study of thirty battered wives and thirty control subjects, Price and Armstrong concluded that the woman who is physically abused within a marriage or a de facto relationship "often comes from a very disturbed background". The majority of "predisposing differences" between the control group and the battered wife group were found in father-related items:

---

17. "Violence" here includes not only violence expressed in physical acts, but also more "sophisticated" forms such as psychological abuse. To date, studies in the spouse assault field have mainly concentrated upon violence in its physical form; psychological abuse is a field as yet unexplored. [Since this article was written, although physical abuse remains a more researched area, psychological abuse is on the research agenda and a greater amount of writing has been produced on it. Economic abuse is also on the agenda. See, for example, Jocelynne A. Scutt, "Of Love, Of Pain and Money – Women and Economic Violence," Paper presented to the Australian and New Zealand Society of Criminology Conference, St Hilda's College, University of Melbourne, 4 October 1991.]
18. John Price and Jean Armstrong, "Battered Wives – A Controlled Study of Predisposition" (1978) 1 *ANZ Journal of Psychiatry* 43.

CURRENT RELATIONSHIP WITH PARENTS

Battered Wives	Father	Mother
Good or fair relationship	5	17
Poor relationship	12	5
Controls	**Father**	**Mother**
Good or fair relationship	9	15
Poor relationship	6	9

Note: Figures do not add to 30 as a number of participants were reared in children's homes or the father died early in the participant's life, etc.[19]

It was concluded that the findings "underscore the specific importance of a poor relationship with the father as predisposing to abuse from the husband in later life". Price and Armstrong then consider:

The question arises as to whether our battered wives provoke their consorts to violent attack or whether they simply pick out more violent men to marry or whether both these factors operate ... It [is] suggested that a spouse whose father has been alcoholic tolerates her husband's drinking better if she has had a good relationship with her father. This raises the possibility that what provokes violence is her objection specifically to the drinking. *To put this a different way, the man she marries may potentially be violent but it may be that what matters is whether she is critical of his drinking or not.* (Emphasis added.)

This type of approach to domestic violence relies on the "blame the victim" concept: the man is "potentially violent", but not responsible, because "what matters is whether [the wife] is critical of his drinking or not". The lack of culpability lying with an abusive husband is again stressed:

A vicious circle may come into operation ... whereby increasing alcohol abuse provokes increasing criticism which in turn leads to increasing alcohol abuse and increased violence, and so on, culminating in the temporary or permanent break up of the marriage. The sequence of events would then be:
1. Marry or cohabit with a violent man.
2. Object to his drinking (particularly to his increasing drinking) because of a poor relationship with a heavy drinking and violent father.
3. Get battered and leave him.

The women are described in patronising terms, in that they proved difficult to trace for follow up, tending to "shoot through": "... either, one suspects, to avoid further involvement with abusers, or for the opposite reason: to go back to them ..." and they are generally depicted as lacking initiative. Nonetheless, according to Price and Armstrong, they lack no initiative in becoming victims of spouse abuse: *they* marry or cohabit; *they* deliberately choose a violent man; *they* object to his drinking; *they* get

---

19. John Price and Jean Armstrong, note 18, p. 19. The immediately following quotations are from the same source.

battered. Indeed, the crude "joke" springs to mind: "She deliberately put her eye in the way of my fist, constable ..."

In this study, even the mothers of the abused women come in for negative comment: mothers of the battered wives were found to be in poorer physical health than the mothers of the control group and this is said to "relate to a statement ... that such a mother is commonly a 'door-mat'":

... that is to say, rather timid and afraid to stand up to her violent spouse. In the present study those mothers who objected to violence by their husbands [expressed] towards the participant [their daughter] were in a minority.[20]

It is not difficult to discover other studies permeated with a similar morality. Again it must be asked why such an approach is adopted. The answer is that this is the "easy way out", one that does not require any restructuring of society or of social interaction.[21]

The wife is responsible for her situation and must "do something" to extricate herself from a situation into which she alone "got herself". As one clinical psychologist and marriage guidance counsellor said:

I have never seen a chronically abused wife who truly objected to being abused. The chronically abused wife is one who permits her husband to beat her, refuses to take punitive action afterward, and remains in the same situation so that she may be beaten again.[22]

Yet it is difficult for the woman to know how she should act. From the viewpoint of the clinical psychologist and marriage guidance counsellor, no course of action is acceptable:

The repeatedly abused wife is one who sends messages to her husband that his physical violence is a legitimate and tolerable activity. In some instances she does not even verbalise an objection, and gives no indication that the beatings are unacceptable. In other cases she will ask or tell him to stop, but takes no action to force him to stop, contradicting her verbal message, and letting him know that her words are for form's sake only.

Ah! She should fight back ... ? No:

Some women see fighting back as a stronger protest, but it may be suggested that unless they are exceptionally strong, well armed, or very well trained in the martial arts, such action is

---

20. John Price and Jean Armstrong, note 18, p. 46.
21. See for example Murray Straus, "A Sociological Perspective on the Prevention and Treatment of Wifebeating" in *Battered Women*, Maria Roy (ed.), 1977, Van Nostrand Reinhold, New York; Murray A. Straus, "Sexual Inequality, Cultural Norms and Wife Beating" in *Victims and Society*, Emilio C. Viano (ed.), 1976, p. 54; Marjorie D. Fields, "Wife Beating – The Hidden Offense" (1976) 175 (83) *New York Law Journal* 1.
22. James H. Kleckner, "Wife Beaters and Beaten Wives – Co-Conspirators in Crimes of Violence" (1978) 15 (1) *Psychology* 54. The four immediately following quotations come from the same source, pp. 54–55, 56. (There is not even a question mark at the end of the title of this article.)

more likely to reinforce the legitimacy of physical violence as a marital interaction than anything else.

She must tread the careful line between retaliation and resistance:

Resistance is necessary lest the husband interpret the wife's passivity as acceptance. A woman who stays passive and allows herself to be beaten, is accepting the validity of beating as a method of communication, and interaction. Resistance, if offered, should be swift and effective. Frequently women offer only token resistance with the explanation that they are aware that it is their husband, and that they do not really want to hurt him ...

Without doubt, the line of the clinical psychologist and marriage guidance counsellor should be acceptable to no one with a real concern for halting violence in the home, particularly where he further states:

Abused wives often explain that they have no place to go (not true), that they don't know where to go (anywhere), that they afraid of losing their financial support (how much per beating?) or that they tolerate beatings for the sake of the children – as if the children really thrive in a violent home. What it all comes down to is that wife beating, like all other crimes against people, must not be tolerated. It can only be stopped through action by the victim or intended victims. It can only occur with the tacit permission of its victims. A wife who has been beaten for the first time may be a victim. A wife who is beaten again is a co-conspirator.

But abused wives frequently have nowhere to go; frequently they have no parents nearby – or if they do, in many cases prefer not to admit to what they perceive as their own marital failure; sometimes they are turned away from refuges as funding is inadequate to provide for those persons requiring assistance.[23] Often women do not know of the existence of refuges – particularly where they live in affluent suburbs, or suburbs with few community services; where they speak little English; or where they have been transferred by the abusive husband's company from interstate. In rural areas, a refuge may not be available anywhere nearby and, if it is, the social opprobrium of going there may so overwhelm a woman in a small country town with no anonymity that she simply cannot go there.

To ignore the "blame the victim/she drove him to drink" approach means society must come to grips with many (most) women's lack of access to financial independence; with the lack of adequate childcare and equal sharing of childcare by husbands that leads to isolation of women and consequently greater dependence upon a spouse. There is equally a need for a total reassessment of male and female roles, so that a woman will no longer be placed in a situation where she plays a passive part, making

---

23. This recently occurred in Western Australia. See Jocelynne A. Scutt, "Domestic Violence – The Police Response" in *Proceedings from the Women's Advisory National Conference on Domestic Violence*, November, 1979, Sydney, published in *Family Violence in Australia*, Carol O'Donnell and Jan Craney (eds.), 1981, Longman Cheshire, Melbourne. [The turning away of women as a consequence of funding inadequacies and cutbacks has not lessened.]

it easier for society to explain away domestic disputes by finding the problem to be victim-provoked alcoholism rather than structural inequalities in society and in social relations between male and female persons.

Rape and Alcohol: The Aggressor

With rape and other crimes of sexual abuse, the "triggering factor" is frequently said to be alcohol: without alcohol, sexual aggression would not be expressed by violence. Here, sexual aggression is seen as unusual or abnormal. It usually results in crimes viewed by society as "horrific" or "unspeakable". Frequently, cases closely approximate the rape paradigm: the stranger (usually from the lower socio-economic strata, frequently Black or of an origin other than anglo-Australian) leaping from the bushes to attack a young, defenceless virgin:

In 1976 Justice Jones said in the Supreme Court, "It was obvious that if there were no limits, the amount of damages would exceed $2,000." He said the little girl had suffered dreadful injuries when she was raped near Roebourne in 1975, by a Thursday Islander, ... aged 35.

She had gross internal injuries and must have suffered a great deal of pain, as well as considerable emotional disturbance.

... The judge said, "The only redeeming feature of the crime was that [the offender] had not displayed deliberate brutality, but rather unthinking animality, aggravated by alcohol. The effects on the child were disastrous. It is a matter of some surprise to me to find that the little girl ... has substantially recovered from what could be long-lasting disabilities, though there is no doubt that she could face some trouble when the time comes for her to have a family."[24]

In some cases the "respectability" of the victim and lack of "attributes worthy of respect" on the part of the aggressor are noted in conjunction with the presence of alcohol. Thus in *Lovegrove's case* the victim, described as a married woman and a mother, was dragged into some bushes by the defendant at night:

The defendant, who was 28 and whose mother was a full blood Aborigine, grasped the victim around the throat and raped her. In sentencing the appellant to imprisonment with hard labour for four years and eight months, Muirhead J. stated, "Your counsel tells me, and this I must accept, that you are addicted to liquor, that you habitually drink during most of your spare time and that you have to some extent been brutalised by your roving type of life and by the necessity of depending on your own resources. I accept the fact that you would not have committed the crime but for the effect of the liquor you consumed but I am afraid that the law would cease to be a protection to the public if this was regarded as an excuse rather than an explanation."[25]

---

24. Statement by Justice Jones, published by Australian Women Against Rape, 1979, Perth; copy held by the writer.
25. Unreported decision of the Northern Territory Supreme Court SCC No. 99 of 1974; cited John E. Newton, *Factors Affecting Sentencing Decisions in Rape Cases*, 1976, Australian Institute of Criminology, Canberra, p. 17.

Unfortunately, the treatment of rape as an exceptional crime – and as one occurring mostly where the assailant is overcome by drink and is acting "out of character", or where the aggressor is "sexually dangerous" as a result of dependence on alcohol combined with psychological problems – will be of little assistance in any attempts to eliminate sexual offences crimes.[26]

The initial problem lies in the discrepancy between the number of persons held in prisons or in psychiatric hospitals as a result of criminal prosecution for the offence, and calculations of the number of rapes that occur in a given population. Between 1958 and 1977 in Massachusetts, 2000 sexual offenders were examined to determine whether they were "sexually dangerous" within the terms of the relevant sex offender law. Of these, 800 were sent to a special treatment centre for intensive study. Of the 800, a group of 240 were found to be "sexually dangerous" under the law and were committed to the centre for treatment.[27] As not all in the study were given this classification, presumably some persons committing sexual offences are not "abnormal". (Indeed, according to the study, the vast majority.) Perhaps those who were not so classified committed the crime whilst intoxicated and, with the passing of the effect of the alcohol, once again became "normal". However, in view of current calculations of rapes in the United States, the number available for study seems low.

In one hospital alone in Boston, Massachusetts in 1973, Burgess and Holstrom gathered information on 191 victims of rape admitted during that year.[28] According to the FBI, rape is "one of the most under-reported crimes due primarily to fear and/or embarrassment on the part of the victim". It has been calculated that "one in five rapes, or possibly one in twenty, may actually be reported".[29] Further, of those rapes reported, as Susan Brownmiller points out, not all result in apprehension and prosecution, nor in conviction, of the offender:

On a national average, police say that 15 per cent of all rape cases [in the United States] reported to them turn out on cursory investigation to be "unfounded" – in other words, they didn't believe the complainant. In reported rape cases where the police do believe the victim,

---

26. These expressions appear in, for example, *Williams* [1965] Qd R. 86; cited John E. Newton, note 25, p. 18; see also *O'Donnell* [1974] SASR 114.
27. See Murray L. Cohen, Ralph Garofalo, Richard B. Boucher and Theoharis Seghorn, "The Psychology of Rapists" (1971) 3 (6) *Seminars in Psychiatry* (August); also in *Forcible Rape – The Crime, the Victim and the Offender*, Duncan Chappell, Robley Geis and Gilbert Geis (eds.), 1977, Columbia University Press, New York, p. 294.
28. Anna Wolbert Burgess and Lynda Lytle Holstrom, "Rape Trauma Syndrome" (1974) 131 *American Journal of Psychiatry* 981; also in *Forcible Rape – The Crime, the Victim and the Offender*, note 27, p. 315. See also L. L. Holstrom and A. W. Burgess, "Rape – The Victim and the Criminal Justice System" (1975) 3 (2) *International Journal of Criminology and Penology* 101, p. 103: "Only a minority of women in the present study contacted the police completely on their own; specifically, only 14 out of 61 did so."
29. Cited Susan Brownmiller, *Against Our Will – Men, Women and Rape*, 1975, Secker and Warburg, London, p. 175; Norval Morris and Gordon Hawkins, *The Honest Politician's Guide to Crime Control*, 1972, Sun Books Pty Ltd, Melbourne, p. 60. The immediately following quotation comes from the same source.

only 51 per cent of the offenders are actually apprehended, and of these, 76 per cent are prosecuted, and of these 47 per cent are acquitted or have their case dismissed ...

It is generally accepted that apprehension, prosecution and conviction rates for rape are lower than for other crimes, not only in the United States and elsewhere, but in Australia. Furthermore in Australia, the victim report rate for rape is approximately the same, proportionately, as that in the United States – 86 per 100,000 in the United States victimisation survey, 95 per 100,000 in the Australia victimisation survey. But police reported rape rates per 100,000 population are four to five times as high in the United States as in Australia.[30]

It is valid, then, to ask why, if sexual offences take place only as a result of psychological instability, "sexual dangerousness" and abnormality caused by intoxication, more offenders are not apprehended. The problem is even more pronounced by acknowledging that inebriated persons are not normally as skilful at eluding detection as are persons fully in control of their faculties. Many offenders go free. This is facilitated by the fact that they do not suffer any disability marking them off from the general run of the population.

Rape occurs in circumstances other than those involving "abnormality". As Smart and Smart point out, the reasons for rape that most frequently are brought to the attention of the public:

... are almost taken from statements by the defending counsel, or the judge in his summing up, or in the passing of sentence. Consequently motivations for rape which are provided with the specific intention of trying to achieve an acquittal for the accused, or in an attempt to reduce his sentence, are reported in the press as the motivations and therefore these statements assume the status of legitimate and reasonable accounts of rape. Thus we find in many newspaper accounts a version of the frustration-aggression hypothesis in which the convicted rapist's responsibility for his behaviour is diminished either by appeal to his "condition" as a sexually frustrated man or by reference to the "uncontrollable" level of his sexual arousal. This kind of appeal assumes many forms from reference to the rapist's wife's pregnancy, to the period of "enforced" sexual abstinence, to the effect of alcohol and drugs, and to the "problems of adolescence ..."[31]

Examples are not hard to discover:

He drank about two gallons of beer before the attack outside the disco ... the pregnancy of [his] wife may have been "one of the reasons for his committing the offence".[32]

---

30. John Braithwaite and David Biles, "Women as Victims of Crime – Some Findings from the First Australian National Crime Victims Survey" (1981) *Australian Quarterly*, 4. See also Paul Ward and Greg Woods, *Law and Order in Australia*, 1972, Angus and Robertson, Sydney, p. 94; Paul Wilson, *The Other Side of Rape*, 1976, University of Queensland Press, St Lucia.
31. Carol Smart and Barry Smart, "Accounting for Rape – The Myth and Reality in Press Reporting" in *Women, Sexuality and Social Control*, Carol Smart and Barry Smart (eds.), 1978, Routledge and Kegan Paul, London, p. 98.
32. *News of the World* 25 January 1976, cited Carol Smart and Barry Smart, note 31, p. 99. The immediately following quotation comes from the same source.

And again:

Two young men ... raped a 14-year-old girl after drinking with her in a pub and a club ... It was not unusual for young men to take advantage of a girl or for young men to behave totally out of character after having something to drink, said the judge.

This form of "analysis" of rape enables society to ignore the reality of rape. In the soporific belief that "ordinary men" do not engage in rape, or that "ordinary men" do so only under abnormal circumstances, separating them off from the men we know and love (or the men we are), we can indulge in fantasies of controlling the offence. To do so, what is necessary is the elimination of "unnatural circumstances" and of substances that encourage "unnatural circumstances". Thus we can indulge in a fantasy that ridding the world of liquor will rid the world of rape: we can ban the sale of alcohol – or ban its sale to "at risk" groups – adolescents and young men. To eliminate the "unnatural state" of "enforced" abstinence from sexual activity, social standards can require all individuals to marry as soon as possible after reaching the "proper" age, or where standards relax, to enter a sexual relationship outside marriage. Nonetheless rape does not – will not – go away. Thus another method of controlling the offence is to focus on the victim and thereby define the crime out of existence.

Rape and Alcohol: The Victim

A second method of relating alcohol and rape is to explain the rape in terms of the victim's relationship to alcohol. This view is most frequently expressed by law enforcement agencies and courts in dissecting the alleged crime: the act occurred because the woman engaged in drinking with her alleged assailant; she became intoxicated and "led him on"; she wished to engage in intercourse, and drinking allowed her to do so without feeling responsible for her "promiscuousness".

In *R v. Ives* the Queensland Court of Criminal Appeal reduced a term of imprisonment given for rape in which the applicant had been present in a hamburger shop where a discussion took place in the presence of the victim, concerning her having to remove all her clothes at a game of "strip-jack-naked". The party consumed liquor and the girl accompanied them to a remote area – where she was raped. Her "complicity" in the affair was seen as a reason for lessening the penalty on appeal.[33] In *Walker's case* the court "was prepared to adopt a more lenient attitude toward the offender" where a student nurse went to the offender's flat after a dance, for a drink, and was raped. The rationale was that the young woman "had been prepared to share the culprit's company in the privacy of his own room"; therefore the penalty should be lighter than otherwise would have been the case.[34] As Newton says:

---

33. *R. v. Ives* [1973] Qd R. 128.
34. *R. v. Walker*, 27 July 1966; 1 December 1966; cited John E. Newton, note 25, p. 14.

[The] type of case which involves either a degree of encouragement by the victim or behaviour on her part which is foolish and may tend towards encouragement of the offender, will usually result in the court taking these factors into account in determining penalty ... In cases where the rape victim may be considered to have contributed to her own downfall the courts are prepared to adopt a more lenient attitude towards the offender ...[35]

Drinking and accepting lifts are frequently linked as "precipitating" factors in rape:

Judges [have] warned women "time and time again" against hitchhiking or accepting lifts with strangers ... such behaviour all too often [leads] to sex attacks.[36]

Two young men ... raped a 14-year-old girl after drinking with her in a pub and a club ...[37]

... imprudent behaviour of many young women [does] not excuse offences committed on them, but lessen[s] the moral culpability of the offender ... There [are] too many young women hitching lifts and accepting rides with cars full of young men they [do] not know. They fraternise and [drink] with men they [do] not know, in bars, and [do] their best to bring disaster on themselves. These foolish young women should behave with more dignity and show some elementary prudence ...[38]

In a study by Menachim Amir on rape in Chicago, "victim precipitation" was enshrined as a legitimate factor in determining responsibility for rape (or "non-rape"). "Victim precipitation" was used to, "... refer to those rape cases in which the victim actually (or so it was interpreted by the offender) agreed to sexual relations but retracted before the act or did not resist strongly enough [sic] when the suggestion was made by the offender". It was also used to describe cases where a victim "voluntarily" enters a situation "charged with sexuality".[39]

Examples of "victim precipitated rape" include those where a woman is raped when she has "teased, led on, or encouraged the man, ... has accepted a ride from a stranger, ... has invited a man previously unknown to her to an apartment for a drink ..."

The presence of alcohol and the involvement of the victim in drinking prior to the act may be used to "explain" rape in two ways. First, the fact that the woman was drinking is employed to depict her as "sexually loose", as unworthy of protection by rape laws, as showing she "deserved" what occurred, or she "brought it on herself". Second, it may be used to show she was truly consenting to the act: she was obliging,

---

35. Commentary, John E. Newton, note 25, pp. 14–15.
36. Begg, J. in Central Criminal Court, New South Wales; cited Ellen Goodman, "The Victim of Rape – What Progress?" (1979) 14 (1) *Australian Journal of Social Issues* 21.
37. *Daily Mail* (England) 19 March 1976; cited Carol Smart and Barry Smart, note 31, p. 102.
38. Justice Jones, Supreme Court of Western Australia, cited Australian Women Against Rape, note 24.
39. Menachim Amir, *Patterns in Forcible Rape*, 1971, University of Chicago Press, Chicago; see also Donal E. J. MacNamara and Edward Sagarin, *Sex, Crime and the Law*, 1977, Free Press, New York, pp. 43 ff. The immediately following quotation comes from *Patterns in Forcible Rape*, p. 43.

wanted the act to occur, and drank to "give herself courage" and an "excuse" for engaging in sexual behaviour.[40]

If women's use of alcohol leads to rape, then the way to prevent rape is for women to cease indulging in the habit of drinking. Although this advice is absurd, too frequently analogous counsel is given on issues such as hitchhiking, walking alone at night and the like:

I don't want to appear alarmist, but women and girls who are forced to walk alone should take a route where there are plenty of people about, even if it means going out of their way …[41]

I wouldn't advise any female to go walking around alone at night … and she should lock her car at all times … Always lock your car [but] of course you don't have to be paranoid about this type of thing …[42]

If women use alcohol to fortify themselves into consenting to sexual intercourse, presumably the way to prevent acts that might be on the "borderline" between "force, suggestion, and persuasion" is for women to cease using the prop of liquor and face up to their sexual responsibilities. Yet again, this advice is of little avail to any woman when analysts of rape write about "the socially approved pattern for feminine behaviour, according to which the woman is supposed to put up at least a token resistance, 'No, no' or 'We mustn't!'"[43] No woman can make use of the advice that she should abjure the social prop, say "Yes" when she means "Yes" and "No" when she means "No", for we learn from the "best authority":

Any reasonably experienced male has learned to disregard such minor protestations [as "No, no" or "We mustn't!"], and the naive male who obeys his partner's injunction to cease and desist is often puzzled when she seems inexplicably irritated by his compliance.[44]

---

40. On the first proposition as it relates to the admission of evidence in rape cases, see Vivienne Berger, "Man's Trial, Woman's Tribulation – Rape Cases in the Courtroom" (1977) 77 *Columbia Law Review* 1; H. Kalven and H. Zeisel, *The American Jury*, 1966, New York; Jocelynne A. Scutt, "Admissibility of Sexual History Evidence and Allegations in Rape Cases" (1979) 53 *Australian Law Journal* 817. The second approach was taken by Kinsey who thought the difference between a "good time" and a rape "may hinge upon whether the girl's parents are awake when she finally arrives home": Alfred C. Kinsey, Wardell B. Pomeroy, Clyde E. Martin, *Sexual Behaviour in the Human Male*, 1948, Saunders, Philadelphia; see also comments in Paul H. Gebhard, John H. Gagnon, Wardell B. Pomeroy and Cornelia V. Christenson, *Sex Offenders – An Analysis of Types*, 1965, Harper and Row, New York; and John McDonald, *Rape – Offenders and Their Victims*, 1971, Charles C. Thomas, Springfield; also Donal E. J. MacNamara and Edward Sagarin, note 39, pp. 44 ff.

41. *Star* (Sheffield, England) 26 June 1976; cited Smart and Smart, note 31, at p. 102.

42. Quoted Susan Griffen, "Rape – The All American Crime" (1971) *Ramparts* (September); also in *Forcible Rape*, note 28, p. 49.

43. Donal E. J. MacNamara and Edward Sagarin, note 39, p. 44.

44. MacNamara and Sagarin, note 39; see also Paul H. Gebhard, et al, note 40; also Alfred C. Kinsey, et al, note 40; *Wigmore on Evidence* Vol. 3A, "Rape and Other Sexual Offences". [These notions continue

cont. next page

Besides, women sometimes "desire to be overpowered and treated a little roughly ..."[45]

Rather than concentrating upon the victim and her use of alcohol or the lack of it, those wishing to end rape would be better engaged in ending the socialisation that inevitably leads to this form of violence against women. As in the case of domestic violence, where women and girls are constantly taught to embrace the "truly feminine" image of passivity-submission, where men and boys are equally often taught to live up to the "masculine" image of aggressive-dominance, the sexual union of male and female is hard pressed not to mirror the rape image.

Rape will not cease by fastening upon isolated aspects of aggressive relations. As Smart and Smart comment on media depiction of rape:

In so far as a press report of rape never seeks to explain or address the existence of the general phenomenon of rape but merely selectively focuses on a specific instance, the account which is produced is structured in terms of the surface details of the specific case concerned. As a result the underlying structuring of social and sexual relations, which both produce the possibility of rape and make specific social locations and circumstances likely venues for rape, remain undisclosed in press accounts. Thereby the conventional wisdoms concerning rape are upheld, namely that women who get raped are in some sense responsible for their own fate, could have in fact avoided their suffering by not putting themselves at risk by entering the specific social space or territory within which the rape occurred ... In other words women are to limit their freedom in order to avoid rape ...[46]

---

44. *cont. from previous page*

to be adhered to in Australian courts. In Victoria in 1993, Judge Bland of the County Court was quoted as saying that in his legal experience "no" did not always mean no, but rather its opposite, "yes": Michael Magazanic, "No to sex can often mean yes, says judge" *Age*, 6 May 1993, p. 1. See further, Jocelynne A. Scutt, "The Voice of the Rapist", paper presented to the Second National Conference on Violence, Australian Institute of Criminology, Canberra, ACT, 16 June 1993.]

45. *Wigmore on Evidence*, note 44. [This notion has a long history in the law – see for example *G. v. G.* [1923] Ch. 21; and it continues to find favour with some members of the judiciary. One of the more publicly recognised examples is that of Justice Bollen of the South Australian Supreme Court, who said in his summing up to the jury in a case involving charges of marital rape:

"Bear steadily in mind – I am sorry to be repetitive – it is for the Crown to prove the lack of consent. "Consent" means free voluntary agreement to engage in an act of sexual intercourse at the time relevant. Submission is not consent. Of course, you may run into considering in this case the question of, shall I say, persuasion. There is, of course, nothing wrong with a husband, faced with his wife's initial refusal to engage in intercourse, in attempting, in an acceptable way, to persuade her to change her mind and that may involve a measure of rougher than usual handling. It may be, in the end, that handling and persuasion will persuade the wife to agree. Sometimes it is a fine line between not agreeing, then changing of the mind, and consenting. You will bear that in mind when considering the totality of the evidence about each act of intercourse." (Quoted in *Director of Public Prosecutions v. Respondent*, unreported, Supreme Court of South Australia, 20 April 1993.)

When the case went on appeal, one of the three Supreme Court judges held that Justice Bollen had not been wrong, in law, in including this paragraph in his summing up. The other two judges said the statement ought not to have been made and was wrong in law.]

46. Carol Smart and Barry Smart, note 31, p. 102. The immediately following quotation comes from the same source.

Thus, the way we think about rape becomes detached from the reality of the offence; rape becomes an isolated, "socially unstructured phenomenon which affects specific categories of women in special social circumstances". In reality, rape does not only occur where a man is "too drunk to know what he was doing", or where a woman drinks in bars, "leading" men to believe she is "easy game", or where she "loses control" through drinking.

The irony of the way rape is depicted through the media, through the court cases, through the so-called objective research literature, is that the false image of rape as an isolated event occurring between strangers, or an event for which the victim must take responsibility, persuades women to cast constraints over our own activity, to limit our independence. It operates to force us more strongly to conform to the passive-dependent, submissive-obliging role that leads initially to violence being exercised against women. It also socialises men into accepting the myth of chivalry and the need for dominance and aggression: it is only in this way that they can "protect" their (female) property from exploitation, maintaining her solely for their own use.

Conclusion

An objective review of studies and legal cases allegedly finding a link between alcohol and rape, and alcohol and domestic violence, discloses that such a link is not so easily established. The studies begin with a premise that the link exists and slant the evidence to bolster the common belief. A feminist perspective on alcohol and its supposed link with crimes of violence against women reveals the sexism implicit in the research and in common attitudes toward violence against women. Far from being "unnatural" or "abnormal", aggression directed toward women is a natural outcome of men and women's socialisation. Rape and domestic violence inexorably occur when men and women have been programmed into interacting in a passive-aggressive, dominant-submissive pattern, particularly in regard to sexual relations.

Rather than concentrating upon alcohol as the culprit, if the aim is to eliminate domestic violence and rape from our society, clearly what must be concentrated upon are the methods by which we socialise boys and girls, men and women, into patterns promoting violence as a way of life. Rather than concentrating upon the "abnormal", we would do better to apply resources toward altering the stereotypical roles that are viewed as "normal" in a social structure that promotes violence against women.

[After the rape] Val took her for vd tests and a general physical. There was nothing wrong with her health. Chris went everywhere with Val, because she would neither go out nor stay alone ... The two women could do nothing. They would, on occasion, turn on TV at night, but within a minute or two there would appear a commercial, a line, a scene, a snatch of dialogue that was intolerable and without looking at each other, one of them would get up and turn it off. When Val tried to read, she would get through a few lines, then throw, literally throw the book against the wall. They could not even play music. Chris growled about rock lyrics and Val growled about Beethoven. "Daddy music" she kept muttering. The entire world seemed polluted ...[47]

---

47. Marilyn French, *The Women's Room*, 1977, p. 578.

8

SEXISM AND PSYCHOLOGY:
An Analysis of the 'Scientific' Basis of the Corroboration Rule in Rape

Published in (1979) 5 (No. 1) *Hecate* 35

In 1979 all Australian states and territories apart from South Australia retained rape laws which were based firmly in the common law of England.[1] The English common law of rape had itself crystallised in the eighteenth century. Although some changes to sexual offences laws generally had been made since that time, the basics of rape law were as they had been pronounced by Mathew Hale, sometime Chief Justice of England. In 1734 in his book, Hale's History of the Pleas of the Crown,[2] *he set down the legal principles applicable to the crime of rape.*

Bluntly, it is difficult to see Hale as anything other than a misogynist. His writings are replete with signifiers of anti-woman attitudes. And whether a judge who believes in witches can be taken seriously on matters of law, particularly where women's evidence and well-being is in question, must surely be in issue. Hale sat on the last trial of women for witchcraft in England, the Lowestoft Witchcraft Trial, where Amy Duny and Rose Cullender were found guilty. Their crime included bewitching some young children so that (amongst other strange symptoms) the youths coughed up pins and nails, in some instances thirty at a time, and some as large as those used to shoe horses. Hale concluded the trial by saying, in his charge to the jury, that there were two

---

1. In the 1970s and early 1980s all states amended their *Evidence Acts* purporting to introduce effective changes to laws of evidence affecting rape cases, but (apart from New South Wales in 1981) the amendments basically admonished the judges to look at the evidence and then to apply the laws as they already existed, if the judge thought that appropriate. Effectively, there was no change and women's prior sexual history and other aspects of her character remained a very real part of rape trials. On this, see Jocelynne A. Scutt, "Admissibility of Sexual History Evidence and Allegations in Rape Cases" (1979) 53 *Australian Law Journal* 817. In the footnotes, square brackets [...] indicate new material added for this edition.
2. *Hale's History of the Pleas of the Crown (Hale's Pleas of the Crown)* was published in 1734 by Nutt and Gosling of London, with numerous reprints through the centuries following.

matters only to enquire after: "First, whether or no these children were bewitched? Secondly, whether the prisoners at the bar were guilty of it?"[3]

Chief Justice Hale had no doubt that there were such creatures as witches for, first, "the scriptures affirmed so much" and, secondly, "the wisdom of all nations had provided laws against such persons, which is an argument of their confidence of such a crime". He went on: "And such hath been the judgment of this Kingdom, as appears by that Act of Parliament which hath provided punishments proportionable to the quality of the offence."[4]

In his Letters of Advice to His Grandchildren, Hale was critical of women saying:

They make it their business to paint or patch their faces, to curl their locks, and to find out the newest and costliest fashions ... The morning is spent between the comb, the glass, and the box of patches; though they know not how to make provision for themselves, they must have choice diet provided for them ... [They] sit in a rubbed [spring cleaned] parlour till Dinner ... After they go either to a Ball or to cards ... They spend their parent's or husband's money or estate on costly clothes, new fashions, and changeable entertainments ... Their house is their prison and they are never at rest in it, unless they have gallants and splendid company to entertain.[5]

At least he recognised the imprisoned reality of the lives of aristocratic or middle-class women.

In the 1970s and 1980s, the Women's Movement continued the agitation of women of the past for greater account to be taken, in the law and the courts, of the realities of rape and other sexually aggressive acts against women and children. In a number of respects, "Sexism and Psychology" is an historical document. Contrary to the position at the time the article was written, the law has been changed in all states (apart from Queensland where the law came under review in the 1990s) and territories in Australia so that rape is no longer, in the law, a crime exclusively associated with the non-consensual penetration of a woman's vagina by a man's penis. Aggressive penetration of mouth, anus and vagina by a penis is now "rape" (or, in New South Wales, "sexual assault"). Aggressive penetration of the anus and vagina by a hand or other part of the body (including tongue), and by a foreign object, is now "rape" ("sexual assault" in New South Wales).[6] The penalty for rape is no longer life imprisonment in any jurisdiction. Women demanded this change, too, on the basis that so long as the statute books

---

3. *A Tryal of Witches at the Assizes Held at Bury St Edmunds*, 1682, William Shrewsbury, London, p. 55. See also Gilbert Geis, "Lord Hale, Witches, and Rape" (1979) 5 *British Journal of Law and Society* 26.

4. *A Tryal of Witches at the Assizes*, note 3, pp. 55–56. Hale has been excused for his approach on the basis that the sentence "was in accordance with the law" and that the "existence of witches was vouched for by the *Bible*". Therefore, the legal historian Holdsworth concludes: "... a man of Hale's mind and temper could hardly be expected to doubt. And these are, after all, small matters": William Holdsworth, "Sir Mathew Hale" (1923) 39 *Law Quarterly Review* 407.

5. Mathew Hale, *Letters of Advice to His Grandchildren*, 1816, Taylor and Hessey, London, p. 119.

6. See generally Jocelynne A. Scutt, "Sexual Assault and the Criminal Justice System" in *Australian Criminal Justice System*, Duncan Chappell and Paul Wilson (eds.), 1986, Butterworths, Sydney, p. 57.

listed such a severe penalty, juries would be reluctant to convict, particularly where the accused was a middle-class, "respectable" man – or even, simply, anglo-Australian.[7] Rape laws were recognised by women not only as being discriminatory against women, but also that they operated so that those most likely to be brought before the courts on rape charges were lower socio-economic status, non-anglo Australian men who could not bring before the courts a trail of middle-class, "respectable" men of anglo-Australian heritage to be character witnesses for them. This led women to agitate for changes which would, hopefully, impinge upon the jury's traditional attitude of recognising as "rape" only the paradigm case of the non-anglo Australian man leaping out of the bushes to ravage and abuse a young girl. Certainly in the 1970s no one received a penalty of life imprisonment for rape; in New South Wales, despite this being the maximum sentence available, the average sentence imposed by judges was four years only. But, it was thought, the very existence of the maximum penalty meant juries would be reluctant to class as rapists men who did not "look" like rapists. Who would want to run the risk of sending a man in a white shirt, tie and dark suit to prison – for life!

Concomitant with this change was that of making rape laws "sex neutral". The Women's Movement hoped that if male jurors and judges had to apply a law which envisaged that a man could be a victim of rape, they may be more likely to understand the realities of the crime, and in turn be more likely to put the law into effect in a way that did not deprive victims and survivors of rights, nor elevate the rights of men accused of rape so that they had privileges which did not extend to accused persons in relation to any other crimes.

Generally states and territories had, by the mid-1980s, abolished the mandatory application of the corroboration rule.[8] Nonetheless, because judges retained a right to give the warning in any sexually aggressive offence case they chose, it was not uncommon for judges to give the corroboration warning anyway, as a matter of course. Thus juries continued to be told that they should study the evidence before them with great care because "a charge of this nature is easily made and hard to be defended against by an accused person, however innocent he is". The idea that a warning was necessary was reinforced outside the criminal sphere. Thus in 1988 in M. v. M., a Family Court case where a father's access to children was in issue and allegations of child sexual abuse were raised, the High Court of Australia reiterated this dictum (devised by Chief Justice Hale) without any analysis or critique.[9] At last,

---

7. For example, in Victoria in 1992 the maximum penalty was set as 25 years; in 1981 it was set at 20 years maximum for "aggravated rape" and 10 years maximum for rape. In 1993 despite considerable opposition from women's organisations including Feminist Lawyers, the Victorian Bar Council and others, statutory provisions were amended to increase penalties for rape so that now, for example, where multiple offences occur the accused will be sentenced cumulatively (each respective sentence being served consecutively) rather than the sentences being made concurrent (two sentences of, say, nine years resulting in a person serving at maximum nine rather than 18 years).

8. See generally Jocelynne A. Scutt, note 6. Queensland is currently considering the matter.

9. M. v. M. (1988) 63 ALJR 108 and B. v. B. (1988) 63 ALJR 112. For a critique of M. v. M. and B. v. B. see Jocelynne A. Scutt, Women and the Law, 1990, Law Book Co., Sydney, pp. 294–305.

in 1989 in Longman v. The Queen *one member of the High Court (Justice Deane) addressed the question whether the content of the warning had any validity. He found that the realities of sexual assault, particularly within the family, militate against the proposition that the charge is made "with ease", and that any proposition as to "the difficulty which may attend its rebuttal" runs the risk of "diverting the jury's attention from the proper working of the onus of proof in a criminal trial".[10] Thus (at least one member of) the High Court now recognises what women (and men) have known for centuries – namely that charges of rape are* not *easily made, and that it is* not *difficult for a man to defend himself against them if they are made.*

Despite the changes, problems in rape laws remain. On the matter of the corroboration warning, for example, although the High Court in Longman v. The Queen *has now said that changes to the law mean that no longer as a matter of course should the warning be given, and that it is wrong in law for a judge to give a warning implying that a whole group – namely women alleging the crime of rape has been committed against them – is suspect, there is one group at least which effectively remains suspect. This is the group comprising adult women who complain of having been raped as children. The import of* Longman's *case is that a warning should be given to the jury in such a case, as a matter of course. This was on the basis that a considerable period of time had elapsed – 20 to 24 years – before the woman in* Longman's *case complained of the sexual imposition she alleged, and which formed the basis of the charges. This means that in every case of child sexual abuse a warning will have to be given. Children's evidence is generally subject to such a warning, so that if the child complains when she is still a child and the trial takes place then, the warning will be given; if the complaint is made when the child is an adult, with the trial taking place at that time, the warning will be given, due to the lapse of time.*

The Supreme Court of South Australia has suggested that there may be a second category of witness whose evidence ought to be subjected to a warning to the jury: women alleging rape in marriage. In DPP v. Respondent Party *the Chief Justice of South Australia said, amongst other matters:*

There are special difficulties in reaching a just verdict where the rape or attempted rape is alleged to have occurred in the matrimonial bed or the bed occupied by the parties to a continuing sexual relationship. There is the risk of motives, disclosed or undisclosed, arising out of tensions in the relationship. There is the risk of misunderstandings as to consent arising out of the habitual physical contact inherent in the relationship. The opportunities for corroboration are slight and an accused can do little to defend himself apart from denying the allegation. These factors, where they apply, are all proper bases for an appropriate warning.[11]

---

10. *Longman v. The Queen* (1989) 64 ALJR 73, 78, 79.
11. *DPP v. Respondent Party*, unreported, Supreme Court of South Australia, Court of Criminal Appeal, 20 April 1993 (this is the "rougher than usual handling" case), judgment of Chief Justice King, p. 6.

This case postdates Longman's case, *and contains all the self-same notions of women in sexual offence cases being a suspect category that permeated the "old" law, the Chief Justice quoting his own judgment in an earlier case,* R. v. Pahuja,[12] *which was referred to (apparently with approval) by the High Court in* Longman's case:

In many sexual cases prudence will dictate the giving of some appropriate caution or warning. If ... the judge cautions or warns the jury as to their approach to the evidence of an alleged victim of a sexual offence, he does so as part of his duty to provide guidance to the jury as to the evidence and the facts. He is free to frame the caution or warning in such terms as he sees fit ...

There are aspects of human nature and behaviour, such as sexual appetite, certain motives for making false complaints and proneness to certain types of fantasies, which have a peculiar bearing upon sexual cases and which may be important in certain factual situations. The ease of making an allegation and difficulty of refutation, often given as reasons for the former rule, are considerations not entirely confined to sexual cases, but are often nevertheless of considerable importance in such cases. The trial judge is not required to ignore such matters in charging the jury and may have a duty in certain cases to remind them of such considerations...[13]

Thus despite "reforms", the law remains imbued with age-old notions of woman as deceiver where sexual offences are concerned. Chief Justice Hale remains firmly in the saddle, the corroboration rule having received only the most mild of jolts.

Jurist Mathew Hale predated Sigmund Freud, psychiatrist, by well over a century. Far from Freud being inventive in promulgating his "theory" of women as congenital liars where they spoke of being raped, as children, by fathers or other family members or family friends, Hale and the English common law were there long before he was.

I began the research that forms the basis of "Sexism and Psychology" in 1974, and completed the writing in 1977–1978. The understanding women have of the deceit practised by Freud in asserting that his women patients were themselves deceitful has appeared in a number of writings, including Florence Rush in 1980 and Elizabeth (Biff) Ward in 1984.[14] In 1984, Jeffrey Masson's The Assault on Truth: Freud's Suppression of the Seduction Theory *reiterated the knowledge women had already put into the public arena.[15] Jeffrey Masson had access to Freud's papers and was able to show, by reference to earlier unpublished work and letters, that Sigmund Freud had indeed acknowledged the truth of rape and sexual abuse of women as children, within the family or family circle, and how he had later renounced the truth for a false position which regained him the support of his mentor Fliess and colleagues generally in the psychiatry movement.*

---

12. *R. v. Pahuja* (1988) 49 SASR 191.
13. *DPP v. Respondent Party*, note 11, pp. 4, 5.
14. Florence Rush, *The Best Kept Secret – The Sexual Abuse of Children*, 1980, McGraw Hill, New York; Elizabeth (Biff) Ward, *Father-Daughter Rape*, 1984, The Women's Press, London.
15. Jeffrey Masson, *The Assault on Truth – Freud's Suppression of the Seduction Theory*, 1984, Harper Collins, London.

The Australian judiciary, as well as crown prosecutors, apparently remain unaware of this literature. There is some evidence that juries are now more attuned to the realities of rape. Yet the reality embodied in the voices of the survivors is, sadly, yet to impinge in any extended way upon the judges.

Rape has been called a "special" offence, a crime that is "different". That the crime is "special" or "different" in psychological, anthropological or sociological terms remains under discussion. That the law relating to the offence of rape makes the crime "different" cannot be denied. On the face of it, at common law, the crime is "special" in that it is "sex-specific": no woman is physically capable of directly performing the act. No man is physically capable of being the object of the crime.[16]

Further confirmation that something about the crime of rape renders it "different" lies in sentencing policy. The stated penalty for rape in many jurisdictions remains as a maximum of life imprisonment or, in some cases, the death sentence. The penalty is more often in conformity with the penalty for the crime of murder than with that for crimes of a seemingly more similar nature – such as non-consensual sodomy. In New South Wales where the penalty for rape is life imprisonment, the penalty for non-consensual sodomy, if classed as "buggery", is a maximum of fourteen years imprisonment only. If classed as indecent assault, the penalty is four years if committed upon a woman, five years if committed upon a man, and six years if committed upon a girl under the age of sixteen years: ss. 63, 76, 79 and 81 *Crimes Act* 1900 (NSW).[17] Where penetration is by way of the mouth, the common law made no provision for punishing the act other than as an indecent assault, with a penalty of four, five or six years depending upon the age and sex of the victim. Similarly, where penetration is not

---

16. See generally Vivienne Berger, "'Man's Trial, Woman's Tribulation' – Rape Cases in the Courtroom" (1977) 77 *Columbia Law Rev.* 1. Susan Brownmiller discusses these issues extensively in *Against Our Will – Men, Women and Rape*, 1975, Secker and Warburg, London, as does J. Rose, "The Rise of the Rape Problem" in *Our Land of Promises – The Rise and Fall of Social Problems in America*, Mauss and Wolfe (eds.), 1978; J. Rose "Rape as a Social Problem – A Byproduct of the Feminist Movement," (1977) 25 *Social Problems* 75. See also discussion in Julia Schwendinger and Herman Schwendinger, "Rape Myths, Legal Theoretical and Everyday Practice" (1974) 1 *Crime and Social Justice* 18. See also, for example, *State v. Flaherty* 146 A. 7, 128 Mc. 141. A woman may be convicted as principal to the act of rape where she procures, aids or counsels a man to commit the act on another woman: *State v. Carter* 182 P. 2d 90, 66 Ariz. 52; *R. v. Ram* (1893) 17 Cox CC 609. Although writers have frequently used the term "homosexual rape" to describe non-consensual acts of buggery where the victim is male, at least in contemporary times (see, for example, A. M. Scacco, *Rape in Prison*, 1975, Thomas, Springfield) in common law parlance "rape" denotes penentration per vagina. Anal penetration where the victim may obviously be female or male has variously been termed "sodomy" or "buggery" at common law and by statute, with penalties usually far below those for rape.

17. ss. 63, 76, 79 and 81 *Crimes Act* 1900 (NSW). [Note that in 1981 major changes were made to rape laws in New South Wales by the *Crimes (Sexual Assault) Act* 1981 which repealed various provisions
cont. next page

effected by way of the penis, but by other bodily means or by artificial instruments, the offence at common law would classify as indecent assault or, possibly, unlawful wounding: ss. 33, 34, 35 *Crimes Act* 1900 (NSW).[18]

This raises the issue of why vaginal penetration was considered at common law to be apart from and "worse" than penetration *per anum* and penetration by way of mouth. Some commentators have contended that the possibility of pregnancy is the operative factor. This stance is not compelling: not all women who are raped are capable of becoming pregnant for, as studies clearly show, many victims of rape are below the age of puberty, and many are beyond the age of menopause. Further, emission of semen is not a requirement for the commission of the crime. A second argument might be that loss of virginity by forcible means requires a severe censure by society – yet this, too, is not a convincing stance. Married women and other non-virgins may, according to the law, be victims of rape.[19]

As for the physical harm caused, that a man cannot become pregnant, or lose his "virginity" in the conventional sense, would hardly seem to be of comfort to the male victim of a sexually penetrating attack. A woman, too, may be just as (or possibly more) severely harmed by anal rather than vaginal penetration. Additionally, the harm caused by penetration could well be worse where artificial means are employed. Yet if a man uses this means he is, at common law, punished less than the conventional rapist. Further, it seems wrong that where a woman assists a man to rape another woman, she may be found guilty as principal receiving like punishment as the actor, yet at common law if a woman attacks and penetrates another by hand or instrument, she is guilty of

---

17. *cont. from previous page*

of the *Crimes Act* and replaced them with new sections. The crime of rape was redefined to include non-consensual fellatio and cunnilingus, non-consensual anal and vaginal penetration by any part of the body (hands, fingers, tongue, for example) or foreign objects, and non-consensual penile penetration of the anus as well as common law rape – non-consensual penetration of the vagina by a man's penis. This meant that many acts which at common law were "indecent assault" or "gross indecency" were now categorised together with common law rape. Rape was then renamed "sexual assault", covering all non-consensual sexual penetrations.]

18. Note that Colin Howard, *Australian Criminal Law*, 2nd edn, 1970, Law Book Co., Sydney, p. 176, contends that the common law crime of buggery applies to consensual acts of anal intercourse only; thus non-consensual acts would have to classify under some other head; see also *R. v. Wardle* [1947] VLR 389. The penalty under s. 33 for malicious wounding with intent to do grievous bodily harm is penal servitude for life. However, it is extremely difficult to prove malice and this would seem particularly so for sexual offences. Thus it is probable that the accused would come under ss. 34 and 35. Under s. 35, if the jury is satisfied that the wounding or grievous bodily harm has been intentionally carried out, but malice is not proved, then they may find the individual guilty of a lesser offence under s. 35, with a maximum penalty of penal servitude for seven years. [With the 1981 changes the maximum penalty for sexual assault was set at 20 years, with grades down to indecent assault with a maximum penalty of seven years. In 1989 further amendments were made to the law, one being to increase the maximum penalty.]

19. "... the law of England ... holds it to be felony to force even a concubine or harlot [to participate in the act of intercourse]": *Blackstone's Commentaries* ss. 213; and see *Patterson v. State* 141 So. 195, 224 Ala. 531; *State v. Beltz* 279 NW 386, 225 Iowa 155 (1938).

and subject to the penalty for indecent assault only, not guilty of rape. If a man assisted her in the act he would be guilty only, as the woman, for indecent assault or as an accessory. Yet the physical and mental damage to the victim and the danger represented by the aggressor might well be equal.[20]

Apart from difference in the substantive law of rape, restricting the common law offence to interaction of a particular type between male and female, rules of evidence confirm the "oddness" of rape. Thus the introduction into evidence of a broad spectrum of the sexual history of the chief witness for the prosecution is allowed. In addition, the jury is admonished to "scrutinize the evidence of the complainant carefully", and is warned of the dangers of convicting an accused of rape where the evidence of a complainant is not corroborated by some other evidence. This proviso constitutes what is called the "corroboration rule in rape". The lack of any corroborative evidence will not mean that a jury lacks the power to bring in a verdict of guilty. However, it has been held that where a corroboration warning has not been given to the jury, a verdict of guilty may be set aside.[21]

At the base of such evidentiary rules lies a distrust of women's truthfulness in regard to sexual encounters with men. This distrust is aggravated by both the isolation of the crime of rape from other crimes of a similar nature, and the severity with which rape is (on paper) required to be treated by the law when the offence is finally proven.

Basic Issues

The determination of whether the crime of rape has occurred is, it is claimed, fraught with difficulty. Unlike the killing of a human being, which in law is inherently wrong, sexual intercourse often takes place with the consent of both parties: thus of two acts that are basically alike, one may attract a criminal penalty due to the lack of consensuality, whereas the other may be no offence at all.[22] How then, to determine whether a crime has occurred? Again, sexual intercourse most often takes place with the two participants, only, present. How to determine guilt or innocence when one party claims the act was consensual, the other party contends that it was not?

---

20. See *Ram and Ram* (1893) 17 Cox CC 609; *R. v. Hapgood and Wyatt* (1870) 11 Cox CC 471; *State v. Burns* 72 A. 1083, 82 Conn. 213 (1989); *State v. Pickel* 200 P. 316, 116 Wash. 600 (1921). [See introduction to this chapter and notes 17 and 18.]

21. On evidence, see generally Vivienne Berger, note 16, and see comments in Tasmanian Law Reform Commission, *Report – Harassment and Embarrassment of Victims in Rape Cases*, 1976, Law Reform Commission, Hobart. On corroboration see generally Andrew Ligertwood, "Failure to Warn in Criminal Cases Where Corroboration May be Required" (1976) 50 *ALJ* 158; *R. v. Graham* (1910) 4 Cr. App. Rep.; 218; R. Watson and H. Purnell, *Criminal Law in New South Wales*, Vol. 1, 1971, p. 103. [Evidence laws and the corroboration rule in rape were subject to modifications in all states and territories at the end of the 1970s and in the early 1980s respectively (Queensland is only now considering the corroboration rule): see introduction to this chapter.]

22. Note however, that this difference may be passing in that there have been increasing reports of "confessions" of assisting terminally ill patients to their deaths, confessions that are apparently often

cont. next page

Despite these difficulties the criminal process, as designed to cover assaults other than rape, should be adequate to deal with problems arising in proof of the commission of the crime of rape. Some acts which without consent would be assault may be rendered lawful by their consensual nature. Individuals buffeting each other about on a football field are not engaged in criminal acts where all parties have agreed to play; however the individual walking across the football field who is set upon by others and pushed or kicked will be the victim of a criminal assault through lack of consent.[23] Thus, if concern about the criminal process is the reason for the introduction of special rules dealing with rape, then the question is why these same rules do not apply to parallel situations. Further, it seems spurious to make a distinction between rape and other crimes on the basis of the private nature of the sexual act, as justification for the creation of special rules. Crimes such as theft and armed robbery which, like rape, involve the element of lack of consent, are not often committed in the public eye: victim and aggressor are frequently the sole participants. The lawful equivalent of such acts – gift-giving – is, like sexual intercourse, often a personal act without audience.

The basis of the introduction of "rules for rape cases" is that the nature of the crime – that it involves sexual activity between male and female – promotes it into the realm of the special:

[We must] be the more cautious upon trials of offences of this nature, wherein the court and jury may with so much ease be imposed upon without great care and vigilance the heinousness of the offense many times transporting the judge and jury with so much indignation, that they are over hastily carried to the conviction of the person accused thereof, by the confident testimony sometimes of malicious and false witness.[24]

---

22. *cont. from previous page*
   ignored by law enforcement authorities. This may indicate an approach toward a revision of the law of murder so that in certain circumstances consent may become relevant to the killing of a human being. In the United Kingdom in 1979 Baroness Wootton of Abinger sponsored a Bill providing for euthanasia under certain circumstances. [In 1989 and 1990 a similar debate took place in Australia, in the Victorian Parliament and in 1993 it appeared the debate was recommencing. See, for example, Bill Birnbauer, "A Woman's Tale – The Kindness in Killing", *Age* 14 September 1993, p. 3.]

23. Although if injury is caused that amounts to grievous or actual bodily harm, consent to play a football match (for example) is irrelevant: the person who inflicted the injury will be guilty of assault occasioning grievous bodily harm or actual bodily harm. [Since this article was written, there has been a noticeable upsurge in prosecutions of football players for injuring their player colleagues during matches.]

24. *Hale's Pleas of the Crown*, Vol. 1, p. 636. See also R. Watson and H. Purnell, *Criminal Law in New South Wales*, 1971, Law Book Co., Sydney, ss. 340 pp. 120–1. The cases cited relate to males involved in the crime of buggery as accomplices rather than as victims: *R. v. Tate* [1908] 2 KB 680; *Davies v. DPP* [1954] AC 378: H. Greenfield, "The Prompt Complaint – A Developing Rule of Evidence" (1972–3) 9 *Crim. Law Quart.* 217.

There is some indication that "offences of this nature" includes not only rape, but also offences with males as victims. Yet the "malicious and false witnesses" most often alluded to in the cases and treatises on criminal law are of the female sex. The peculiarity of the rules, their growth and adoption in most common law jurisdictions, is attributable to the view that false accusations of disappointed, thwarted, or simply neurotic women abound in the sphere of the sexual offence and must diligently be guarded against:

It is true that rape is a most detestable crime, and therefore ought fairly and impartially to be punished with death: but it must be remembered that it is an accusation easily to be made and hard to be proved and harder to be defended by the party accused, tho never so innocent.[25]

This statement, made by Hale (Chief Justice of England in the eighteenth century), is constantly quoted in legal treatises and in the courts. Emphasis is invariably placed upon the "ease" with which a rape accusation may be made, and the difficulty in defending against the charge. Little is said of the difficulty in bringing a case. Psychological factors may prevent women from accusing a man of rape. Reports of rape made to the police are often disbelieved. Juries are not noted for accepting rape allegations "with ease". Nonetheless, lawyers and others continue to adhere to a belief that the law is "peculiar" because rape is a charge "easily brought" and "difficult to defend."

Many weighty authorities have put the view that rape is a "special" crime; that special rules are required; that false accusations are frequent. Are these authorities right? Should the sexual offence where a woman is the victim be hedged with special rules in order to guard against what is seen as women's psyche?

Wigmore, the doyen of United States' evidence law, has said:

No judge should ever let a sex offense charge go to the jury unless the female complainant's social history and mental makeup have been examined and testified to by a qualified physician.[26]

Wigmore contended that "the modern realist movement" had "insisted" on removing the "veil of romance" which had enveloped all womanhood since the "days of chivalry" so that judges could "look at the facts". In the 1940s Wigmore, the pre-eminent United States jurist and writer on evidence law, recommended the psychiatric examination of all female victims of sex offences upon a rape case coming to trial. This examination should, he said, be mandatory. Yet despite Wigmore's assertion that a "veil of romance" shrouded women in rape trials, any such veil is difficult to find, particularly when the legal authorities on sexual offences against women are consulted. Thus Hale and Bracton, English jurists writing in the days of "chivalry", were under no illusion as to the "realities" of female complainants in sexual crimes; even lacking psychiatric "expertise" as is liberally dispensed in Wigmore's treatise, they advocated measures directing judges' and juries' attention to the "realities" of

---

25. *Hale's Pleas of the Crown*, note 24, p. 636.
26. 3A *Wigmore on Evidence*, 1940 edn, ss. 924a, p. 737.

womanhood. "False and feigned witness", "caution", "malicious contrivance" and "great care and vigilance" were each alluded to.[27] It was the development of the law under the direction of early judges that led to the introduction of the corroboration rule so that "feminine wiles" could not found a rape charge, or at least that it should be made the more difficult to make a charge.

Nevertheless it could be put that, in the past, courts were forced to grapple with amorphous concepts of the female psyche and might easily have been lead astray by particularly subtle complainants. The "realism" of today may lie in the use of the "expert witness" who can better illustrate to judge and jury the nature of the prosecutrix – the psychiatrist.

Such a proposition cannot be accepted without misgiving. The problems of expert testimony in the courtroom have been recognised as a general issue. Psychiatrists as experts cause not the least of these problems. One of the most problematic areas is that of terminology: what do terms such as "neuroticism", "schizophrenia", "psychotic" and the like mean? In writing of their value in the courtroom, psychiatrists themselves have sometimes declared that too much significance is given to psychiatric pronouncements; even that the judicial system is no place for the psychiatrist.[28] Even the much-cited Freud can be found making the following statement about his sense of lack of expertise in dealing with the psychology of women:

If you want to know more about femininity, enquire from your own experiences of life, or turn to the poets, or wait until science can give you deeper and more coherent information.[29]

Freud's theory of sexuality was founded on the role of the male in nineteenth-century Vienna; his theory of female sexuality was set up as the antithesis of male development. His published works relating to the female psyche as such are few. Those works may be subjected to criticism and appear sometimes to be distorted by members of his own profession and by popular thought. Freud believed that women are prone to sexual fantasising, which in turn may lead to their making untrue statements about their being the object of sexual attack. Very often, it seems, the "victim" of a woman's sexual fantasising will be her own father – whom she sees as having seduced or attempted to seduce her.[30]

---

27. Wigmore cites various psychiatrists of the Freudian school, including Karl Menninger, Otto Monkmoller, W. E. Lorenz and William Healy and Mary T. Healy. See further text accompanying notes 38–40 herein.
28. See for example Allen Bartholomew and Kerry Milte, "The Reliability and Validity of Psychiatric Diagnoses in the Courts of Law" (1976) *ALJ* 250; Ennis and Litwack, "Psychiatry and the Presumption of Expertise; Flipping Coins in the Courtroom" (1974) 62 *Calif. L. Rev.* 693; Hussey, "Psychiatrists in Court" (1931) 22 *Amer. Mercury* 342; Thomas Szasz, *The Myth of Mental Illness*, 1961, Harper and Row, New York.
29. Sigmund Freud, *Femininity*, 1932, p. 22, republished in Jean Straus (ed.), *Women and Analysis*, 1976, Penguin Books, Harmondsworth.
30. See an extensive discussion and critique of various of Freud's papers in Jean Straus, note 29; Robin Morgan (ed.), *Sisterhood is Powerful*, 1976, Vintage, New York, p. 161 ff; Juliet Mitchell, *Psychoanalysis and Feminism*, 1975, Penguin Books, Harmondsworth.

Yet can it so easily be said that allegations of women in terms of sexual attack by their own fathers are patently false? Sometimes, at least, there may be foundation in the tale. In "Femininity", a paper delivered in 1933, Freud discussed the pre-Oedipal period in girls and boys.[31] Arising out of his study during the time in which his interest was directed towards the issue of infantile sexual traumas, Freud declared "almost all my women patients told me that they had been seduced by their fathers". Finally he was "driven to recognise ... that these reports were untrue and so came to understand that hysterical symptoms are derived from phantasies and not from real occurrences". Later he was able "to recognize in this phantasy of being seduced by the father the expression of the typical oedipus complex in women". However, another view of the recounted experiences might be that there was some truth in them. Of course, the programmed response to an allegation that fathers in nineteenth-century Vienna were guilty of sexually molesting their daughters is that it is unthinkable. Yet with the increased investigation into child abuse in recent times, it has been found that such abuse is not an isolated occurrence. Further, it seems that often sexual abuse and physical abuse are companions.

A study by Gagon and Simon at Indiana University Institute of Sex Research in 1966 calculated that approximately half a million female children per year are the subject of incestuous sexual abuse. In New York City some fifteen years later, three thousand such cases were reported each year. Those who have studied accepted cases of sexual abuse within the family have estimated that in the United States "one in every ten people" in the total population have at one time or another been involved in incestuous activity. The conclusion of Woodbury and Schwartz is that this is "far more common and far less traumatic than we have been led to believe".[32] The statement directly contradicts Freud – for his belief was that false allegations of the activity were common and it was the fantasy of incest which led to certain traumas, rather than the truth of the allegation being founded in fact, with no consequent trauma! Yet a third stand presents itself: that incestuous happenings in fact occur, and that they are traumatic. The very problem here is that there is too ready acceptance of a particular type of analysis, an acceptance of long-held beliefs which may not necessarily be true.

Again this approach appears in Freud's paper "The Taboo of Virginity", where the roots of primitive tribal customs of defloration were found in the "ambivalence" of women towards those with whom they may first engage in intercourse. Where custom

31. Sigmund Freud, note 29, p. 80. For the contrary view – that sexual abuse of children by family members is real, see for example John Bremmer (ed.), *Children and Youth in America – A Documentary History*, 1971, Thomas, Springfield; Anne W. Burgess and Linda L. Holstrom, *Rape – Victims of Crisis*, 1974, Robert J. Brady Co., New York; J. Burton, *Vulnerable Children*, 1968; Paul Gebhard et. al., *Sex Offenders*, 1965, Thomas, Springfield; Phyllis Chesler, *Women and Madness*, 1972, Doubleday, New York; Yvonne M. Tormes, *Child Sexual Assault – Confronting Rape in America*, 1976, John Wiley and Sons, New York.

32. J. Woodbury and R. Schwartz, *The Silent Sin*, 1971, Hawthorn, New York; See also Jon H. Gagon and William Simon, *Sexual Conduct – The Social Sources of Human Sexuality*, 1973, Hutchinson, London. (The study was set up under the original guidance of Alfred Kinsey.)

requires that a woman should be deflorated by a priest or other tribal dignitary, the reason (according to Freudian analysis) is that the female psyche is such that the man who is to be her husband cannot risk an adverse reaction from her by performing the act himself; thus the responsibility for doing so is cast on the elders of the tribe. This conclusion was reached by Freud with no research into the minds of "primitive women".[33] It is legitimate to ask what role the male psyche plays in the tribal custom. An equally (or more) valid explanation is that the tribal elders take some pleasure in the activity. It is a very one-sided view which looks only to the female as setting the scene, solely to the (alleged) female reaction as relevant. A parallel arises with studies of father-daughter incest in contemporary life. Fathers justify sexual relations with their daughters by persuading themselves that they are "teaching them the facts of life" or "making a woman out of her." Thus the act on the part of the father becomes a "responsibility" or "duty" and any sexual motivation or abuse of power on his part is denied or ignored.[34]

Another Freudian theory giving support to the notion of "false complaints" is that "the feminine wish to be subject to a sexual attack may become the subject of an hallucination". As a result, she may believe the act has taken place and falsely accuse. This idea rests upon the foundation of "feminine masochism" as essential to the female psyche, a concept that Freud is said to have established and which Helene Deutsch and others accepted as "a constant factor in female development and as an indispensable constituent in woman's acceptance of the whole of her sexuality". Without it, a woman is hardly "a woman".[35]

Freud said masochism is determined by a combination of factors: one, the constitutional disposition of the female; two, her observation of the coitus of her parents, where the act is seen as aggressive, an attack of male on female. However, in returning to the source from whence the idea of masochism as a female attribute has come – the writings of Freud – it is shattering to the concept to realise that he described it as it occurred in men: he studied the way male homosexuals act and the way they modelled themselves on women as they perceived women to act:

---

33. Sigmund Freud, "The Taboo of Virginity" in *Collected Papers*, Vol. 11, 1918, p. 204. Even where devising a "global theory" it would seem incumbent upon the theorist to seek some empirical back up.
34. See C. Schutt and N. Gager, note 31, p. 40; C. Bagley, "Incest Behaviour and Incest Taboo" cited C. Schutt and N. Gager, note 31.
35. Sigmund Freud, *Collected Papers*, Riviere's Trns., 1948; cited Carol Bohmer and Anne Blumberg, "The Rape Victim and Due Process" (1974) 80 *Case and Comment* 3, fn. 9. See Helene Deutsch, *The Psychology of Women*, Vols. I and II, 1942, Basic Books, New York; I. Bieber, "The Meaning of Masochism" (1953) 7 *Am. Journ. Psychotherapy* 433; Marie Bonaparte, *Female Sexuality*, 1953, Basic Books, New York. Freud's major works dealing with this issue are found in Femininity, 1932; "The Masochistic Character" (1959) 7 *Jrn. Am. Psycho. Assn.* 197. From Helene Deutsch in "The Psychology of Women in Relation to the Function of Reproduction" in *Psychology and Women*, Vols. I and II, 1973, Bantam, New York, we learn: "In actual fact parturition is for the woman an orgy of masochistic pleasure". (Her assertion may not be echoed by women going through childbirth.)

Feminine masochism ... is the form most accessible to observation, least mysterious, and is comprehensible in all its relations. We may begin our discussion with it. In men (to whom for reasons connected with the material I shall limit my remarks) ... if one has an opportunity of studying cases in which the masochistic phantasies have undergone specially rich elaboration, one easily discovers that in them the subject is placed in a situation characteristic of womanhood, that is they mean that he is being castrated, is playing the passive part in coitus, or is giving birth. For this reason I have called this form of masochism fortiori feminine although so many of its features point to childish life.[36]

Once more it is through the eyes of the male that the psyche of the female is determined. Although men might interpret the woman's situation as "passive", filled with suffering and so on, this is no assurance that women view themselves in this way. Even if Freud's basic premise of feminine masochism were accepted, would questions arise: how many children observe parental coitus; did the theory later gain credence through clinical observation of sufficient female persons to make its universal application tenable? Or could it be said that this would be another case of finding the theory, then interpreting actions to fit it? Even if some women were to conform to the Freudian ideal, would this mean that all women who are found to charge men with rape conform to it and thus, being predisposed to falsify, do so? Would it mean, even, that so many women could be thus predisposed as to justify special rules in the rape sphere, in order to protect those at whom the false accusations are directed.[37]

Generally, psychiatrists cited in support of theories of the frequency of (or potential for) false accusations of rape made by women appear biased. Wigmore calls on various psychiatrists. One is quoted as saying "fantasies of being raped are exceedingly common in women, indeed one may almost say they are probably universal".[38] This statement must be taken on trust; no numbers of patients – or, for

---

36. Sigmund Freud, "The Economic Problem in Masochism" in *Collected Papers* vol. 11, at 255; see also Ethel Person, "Some New Observations on the Origins of Femininity" in *Women and Analysis*, note 29, p. 250.

37. A quick verbal quiz conducted among twenty women students and undertaken by the writer revealed that women may have sexual fantasies but these involved acts of a consensual (and pleasant!) nature, not non-consensual and damaging acts, which those questioned would not care to have in fact, nor in fiction. The work of Shere Hite, published in *The Hite Report*, 1976, Macmillan, New York, similarly appears to bear out the fantasising of women in relation to acts that are pleasurable. Even were the truth borne out that women fantasise about acts of an aggressive nature, it is questionable whether women want to be hurt in reality and, anyway, whether such fantasising would lead women to say they'd been raped when they hadn't. Surely if (a) (some) women *fantasise* about being attacked aggressively; (b) (these) women *want* to be attacked aggressively; (c) (these) women *are* attacked aggressively; (d) (these) women *enjoy* being attacked aggressively – they would hardly be likely to complain that the (desired and pleasurable) aggressive acts were rape. To them, because (according to this theory) the women wanted the aggressive acts to be done to them, the acts would hardly be defined by them as rape. If, on the other hand, women fantasise about aggressive acts being done to them but aggressive acts done to them in reality are not what they want, the fantasising cannot make the reality "not rape".

38. Karl A. Menninger, cited 3A *Wigmore on Evidence*, 1970 edn., ss. 924a, p. 744. The three immediately following quotations are from Otto Monkmoller, cited 3A *Wigmore on Evidence*, ss.

that matter, women not in analysis – are cited in support. Another declares a complainant will show her falsity where she exhibits an "intensely erotic propensity ... in [a] wanton facial expression ... sensuous motions, and manner of speech." However, deceit may also be concealed by "a madonna like countenance that such a girl can readily assume ... [a] convincing upturn of the eye, with which she seeks to strengthen her credibility." This manner of deceit appears to be limited to the female, as shown in the case cited by one of Wigmore's psychiatrists, where a young girl alleged an act of incest by her brother, but the "character sustained by the brother ... was quite out of keeping with the grave accusations against him" – no suggestion that a male person guilty of the crime of incest might dissimulate.

Not only is bias revealed in the assumption that it is women who are likely to deceive, but also in the support alleged to exist in female sexual fantasies at the base of false accusations. Thus "hysterical girls ... living through fantastic sex dramas" are cited; so, too, is the case of those women whose sex urge is "strongly developed" so that "if some man comes within their vicinity, they may dally with a secret wish to have some sex relation with him, and then his most harmless conduct is transformed by these sex-imaginative witnesses into acts which charge him as a criminal"; and the "erotic imagination of an abnormal child of attractive appearance may send an innocent man to the penitentiary for life".[39]

For the male sex it is confidently said, "In male youths this particular sex-disposition plays a far smaller part."[40] Yet even a less-than-critical reader or analyst is surely led to ask how often this dichotomy really presents itself. Could it not equally be said that many male persons have a sex-urge which leads them to fantasise, so that sometimes these fantasies may lead them to believe that a particular female is interested in joining a sexual dalliance – when in fact she is not, and has not even considered the proposition. Are males not capable of "transforming ... the woman's most harmless conduct" into an invitation, and persisting in this belief in spite of any protest she might voice?[41]

The vision of female as seductress is yet a further expression of a built-in refusal to view sexual relations objectively. Thus, in incest cases, the psychiatrist's view most often expressed is that the child, not the father, is responsible for the activity; the child is "collaborative", "encouraging", "fully participating"; "repeated sexual involvement

---

39. W. E. Lorenz, cited 3A *Wigmore on Evidence*, ss. 924a, p. 744; Otto Monkmoller, cited 3A *Wigmore on Evidence*, ss. 924a, p. 774; 1937–38 *Statement Am. Bar Assn. Committee on the Improvement of the Law of Evidence*, cited 3A *Wigmore on Evidence*, ss. 924a, p. 747.

40. Otto Monkmoller, cited 3A *Wigmore on Evidence*, note 20, ss. 924a, p. 744.

41. Reported rape cases and pornographic films certainly suggest this is true. Only fantasy could lead a male person to suggest that he considered a woman to be consenting to sexual intercourse when he had climbed, unacquainted with her and uninvited, through her window at night: *R. v. Stapleton* [1975] 2 All ER 747; *R. v. Collins* [1972] 2 All ER 1105. [For an account of the way judicial courtroom voices echo the words of men absolving themselves from responsibility for rape, see Jocelynne A. Scutt, "The Voice of the Rapist", paper presented to the Second National Conference on Violence, 16 June 1993, Australian Institute of Criminology, Canberra.]

with the same person says clearly that at some level the child wanted the relationship to continue …"[42] Surely, the authority relationship of father to offspring has some effect on the submissiveness of the child and her frequent refusal to make the activity known. Similarly, other authority relationships involving sexual activity create identical responses. Yet the traditional view is that the child is responsible, not the father. Responsibility is also attributed to girls and women in other authority relationships. Thus, in an oft-cited study by the Group for the Advancement of Psychiatry, "Sex and the College Student", the unanimous view expressed is that where a sexual involvement takes place between female student and male teacher, it is the student upon whom the onus for initiating the sexual relationship lies. A typical case:

At a small party in the instructor's apartment, Betty, a junior, became intoxicated and the teacher had intercourse with her after the party. He thought little about it, and was surprised and distressed to be summoned by the Dean. The girl had reported him, saying that her condition made it impossible for her to protest effectively. He said he had not used force, believed the girl had been an active participant, and finally indignantly protested that he had been framed.[43]

The issue here is not whether in fact the girl was the victim of non-consensual sexual intercourse; nor whether in fact she was a willing participant; nor that the teacher was an unprincipled Lothario; nor that her report to the Dean might have been motivated by shame and an attempt to transfer guilt. The issue to address is that invariably the view taken by the psychiatrist in this and similar instances was that the conclusion was incontrovertibly writ: the female plays the part of seductress; for varying reasons she falsely reports rape.[44]

In too many psychiatric writings on the sexuality of females no effort is made to take an unbiased stance. Explanations conform with folk tales of women as the deceitful sex, and every case cited shows that, in whatever manner she deports herself, the cry of "feigning it" will arise to justify special rules in the judicial area. Even Hale, who had no science of psychiatry at his disposal, produced a typically ambiguous case to support his theory of false or feigned charges to be guarded against – and could not even contemplate an alternative explanation. He instanced the case of a child who

---

42. See for example Jo Woodbury and R. Schwartz, 1971, note 32; N. Gager and C. Schutt, note 31, p. 37 ff. L. G. Schultz, "Psychotherapeutic and Legal Approaches to the Victimised Child"; C. R. Kiefer, Director of Child Mental Health, Indianapolis cited N. Gager and C. Schutt, note 31, pp. 48–49.

43. Group for the Advancement of Psychiatry, Sex and the College Student, *Report No. 60*, 1965, USA.

44. The irony is that the word "seduction" was originally used to describe the activities of males in "luring and enticing females to submit to 'defloration'", see C. Schutt and N. Gager, p. 47: "Psychiatrists, psychologists, anthropologists, sociologists, and criminologists – reversing the actor and the acted-on – now apply the term almost exclusively to the female." Again it is ironic that, on the one hand, the myth is that women have no sex urges at all, conforming to the "real Victorian woman" type; on the other hand she is seen as having a voracious or insatiable appetite! See Kramer and Sprenger, *Malleus Maleficarum (The Anvil of the Witches)* published in the 14th century; H. R. H. Hays, *The Evil Sex*, 1968; published as *The Dangerous Sex – The Myth of Feminine Evil*, 1972, Pocket Books, New York.

alleged rape, when the accused suffered from a physical disability precluding him from the act of intercourse.[45] Yet other explanations are available that are not beyond belief. The girl might not have understood that "rape" means "penetration" and the act might have been something less than this; the girl may have been sexually fondled by the man – an occurrence not unknown. Certainly the girl may have been lying: the tale may have had no foundation in fact. Certainly in all trials every effort must be made to ensure that innocent persons are not convicted or that the conviction is appropriate in terms of the act committed. Nonetheless, it is clear that there is an almost automatic presumption on the part of the criminal justice system that a female complainant is not to be trusted and that this mistrust renders sexual offences against women different from the general run of the criminal law.[46]

There is automatic acceptance of statements and records by police putting the view that, say, 65 per cent or 80 per cent or 50 per cent of complaints coming before them for investigation are unfounded. For the authorities, no research into the methods by which the police come to this determination appears to be necessary. Or worse, there is an unquestioning acceptance of anecdotal information as to the frequency of false tales by women and their lack of veracity as victims in a rape offence. However, more recent views of female sexuality and studies of rape victims not previously undertaken (anecdotal information being preferred) appear to herald a need for swift revision of attitudes – or at least an objective look at the system that has been created.[47]

---

45. *Hale's Pleas of the Crown*, Vol. 1, p. 636.

46. In a New York study of child abuse it was found that the most prevalent sexual crime (45%) was rape or attempted rape; indecent or immoral practices involving sex organs of a child constituted 19 per cent; "impairing morals" accounted for 12 per cent; 14 per cent involved sodomy; 9 per cent involved incest. In 75 per cent of the cases studies, the offender was the girl's father, stepfather, a lover of the mother, a brother, uncle or "friend" of the family. Other studies show similar results: see Victor de Francis, *Protecting the Child Victim of Sex Crimes Committed by Adults*, 1969; Yvonne M. Tormes, *Child Victims of Incest*, 1969, The American Humane Society, Denver. Similar studies carried out in Britain, Germany, Canada and South Australia are cited in the Royal Commission on Human Relationships, *Final Report*, Vol. 5, pp. 223–4 and see that *Report* generally p. 222 ff.

47. The Royal Commission into Human Relationships reported: "Forty-four experienced Queensland police officers were interviewed. Twenty-eight said that when they first received a rape complaint, the possible falsity of the complaint was uppermost in their minds ... [We] do not have precise figures for complaints rejected by the police, but the Victorian Rape Investigation Squad report that of twenty-two complaints received during its first five months of operation, only twelve were accepted as rape cases. This is consistent with the Victorian Law Reform Commission's analysis into the job books of four districts, covering the period between January 1975 and November 1975, which showed that 50 per cent of rape complaints were accepted as genuine." (At p. 178.) See also Note, "Rape and Rape Laws – Sexism in Society and Law" (1973) 61 *Calif. Law Rev.* 919: Carol Bohmer and Carol Blumberg, "The Rape Victim and Due Process" (1974) 80 *Case and Comment* 3, p. 10, fn. 9. The unthinking acceptance of the police view is all too clearly revealed in the Report of the Victorian Law Reform Commissioner, *Rape Prosecutions (Court procedure and rules of evidence)*, 1976, Government Printer, Melbourne, Australia, where the rape complaints accepted as genuine and those accepted by the police as false were accepted without demur. For a criticism of police views of false complaints
cont. next page

The Psychology of Women Reassessed

In the past the failure of a rape victim to make what the police or courts considered to be a sufficiently "prompt complaint" supported the belief that an allegation of rape was untrue. Today the view has been put:

> ... it is no longer true, if it ever was, that a woman who is raped necessarily raises a hue and cry. Whether she complains at the first opportunity or not depends very largely upon her personality and her temperament. It is a false assessment to assume that every women who is raped will necessarily immediately complain to her parents or her husband or some close relative. The fact that a woman may decide to give mature consideration to whether she will or will not report the rape to the police does not of itself indicate that she is untrustworthy ... [The] admission of the evidence of the complaint serves no useful purpose and is likely to mislead the jury.[48]

This reassessment of the role of the female in sexual offences is no doubt due to a general reassessment of the female role. A catalyst to the current "new thought" was a study conducted in 1970 amongst 79 clinicians, 46 being male, 39 female. When asked to define the "normal" male the result was to portray him as independent, aggressive, dominant, objective, competitive. For the "normal" female, the traits attributed to her were that she is more dependent than the male, more submissive, less competitive, more excitable in minor crises, more easily hurt, more emotional, more vain, less objective. The definition of the "normal" human being was that such a person is independent, aggressive, dominant, stable, objective, competitive.[49] Obviously the woman is in an untenable position. If she conforms to the "normal" female pattern she automatically places herself outside the realm of the "normal" human being. If she conforms to the pattern of the "normal" human being she is automatically excluded from the definition of the "normal" human female. The conundrum has been addressed by "non-traditionalists", "... whether they accept or reject the female role [women] are psychiatrically impaired – simply because they are women ..."[50]

---

47. *cont. from previous page*
    see the recent report of the task force of the New South Wales Premier's Department, *Care for Victims of Sexual Offences*, 1978 pp. 9, 10. The *Final Report* Vol. 5, p. 178 of the Royal Commission into Human Relationships also questioned police statistics and the too-easy acceptance of them by those in authority. See also comments in Duncan Chappell, "Reforming Rape Laws (and attitudes ...?)" (1977) *Legal Service Bulletin* 217; also *R. v. Hinton* [1961] Qd. R. 17; *Hopkinson v. Purduc* [1904] AC 286 at 296; *Baccio v. People* 41 NY at 265–268. For the traditional view, see *R. v. Hinton* [1961] Qd. R. 17; *Baccio v. People* 41 NY at 265–268.
48. South Australian Criminal Law and Penal Methods Reform Committee, *Report on Rape and Other Sexual Offences*, 1976, Government Printer, Adelaide, p. 48.
49. I. Broverman, D. Broverman, F. Clarkson, P. Rosencrantz and S. Vogel, "Sex Roles, Stereotypes and Clinical Judgements of Mental Health" (1970) 34, *Jrn Consulting and Clinical Psychol.* 5.
50. Phyllis Chesler, note 31, p. 115.

The traditional psychologist's view has set up femininity as a "sort of natural pathology".[51] Non-traditionalists say:

We learn from a good analytic authority that not only is a woman to be dominated but she will become neurotic if she is not. To be dominated then becomes an imperative for mental health for women; this, the doctor's prescription.[52]

The easy way of acceptance of stereotypical views of the female psyche is to be guarded against. So, too, is the belief that there is only one way for an honest and chaste woman to act when confronted by an attacker. In the past, the stereotype having legal sanction was that of the raped woman who is so humiliated, hurt, outraged that she immediately reports it. However, a diversity of reactions is possible and should now be recognised: the woman may be so hurt and humiliated that she chooses not to reveal the damage to others; she may believe herself to be in some way guilty – a not uncommon reaction, despite a patent lack of participation on her part. It is more likely that she does not report rape than that she does.

A second stereotype given the sanction of the law is that of the virtuous female who truly believes rape to be a "fate worse than death". If she does not resist and fight to the utmost, then the act was not rape. Yet there is not one pattern to be followed representing "innocence", all others denoting "falsity" or "deceit". Some women, faced with an assailant, may prefer to live; some to suffer no damage beyond the act of non-consensual intercourse; some to suffer no damage beyond the act of "complying" until they can escape; some may be programmed into compliance, believing that they have no ability to resist, never having taken part in fisticuffs, nor having been required to develop self-defence skills.

A third stereotype of the female finds too ready a place in the law books and judicial mind: that of the seductress, an individual having little control over her sexual urges and fantasies. This stereotype must be re-examined in the light of the new psychiatry and new ideas and understanding about sexuality. Not only women have sexual fantasies; most people are able to distinguish between fantasy and fact; the very essence of a fantasy is that it is just that – and remains so. One view is that sexual (and other) fantasies fulfil a particular human need, the very essence of that need being that fantasies should remain unfulfilled in fact. If fantasy is a human need (whether "natural" or socially constructed) which most people access, then it is difficult to blame fantasy for allegations of rape; otherwise, why aren't all women *and all men* constantly making (false) allegations of rape?

With changing social mores, the fourth stereotype playing a role in forming attitudes of courts and designing of rules is that of the "unchaste woman". Thus any

---

51. Judith Bardwick, *The Psychology of Women*, 1970, p. 21.
52. John Seidenberg, "Oedipus and Male Supremacy" in *The Radical Therapist Collective*, 1971, p. 147, and see Judith Roth, Jonathan Daly, Judith Lerner, "Into the Abyss – Psychiatric Reliability and Emergency Commitment Statutes" (1973) *Santa Clara Lawyer* 300, p. 409.

attempt to endorse a distinction between the sexes, in terms of what type of characteristics affect their veracity, should be reviewed. It can no longer be accepted, at least as a legal concept, that:

... it is a matter of common knowledge that the bad character of a man for chastity does not even in the remotest degree affect his character for truth, when based upon that alone, while it does that of a woman.[53]

Just as sexual activity and honesty have no correlation in the male, so too should this lack of any relationship in the female be recognised.

No furtherance of justice is apparent in accepting female stereotypes as relevant to the criminal justice system. Similarly, current reassessment of the female psyche with reference to the crime of rape should be accompanied by a reassessment of the male in terms of the crime. Thus, the attitude depicted in the statement that current laws are responsible for a "waste of human resources through this excessive penalisation of what may be a nominal behaviour in a man's cultural, social or racial milieu" demands objective review.[54] (Such as what might be required or expected in a human milieu!) The stereotype of the rapist as a sex-crazed fiend advances no cause. There must be real debate around the concept of the "ordinary, everyday" man as a rapist. Contrary to popular thought, rape is not the result of pent-up sexual desires, but an act of sexual violence which should take its rightful place in criminal law in the general run of violent acts against the person, rather than being isolated in some separate category of "sexual offences against women and girls".

Conclusion

The legal system is slow to change. In the 1970s and 1980s debate on reform of the rape laws, this view was put:

There are, unquestionably, some aspects of the offence of rape which call for remedial legislation. However [it does not seem] that the basic framework of existing legislation is "ill designed" ... A starting point for any reform must ... be that, while there may be areas needing specific reforms, at present substantial justice is being effected – as it has been for many generations past. It is all too easy to overlook the consideration that existing laws – unlike many of the radical proposals currently being advanced – have stood the test of time.[55]

---

53. Per Burgess J. in *State v. Sibley* 33 S.W. 167, 171, 130 Mo. 519, 531–532 (1895).
54. Martin Ploscowe, *Sex and the Law*, 1951, Thomas, Springfield. Ploscowe was a member of the Criminal Law Advisory Committee set up to draft the United States *Model Penal Code*.
55. Department of the Attorney-General and of Justice, Criminal Law Review Division (NSW), *Supplement to Report on Rape and Various Other Sexual Offences*, 1977, Department of the Attorney-General, Sydney, p. 22.

This approach begs the question: can it be so confidently said that "substantial justice is being effected" when it is clear that many rapes go unpunished because they are not prosecuted, or where criminal offences go unreported because many victims of the crime are afraid to report that an offence has occurred since, among other reasons, they consider the criminal justice system will be unsympathetic?[56] Have existing rape laws really "stood the test of time?"

What may be said to have "stood the test of time" are attitudes of a highly biased nature directed towards victims of a particular type of sexual offence, classified as "rape" under traditional laws (if those laws are brought into play). The issue is whether these attitudes are to be approved of, supported and "given the blessing" of the legal system. Singling out the female victim of a male sexual attack as requiring special conditions in bringing the offence to court shows that justice fails to act in a neutral manner. When the "evidence" upon which such a lack of neutrality is based is studied, those individuals who have been victims of sexual offences can equally be said to become victims of the criminal justice process.

And where rape laws have been at all modified – as in South Australia, where changes to the substantive law were approved in 1976, or in Western Australia, Tasmania, Victoria and Queensland, where changes to the rules of evidence were introduced in the 1970s – legislatures and "reformers" have not accepted that any change to the corroboration requirement should be made.[57] Juries can continue to be confused by the direction of the judge: that they must not only find the crime proved beyond a reasonable doubt, but that they must look for corroboration of the victim's story. Nothing can be more mystifying to a jury than to be directed to "find something extra" than that the accused is guilty beyond reasonable doubt. For this is, effectively, what jurors are told by judges urging that they seek corroboration, and the inference that the "beyond reasonable doubt" standard is not (whatever the jury thinks of her evidence) met by the victim telling of the acts against her. Jury studies show that there

---

56. Investigations as revealed in the most recent literature on the subject clearly show this. See comments in Royal Commission into Human Relationships, *Final Report* Vol. 5, 1977, AGPS, Canberra.

57. See *Criminal Law Consolidation Act (Amendment) Act* 1976 (SA) and also *Justice Act (Amendment) Act* 1976 (SA); *Rape Offences (Proceedings) Act* 1976 (Victoria); *Evidence Act (Amendment) Act* 1976 (WA); *Evidence Act* (No. 3) 1976 (Tasmania); *Criminal Law (Sexual Offences) Act* 1978 (Queensland). [More prescriptive changes were made to New South Wales evidence laws in 1981, simultaneously with the changes to the substantive law of rape. Rather than using the "loop hole" approach of incorporating restrictive rules with a catch-all at the conclusion, allowing admission of any evidence determined by the court to be relevant and admissible in all the circumstances of the case, which essentially led to little change, New South Wales proscribed certain stipulated types of evidence from admission into rape trials. Still, problems remained. See generally Liza Newby, "Rape Victims in Court – The Western Australian Example" in *Rape Law Reform*, Jocelynne A. Scutt (ed.), 1980, Australian Institute of Criminology, Canberra, p. 115; Rosemary O'Grady and Belinda Powell, "Rape Victims in Court – The South Australian Experience" in *Rape Law Reform*, p. 127; Jocelynne A. Scutt, note 1. The corroboration rule was changed in the 1980s, by the inclusion of a provision in the relevant statutes that the corroboration warning was not mandatory; this left it to the discretion of each judge, in the particular case. See generally introduction to this article.]

is a reluctance upon the part of the jury members to accept the uncorrobo-rated story of a victim of rape, or even to accept a tale of rape where seemingly clear evidence bolsters the occurrence of the crime. Thus, in stating the rule, the judge is not engaged in bringing neutrality or fairness into the rape courtroom; rather, the direction serves only to confirm the jury in the commonly held belief that victims of rape lie.[58]

Where false accusations of crime occur in the legal arena, it is accepted generally that the legal process without special modifications will serve the course of justice and expose the falsity of the allegation – at least where the crime is robbery, theft, (non-sexual) assault, even so serious an offence as murder. In arguing that the usual procedure should apply in the case of rape, no one contends that no false accusation will ever be made. Just as false accusations of other crimes are sometimes made, so some few accusations of rape may be mistaken, but ordinary procedural rules will cover the case.[59]

Mistrust of "scheming women" has no place within our criminal justice system; the implication that deceit is a sex-linked characteristic must not be countenanced in courts of law; the legal process should adopt an unprejudiced stance where the crime is rape, the victim a woman. Clearly, although "justice" demands that no innocent person should be found guilty, so too it requires that those persons who are guilty should be punished: not that they should escape conviction as a result of rules linking us to a misogynistic past.

---

58. See Michael Soler, "Women's Place ... Combating Sex-Based Prejudices in Jury Trials Through Voir Dire" (1975) 15 *Santa Clara Lawyer* 535; Hans Kalvan and Henry Zeisel, *The American Jury*, 1966; Shirley Feldman-Summers, "Conceptual and Empirical Issues Associated With Rape" in *Victim and Society*, Emilio Viano (ed.), p. 177. Shirley Feldman-Summers and Janet Lindner, "Perceptions of Victims and Defendants in Criminal Assault Cases" (1976) 3 *Criminal Justice and Behaviour* 135; Jones and Aronson, "Attribution of Fault To Rape Victims as a Function of Respectability of the Victim" (1973) 26 *Jrn. Personality and Social Psychology* 415. [Note that jurors' views appear to be changing so that the reality of victims/survivors is granted greater credence. See Jocelynne A. Scutt, 1993, note 41 this chapter.]

59. The prime case-support for the offence of "false reporting" or "causing a public mischief" by making a false complaint is *R. v. Manley* [1933] KB 529 where the crime falsely reported was not rape, but robbery.

9

ANZAC DAY AND WOMEN RAPED IN WAR
Or, Women Don't Have a
'One Day of the Year'!

Paper presented to Anzac Day Forum for Women – Thinking About the Future
Melbourne YWCA
25 August 1984

*In the mid-1970s and into the mid-1980s women around Australia debated the rape of
women in wartime, the use of women as "spoils of war", the damage inflicted upon
women as women – because women are women – in the course of war and its
aftermath, and the grossly abusive objectification of women as a means of "getting
back" at the enemy during wartime. One year, early on, news reports were heard
throughout Australia of flowers laid and slogans slashed upon the war memorial in
Kings Park, Perth, early on Anzac morning, just before the "official" marchers
arrived. The flowers remembered the women raped in war; the slogans protested
against the masculine ethos which supports death and dying, physical and psychological, not only as a result of bombs, shells and rifle fire, but through the stark
brutality of rape. This is brutality not at a distance, made clinical by the height of
planes dropping bombs from the air, or remote guns blasting depth charges from the
holds or the decks of a ship, or even pulling a trigger from several yards – or even
more – away. It is as close as one human being can come to another. Pain and terror,
close up.*

*Later, the memorial in Martin Place, Sydney, was the scene of passionate claims
by women to march and mourn for women raped in war. The shrine in St Kilda Road,
Melbourne, became the stage for verbal sparring about who did – and who didn't –
have "the right" to march on Anzac Day, whose death, whose agony, had a right to be
spoken of and to be mourned. In Darwin, Alice Springs, Townsville, Adelaide,
Brisbane ... women were marching.*

*I admired the women who stood, and marched, by their ideals and ideas, joining in
the Anzac Day march despite the best efforts of "the authorities" to exclude them –
sometimes violently. Yet I could not join in a protest linked to a day centred around*

masculine warring. "Anzac Day and Women Raped in War" was written years long after I had formed the view that Anzac Day is not a remembrance that speaks to women raped in war. That it cannot hear women's voices raised in anger and agony for women's deeply centred anguish founded in the course of war. I appreciated being asked to speak at the Anzac Day Forum for Women – because it made me commit to writing views I had been expressing for some time. I was glad Anzac Day and the organisers of the Forum gave me the opportunity and the impetus to write "Women Don't Have a 'One Day of the Year'!"

[Those women should] pick another day when there has been a lot of rape victims and make that their day …

Bruce Ruxton, President, Victoria RSL.[1]

In 1978 in Canberra a handful of women took to the street on Anzac Day to march in protest and mourning for women raped in war. They were arrested and tried on grounds that the police had a right – indeed a duty – to arrest and keep them in custody, on the basis that their presence on an Anzac Day march created a likelihood of riot or affray. Yet the marchers had no intention to riot, nor to cause an affray. It was the men who were marching on Anzac Day who claimed that if the women marched, they would be attacked and prevented from doing so. This was evident in all evidence given to the court when the women were tried.

The following year, hundreds of women took to the streets, despite protests from the Returned Services League (RSL) and a significant police presence, as well as the famed *Anzac Day Ordinance* which came into effect rapidly, in a Territory where much outstanding legislation has been "in the pipeline" for years – including rape reform legislation, which has been gestating in the Department of the Attorney-General for five or more years.[2]

Each year since, women have protested in hundreds in Canberra, Sydney, Melbourne, Perth, Adelaide and elsewhere in Australia. In no year have I marched in the protests.

---

1. Quoted Adrian Howe, "Anzac Day – Rethinking Feminist Strategy" in *Anzac 1984 – The Issues For and Against*, 1984, UWU, North Fitzroy, p. 9. In the footnotes, square brackets [...] indicate new material added for this edition.
2. See Arthur Watson, "Reform of the Law of the Australian Capital Territory Relating to Rape and Other Sexual Offences" in *Rape Law Reform*, Jocelynne A. Scutt (ed.), 1980, Australian Institute of Criminology, Canberra, p. 67. [In the year this paper was written, the Australian Capital Territory reformed its rape laws, making rape in marriage a crime (an earlier proposal extended immunity from prosecution to men raping women with whom they live in a de facto relationship) and, amongst other matters, introducing an extensive definition of what consent is *not* where acts of sexual aggression against women are in issue. The definition incorporates provisions proposed by the Women's Electoral Lobby in its 1976/1978 *Draft Bill on Sexual Offences* and associated law reform proposals, see Appendix II, *Rape Law Reform*, p. 265.]

This is not because I deny the right of women to march in protest, and/or in mourning for women raped in war. It is because I believe that Anzac Day signifies so clearly everything that is masculine about Australian society – indeed about the world – that to participate in any way in an Anzac Day march is to participate in the glorification of war.

Why do women protesting or mourning women raped in all wars march *toward* a symbol of patriarchal damage and glory – which is what the "shrine of remembrance" is? Why should *women* march toward such a symbol – in Melbourne or in Sydney, an even more obviously phallic protrusion in Martin Place – to lay a wreath in parody of armies laying wreaths?

What does the day symbolise? What do the ceremonies symbolise? What do the male erections – be they named shrines of remembrance, cenotaphs, or memorials – symbolise? Do women want to be associated with those symbols? Indeed, *can* we be associated with them?

Anzac Day symbolises "the birth of a nation". On that day, what is celebrated is Australia's "coming of age". According to the pundits – and the message has become inextricably entwined with that day and the ceremony – Anzac Day was the day upon which Australia and Australians gained a maturity which entitled "us" to call ourselves a nation. The war at Gallipoli was a disaster. It was a disaster in human terms, in tactical terms. Men were killed. Any "heroism" related to men trying to save their mates from the bullets, or plunging on in terrain that was impossible, to inevitable death. It was an exercise in madness of a particularly male kind. Those who gave the orders (interestingly enough, at the head of the order-giving was that old "hero" of a later war, Churchill) lived to make war again.

Anzac Day is an important symbol – and a clever symbol in patriarchal terms. It combines the male ideal of heroism with the worst form of sentimentality. The day can appeal to women on the basis of loss, death, failure, sorrow, horror – all of which women have no trouble identifying with. No doubt that is why the protests against women marching on Anzac Day for women raped in war come not only from men, but from women – and sometimes most vehemently from women.

In Canberra, since the protests by feminists began, an Anzac Day that was dying with the aging of soldiers who found a strong and important symbol in that day, has revived with a vengeance. Today, scouts and guides have joined the march at the invitation of the RSL hierarchy. What are these scouts and guides learning about Australia, about society, about Anzac Day and about the protesting women who are surely depicted to them in the most negative light possible? A whole new generation which might hopefully have been lost to Anzac Day is now growing up with an RSL view of the day. In Canberra, women are now "allowed" to lay a wreath – as long as they do it before the "real" march begins – or after it ends.

How can laying a wreath on a symbol of male warfare and killing, and a glorification of war and killing (or a horrible sentimentality about war and killing that is almost as bad – if not worse) mourn women raped in war? Bruce Ruxton is reported as saying feminists should pick another day for marching and wreath-laying, when a lot of rape victims have been ravaged, and make that our day. Certainly we could pick any day and find there were "lots of rape victims". We could march on Mother's Day, for women raped in marriage. Father's Day, for women raped by their fathers. Australia Day for women raped by the colonial invaders. Hiroshima Day for women raped by the winners of Nobel Prizes. Good Friday, Easter Day, Easter Sunday and Christmas Day for women raped by religious bigots.

The problem is that women could find every reason for marching on every day for women raped in war and in so-called peace time.

Surely, male celebratory days are not meaningful in a feminist way for women. Just as women do not have to go to prison to be raped, women do not have to live through war to be raped. The male dichotomy which divides space and time in accordance with terms like "war", "prison", "coming of age", "realisation of nationhood" has no relationship to women's activity, time, space, being.

If we are concerned about the issue of rape, it would make more sense to protest rape on days when we know thousands of women are being raped, have been raped, will be raped ... all day, every day. There is no special day for women and rape. If we choose to march on Anzac Day for this purpose, and alone on that day, we are being subsumed into a time/space dimension that has been chosen by men and defined by men. Talk of our redefining it does not make sense – because its entire rationale is masculine; it is wholly linked with masculine meaning. The choice for the celebration is theirs; the rationale of the day is theirs; it is *their* Day; with *their* meaning. If they let us march on that day, even lay wreaths, it is their day we are joining. We cannot convince ourselves we are creating our own.

Women don't have a "One Day of the Year".

10

WOMAN AS PROPERTY:
Prostitution, Pornography
and Sexist Advertising

FEMINIST IN RESIDENCE, KEYNOTE SPEECH
Women's Studies Summer Institute, Deakin University, Geelong, Victoria
14–26 January 1990

On 13 August 1984 I made my first public speech on the issue of pornography.[1] Prior to that time, I had spoken publicly, on the radio, television and in the press, against the sexual objectification of women which is pornography. When invited to speak at "Speaking the Truth About Pornography", a public meeting in Canberra, I was well aware of the extended risk of being labelled "sexually repressed" and "sexually repressive". There is no doubt that when women speak out against pornography, some people are poised to brand us as what we are not: "right wing" moralists, determined to stop "people" from "having a good time". What we know is that women are not having a good time in pornography and because of it. And if a few women profess they are, there is a bigger question here. What of the right of all women not to be oppressed by images of women which subjugate, demean, humiliate and too often physically injure the women on the screen, who are the "images", at the same time as locking all women in to stereotypical notions of womanhood, ideas of being "women" that are injurious to us all.

It was the need for a feminist view to be put publicly that made me accept the invitation to speak at "Speaking the Truth About Pornography". This too is what makes

---

1. "Women and Pornography" was the title of the paper I presented at the public meeting held in Canberra, ACT, on 13 August 1984. On 28 August 1985 I presented another paper, "Pornography: How Civil? Whose Liberties?" to the ANZ Society of Criminology Conference in Melbourne, Victoria, and an edited version of this paper was presented by me to the Annual General Meeting of VACRO (Victorian Association for the Care and Rehabilitation of Offenders) on 21 November 1988, also in Melbourne. A shorter version was published as "Putting Porn in Check" in *Cinema Papers*, March 1987, Issue 62, p. 22. The ideas in these papers were combined, together with new material, for the Keynote Speech "Woman as Property: Prostitution, Pornography and Sexist Advertising". In the footnotes, square brackets [...] indicate new material added for this edition.

me continue to speak out. As Feminist in Residence at the 1990 Women's Studies Summer Institute at Deakin University, I chose to speak on "Woman as Property", arguing against the silencing of women's voices where pornography is in issue. It is ironic that our speaking out against the censoring of ourselves as women is in turn labelled "censorship". How women's speaking publicly against the vilification of women can be said to interfere with other people's freedoms is difficult to fathom. Or is it? The problem here is that one group, the dominant group seeking to retain power, wishes not to acknowledge another group – the 52 per cent who are women – as human beings with equal rights. "Freedoms" that are contingent upon violating the fundamental human right of bodily and psychic integrity, the right not to be violated, are not freedoms at all; they are aggressions.

As soon as a woman speaks out against the sexual vilification of women, she is accused of censorship. On one hand, this is a diversionary tactic, designed to avoid the very issue women seek to address: why are women's bodies used so frequently to sell products, to add "titillation" to movies; why are women's bodies so often the target of sexual violence in film? Certainly men are targets of film violence – Rambo is one of the categories of film which speaks so well of the way racism and ethnophobia can be promulgated in "action movies". At the same time, men are not generally violated and abused in sexual ways. The violence they suffer on the screen may be punching, hitting, kicking, shooting, bombing and other warlike means of destruction. But it is not directed to them in the sexualising way that violence is directed against women in film.

It is virtually impossible to think of any film where violence against women has occurred, and the violence has not been directly connected, or at least associated, with the fact that she is a woman; her sexuality is the target of the violence. As women, we get used to seeing ourselves on screen as targets of male violence; we get used to seeing ourselves in film as sexually objectified; we get used to seeing ourselves in the movies as sexual beings – one-dimensional, and that dimension is there to provide the "love interest", or the "reason" for a man's aggression and violence, or to utter the obligatory squeals – even shouts – and cries of sexual arousal that indicate to all that the man (who maintains a powerful silence or, at most, discreet, manly grunts, whilst she squeals and shouts and cries) is a real man – in control.

Since writing "Women as Property" I have argued that a sexual vilification law should be incorporated into the federal Sex Discrimination Act and state and territory equal opportunity, anti-discrimination and sex discrimination legislation. This law would provide that woman vilification is unlawful, stating:

It is unlawful for a person, by a public act, to incite hatred towards, serious contempt for, or severe ridicule of, a person or group of persons on the ground of the sex of the person or members of the group.[2]

---

2. These provisions are based directly on the New South Wales race vilification sections of the *Anti Discrimination Act* 1977 (ss. 20B, 20C and 20D).

The draft law then states that a person:

... shall not, by a public act, incite hatred towards, serious contempt for, or severe ridicule of, a person or group of persons on the ground of the sex of the person or members of the group by means which include:

a. *threatening physical harm towards, or towards any property of, the person or group of persons; or*

b. *inciting others to threaten physical harm towards, or towards any property of, the person or group of persons.*

"Public act" is defined to include:

a. *any form of communication to the public, including speaking, writing, printing, displaying notices, broadcasting, telecasting, screening and playing of tapes or other recorded material; and*

b. *any conduct (not being a form of communication referred to in paragraph [a] observable by the public, including actions and gestures and the wearing or display of clothing, signs, flags, emblems and insignia; and*

c. *the distribution or dissemination of any matter to the public with knowledge that the matter promotes or expresses hatred towards, serious contempt for, or severe ridicule of, a person or group of persons on the ground of the sex of the person or members of the group.*

Public acts are not unlawful as sex vilification where they amount to:

a. *a fair report of a public act inciting hatred towards, serious contempt for, or severe ridicule of, a person or group of persons on the ground of the sex of the person or members of the group; or*

b. *a communication or the distribution or dissemination of any matter which is subject to a defence of absolute privilege in proceedings for defamation; or*

c. *a public act, done reasonably and in good faith, for academic, artistic, scientific or research purposes or for other purposes in the public interest, including discussion or debate about and expositions of any act or matter.*

Racial vilification is outlawed in some Australian jurisdictions and laws are proposed in others.[3] For many women, racial vilification is combined with sexual vilification. For all women, sexual vilification is a reality that damages and distorts our lives.

---

3. In 1989 New South Wales amended its *Anti Discrimination Act* to insert Division 3A – Racial Vilification. In 1992 debate took place in Victoria and at federal level as to the incorporation into the *Equal Opportunity Act* 1984 (Vic.) and the *Racial Discrimination Act* 1975 (Cth) of race vilification provisions. It appears that with the change of government in Victoria in October 1992 race vilification legislation will not be proceeded with, as the present Liberal government does not favour it. Western Australia makes racist vilification an offence under the criminal law.

In 1983 in Minneapolis, Minnesota, a woman named Linda Marchiano appeared before a City Council hearing to testify about the abuse she had suffered at the hands of her husband, Chuck Traynor. She described a life that began with enforced prostitution, progressed through enforced participation in group sex, bashings, beatings and marital rape – and ended with her escape. In her book, *Ordeal*, she wrote:

Often I am asked why I didn't escape [earlier]. Behind that question there's an attitude, a presumption. I can see it in the face asking the question. The questioner always has the sure knowledge that this could never happen to him or to her. They would have been strong enough and smart enough and resourceful enough to have gotten away ... Once, during a grand jury hearing in California, I was asked the question point-blank: "How come you never got away?"

And I answered point-blank: "Because it's kind of hard to get away when there's a gun pointed at your head."

There was always a gun pointed at my head. Even when no gun could be seen, there was a gun pointed at my head. I can understand why some people have such trouble accepting this as the truth. When I was younger, when I heard about a woman being raped, my secret feeling was that that could never happen to me. I would never *permit* it to happen. Now I realised that can be about as meaningful as saying I won't allow an earthquake or I won't permit an avalanche ...

At first I was certain that god would help me escape but in time my faith was shaken. I became more and more frightened, scared of everything. The very thought of trying to escape was terrifying. I had been degraded every possible way, stripped of all dignity, reduced to an animal and then to a vegetable. Whatever strength I had began to disappear. Simple survival took everything; making it all the way to tomorrow was victory.[4]

Linda Marchiano will no doubt be recognised more readily by the film name of her past – "Linda Lovelace". The film for which she is renowned is *Deep Throat*. Her husband was her "agent".

In 1973 when I was at university in the United States, *Deep Throat* played to a picture theatre audience of some 600 university students, two nights running. The queue of students waiting to enter the theatre wound around two blocks, with the temperature standing at less than 10 degrees fahrenheit. As they waited, male and female students laughed with each other about the erotic fantasies they thought they would see. At the Minneapolis hearings in 1983, Linda Marchiano testified to the force and coercion to which she was subjected in the making of that film. She told of two years of confinement by Chuck Traynor, while he forced her into prostitution and pornography through beatings, constant sexual terrorism and abuse, psychological brutality, and threats to her life and the lives of members of her family. Her story was unusual, she said, only because she survived to tell it.

Recording Linda Marchiano's testimony, Diane Barkey writes:

Many women forced into prostitution and pornography are killed. Those who survive are usually so damaged and terrorised they cannot speak about it, or if they do speak, they are not believed.

---

4. Linda Marchiano (with Mike O'Grady), *Ordeal*, 1980, Citadel Press, Secaucus. See also Gloria Steinem, "The Real Linda Lovelace" in *Outrageous Acts and Everyday Rebellions*, 1984, Jonathan Cape Ltd, London, p. 243.

[Linda] Marchiano described her struggle to use the legal system to hold those who abused her accountable, and to stop the pornography made from her coerced performances from being shown. She said that the [existing] statutes of limitations – [limits on] how soon after the injury an individual must file charges – do not reflect an understanding of the amount of damage sustained by a victim or the time it takes to rebuild her physical and psychological health to be able to begin legal proceedings.[5]

Linda Marchiano told the hearing that there is no way to use the law to stop products such as *Deep Throat* from being shown. She said:

... the fact that this film is still being shown and that my children will one day walk down the street and see their mother being abused makes me angry, makes me sad. Every time someone watches that film, they are watching me being raped.

What is the nature of a society which can allow this to happen – that leads to some people finding pleasure in watching a woman being raped on film? That produces human beings who are capable of exploiting women (and do) by forcing them to participate in sexual activity, filming their exploitation, canning the film and marketing it around the word? What is the nature of a society which provides no legal avenue of redress for a woman, forced into participating in pornographic "entertainment", so that the evidence of her exploitation and abuse can be withdrawn from the marketplace?

It is a world where courts have no definition of pornography, only a definition of obscenity, which is evidently a very different thing. The test for obscenity is:

... whether the tendency of the matter said to be obscene is to deprave and corrupt those whose minds are open to such immoral influences and into whose hands a publication of this sort may fall.[6]

So, if one is already depraved and corrupted, and it is only into the hands of the depraved and corrupted that an item falls, then that material is not obscene. It is not pornographic, whatever its content, however it depicts the woman appearing in it.

Our heritage is that of a world where obscenity is defined as "appealing to the prurient interest" – titillating, sexually provocative, tempting. Yet this in itself confirms there is something amiss: the very material which is the most sexually violent, the most exploitative of women, could hardly fall within this prohibiting definition. Or if it does – if men are tempted, provoked, titillated by pictures of women bound, gagged, bleeding, wounded, open to sexual display and smiling, smiling, smiling through the agony as if we liked it – if that is what is sexually stimulating to men, then the hope that the exploitation of women may be eradicated can hardly be

---

5. See Andrea Dworkin and Catharine MacKinnon (eds.), *Pornography and Sexual Violence – Evidence of the Links*, 1988, Everywoman Pty Ltd, London.
6. *R. v. Hicklin* [1968] LR 3 QB 360; see also *Roth v. United States* 354 US 476 (1957), 487 per Justice Brennan – pornography is that which "appeals to prurient interest".

realised. The nature of such a society arises out of a patriarchal inheritance. Our heritage is that of a world which encourages male domination of women.

What are the countervailing arguments in the pornography debate? One asserts a concern for women, in the same way that arguments supporting the selling of women's bodies through prostitution purport to support women: the notion that if we do not enable men to have sexual access to prostitutes, we will become victims of rape; that if we do not enable men to view pornography, then men's "natural urges" will erupt into sexual violence against real, live women. The underlying threat seems to be: "Allow your sisters to suffer exploitation and degradation in pornographic depictions and allow your bodies to be paraded vicariously on screen in writhing agonies of sexual display – or else, ladies, you will suffer those indignities, that exploitation and degradation of your own bodies. Let us own their bodies, lest we own yours."

But this argument does not protect any woman from exploitation. Through the assertion of ownership of the bodies of women as prostitutes, or ownership of the bodies of women depicted on the screen, is derived (and reinforced) the notion that all women's bodies are there for the taking, there to be owned, commodities to be bought. And contrary to another view, it is not women who sell our bodies: it is the male pimps, brothel owners, makers of the movies, agents, who sell women's bodies to men as customers, clients, film goers, television viewers.

Another argument revolves around the privacy of the home. Here, one sector of society states that viewing pornographic material in the privacy of one's own home is and should be acceptable; it is not, say this group, for the state to intrude upon the hearth to enforce standards; what a person looks at in his own home is for him alone to determine. For the other side, the argument is that allowing pornographic videos and films into private homes grants the possibility that children may view them: children are the great television watchers of the age; how are they to know that a video cassette lying innocently on the table-top contains graphic depictions of violence against women? Children may inadvertently view pornographic films and videos at home, or in someone else's home. Children may be tempted into viewing a private video library of pornography, lured by the stealth that surrounds it.

How much validity is there in the "privacy of the home" proposition? This is the argument used by some in our society to bolster the idea that there should be no intervention in the home when women are raped, battered, bashed and abused by their husbands. Notably, when Linda Marchiano spoke of her years of pornographic coercion, the crimes she cited involved rape, bashing, beating – by her own husband, in her own home. The final outcome was that she was forced to make a pornographic film that has gained notoriety both inside and outside her own country.

No human being should be forced to endure abuse – whether it be the physical abuse involved in rape and wife-beating, or the psychological abuse in being forced to look at pornographic videos, or to live in one's own home without the freedom to move about in it, because the television room is out of bounds. When some people talk of the privacy of the home, they omit to recall that, unless it is a single-person household, there are other human beings with equal rights of enjoyment of the homeground.

A second argument with alleged civil liberties underpinnings is that of freedom of speech. One side declares that it is an individual's right to speak as he wishes, to read and view what he wishes; that the state has no right to restrict that freedom. The opposing side states that there is some material so offensive that it should not be available for anyone to read or to view; that it should not be depicted. Some on this side restrict the banning approach to material involving child pornography, or material being disseminated to children. (Under present federal laws, child pornography is banned from entering Australia.)[7]

Yet when alleged civil libertarians protest about freedom of speech in defence of conglomerates to peddle pornography; or of a newsagent to load his shelves with magazines depicting women as lumps of flesh with no name, no personality, no autonomy – as commodities; or of a cinema to show endless streams of women writhing in agony on the screen, a smile on their lying lips; or of a video pirate to sell his wares in a street market, their voices are almost drowned out in the clinking and chinking of money, the swish of $100 bills.

Back in the days of restrictive censorship in Australia, which have nothing to recommend them, despite any restrictions the speech of the pornography peddlers continued. They whispered in blue movie houses. They spoke through magazines mailed in brown covers. They shouted through profitable avenues of bucks parties, porno movie nights. As Gloria Steinem reports:

In the United States the last screening of a snuff movie showing a real murder was traced to the monthly pornographic film showings of a senior partner in a respected law firm; an evening regularly held by him for a group of friends including other lawyers and judges.[8]

The freedom of speech of the purveyors of pornography will never be at risk, as long as we live in a society that glorifies the domination of men and enforces the subordination of women.

But there is a third aspect of the freedom of speech debate that is little spoken of. That is the right of persons who traditionally have been silenced, to speak. The freedom of speech which is threatened in the pornography debate is the freedom of those who would want to protest against the exploitation of women and whose demonstrations are the subject of physical attack by male onlookers, and of other forms of abuse. The freedom of speech that is at risk is that of women seeking to protest who do not have the funds of the conglomerates and who are unable to market non-sexist films and other non-sexist materials; worse, who are not able to make non-sexist films and videos, because they do not have the money, or do not have the training – because they did not have the educational and work training advantages of their male counterparts –

---

7. *Customs Act* 1960 (Cth).
8. Gloria Steinem, "Erotica vs. Pornography" in *Outrageous Acts and Everyday Rebellions*, note 4, p. 230.

or if they do have the training, discrimination in the workplace denies them the right to inject their own non-sexist views into the world of "free speech".

Positive action is being taken, through the efforts of women, to remedy the lack of freedom and lack of rights women possess. Sex discrimination, anti-discrimination, equal opportunity and affirmative action legislation have been introduced at state level and federally, or are projected, in the private and public sectors; efforts are being made in the education of women and girls. These are a beginning, although there are many backward steps too. Even these beginnings are fraught. The loading against women's right to speak out against the degradation and exploitation inherent in sexist literature and film and advertising is not neutralised by legislating for equal opportunity. Our sheer inability in terms of access to the media and to other channels to protest against the sexist magazines and movies which culminate in pornographic films and video impedes our speech and our right to be heard. Affirmative action does not extend to accessing television, radio and the press. It is women's freedom to speak out that is more than at risk. In many cases it simply does not exist, just as women's right to speak out against physical abuse inflicted directly upon her is inhibited by lack of support in a society that condones that violence. And in Australia, until the 1980s, women were seen as having no right to speak out against rape where the rapist is a husband: his acts were, until the late 1980s (when finally Queensland recognised rape in marriage as unlawful), in traditional interpretations of Australian *Crimes Acts* and in *Criminal Codes* and their equivalents elsewhere, above the law. Should the woman speak out, no court would hear her.[9]

In talking about privacy and freedom it is odd that, where women are concerned, the words are most often used where they involve the real or potential exploitation of women's bodies and sexuality. Those talking about "freedom" in the pornography context talk about a woman's right to participate in prostitution or in pornographic movies. But what is the validity of the professed choice women have, in a country where women still earn only 66.7 per cent of men's pay (where women earn any money at all), despite decisions allegedly securing equal pay for women. The truth is that many women are forced into prostitution or pornography through economic reality or through physical brutality.

Andrea Dworkin has noted:

... the bitter fact that the only time that equality is considered a value in this society is in a situation where some extremely degrading transaction is being rationalised. And the only time that freedom is considered important to women as such is when we're talking about the freedom to prostitute oneself in one way or another.[10]

---

9. On rape in marriage and the law, see Jocelynne A. Scutt, "Consent in Rape – The Problem of the Marriage Contract" (1977) 3 *Mon. Law Rev.* 255.

10. Andrea Dworkin, quoted Gena Corea, *The Mother Machine*, 1985, Harper and Row, New York. The immediately following quotation comes from the same source.

The "freedom for women" argument is conspicuously absent in the speeches of establishment people when they are talking about other aspects of women's life. "You never hear the freedom to choose to be a surgeon held forth with any conviction as a choice women should have, a choice related to freedom," Dworkin says:

Feminists make that argument and it is, in the common parlance, not a "sexy" argument. Nobody pays any attention to it. And the only time you hear institutional people – people who represent and are a part of the establishment – discuss woman's equality or woman's freedom is in the context of equal rights to prostitution, equal rights to some form of selling of the body, selling of the self, something that is unconscionable in any circumstance, something where there usually is no analogy with men but a specious analogy is being made.

The state has constructed the social, economic and political reality in which the sale of some sexual capacity is necessary to the survival of the woman. It fixes her social place so that her sex capacity is a commodity, says Dworkin.

The civil libertarians endorse the establishment position by loudly professing the individual woman's right to choose to sell her body in this way. Do the civil libertarians of the establishment with equal force profess the right of women to express our own sexuality in an autonomous way? Do the pornographers profess this right of women? It is the civil libertarians who clamour against reforms to rape law to grant women victims and survivors of rape equal status in the legal system with victims of other crimes. Their argument is that the rights of rapists are in danger, if the rights of women victims are raised to the level of all other victims in the criminal justice system. The pornographers clamour effectively in favour of rape; as women escaping from pornographic confinement tell, the reality of their so-called consensual participation in pornographic movies is rape and sexual coercion. The pornographers clamour loudly for films depicting women participating endlessly in sexual contortions with men, and clamour equally for films depicting women participating endlessly in sexual contortions with women. But their aim is not to grant women sexual freedom. Rather, it is to commoditise women's bodies and women's sexuality. Their very aim is to provide voyeuristic "experiences" for men viewers, not to enable women to have the freedom to have, nor to enjoy, autonomous sexual relationships with persons of the same or opposite sex.

The individual woman, whom the pornographer and establishment civil libertarians use as the means of supporting their argument for men's free access to pornography is, as Andrea Dworkin points out, a fiction:

... as is her will – since individuality is precisely what women are denied when they are defined and used as a sex class. As long as the issues of female sexual destiny are posed as if they are resolved by individuals as individuals, there is no way to confront the actual conditions that perpetuate the sexual exploitation of women.[11]

---

11. Andrea Dworkin, note 10.

Gloria Steinem says:

The problem is there is so much pornography. This underground stream of anti-woman propaganda that exists in all male-dominated societies has now become a flood in our streets and theatres and even our homes. There is hardly a news-stand without women's bodies in chains and bondage, in full labial display for the conquering male viewer, bruised or on our knees, screaming in real or pretended pain, pretending to enjoy what we don't enjoy. The same images are in mainstream movie theaters ... they are brought into our own homes not only in magazines, but in the new form of video cassettes. Even video games offer such features as a smiling, ropebound woman and a male figure with an erection, the game's object being to rape the woman as many times as possible ...

[But] perhaps that's better in the long run. Women can no longer pretend pornography does not exist. We must either face our own humiliation and torture every day on magazine covers and television screens or fight back.[12]

And so – what are we to do about it? How do we fight back? There are avenues of demonstration, making our own non-sexist films with the resources we have, taking action against sexist advertising as women in the film industry are currently doing, continuing our activism in the political arena and the workplace: for the upgrading of women's work and skills, and the acknowledgment of women's work and women's right to equal pay and equal access to jobs. The law can also be used. Laws must be changed to address the harm done to women in the making, distribution, and consumption of pornography. Andrea Dworkin and Catharine MacKinnon point out that since pornography is central in creating and maintaining women's inferior social status, it is a form of sex discrimination, a practice infringing on the civil rights of women. It is necessary to take a new, civil rights based, legal approach. A definition of pornography as sex discrimination must be included in equal opportunity and anti-discrimination legislation, and the *Sex Discrimination Act* 1984, to provide that material which emphasises the explicit subordination of women in a dehumanising way as sexual objects, grants a right of action for legal claims. The definition of pornography to be included in the Act should be that pornography is:

... the sexually explicit subordination of women, graphically depicted whether in pictures or in words, that also includes one or more of the following:
* women are presented dehumanised as sexual objects, things or commodities; or
* women are presented as sexual objects who enjoy pain or humiliation; or
* women are presented as sexual objects who experience sexual pleasure in being raped; or
* women are presented as sexual objects tied up or cut up or mutilated or bruised or physically hurt; or
* women are presented in postures of sexual submission or sexual servility, including by inviting penetration; or
* women's body parts – including but not limited to vaginas, breasts, and buttocks – are exhibited, such that women are reduced to those parts; or

---

12. Gloria Steinem, "Erotica vs. Pornography", note 8, pp. 222–223.

- women are presented as whores by nature; or
- women are presented being penetrated by objects or animals; or
- women are presented in scenarios of degradation, injury, or torture, shown as contaminated or inferior, bleeding, bruised, or hurt in a context that makes these conditions sexual.[13]

Excluded from the definition is erotica that does not rely on the dynamic of submission and domination, but is based on sexual equality.

If material meets the definition of pornography, the Act should provide four legal claims of discrimination:

1. *Coercion into performing for pornography*

   Women coerced into performing for pornography would have a cause of action against the makers, sellers, exhibitors, or distributers of pornography. Redress would be in the form of damages, elimination of the products of the coerced performances from public view, or both.

2. *Forcing pornography on a person*

   Women who have had pornography forced upon them would have a cause of action against the perpetrator.

3. *Assault or physical attack due to pornography*

   Women who are assaulted, attacked, or injured in a way that is caused by a specific example of pornography could seek damages from the maker, distributor, seller, or exhibitor of the material.

4. *Trafficking in pornography*

   Any woman or group of women could bring a complaint against traffickers in pornography as a woman acting against the subordination of women.

These new remedies would exist alongside any already existing criminal remedies – for example, sexual assault or rape legislation.

---

13. For an outline of the Dworkin/MacKinnon proposal, upon which this section is directly based, see Catharine MacKinnon "Not a Moral Issue" (1984) *Yale Law and Policy Review* 321; also published as "Pornography – Not a Moral Issue" (1985) 8 *Women's Studies International Forum* 106. See also "Is One Woman's Sexuality Another Woman's Pornography? It's the Question Behind the Newest Legal Battle Facing the Country" in *Ms. Magazine*, April 1985. [I now use the term "vilification of women" in preference to "pornography". The definition of "pornography" given here could be incorporated into a definition of "vilification of women". Vilification of women is more descriptive, as a term, of what we complain about as pornography. The latter term is imbued with masculine meanings and has such a potential for misunderstanding. Much of this misunderstanding is deliberate obfuscation and often extends to attempted harassment of women speaking out against the vilification of women. It is deliberate on the part of pornographers and supporters of pornography who wish to continue doing what they are doing: making lots of money, and vilifying women by confusing (or attempting to confuse) the issues. Rather than enter into a debate about what is, or is not, "pornography", it may be better to speak of the vilification of women which is less susceptible to the "double speak" of pornographers and their supporters.]

Advantages of this Approach

This approach means:

- by providing an avenue of action and redress for women whose rights have been infringed by pornography, the state declares clearly that pornography does not have state sanction;
- by providing a right in the person whose liberties have been infringed, the law maintains its concern for the autonomy of women;
- by providing a right in the person whose liberties have been infringed, the role of the state in enforcing standards is limited to the rights of that individual and others in the group "women" – it is for the woman or group discriminated against to decide whether or not the subject of complaint meets the standards, and on that basis to approach the legal system for redress;
- complaints about pornography are made in the public arena and standards are not enforced by administrative measures that are not open to public view, or are not as open to public view as the courts;
- if women believe that the outcome of any case which goes through the tribunals, boards or courts is wrong, then women maintain the right to protest against the decision, by explicitly describing to the public the nature of the pornographic exploitation and showing how out of touch with feminist standards courts and tribunals are.

The feminist approach to ending pornography is premised on feminist principles. As Dale Spender has said:

Feminism is based on values, on values of self identity, responsibility, autonomy, equality and the absence of dominance, coercion and oppression. Understandings which do not respect these values, no matter from whom they emanate, are not tolerated.[14]

Sexual Harassment

It may be argued that courts are not friendly places for women and we do not control the standards enforced therein, so such an approach will not work. There are many responses to this argument, which is designed to deprive women of the will to take action. I would not profess to believe that courts are woman-friendly, nor friendly to any subordinate or oppressed group. Nor is the law. But nor is any institution existing in our current society. Do we therefore give up and bow down to all existing institutions, confessing our inability to change them or use them?

On the contrary, to overcome the subordination of women, we must, simultaneously with working outside the system, use those institutions already existing to shape a society where women can be truly autonomous. In this world, no one will own women,

---

14. Dale Spender, *For the Record*, 1985, The Women's Press, London, p. 203.

nor women's bodies, nor women's sexuality, nor women's sexual identity. Men will not own women's bodies. Women will not be property. We as women will not *own* our own bodies. Rather, there will be a recognition that *we are our bodies ourselves* and minds.

If there were no legal system, in society as it is now, would women be better off? The answer surely cannot be "yes". Although the legal system does not usually advance our cause, at minimum rules exist within that system which profess to live up to standards of justice and fairness. The rules may be unfair. They may be manipulated. They may be used against us. But rules may be changed. And in the world outside the courtroom, where no rules exist, women are not better off. Within the legal system it is also true that sometimes, the rules may be used in favour of oppressed groups. It is foolish to assume that the legal system is so blindly monolithic that it admits of no "errors" where the subordinated group actually wins.

An example closely paralleling that of pornography (and overlapping with it at some levels) is sexual harassment on the job. In the past it was asserted that women protesting sexual harassment of themselves and others were "wowsers" or "killjoys". Some called the protestors "god's police". Feminists were regarded as without humour, not able to understand "a bit of fun", and determined to ruin working relationships, setting men against women and women against men. Yet this approach to sexual harassment has not been able to surface of late with any real public support or respectability. One might ask why. One reason most assuredly is that in various states in Australia and federally, sex discrimination and equal opportunity legislation has been interpreted or drafted to include sexual harassment as sex discrimination. Around Australia, cases have been fought – and won – on this very issue. Sexual harassment is seen as a legitimate legal problem demanding redress, and women receive damages in response to tribunal rulings that they have been sexually harassed at work.

Even with the infamous *Loder case* in New South Wales, where the Commissioner for Main Roads, Mr Loder, was found not to have sexually harassed an employee, a woman lift driver, the memory remaining with many men is that the matter was cause for alarm, in that it went through a public hearing for days.[15] Can anyone imagine Mr Loder, Commissioner for Main Roads and sometime alleged sexual harasser was, whatever the outcome of the case before the Equal Opportunity Tribunal, free to sexually harass female employees of the Main Roads Department? How many men were affected by that case, so that they now harbour a real fear of having action taken, should they decide to impose themselves sexually upon a female employee? And has it resulted in a breakdown of friendliness (in the real sense of the word) in the paid workplace?

There can be no illusions. It would be ridiculous to imagine that sexual harassment will cease simply because of a few cases and attendant publicity. Nonetheless there is no going backwards, and something has been gained. Women have an avenue of

---

15. *O'Callaghan v. Loder* (1984) EOC 92-023.

redress previously not open. Although sexual harassment is covered by criminal laws and civil laws providing for suing the harasser, these avenues are little used. Equal opportunity and sex discrimination legislation provide a clear statement in the law that sexual harassment is unacceptable conduct and that those carrying on in this way open themselves to legal action, taken by women ourselves, asserting women's right to engage in paid work free of harassment – our right to autonomy.

Sexist Advertising and Soapies

There is every reason to believe that the cause of equal rights for women will be advanced if a definition of pornography is included in sex discrimination legislation. Feminists do not want or need censorship, which allows others to impose sexual standards, standards over which it is certain feminists would have no control. What women need is forums in which our right not to be regarded nor treated as property can be expressed. We need public platforms inside and outside the legal arena where we can speak out loudly against the exploitation of women through pictorial depictions. Surely this is what freedom of speech means.

There is no doubt other wrongs require redress. Oppression of women is not manufactured through pornography alone. Ownership of women is not expressed solely through pornography. Other pictorial depictions are equally harmful: sexist advertising; that women appear in foolish guises in soap opera; that women less often read serious news (although this is changing); and that women are used in trivial roles in the media generally. We must fight back against sexism in magazines such as *Pix* and *People* as well as *Penthouse* and *Playboy*. As an example of the notion of ownership, of women being represented as commodities in these magazines, promotions in *The Picture* have included:

- a poster of a large-breasted blonde woman with a gun to her temple and the headline: "Buy this magazine or we shoot this girl [*sic*]";
- a competition to match photographs of women's naked bottoms to their faces "and win $1,000";
- a cover photograph of a woman with three breasts (faked).

The editor of this magazine, and editors of the *Post*, *Pix* and *People*, are described by a (male) journalist in these words:

[They are] four men in their 40s. Whatever you think of their publications, they are all highly skilled and highly inventive journalists.[16]

The level of journalism exhibited by those who are not "highly skilled" hardly bears thinking about.

---

16. Richard Glover, "Full-Frontal Farce", *Good Weekend* (accompanying *Age* and *Sydney Morning Herald*), 5–6 December 1989, p. 20.

Conclusion

What remains astonishing and at the same time instructive in this world of owning women is that whenever women speak out against the sexual oppression of women, the charge laid at our door is that we are engaging in sexual oppression of men, arising out of our own alleged sexual repression. We live in a world where the liberation of women – the lifting of women's sexual oppression – is viewed by the dominant group, men, as an encroachment on their liberties. We live in a world where women's repression is bound up with the "liberation" of men. Their liberty to do as they want, with and to women and women's bodies, is seen as at risk when feminists protest women's right not to be done to. This risk is seen in feminists protesting against the using of women's bodies as objects and receptacles, whether the using is of ourselves – *our* bodies, or the real bodies of women depicted on the screen and who represent *all* women. The civil liberties of women are inextricably interwoven with the civil liberties of men. The traditional (male) view of their own civil liberties is a view denying women freedom of speech and freedom to define our own sexuality so as to be sexual subjects rather than sexual objects. These sexual objects grotesquely fill the porno movie houses, the blue videos, the sexist advertising screens. These pornographic depictions picture and mirror our world. They provide a view centred in the notion that women's bodies are for owning, when they are – we are – ourselves.

Ultimately, the wrongs of violence against women, the exploitation of women, the ownership of women, will be ended only when patriarchal values cease to order the way of life lived the world over. Only then will the buyers of pornography cease to buy, the sellers cease to sell, and the makers cease to make. Only when the value system promoting woman as a sex object to be bought, bartered, used and abused is ended, will women become what women can truly be. Only when that system, which simultaneously promotes the equally undesired reverse – woman as paragon on a pedestal – ceases to be, will women be ourselves. It is only then that a vision of woman as equal with man, as equally worthy, will become the reality, and pornography and the notion of woman as property cease to be.

11

WHAT IS A WOMAN'S LIFE WORTH?
In 1989 Australia – Not Much
(Except to Us)

SPEECH PRESENTED TO COMMEMORATION EVENT FOR WOMEN AND CHILDREN
WHO HAVE LOST THEIR LIVES AT THE HANDS OF THE MAN IN THEIR LIVES
Melbourne Town Hall, Victoria
31 May 1989

The Domestic Violence and Incest Resource Centre, located in Melbourne, Australia, has played an important role in counselling victims and survivors of these crimes and raising community awareness of the facts and the issues surrounding them. When the centre began the "Family Murders Project" I had discussions with workers about the project generally, and its progress. In mid-1988 we discussed the possibility of holding an inquest to highlight the number of unlawful killings occurring in households, or upon the breakup of households, the killers being husbands, de facto husbands, boyfriends or ex-husbands, ex-de facto husbands or ex-boy"friends" of the woman killed, and men in a paternal role to the children whose lives they so abruptly brought to an end. In the upshot, the centre organised a Commemoration Event to celebrate and to mourn the murderously shortened lives of women and children killed, and to condemn the killing.

Speakers included relatives of women whose "loved" ones had ended their lives. One woman spoke of the fears she harboured, as a child, when her father went to prison for manslaughter, having killed his wife – her mother. Her overwhelming fear was that upon his release from gaol her father would claim custody of herself and her siblings. Another woman spoke of her sister's death, the killing carried out with a gun brought to the scene for the purpose, the shooting conducted in front of her sister's children. Her sister's killer, sentenced to a short term of years for manslaughter, not murder, was in the midst of claiming rights of access to the children – and making application for legal aid to enforce his "rights". Upon his release, he was granted legal aid to pursue a claim through the Family Court of Australia for the children's custody. He was deported to the country of his birth, protesting all the while about the injustice that was being done to him! A man spoke of his sister's killing, and the iniquities of the legal arguments about provocation that had reduced her death to manslaughter rather than murder. She had had the temerity to leave the man with whom she had been living, and to retain ownership of her own motor vehicle – both acts, apparently, of such moment as to qualify her killer for a conviction for manslaughter only, not murder. Oh – and she had (according to him) told him to "fuck off" immediately before he stabbed her with knives he had brought to the scene – the kindergarten where she worked. (Her family denied she would have used this expression – but even had she, what nonsense that any court would tolerate a notion that this should enable a man to argue he was provoked to kill.) Why had this man brought the knives? To slash the tyres of the car, he said. Why had he used them to end her life? "I was provoked," he said.

The Commemoration Event for Women and Children Who Have Lost their Lives at the Hands of the Man in their Lives was a strong public statement of support for unlawfully killed woman and children. It was a strong public statement against a society and a system that does not say stop. No more. Cease it. Stop it. End it. STOP.

This was a landmark in the fight-back, by women and children, survivors and supporters, against the brutality of men who are too often given imprimatur, by the legal system, to continue with their aggressive and cowardly acts. How long will it take courts of law to recognise the lives of women and children are equally important as those of men? How long will it take the legal system to acknowledge as the murderous activity it is, the acts of men who believe they have a right to "claim" their wives and children as their possessions – alive and dead?

All of us would prefer that such a commemoration would never have occasion to be held. In speaking at the event, I was pleased to be working together with women of determination and courage in their work and their lives, and who exhibited that same brave determination in the planning and execution of the Commemoration Event.[1]

WIFE FOR SALE –

Gentlemen, I have to offer to your notice my wife, Mary Anne Thomson, otherwise Williams, whom I mean to sell to the highest and fairest bidder. Gentlemen, it is her wish as well as mine to part for ever. She has been to me only a born serpent. I took her for my comfort, and the good of my home; but she became my tormentor, a domestic curse, a night invasion, and a daily devil.

Gentlemen, I speak the truth from my heart when I say – may God deliver us from troublesome wives and frolicsome women! Avoid them as

---

1. "What is a Woman's Life Worth?" was presented in part in an extended version to a conference on Violence Against Women held at the YWCA in Adelaide, South Australia, in 1982, and organised by the Christies Beach Women's Collective. See generally Dawn Rowan, "Beware, Oh Take Care" in *Breaking Through – Women, Work and Careers*, Jocelynne A. Scutt (ed.), 1992, Artemis Publishing, Melbourne, p. 139. In the footnotes, square brackets [...] indicate new material added for this edition.

you would a mad dog, a roaring lion, a loaded pistol, cholera morbus, Mount Etna, or any other pestilential thing in nature.

Now I have told you her faults and failings, I will introduce the bright and sunny side of her, and explain her qualifications and goodness. She can read novels and milk cows; she can laugh and weep with the same ease that you could take a glass of ale when thirsty ... She can make butter and scold the maid; she can sing Moore's melodies, and plait her frills and caps; she cannot make rum, gin, or whisky, but she is a good judge of the quality from long experience in tasting them. I therefore offer her with all her perfections and imperfections, for the sum of fifty shillings ...

After waiting about an hour, Thomson knocked down the lot to one Henry Mears, for twenty shillings and a Newfoundland dog; they then parted in perfect good temper – Mears and the woman going one way, Thomson and the dog the other.

> Quoted from THE ANNUAL REGISTER for 1832
> in *The Book of Days*, 1886, by Robert Chambers

This – an excerpt from THE ANNUAL REGISTER for 1832, when women were bought and sold as chattels. It has no literal application in Australia today; figuratively, however, we are bound to acknowledge that women are still held in low regard in Australian society, and that women's lives are worth little, particularly within the home and in our courts, not least when women are criminally assaulted at home, and killed.

The anglo-Australian system of justice has always accorded men's lives greater value than the lives of women. The twelfth editor of *Blackstone's Commentaries*, the legal bible of the past, in 1793 commented upon the practice of terming a wife "femme", a husband "baron", saying that it is wrong to consider these terms "unmeaning" and "technical". He wrote:

... we [must] recollect that if the femme kills her baron, it is regarded by the laws as a much more atrocious crime; as she not only breaks through the restrainings of humanity and conjugal affection, but throws off all subjection to the authority of her husband. And therefore the law denominated her crime a species of treason, and condemns her to the same punishment as if she had killed the king. And for every species of treason (although in petit treason the punishment of men was only to be drawn and hanged) ... the sentence of women was to be drawn and burnt alive.[2]

It is no longer true that our system of justice holds a woman who kills her husband to be classifiable as guilty of petit treason, whilst a husband who kills his wife is a murderer only. However, when one looks beyond the simple statement of what the law is, to the issues underlying it and its application, it is not difficult to discover that different standards are applied against those who kill husbands and those who kill wives. At first glance, the law might appear to be neutral or egalitarian, but in interpretation and application it is not. This results in a differential treatment, still, of husband-killing and

---

2. *Blackstone's Commentaries*, 12th edn, 1793.

wife-killing. A woman is highly likely to be prosecuted for, and convicted of, murder. If prosecuted, a husband is likely to be prosecuted for manslaughter, rather than murder; or to be convicted of manslaughter, rather than murder.[3]

That the law acts differentially is illustrated well in analyses of the law relating to homicide. Where a person is prosecuted for murder, if it can be shown that the person acted in self-defence, then there will be no conviction: the accused is acquitted entirely. If it is shown that the accused acted in self-defence but used excessive force, or that the accused was provoked into killing, then the accused will be convicted of manslaughter only, not murder. This is highly relevant in states where the mandatory penalty for murder is life imprisonment, because if convicted of manslaughter only, the accused can be sentenced at the discretion of the judge – to a term of years, a bond, or whatever penalty the judge thinks appropriate; it will not be life imprisonment. In states like Victoria and New South Wales, where life imprisonment is not mandatory for murder, a conviction for manslaughter remains relevant to sentence. Because murder is a more serious crime than manslaughter, the man convicted of manslaughter rather than murder must, in the general scheme of things, receive a lesser penalty than he would if convicted of murder. The sentence is at the discretion of the judge, but the judge will have to take into account the conviction for manslaughter, not murder.

The classic case of provocation noted by the textbook writers is that of a man coming home to find his wife in the act of adultery with another man.[4] The question has never arisen in the courts of a woman coming home, finding her husband in the act of adultery, and killing him (or his lover). It might be that no woman has discovered her husband under those circumstances; that no woman is so aroused to passion at discovering her husband in these circumstances that she is minded to react and kill. It cannot be that no man commits adultery. The better assessment is that, should a wife return home to find her husband in the adulterous act, it is unrealistic to suppose she can whip out her trusty hunting knife and kill husband, adultress or both; or that she can retrieve her gun from the wardrobe and kill. The gun and hunting knife are likely to be somewhere in the house, but known to him, not her. So many men own guns (whether legally or illicitly) and hunting knives; few women do. If these implements were available to women many would be unable to use them at all, or with skill, through lack of training or self-confidence, or lack of will to kill by these methods, and in these circumstances. The knife and the gun will invariably be his, to use and abuse.[5]

---

3. See Jocelynne A. Scutt, *Even in the Best of Homes – Violence in the Family*, 1983, Penguin Books Australia, Ringwood, Chapter 7, "Marital Murder", pp. 174–88. [See further Jocelynne A. Scutt, *Even in the Best of Homes*, reprint 1990, Chapter 13, "The Politics of Violence", pp. 286–323; Patricia Easteal, *Killing the Beloved*, 1993, Australian Institute of Criminology, Canberra.]
4. *Attorney-General for Ceylon v. Perrera* [1953] AC 200.
5. Certainly kitchen knives are available to women, but women have not been trained to use knives in a way that, generally, promotes using these implements for killing. Anyway, the distance between kitchen and bedroom that would have to be negotiated by a woman wanting to use such a knife would

cont. next page

It is more probable that the woman would go to the kitchen, make herself a cup of tea, and sit distraught, thinking of her own inadequacy and error: why else would he seek sex and comfort elsewhere? Then she might think of ending her husband's life for the humiliation he has caused her, although this is an uncommon response from women to this situation. (She is more likely, if thinking of death, to contemplate her own.) What means are available to a woman? She could effect the act more easily when the man is asleep, or by some method other than gun, knife or other weapon: not an immediate lashing out. But once the step is taken, of sitting, thinking, wondering what to do, it is impossible under the law of provocation to argue that the act of killing was done in the heat of passion; rather, the court interprets it as being a coolly contemplated and executed crime; intentional killing; murder, not manslaughter; life imprisonment, not a bond. But for a man, equipped with gun or knife and well able to use them, or having recourse to his simple strength for strangling, a quick retaliation is realistically imagined: he therefore qualifies for the provocation argument, to be convicted not of murder, but of manslaughter, if of that.

The more recent and growing excuse used by men as provocation in wife and other woman-killings is that of the woman telling the man she no longer loves him, is leaving him. The ludicrous position is adopted under the law of provocation that a man has an "excuse" for killing a woman because she signifies a relationship is at an end. Several judges of the Supreme Court of Victoria have spoken out against the law of provocation as it currently stands. The law proclaims, under this nonsense "excuse" for woman-killing, that a woman must stay with a man. If she does not, it asserts she takes upon herself the risk of death by presuming to act autonomously and to believe this society gives her a right to determine whether or not she will live with, or continue a relationship with, a man. The law is saying that a woman must stay with "her" man, although we know the risk (where staying) in being killed is enormous. The law backs the view that it is up to the man alone to terminate the relationship. If she seeks to terminate it, he is excused for putting himself back in the power position, by recovering control and choosing the method of termination: by electing death for her, rather than her separation from him and her continuing life.

With self-defence, the elements to be satisfied in law are that the accused who killed must have been in apprehension of attack from the party killed; must have retaliated in fear of that attack; and that retaliation must be proportionate to the apprehended attack. That is, if one is attacked by fists, then fists must be met with fists, force is to be met with force, blow to be matched with blow.[6] So, where do women fit in? First, the

---

5. *cont. from previous page*
   militate against the notion that she was acting under provocation. Being sufficiently in charge of her faculties to determine to go to the kitchen, collect a suitable knife, then return implies an intention to kill. And would her husband await her return, unguarded against any weapon, anyway? [On gun ownership and use of guns in marital killing, see Law Reform Commission, *Discussion Paper on Firearms*, 1990, Government Printer, Melbourne.]
6. *Zecevic v. DPP* (1987) 162 CLR 645.

apprehension of attack: if a man attacks a woman with fists, it is unrealistic to imagine in most cases that her "fighting back with fists", "blow for blow" would really avail her much protection. It is more likely that a woman may take up a knife from the kitchen table and protect herself with that. But once a weapon comes into the fray, wielded by a woman, she is immediately at risk of being classed as a person with intention to kill or inflict grievous bodily harm, and therefore guilty of murder, or (under the common law prior to *Zecevic's case* in 1987) at the very least, of having used too much force in repelling the attacker, and therefore risking conviction of manslaughter (or murder), not acquittal.

Women suffer from the very fact that women are less likely to be brutal, violent and aggressive towards others than are men. Weapons in men's hands are "normal". In a woman's hands, a weapon immediately gives rise to suspicions of her intention to inflict harm. If she picked up a weapon, it runs, she must have been serious, must have intended harm. For a woman to have a weapon, much less use it, is extraordinary. If he intrudes with a weapon, this has the flavour of normality: men and weapons go together; men therefore are advantaged again in the application of laws relating to self-defence and unlawful killing.[7]

What if the woman endures a beating without retaliating or protecting herself, or fighting to protect herself as best she can, by fists alone, or biting, or kicking? She will not be exonerated from guilt by way of any self-defence rule if she chooses to take a knife or gun while her husband sleeps, and kills him. It is here that lawyers, sociologists and many members of the community say that her way out is not to kill the husband and seek to have a rule developed to cover the case, but to leave him, seeking a divorce. Although this might seem a "solution" to outsiders, for the woman who is confronted daily with a man who beats, bashes and abuses her, her only protection against it may be ridding herself of his ability to do this to her. Contrary to the view of the court and the jury, as he lies asleep on the couch he is not a totally powerless person. Rather, he is all-powerful, though asleep. He polices her every move. He beats, bashes and brow-beats her into submission. He creates, by his actions, a gaol of potent reality: she is the gaoled, he the gaoler. She, like men in prison, can escape only by desperate measures. And she has done no wrong to be placed in this prison. She merely said "yes" when she married him.

But the courts do not recognise this reality, or women's rights. The reality and rights lawyers and courts recognise is that of the person in power, the gaoler; not the prisoner. And women are too often prisoners and victims of "love". That odd male-defined condition that justifies killing; that odd male-defined condition that leads courts to say, and the papers to report, cases of "the Man Who Killed the Wife he Loved", the "tragic court story" of the man "who loved his wife so much he killed her":

---

7. Jocelynne A. Scutt, note 3. [Also Patricia Easteal, note 3, and Jocelynne A. Scutt, *Women and the Law*, 1990, Law Book Company, Sydney, pp. 459–465, particularly pp. 463 ff, and pp. 414–421.]

The judge who sentenced him yesterday to three years jail, but with a six month non-parole period, said: "My sympathy is clearly in your favour."

John Clarke, 37, of Penrith, stabbed his wife in the heart when she said she was leaving him … The court was told he drove his wife to hospital after he stabbed her and then surrendered to the police. His wife's threat to leave him had been the ultimate blow, and he had struck out in despair and frustration.[8]

The judge went on to say that gaol was likely to punish not only the offender, "but also his three children who had lost [sic] their mother".

And how did they "lose" their mother? That euphemistic word that disguises the cause of the "loss": a knife, a man wielding it; that man, their father, abusing their rights along with their mother's right to live; engaging in not only murderous conduct, but the most maliciously abusive conduct that can be inflicted on a child apart from direct physical abuse – the killing of her (or his) parent.

This gathering today is to commemorate the lives of women and children lost in the nightmare of the "normality" of wife and child-killing by husbands who know no better than power, possession and permission. Men have the power to kill; they indulge that power on "their" human possessions; and society gives them permission by failing to enunciate, clearly and without demur, that wife-killing is murder, that wife-killers are murderers, that the murder that is wife-killing is wrong.

As the United States feminist Andrea Dworkin has said:

Under patriarchy, no woman is safe to live her life, or to love, or to mother children. Under patriarchy, every woman is a victim, past, present, and future. Under patriarchy, every woman's daughter is a victim, past, present, and future …[9]

But under patriarchy, women are fighting back, to be victims no more. That fighting does not take the masculinist approach of violence, degradation, selfishness, abuse, bullying and bludgeoning, brutality and beggardliness. Women's way of fighting back is to remember the lives of women and children lost to patriarchy, so that those lives will be lost no more, but reinstated in our memories, in our recollections, in our own

---

8. Quoted Jocelynne A. Scutt, note 3, p. 181.

9. Andrea Dworkin, "Remembering the Witches" in *Our Blood – Prophecies and Discourses on Sexual Politics*, 1982, Women's Press, London, p. 20. [Note that in 1991 the Supreme Court of South Australia ruled that expert evidence on the "battered woman syndrome" (more accurately described as the battered woman reality) was admissible where a woman is charged with false imprisonment and causing grievous bodily harm with intent (and thus also in charges of murder or manslaughter): *R. v. Runjanjic; R. v. Kontinnen* (1991) 56 SASR 114, Chief Justice King and Justices Leggoe and Bollen. The restrictive nature of the interpretation of the battered woman reality was evident in *R. v. Buzzacott*, unreported, Supreme Court (SA) 15 July 1993, Justice Bollen. On the "battered woman syndrome" see Patricia Easteal, note 3; on the importance of avoiding the notion that the woman who fights back to save herself is sick, and the crucial point of acknowledging that she acts to kill according to the *reality* of her circumstances, and thus in self-defence, see Jocelynne A. Scutt, "No Syndrome – The Battered Woman Reality" (1992) *Impact* (June) 18.]

lives as valuable, worthy, worthwhile, to be remembered. In remembering the lives of women and children battered, abused, psychologically beaten, killed, we take back for them, and for ourselves, some small measure of their right to have lived.

In the midst of our one minute's silence, in the midst of the flowers, we need to take up the energies of those women and fight back for every woman and child on this earth.

The men who have killed, the men who have degraded, the men who have stood by and in their encouragement or lack of concern, in their denial of women's worth, in their ignorance of the realities of women's lives and women's deaths – all are responsible for the loss of women's lives, and for the loss of the lives of the children. Until all men renounce the way of life from which they have profited, and women have suffered, the killing of women and children in the name of love will continue.

Women are fighting back, and working to create a new society. Whatever men do, women will not resile from this.

In the midst of our one minute's silence, in the midst of the flowers, we take up the energies of our sisters, our mothers, our children, our friends, our colleagues. As long as there is one woman to speak out, as long as there is one woman to speak up, those energies will not be lost. We commemorate today the fight back for every woman and child who has lost a life. We take back from men the power, the possession and the permission. We renounce patriarchal power. We possess ourselves. We deny the permission to kill.

PART III

UP FROM UNDER

12

THE ECONOMICS OF SEX:
Women in Service

Published (1979) 51 (No. 1) *Australian Quarterly* 32

I left Australia in May 1973, less than six months after the election of the Whitlam Labor government, to study abroad. More than three years later I returned to a very different Australia, one that had been profoundly affected in so many lasting ways by the promotion and acceptance of new ideas through the short years of two Labor governments. There were the Racial Discrimination Act *1974, the* Trade Practices Act *1974, the* Family Law Act *1975, the Australian Legal Aid Office, the Office of Women's Affairs, federally funded women's refuges and rape crisis centres, the Schools Commission, the Office of Childcare. In September 1976 the Liberal-National Country Party Coalition was once more in power.*

Early in 1977 the then parliamentary leader of the National Country Party in New South Wales (Mr Leon Punch) expounded his view of why so few women were members of parliaments around Australia: at the time, only four per cent of all parliamentarians (state, territory and federal) were women; there were no women members of the House of Representatives. Mr Punch's theory was that women "do not vote for women". Not long after, the Women's Electoral Lobby held a "Women in Party Politics" conference at Sydney University, highlighting the fact that women rarely took parliamentary seats because the major political parties rarely pre-selected women for winnable seats. Pre-selected for marginal, swinging, or unwinnable seats, once a woman had made a seat winnable, a man was invariably put forward by the relevant political party to take advantage of the woman's work in making it so.[1]

At the conference, the number of women wishing to speak in the period available for questions and discussion was so large that a queue had to be set up to the left of the

---

1. "Women in Party Politics – Papers from the Women's Electoral Lobby seminar held in Sydney July 1977" (1977) 49 (3) *Australia Quarterly* (September) 3. Note that the Country Party (as it was originally titled) went through a transition stage of being titled "National Country Party" before it became the present-day National Party. In the footnotes, square brackets [...] indicate new material added for this edition.

platform and microphone. Some speakers suggested that the problem of low numbers of women in parliament would soon change, with the general movement of women into the paidworkforce. I joined the queue to voice the concern that women had always been in paidwork, whether in the factories or fields, as charwomen or washerwomen, or governesses, or taking in "paying guests"; what was new was the acknowledgement that women were there, and were recognised as being paid (albeit abysmally, in comparative terms) for the labour. Would this necessarily make any difference to political power and power relations between women and men? My concern was that there is a discernible shift, over time, in power, which means that having women in the public world of paidwork does not presage any general increase in women's power. I expanded on my theory of men, women, paidwork and power, pointing out that in the pre-industrial, manorial system, men in the upper socio-economic levels gained power through "being in charge" of households. The manorial household was the manor – comprising the lord's immediate retinue and the workers living on the estate. With the industrial revolution, power shifted so that men gained prestige and control through their identification with their roles in the professions and trades. For women, a shadow of the power held by the head of the manor came during the eighteenth and nineteenth centuries, when male power moved out into the greater world and the mistress of the house wielded (secondary) control over the domestic servants. Now, women were moving into professional and trade roles. But to think that this meant women would thereby gain power akin to men was wrong. The men were, no doubt, moving on – on to some new accumulation of power.

Jennifer Aldred, then Executive Officer with the Australian Institute of Political Science, heard me speak and wrote to me, asking would I construct my argument into an article for the Australian Quarterly. *I promised to do so, but wrote "The Economics of Sex" first. "Women and the Economics of Power" remains to be written.[2]*

Introduction

A recurrent argument within the ambit of the "equal rights for women" campaign arises between those who see feminist aims as inextricably bound up in the march toward socialism, and those contending that socialist and feminist ideals need not necessarily be contiguous. The dispute relates to whether, come the socialist revolution, women will automatically be classed "equal", the feminist cause achieved; or whether on the contrary the feminist revolution will still have to be won in order that "true equality"

---

2. In reading through this piece, I am reminded that through the 1970s I adopted the habit of referring to "men" as "male persons". This was possibly a reaction to the refusal to include women in the term "persons" in the cases rejecting women as voters in elections in Australia and Britain in the nineteenth and early twentieth centuries, as well as the denial of rights to practise law which was again based on the notion that women were not "persons". I had immersed myself in this history and at this time began writing an analysis of the cases.

between the sexes may be realised.

If the group "women" contains class divisions along the same lines as those of the group "men", and these class lines are the most distinctive feature of the grouping, then presumably socialism will bring about equality amongst all, regardless of sex. Yet the more compelling proposition is that rather than any distinctive class line attaching to women (as persons and not in relation to their attachment to male members of society), women fall more easily into a system of caste. That is, woman's intrinsic worth is seen in her value as sex object. Her socio-economic position is measured in terms of her sexuality.

Effectively, a woman trades her sexuality for sustenance under the contract of marriage. If she does not take this route, a woman may become a prostitute, where again the exchange is of sex-for-money. Even where she enters a legitimate career, the fact that a woman is female plays an important role in career choice and in the dimensions of work. Thus, women exchange their sexuality for cash by way of the screen or the stage: acting was one of the first careers opened to women. Here the (young) woman succeeds (ostensibly) by way of the "casting couch". In the business world the secretary is often chosen because of her sexual characteristics. Frequently rewards for women on the job are related to sex: hence the current uncovering of the problem of sexual harassment at work. If she does not get money for value where her body is concerned, a woman becomes the subject of derision or pity. Where she is labelled "promiscuous" there is a tacit agreement that no value need be given in exchange for her favours: she has lost her bargaining power. If sexual intercourse is achieved by another without her consent (in other words, if a woman is raped), the act is classified in law as akin to robbery or theft and the woman is scorned due to her failure to barter: no dinner, no marriage, no money in exchange – she has lost "everything".

"Woman as sex object" is the prime mover in framing woman's role in society. Woman's value is measured by an unchanging (and unchangeable) characteristic: whatever her role, she is "paid" for her sexual nature.

If this is correct, then the feminists who see "women's liberation" as requiring something more than socialism are right: until all women cease to be seen as sexual beings for (re)production purposes, any professed equality between males and females will remain illusory.

Marriage as Career

"Marriage is legalised prostitution," Bernard Shaw said.[3] As has been pointed out:

The channelling of sexuality into marriage is crucial to all societies and espoused as a desirable goal by virtually all component sub-groups. In our society, sexual taboos, often enacted into law, buttress a system of monogamy based upon the "free bargaining" of the potential spouses.

---

3. George Bernard Shaw wrote extensively on marriage and women's position in it. See, for example, *Getting Married*, reprinted 1986, Penguin, Harmondsworth; *Misalliance*, reprinted 1984, Penguin, Harmondsworth; *Man and Superman*, reprinted 1985, Penguin/Viking, Harmondsworth; *Maxims for Revolutionists*, reprinted 1972, Penguin, Harmondsworth; *The Intelligent Women's Guide to Socialism, Capitalism, Sovietism and Fascism*, reprinted 1971, Penguin, Harmondsworth.

Within this process, the woman's power to withhold or grant sexual access is an important bargaining weapon ... It is interesting to note that we do not recognise this function of sex in the man. He is not considered to have the same "economic" right in his sexual capacities, and the law does not protect him from the invasion of the "right" by a woman.[4]

Marriage is the major legitimate path a woman can take in order to make money – or at least to be secure (although the security may often be deceptive). Marriage is the legal way in which a woman sells her sexuality and gains sustenance simply because she is a woman.[5]

The "natural promiscuity" of human beings is asserted through the history of man, beginning with tribal living. In an argument seeking to refute the proposition, Westermarck points to "woman as commodity", "selling" her sexuality. His argument is that it is not promiscuity; it is survival or profit. Yet here it is the father of the girl who first benefits from the trade: it is her father who is the recipient of the bride price usually paid by the warrior who becomes the husband:

Among the Wapore of Usambra unmarried daughters are strictly guarded, because a false step on their part reduces the price paid for them ... Among the people of Madison's Island a handsome daughter is considered by her parents as a blessing which secures them, for a time, wealth and abundance.[6]

Where a woman is seduced before marriage, often a fine will be payable as the value of her sexual being is lessened by prior sexual contact:

Of the natives of the Sese Archipelago ... we are told that "if a young woman was seduced, the man was obliged to marry her, and in addition to pay a fine of two goats, and of the Lendu, that for the seduction of a girl a fine of four cows is payable to her father ..."

When a Nasamonian first marries, it is the custom for the bride on the first night to lie with all the guests in turn and each, when he has intercourse with her, gives her some present which he has brought from home.[7]

However, the ultimate gain in marriage for the woman herself is that, all being well, she has secured a livelihood ... no longer will she be dependent upon her father for support.

That a woman must find a means of support, and that marriage is that means, is

---

4. Comment, "Forcible and Statutory Rape – An Exploration of Operation and Objective of the Consent Standard" (1952) 62 *Yale Law Journal* 55, p. 70 and note 108.
5. For an outline of current problems arising in the instance of divorce, maintenance and property settlement, see Women's Electoral Lobby, *Submission on Family Law to the Federal Attorney-General*, 1988, WEL, Sydney. [See further, Jocelynne A. Scutt and Di Graham, *For Richer, For Poorer – Money, Marriage and Property Rights*, 1984, Penguin Books Australia, Ringwood.]
6. See E. Westermarck, *The History of Human Marriage*, 5th edn, Vol. 1, 1951, Macmillan, London, pp. 136, 152. The immediately following quotation comes from the same source, p. 153.
7. Westermarck, note 6, p. 197.

intrinsic to European society. Of the position of women in England during feudal times and leading up to the present, Helen Bosanquet says:

... the most characteristic survivals of the feudal family are not the sons but the daughters of the house. In feudal days ... there were three courses open to them: marriage, the cloister, or the corner of the eldest brother's house. In families where the aristocratic traditions still prevail, the position is not greatly altered.[8]

In a society where property was perpetuated through descent from father to eldest son, the problem inevitably arose of providing for the younger male children:

Chiefly, they found their way into the established professions: the army, the navy, the Church, law and the diplomatic and consular service.[9]

The female children had also to be provided for. Chiefly, they went into the established profession of marriage. So the woman ceased to be a burden upon the assets of the father, provided a sexual outlet for the husband and fulfilled the needs of a property-orientated society by producing an eldest son to inherit.[10]

Today marriage as a profession is preached not only to daughters of the rich, but to the general populace. The idea that girls will eventually take up the role of wife and mother (any paidwork prior to this being of a temporary nature, only "filling in") may be specifically alluded to in educational material, may be a part of the "hidden curriculum" and may be adhered to be the recipients of the information – the girls themselves.

In a report by a United Kingdom committee given the task of devising directions for girls' education, the "home-making" aspects of the female were emphasised:

One line of advance lies in courses built around broad themes of home making, to include not only material and practical provisions but the whole field of personal relations in courtship, in marriage, and within the family ... Girls can be brought to see that ... they will themselves have a key role in establishing the standards of the home and in educating their children ...[11]

Any perusal of current curriculums and of the numbers of female students taking such subjects as home economics shows little need for schools to concentrate upon these types of subject (at least in their present form) to any greater degree, in order to persuade girls that this is the field for them.[12]

---

8. Helen Bosanquet, *The Family*, 1906, Macmillan, London.
9. Ronald Fletcher, *The Family and Marriage in Britain*, 1969, Penguin Books, Harmondsworth.
10. On the wife as "sexual" outlet see, for example, the oft-cited case of Soames and Irene, in J. Galsworthy, *Forsyte Saga*, Book 1, Part III, chapter 4, quoted in Terry Budden, "Revision of Sexual Offences Legislation – A Code for New South Wales?" (1977) 2 *UNSWLJ* 117, p. 130.
11. John Newsome, *The Newsome Report*, 1967, HMSO, London.
12. *Report of the Committee on Sexism in Education*, 1978, Government Printer, Sydney, particularly Underwood, K., Bureau of Statistics. See also Frances H. Lovejoy, *University Discrimination Against the Feminine High School Student – Matriculation and Domestic Studies*, 1979, unpublished paper.

The saying that the "way to a man's heart is through his stomach" is embodied in the school curriculum in the shape of teaching girls the "cookery method of catching her man". The curriculum, backed up by the media and general social attitudes, also teaches that the cook must be pretty. This has led one writer to surmise:

There are few women who fail to understand that their sexual charms can secure for them a "position in life" which puts them above the need for independent exertion. When calculating her chances in the struggle for existence, a girl puts on the credit side her personal attractions, the "sex appeal" which will induce a man to work for her so that, forthwith or by degrees, she will secure money, status, leisure. Far from being ashamed of her sex (as some facile theorists would have us believe), woman is extremely proud of her genital organs. They are the centre of her power to give men incomparable pleasure. She would be amazed if they were neglected, undervalued, despised; and she counts on them to provide for her future, and perhaps lead her to unexpected heights.[13]

In schools, in technical colleges and in prisons women are enrolled in fashion courses, dress-making and beauty programs: dressed to kill, she will secure that meal ticket for life that enables her to cook the meals made from ingredients bought by another's purchasing power, bartering her own sexuality in exchange.

The law, too, supports this mechanism for survival of the female. Under the marital contract at common law the male partner is required to support his wife and children. In traditional law, consideration on the part of the woman making the contract is that of her sex role. In exchange for support the law sees the wife as giving up any control over her character as sexual partner. Inextricably bound up in her consent at the time of marriage is, it is alleged, the woman's consent to sexual intercourse with her husband at all times. After marriage, it is he who dictates the use of her sexual capacity. Furthermore, until recently the husband had a right, measured in money terms, to exclusive use of his wife's sexual nature: were she seduced by another, he could recover damages.[14]

Social attitudes combined with the operation of the law conspire to lead girls to believe that their hope for the future lies within the confines of marriage. School books and books-for-girls continue to emphasise the princess-wife-mother fairy-tale.[15] If she does not take this path, the future is bleak. "Womanly assets" have a short life-span, to

---

13. Comment, note 4, p. 71, note 113.
14. For a discussion of the development of the law relating to rape in marriage and a contradiction of the idea that a man cannot be prosecuted for rape simply by reason of the fact that the victim is his wife, see Jocelynne A. Scutt, "Consent in Rape – The Problem of the Marriage Contract" (1977) 5 *Mon. ULR* 255. For seduction and damage see *Winsmore v. Greenbank* (1745) Wills 577, 125 ER 1330; *Best v. Samuel Fox and Co.* [1951] 2 All ER 116. Under s. 120 *Family Law Act* 1975 (Cth) no action lies for criminal conversation, damages for adultery, or for enticement of a party to a marriage. [In all Australian states and territories rape in marriage is now a crime. In 1989 Queensland was the last state to effect this legislative recognition that a husband could be prosecuted for wife rape.]
15. See *Report of the Committee on Sexism in Education*, note 12, p. 30; Schools Commission Report, *Girls Schools and Society*, 1975, AGPS, Canberra.

be cashed in at a relatively early age. If she does not invest advantageously, the woman may miss out on security, for her husband may fail to maintain her without further exertion on her part. Further, with the passing of time the original agreement – of her sex for his money – may begin to appear unfair, for the husband's value will almost inevitably have increased through promotions, wage rises and the like, whereas her value has a fixed or descending rate. However, in both cases the woman is better equipped having sold her sexuality than having refused to sell. Social and economic conditions are structured so that in the latter case, her prospects in the normal course are limited to a mundane job in the work world and a (state) pension on retirement. Where she marries, she attaches to a male career, which in almost every case will be financially more sound than hers would have been, had she not married. Further, she may consolidate the initial gain by the production of children, to guard against a time when another sex object may appear more attractive, as a financial proposition, to her husband. Thus, the market demands that she should sell.

Career as Prostitute

The classic example of the sex object receiving payment is that of the woman as prostitute:

Prostitution along with beauty contests and pornography ... is seen as the ultimate way in which a woman can sell herself ...[16]

Where she exchanges sex not for marriage but solely for money, the woman again stands to profit more from the transaction than if she had chosen not to enter the market place.

The prostitute may be – and usually is – looked upon as degraded. A parallel to present day attitudes may be found in the tribal customs of the Omaha where, Westermark says, the prostitutes, being chiefly divorced wives, were "looked down upon". Whiffen describes a tribe from the north-west Amazon region, where "very frequently widows become the tribal prostitutes, a custom that is not recognised, but is tolerated, and is never practised openly or immodestly". Similarly in northern Queensland among traditional aborigines, it was said that a prostitute, "though her frailty is usually due to the death or desertion of her husband, is despised, and has a special name applied to her ..."[17] Nonetheless, despite the degradation, she has an independent income and the possibility of increasing her living standard beyond that of the woman who does not marry (or marry again) and yet does not take up the trade; prostitution can be lucrative for a woman. (Men are not forced into this way of life: far more lucrative careers are open to them in numerous fields.) Furthermore, the

16. Jan Aitkin, "The Prostitute as Worker" in *Women and Labour Conference Papers*, Vol. 2, "The Experience of Work", 1978, Macquarie University, Sydney, p. 9.
17. Westermarck, note 6, pp. 137–38; see also T. Whiffen, *North-West Amazons*, 1915, London, p. 167.

unmarried woman or spinster is "looked down upon" as being "unnatural" or having "missed out", "on the shelf", and due to sex-based discrimination in the world of "legitimate" work, does not have the recompense of a large (or potentially large) income.

Just as our school system trains young women to be sexual objects for the purpose of succeeding in the career of wife, it trains women to be prostitutes if they choose not to take upon themselves the acceptable career of marriage, or if marriage-as-career fails in its expectations.[18] An emphasis upon beauty courses, things feminine, fashion, and short-term expectations is well suited to the call-girl, escort service, massage parlour and street-walker trade. As well, the perpetuation of the idea that girls are "good" at undertaking "helping professions" must surely serve to foster any drift of women toward a career of prostitution, the trade being generally regarded as a "necessary social service". (In one survey 70 per cent of those persons questioned "thought that prostitutes were rendering a public service". The New South Wales Council for Civil Liberties has opined: "Most communities need the service.")[19]

In addition to training for the trade, girls are encouraged to take it up as a means of making good money, when their opportunities for independent careers are so limited. Thus in the past laws have been (and remain) framed so as to exclude women from participating in certain professions and trades. Even where they have not been prevented from entering, some laws have been (and remain) framed in such a way as to exclude women from the most profitable career paths within certain industries, by means such as "protecting" them from night-shifts – night-shift being the most highly paid in the industry. In many professions customs and attitudes stand in the way of women succeeding to the most highly paid and rewarding positions.[20]

The law further fosters the climate that the commodity to be sold by women is sex, and that women are alone in selling that commodity. The law concentrates upon the sexual bargaining power of women by (in some countries) outlawing the direct exchange of sex for money, or (in others) outlawing those acts leading up to the sale of sex, such as soliciting. At common law, males are not specifically penalised for soliciting where they wish to sell the sex act, nor under English law are they penalised for seeking to purchase it. Yet again, women are seen as the sexual component in society and the exclusive commercial value of their sexuality is fully (though not in

---

18. Whether this is a new phenomenon or whether research is simply exposing a characteristic of prostitutes from times past, in Gail Sheehy's book *Hustling*, 1976, Random House, New York, it seems that "ordinary housewives" form a large part of the daytime prostitute population, "fitting in" the job between "household duties". Here, the legal (marriage) and the illegal form of prostitution are being combined.

19. The research project was carried out by the Royal Commission into Human Relationships and is cited in the *Final Report* Vol. 5, 1977, AGPS, Canberra, p. 63. See also Submission 436, NSW Council for Civil Liberties, cited Royal Commission into Human Relationships, *Final Report*, p. 63.

20. See generally *Report of the Anti-Discrimination Board*, 1978, Government Printer, Sydney, particularly the volume Discrimination in Legislation, Vol. 1, at Chapter 4, pp. 188 ff, also *Directions for Change* (Wilenski Report 1977, NSW Government Printer), Part E Equal Employment Opportunity, pp. 179 ff.

adequate monetary return) recognised.[21] Simply because our society values women solely for their sexual nature, setting up the system of marriage as a legitimate recognition of this characteristic, it has been necessary at the same time to outlaw legislatively the socially unacceptable commercial enterprise where the women may directly profit, each time on an independent basis, from her sexuality. The acceptable route of the woman's sexual bargain is through marriage; the unacceptable route is through prostitution.

Sex on the Job

Snide remarks of the "career begun on the casting couch" testify to the thesis that women's talents are seen as unidimensional. That this is no new development is implicit in memories of times past:

When I was a girl of seventeen ... writes Miss Kidd my then employer, a gentleman of good position and high standing in the town, sent me to his home one night, ostensibly to take a parcel of books, but really with a very different object. When I arrived at the house all the family were away, and before he would allow me to leave he forced me to yield to him. At eighteen I was a mother.[22]

Social conditions of the nineteenth century conspired to perpetuate a system where women were used for sexual purposes under the guise of legitimate employment:

During the first years of my boy's life my employer compelled me by threats to keep [the knowledge of his part in the affair] a secret, and I had to bear the whole of the burden myself. My people, who were also in his employ, suspected him but did not dare to charge him, consequently the real truth never transpired.

---

21. Many United States jurisdictions outlaw sex-for-money sales: *US v. Moses* (1972) Crim. Nos 1778-72, 21346-72 (DC Sup. Ct, November 1972). See discussion in A. Dorsen, "Women, the Criminal Code and the Correction System" in *Women's Role in Contemporary Society – Report of the New York Commission on Human Rights*, 1972, Avon, New York, p. 505. Soliciting for sex, for money is outlawed in the United Kingdom and in Australia, see generally R. Wilkinson, *Women of the Streets*, C. H. Rolph, ed., 1961, London. For male (customer) solicitation, see discussion in *Crook v. Edmondson* [1966] 1 All ER 833; and see an outline and history of the New York statute attempting to prohibit customers from seeking prostitutes to fulfil the service in A. Dorsen, in *Women's Role in Contemporary Society – Report of the New York Commission on Human Rights*, p. 507. [A number of Australian jurisdictions now "catch" the male customer under legislative provisions. Victoria took this approach in the 1970s. See for example, Jocelynne A. Scutt, "Sexism in Criminal Law" in *Women and Crime*, S. K. Mukherjee and Jocelynne A. Scutt (eds.), 1981, Allen and Unwin, Sydney; Jocelynne A. Scutt, "The Economic Regulation of the Brothel Industry in Victoria" (1986) 59 (7) *ALJ* 399.]

22. See "A Guild Office Clerk" in *Life as We Have Known It by Cooperative Working Women*, Margaret Llewelyn Davies (ed.), republished 1977, Virago, London, p. 76. The immediately following quotation comes from the same source, p. 77.

The implication that a woman may "succeed" in a career simply because she is a woman cannot be ignored in today's terms either. For women in employment, sexual identity is a live issue – at least as far as the employer is concerned. Apart from the most obvious areas in which the charge will be made – acting, photographic modelling, "showbiz" generally – recent research supports the view that the "secretary as sex object" goes beyond hiring a good-looking girl for the front office. The *Diaz v. Pan American World Airlines, Inc.* argument, that males acting as "stewardesses" would not be acceptable to airline passengers, is an extension of the notion that a woman-on-the-job fulfils a role as a sex object. The case was eventually lost by Pan Am; it was held that the attendants could be male.[23]

In 1975 the Working Women United Institute was established in the United States, focusing on "the specific problems of sexual harassment on the job". After completing several small surveys in order to determine individual and institutional attitudes towards sexual harassment and to study its effects on its victims, the Institute began a national survey of working women, to compare women's experiences with harassment "across regions, jobs and other relevant categories". The Institute is only one of many organisations directing their attention toward the issue of job-related sexual harassment.[24]

Time, money and effort are being expended upon what is seen as a real area of concern. Surveys have shown that women are employed as secretaries, clerks and in professional capacities only to be confronted with the realisation that it is their sexuality which is being employed along with, or in preference to, any truly job-related talents they may possess. To succeed in the business, or even simply to co-exist with the employer, it is necessary for the woman to endure sexual innuendo, "groping", intimate lunches or dinners, taking the role of "sympathetic friend" to the employer, "working back late at night" – which eventually becomes a euphemism for participating in sexual intercourse with the boss. Cases have already been fought in the United States on the question of whether dismissal on the grounds that the particular woman would not engage in sexual activity with her employer was unfair, as being in contravention of Title VII's provisions on sex-based discrimination. It remains to be seen whether Australian legislation will be used to counter sexual harassment on the job; it has already been shown that the phenomenon exists.[25]

The individual who wishes to ignore her sexual bargaining power, seeking recognition, advancement and economic gain for reasons other than her sexual characteristics,

---

23. 311 F. Supp. 559 (FD Fla. 1970); reversed, 442 F. 2d 385. See also discussion in Karen de Crow, *Sexist Justice – How the Legal System Affects You*, 1974, Random House, New York, Chapter 5, "Money and Employment (2) – Sex and the Job Market", pp. 87 ff.

24. Circular distributed by Working Women United Institute. Most rape crisis centres appear to have become involved in helping women who have been molested or harassed on the job. For example, a recent report from the major centre in London reported a high rate of persons contacting them from this group, and the Rape Crisis Centre in Sydney confirmed that their contacts also suffered from this sort of abuse (personal communication, Sydney Rape Crisis Centre, Chippendale, NSW).

25. In a recent interview, an executive consultant with a large managerial firm stated: "Many senior executives are willing to pay big money for a secretary without being able to define what the

cont. next page

discovers that she is not allowed to do so. Like the black man, who cannot escape the notion that he has "rhythm" or his characterisation as a "stud" who should perform, the female – black, white and brown – cannot escape the "sensuous weight" and "shadowy invitation" of her body,[26] her characterisation as a sexual being whose productivity is concentrated in this aspect of her existence. The work world is, apparently, set up to accommodate women within its ranks basically on the level of sex objects.

Very few women "succeed" in the world of business, at least at the level of managerial and executive positions – positions of power. This has been attributed to basic differences in the upbringing of male and female persons.

---

25. *cont. from previous page*
   secretarial function really entails". He went on to say: "The majority of bosses seem to need, if they are honest, a good tea and coffee maker, a good copy typist or simply a sympathetic friend". What was involved in "being sympathetic" and "friendly", was not stated. See "Bosses Slammed Over 'Tea Girls'" *Daily Telegraph* 5 October 1978. In the United States revelations of sexual harassment on the job have led to media coverage of the problem In *Ms. Magazine* December 1977 a series of leading articles revealed that many positions for women with the United Nations Organisation were dependent upon sexual favours. Similarly the 1979 "sex-scandal on the Hill" showed that many secretarial positions for Members of Congress involved a very high degree of sexual activity. In Australia, the magazine *Cleo* has carried an extensive coverage of the problem: *Cleo* March 1978; also "'Wanted: Secretary with good speeds and a friendly nature ...' How to say 'No' to the Boss and keep your job", *Woman's Day* 9 October 1978, pp. 62, 65. See generally Karen de Crow note 23. [In the 1980s, cases of sexual harassment began to go through the equal opportunity/anti-discrimination/sex discrimination route provided by legislation passed by the states (apart from Tasmania) and territories, and the federal government. (In Tasmania, where there is no equal opportunity/anti-discrimination/sex discrimination legislation, the civil law route has recently been taken, a woman suing individuals and the local council for sexual harassment. She was awarded $120,000. Ms Barker was reported to have said her court victory "should show other women in similar situations that help is available": "$120,000 to sex harassment victim", *Courier Mail* 12 July 1993, p. 3.) In 1984 the first case of sexual harassment dealt with by a discrimination or equal opportunity tribunal or board was heard by the Equal Opportunity Tribunal of New South Wales: *O'Callaghan v. Loder* (1983) EOC 92–203. On this issue, see further Chapter 10, "Woman as Property – Prostitution, Pornography and Sexist Advertising" this volume, pp. 165 ff.]

26. Henry Fairlie, "Woman's Place is on a Pedestal", *Sydney Morning Herald* 16 September 1978, pp. 7–8 (in the "Good Weekend" section). [In the 1980s this phenomenon became a matter of concern in the context of "mail order brides" – the expression often used to describe the exploitation of women from countries such as the Philippines and Thailand, by men from countries such as the Australia, Germany, Austria, the Netherlands, Britain and Japan. In early 1993 Filipinas living in Australia requested a number of women lawyers to work together with them to prepare a brief calling for the Human Rights and Equal Opportunity Commission to institute an enquiry into the deaths of eighteen Filipino women who had been unlawfully killed or who had disappeared in Australia since 1987. Ms Melba Marginson, a leader of the group, was reported as saying: "Some of these women have been treated like objects and nobody seems to care. Some people think of Filipino women only as mail-order brides, as something less than human." The group makes it clear that many marriages between Australian nationals and women from Asian countries are as egalitarian as any Australian–Australian relationship, but that the notion of Asian women being submissive, young, beautiful, compliant, underlies the trade in women. See Heather Kennedy, "Probe pleas on killings", *Sunday Herald-Sun* 15 August 1993, p. 3; Chris Johnston, "Local play tells of mail-order brides", *Western Independent* 7 September 1993, p. 5.]

Girls tend to be raised with far more limited expectations than boys about the roles they will have open to them in life, and they tend to have a general expectation of being an adjunct to men, if not through marriage then through the power behind the throne. And they are not given the expectation they will have to work.[27]

Furthermore, boys and girls are subjected to contrasting treatment in regard to competition and risk:

Boys are encouraged not only to be competitive, but to place a high value on winning. And they are given plenty of opportunity through team sports, if nothing else, to test and hone themselves. Girls, on the other hand, tend to have a higher priority placed for them on the means rather than the end, and it is not so much winning as getting there gracefully. And without too many waves.

However, these sorts of explanation do not necessarily ring true. They may be correct in relation to the business world of work as conceived by male persons and as conceived in terms of male-type achievements. However, girls *are* taught to be competitive, and are taught that the main aim is to succeed. But the notion of competition and success as viewed through the eyes of the male is not identical with the sort of "success" and "competition" that is seen as appropriately striven for by girls. Girls are taught to compete and succeed on a level which is, basically, sexual. Girls learn that sexual characteristics are valuable not only in relation to the girls themselves, but vis-a-vis other parties. The competitiveness and success rate of women cannot be equated with the competitiveness and success rate of men. Women are taught to "sell" sexuality as a means of gaining success. Women learn that competition means being "prettier than", "sexier than", "more beautiful – more curvaceous – better dressed – a better hostess – more stunning – a better wife – a better sex-kitten ..." The man sells a multiplicity of talents. He is encouraged to develop capabilities necessary for "running the show" from the top, rather than achieving by way of attachment to some other person. That women

---

27. See Joan Linklater, "Why women rarely hit the top", *Rydge's*, January 1978. The immediately following quotation comes from the same source. Even where girls do compete on the same level as boys, their success is rarely recognised. Thus, in a study of competition at sport, psychological testing showed that both boys and girls often refused to recognise a girl's greater sporting ability, where girls were competing in group games together with boys. The test involved a game where boys and girls played together, each player being permitted to give turns away by passing the ball to another team member whom she/he thought could score more points for the throw. Two conclusions were reached:

  i. Girls who were the highest ability players on their teams gave away twice as many passes as boys who were the highest ability players on their teams. (There was group pressure for girls to pass to the boys.)

  ii. Even after a boy failed to score any points several times, other children continued to pass to him. On the other hand, after girls hit the bull's eye (a rare achievement for either sex), they got no increase in passes. A few failures didn't seem to damage a boy's reputation whilst succeeding a few times didn't seem to improve that of a girl's. See "It's Not How She Plays the Game – It's How She Loses", Ms. Gazette News, *Ms. Magazine*, May 1978, p. 20. (Study carried out by Helen H. Solomons, PhD.)

are taught to compete and desire success – not on the same "business" level as men, but in terms of their own sexuality – is abundantly clear in any perusal of manuals for training receptionists, office workers, secretaries, (female) assistants to the director and so on. In training for these positions, considerable emphasis is laid upon such matters as grooming and deportment. Training manuals contain the predictable admonition:

Receptionist is your chosen career – be a credit to it and yourself, by always looking your best … good grooming, graciousness and charm play an important part in the success of the receptionist for the Public Service.[28]

Manuals for job-training consist of paragraphs relating to deportment – standing, walking, sitting, entering and leaving a room, getting into a car. Grooming sections include pages covering the important use of complexion, as well as hair, legs and feet, hands, perfume, makeup. Wardrobe is essential to the job. And that these items are significant in a receptionist's work, even vital to that work, shows clearly through in this training manual analogy with another profession:

One of the most difficult things to learn if you are an aeroplane pilot is to make a smooth landing so the passengers are not jolted. This takes skill and practice. Likewise you must learn to sit so gently that people will not realise the moment you have settled yourself into a chair. No doubt you have watched some inelegant female come in who has literally fallen into the seat next to you. When this sort of thing occurs you certainly know when she has "landed" … Let us now practice sitting in an elegant manner.

Under the heading of personality, potential women workers are told that "office personality does play an important part in [their] success … both socially and financially". The readers are admonished to "try and develop" a number of special traits or characteristics. Being "interesting", "enthusiastic", and "happy" are the prerequisites for success. Furthermore, the ultimate is to "be feminine":

Make the most of your face and figure. Achieving this can be lots of fun, and it is up to you to make the end result attractive, natural and worthy of attention. Looking feminine is an art, which if you develop it, can be one of the keys to your happy and successful existence. It has been said the wise woman regards being good looking and as attractive as possible an essential part of her job of being a "delectable creature" of charm and magnetism …

Just as the sale of sexuality is the keynote to the woman's career as wife or prostitute, so too is it her keynote to success in business.

---

28. *Receptionist Course Manual of the Public Service Board*, Sydney, NSW – used as a teaching tool until August, 1978. The manual has now been eliminated from the course. The four immediately following quotations come from the same source. [The removal of the manual from the curriculum came after it was (as rumoured) "leaked" and an extended quotation from it appeared in "Clancy", a column in the (now defunct) *National Times*, which had as its goal "taking the mickey" out of individuals and institutions to effect change. On this occasion it succeeded.]

Rape as Robbery

The taking of sex from the female where she does not bargain for the taking – rape – is in law very much akin to robbery and theft. Simple larceny is committed where an accused person takes and carries away the personal goods of another, with the felonious intent to convert them to her/his own use and to make them permanently her/his own, without the consent of the true owner. As for robbery, the elements of the crime are that it is the unlawful taking and carrying away of property of some value from the person of another, or in her/his presence, from under her/his immediate and personal care and protection, against her/his will and either by force or putting her/him in fear. Rape, like robbery, "may be committed by threats of imminent harm ...". It is the act of "having carnal knowledge of a woman without her conscious permission, such permission not being extorted by force or fear of immediate bodily harm". It is no mitigation of the offence "that the woman at last yielded to the violence, if such her consent [*sic*] were forced by fear or duress".[29]

The parallel is further emphasised in the law governing the husband-wife relationship. Just as in common law it is alleged that a husband cannot be prosecuted for the rape of his wife, for she has consented irrevocably to engaging in sexual intercourse with him at his choosing, in common law a prosecution for theft cannot take place between a husband and wife, upon the basis that possessions of the one spouse are possessions of the other. The law has introduced rules lessening a husband's right to squander his wife's property and eventually legislation was passed making the prosecution of a husband for theft of his wife's goods possible. But it is clear that the original rules made a wife's sexuality or sexual capacity into a "thing" to be used by her husband ("purchaser" and "owner").[30]

A woman's right to consent or to refuse consent to sexual intercourse is "significant as an item of social currency for women", in giving her a degree of bargaining power in a competitive world. But that is not its only function. The consent standard:

... fosters, and is in turn bolstered by, a masculine pride in the exclusive possession of a sexual object. The consent of a woman to sexual intercourse awards the man a privilege of bodily access, a personal "prize" whose value is enhanced by sole ownership. A man may feel loss of

---

29. See generally Raymond Watson and Howard Purnell, *Criminal Law in New South Wales*, Vol. 1, Indictable Offences, 1978, Law Book Co., Sydney, pp. 143 ff, 167 ff; R. Gordon, *The Criminal Law of Scotland*, 1967, p. 830; James Stephen, *A Digest of the Criminal Law*, 9th edn, L. Sturge ed. 1950, Art. 318; I. E. East, *A Treatise of the Pleas of the Crown*, 1803, James Ridgway, c. 10 s. 7, p. 444. See also Jocelynne A. Scutt, "Consent Versus Submission – Threats and the Element of Fear in Rape" (1977) 13 *UWA Law Rev.* 52, pp. 54 ff.

30. See generally John Eekelaar, *Family Security and Family Breakdown*, 1971, Routledge and Kegan Paul, London, pp. 98 ff, for an account of this development; and also Richard E. Megarry and Harold W. R. Wade, *Law of Real Property*, 1966, Sweet and Maxwell, London, pp. 986 ff. On theft see for example *Theft Act* 1968 (UK) s. 30 (1) – each can also be charged and convicted of obtaining the property by deception, etc. one from the other; also theft by one partner of property owned jointly. See generally P. M. Bromley, *Family Law*, 2nd edn, 1971, Butterworths, London, p. 129; also Jocelynne A. Scutt, note 14, pp. 269 ff.

the woman's sexual consent to a competitor ... A reason for the man's condemnation of rape may be found in the threat to his status from a decrease in the "value" of his sexual "possession" which would result from forcible violation ...[31]

But it is not only a husband who may feel a threat to status if his wife is raped. Society as a whole involves itself in the event by upholding the view that the woman raped is a person "ravaged", "worthless", "despoiled", a "thing" devoid of value. Not only men subscribe to this view, but women have been so imbued with masculine values and the ethics of competition that they too view the rape victim as a being to be shunned. Further, because they are forced into a position where the sale of sexuality is their keynote for success, women are consistently trained to think of themselves as responsible for those occasions upon which no material or security benefit comes from their being sexually used: rape. Thus it can be said:

... there certainly are ways in which women contribute to their vulnerability to rape. The most obvious is an ambivalence about being treated as sexual objects. On the one hand women have learned that it is very hard to get any benefits from men if they don't play into this aspect of male sexism. On the other hand, they feel depersonalised by it. In addition, many women have internalised male notions of attractiveness, and so in order to feel good about their appearance, they have to pile on makeup, and display their breasts, legs, or behinds. This need contributes to their own objectification, which in turn contributes to the rape problem.[32]

However, this is not the full story. The truth is that in order to survive, women have had to internalise male notions of attractiveness. Because society is not structured to enable women to achieve in their own right, but requires women to achieve as an attachment to man, a woman needs to emphasise those traits and characteristics which will result, ultimately, in her success. She is therefore programmed to utilise her sexuality in the bargaining game and to lose out completely where a potential partner in the exchange refuses to "pay up".

It is instructive to look at the attitudes of those men who commit the act of rape. Some rapists conform to the typical view of thief or robber. The motivating element is that the individual wants "something for nothing". Thus in an interrogation rapists make such remarks as:

All I wanted was a convenient place to get rid of my desire for a thrill ... The easier the better ... I wanted this beautiful fine thing and I got it ... I wanted things as easy as I could get them ...

Other rapists are intent on exchanging "gifts" for the use of their victim's sexuality. Victims sometimes hear the offender asserting his "love" or desire to continue the relationship, even to the extent of proposing marriage. They appear to have taken to

---

31. Comment, note 4, pp. 72–73.
32. Diana E. H. Russell, *The Politics of Rape – the Victim's Perspective*, 1975, Stein and Day, New York, p. 273. The immediately following quotation comes from the same source, pp. 245–246.

heart the idea that a woman's sexuality should, ultimately, be "paid" for, even if "taken for nothing" initially.[33]

The offence of carnal knowledge or statutory rape also bears out the view that a woman's sexual capacity is something to be bartered. Under the age of consent the law ignores that the girl has in fact consented to sexual intercourse. It is considered that below the set age she has no ability to give an understanding acquiescence to the act of sexual intercourse; her consensual participation will be ousted and the person engaging in the act with her is penalised.[34]

An obvious parallel lies in the world of commercial trading, where the contracts of minors are voidable at law. Again with the law of marriage, there is a legal prohibition against the marriage of minors. The comparison suggests that the law sees young women as not being in a position to sum up properly their own sexual value and not being able to calculate the rate of exchange that should be demanded from a sex (or marriage) partner.[35] In support of this it has been said:

A popular conception of a girl's sexual indulgence or virginity as a single "thing" of social, economic, and personal value explains, in part, the law's concern with her capacity to "understand". An "unwise" disposition of a girl's sexual "treasure", it is thought, harms both her and the social structure which anticipates certain patterned uses. Hence, the law of statutory rape must intervene to prevent what is predicted will be an unwise disposition.[36]

As in our past and current climate, careers for women are centred upon the sexual character of woman, and the law acts in a paternalistic manner to prevent too early, too easy trading: "You mustn't open your presents before Christmas ..."[37] The law intervenes in an attempt to prevent the young girl from giving up "everything in exchange for nothing", leaving her barren of "the goods".

---

33. See John McDonald, *Rape – Offenders and Their Victims*, 1905, Charles C. Thomas, Springfield, p. 6; evidence from the Royal Commission into Human Relationships quoted in Anne Deveson, *Australians at Risk*, 1978, Cassell Australia, Sydney, pp. 183, 184; Diana E. H. Russell, note 32, and Note, "The Victim in a Forcible Rape Case – A Feminist View" (1973) 11 *Am. Jrn. Crim. Law* 335.

34. In the United States the crime is generally termed "statutory rape", in Australia it is "carnal knowledge". See generally Raymond Watson and Howard Purnell, note 29, pp. 110 ff.

35. See D. Harland, *Law of Minors in Relation to Contracts and Property in NSW*, 1975, Butterworths, Sydney. See *Marriage Act* (Cwth) 1961; also T. E. James, "The English Law of Marriage" in *A Century of Family Law 1857–1957*, R. H. Graveson and F. R. Crane (eds.), 1957, Sweet and Maxwell, London, p. 20.

36. Comment, note 4, p. 76.

37. See "Research Report, Attitudes to Sexuality, Sydney" by Sue Wills, Eva Cox, Gaby Antolovich: Comments made during group discussions (these were words used by a teacher to pupils at an all-girls school); quoted in Anne Deveson, note 33, p. 198.

Conclusion

The property value of a woman's sexuality is not only accepted by the dominant group, males. Women have internalised masculine notions of woman's value as sex object – "damage" to her body, such as the "loss" of virginity signifies loss or damage to or of a commodity.[38] Capitalism, which measures everything in monetary (or "money value") terms, permeates all human values: it sets a monetary value on women, or women's bodies. If the "market mechanism" of capitalist society is to be dispensed with, significant issues of how women will survive are inevitably raised. In "Waiting for Lefty", R. E. Lane says:

… the market is a very imperfect mechanism for fitting the variety of human needs to the demands of economic institutions. For all its claim that it maximises satisfaction, some contemporary estimates of sources of satisfaction state that five sixths of the sources of these satisfactions escape the market mechanism. The satisfactions that contribute most to an overall sense of well being rank family and leisure above standard of living; and friendship and freedom from stress contribute more than income.[39]

Certainly current marketing serves few needs for women. Because, in the final analysis, every woman possesses the sole characteristic that she is seen to have for sale, a sole talent, so the market price will always remain depressed.[40] Even where it seems that she has the greatest opportunity for maximising the value of the commodity (through outright sale as a call-girl/prostitute) the market remains in the control of the male – both because the customer is always male and because the system is controlled by male institutions: the police force, the law. However, women are also unable to participate in those satisfactions escaping (in men's eyes) the market mechanism. Because all women possess one talent the system inevitably gives rise to competitiveness between women, making friendship difficult if not illusory.[41] Because the family unit arises, for the woman, out of the market-place and is a direct result, for her, of her marketing activities, family and income are concomitant: thus she has no escape route in the way the man does.

---

38. In studies of simulated juries, both male and female subjects viewed the "loss" of the victim in a rape case in a similar manner. See Shirley Feldman-Summers, "Conceptual and Empirical Issues Associated with Rape" in *Victim in Society*, Emilio Viano (ed.), 1977, New York; Shirley Feldman-Summers and P. Lindner, "Perceptions of Victims and Defendants in Criminal Assault Cases" (1976) 3 *Crim. Justice and Behaviour* 135.
39. R. E. Lane, "Waiting for Lefty – The Capitalist Genesis of Socialist Man" (1978) 6 *Theory and Society* 1, p. 4.
40. Even where there is a scarcity of the commodity through the scarcity of women in a society, the price of the commodity as held by women does not necessarily increase: as in prison communities, men take over the role. Noticeably in early Australia, the shortage of women did not result in their being revered, or in the fortunes of those who were dwelling in Australia to be increased beyond the fortunes of those women living in societies where such a shortage was not the case. See generally Marilyn Dixon, *The Real Matilda*, 1974, Penguin Australia, Ringwood.
41. The feminist movement clearly recognises this, one of its major aims being to foster sisterhood.

If the socialist alternative is to be embraced, again women stand to lose out. Under a socialist system, we are told, the average human type "will rise to the heights of an Aristotle, a Goethe ..."[42] – not much hope for women there. Further:

... incentive systems in a socialist economy must rely on ... self-interests, ... but there are more demands upon individuals for other motives, and rhetorically, a chorus of voices raised against what is called "selfishness". Owen called it "immoral", Fourier a "perversion", Marx thought it worthy only of an animal, William Morris equated it to "hell", Mao calls it "poison", Castro "the beast instinct". Marx hoped that in true communism men would be guided by the principle "From each according to his ability, to each according to his needs." But setting aside the rhetoric, the socialist principle of a guaranteed income, the extension of the progressive income tax to equalise incomes (changing the effort/reward contingency relationships), within the bureaucracies common to both systems the extension of civil service security to those previously vulnerable to unemployment, and the enlarged participatory demands made by "worker self-management", all these institutional changes also change the incentive system to dilute the clear contingency reinforcement system of the market.[43]

Yet sadly, each of these changes could take place without woman losing her position within her caste. Effort/reward relationships may be changed; social security extended to the woman in the home; women may demand "self management" of their own sexuality;[44] incomes may be guaranteed. None of these achievements give any assurance that women will be contained within the "brotherhood of man". Even were class divisions eliminated, women would remain in the position of having to contend with their overriding classification as "women".[45] As Marx said:

What we have here to deal with is a communist society, not as it has developed on its own foundation, but, on the contrary, as it emerges from capitalist society; which is thus in every respect, economically, morally and intellectually, still stamped with the birthmarks of the old society from whose womb it emerges.[46]

Sadly, the old society gives rise to the attitude succinctly expressed by a so-called radical in the movement for (class and racial) equality, an alleged progenitor of social change, harbinger of the "new society", in the United States, Stokely Carmichael:

---

42. Leon Trotsky, quoted in Michael Harrington, *Socialism*, 1973, Bantam, New York, p. 543.

43. Lane, note 39, pp. 10–11.

44. As in the current agitation for abortion law repeal – "the right to choose", and the current debate on reform and interpretation of rape laws so as to recognise woman's right to choose her own sexual partners in terms of "real" choice rather than in the traditional manner of interpreting "consent" to sexual relations as males view consent. On abortion, see "NZ Abortion Bill – Legalised Inquisition and Item 6469 – Back to Backyarders?" *National WEL Newsletter* 18 October, 1977, p. 14. On rape, see Jocelynne A. Scutt, "Consent Versus Submission ...", note 29; and "The Rape of One Woman is the Rape of All Women – Report of the Adelaide Conference on Rape", *National WEL Newsletter* 18 October 1977, p. 23.

45. Significantly socialists continue to refer to brotherhood; sisterhood is a peculiarly feminist concept.

46. Cited Lane, note 39, p. 1.

The place for women in the movement is prone.[47]

It is thus impossible to escape the conclusion that it is our own movement, the development of feminist consciousness, that provides the only path to the creation of a society where women can stand, literally and figuratively, perpendicular with the rest. Realisation of feminist goals is our sole chance to get off our backs.

---

47. See Judith Hole and Ellen Levine, *Rebirth of Feminism*, 1971, Quadrangle/New York Times Book Co., New York. In 1964 a small group of women from the Student Non-Violent Co-ordinating Committee (SNCC) began to meet and talk about their role in the organisation. At a SNCC staff meeting that year, Ruby Doris Smith Robinson presented a paper resulting from the talks and analysis of that group and titled "The Position of Women in SNCC." It elicited comment from Stokely Carmichael "the only position for women in NCC is prone", p. 110. For a discussion on the place of women in Australian Communist Movement see "Women and Labour Conference" (1978) 65 *Aust. Left Rev.* 12, pp. 17 ff. [On the latter issue, see also Joyce Stevens, "A Reasonable Exchange" in *Glorious Age – Growing Older Gloriously*, Jocelynne A. Scutt (ed.), 1993, Artemis Publishing, Melbourne, p. 192.]

13

WOMEN, HOUSING AND PATRIARCHY:
More Than an Emergency

ADDRESS TO WOMEN AND HOUSING CONFERENCE
Adelaide, South Australia
16 May 1985

In 1978 Di Graham, long-time member of the Women's Electoral Lobby (WEL) and who had been very much involved in the strong lobby for rape law reform in New South Wales, began receiving telephone calls from women who were concerned about their rights to property accumulated during marriage. They were concerned about the outcome, or possible outcome, of their litigation in the Family Court of Australia.[1] Under the Family Law Act *1975 (Cth), non-monetary contribution to the accumulation of marital assets was acknowledged for the first time. Prior to this, the economic value of unpaid work in the home was not recognised in the distribution of property upon divorce. At the time, Di Graham, Kerry Heubel and myself were still very much engaged in the struggle to ensure that the WEL Draft Bill on Sexual Offences would form the basis of rape laws, which were under review.[2] I was reluctant to be drawn into a new arena of sex discrimination, although it was clear that women's rights were under severe challenge.*

Di Graham was persistent, as were those telephoning her. With Di as convenor of the newly constituted WEL Family Law Action Group, she, Kerry Heubel, myself and others began to analyse the complaints. Di Graham continued to collect them. We

---

1. See Di Graham, "Through Life in Pursuit of Equality" in *Different Lives – Reflections on the Women's Movement and Visions of Its Future*, Jocelynne A. Scutt (ed.), 1987, Penguin Books Australia, Ringwood, p. 178. In the footnotes, square brackets [...] indicate new material added for this edition.
2. For the WEL *Draft Bill* see Appendix to Criminal Law Review Division, Department of Attorney-General and of Justice, *Supplementary Report on Rape and Other Sexual Offences*, 1977, Department of Attorney-General and of Justice, Sydney. Many provisions of the Bill are now law in a number of Australian jurisdictions, for example, NSW (in the 1981 rape law reforms), ACT (in the 1984 rape law reforms), Victoria (1991 rape law reforms).

wrote submissions to the federal Attorney-General, with copies to each Member of Parliament and the Chief Judge of the Family Court, Justice Elizabeth Evatt. We filed a submission with the Joint Select Parliamentary Committee of Enquiry into the Family Law Act, chaired by Phillip Ruddock, MP, and appeared before the committee to give evidence. (The enquiry reported in 1979.)[3] *We visited the Parramatta Registry of the Family Court, sat in on a number of cases, and spoke with the judges who were assigned to that court.*

Our work convinced us that the discretionary powers of judges, which enabled them to make disparate determinations as to property division between divorcing parties, were at the base of the differential treatment women received at the Family Court. Because the Family Court judges had been trained under the old law embodied in the Matrimonial Causes Act *1959, or even before that Act, when men had greater rights than women in divorce and matrimonial causes, it was, we believed, unrealistic to expect them to abandon sexist notions of "male right". If sexism existed in the world outside the Family Court (as we knew well that it did), it was hardly likely that it would not be entrenched in family law.*

A system of equal rights to marital assets – distribution of all *assets equally between divorcing parties – would ensure that discriminatory treatment of women would be less likely to occur. As it was, some women believed that women were treated fairly in property distribution. It was even said, by some, that women received 60 per cent of the assets. Our research showed that this assertion was wrong. Superannuation, cars, business assets, the spare block, the caravan – these were not being taken into account as assets properly to be divided between the parties. Rather, they were seen as the property* of the husband. *The matrimonial home (where there was one) was the "property" so far as too many of the Family Court judges were concerned.*

We presented a tightly argued paper to the 1981 WEL National Conference in Sydney. We continued lobbying federal parliamentarians. We wrote a book setting out the arguments.[4]

"Women, Housing and Patriarchy" was written with the research Di Graham, Kerry Heubel and I had done on the Family Court and property division firmly in mind. I was determined that the Women's Movement should deal front-on with the question of women's lesser economic power and the fact that women had fewer economic rights than men. I was equally determined that the welfare-ist approach to women should be confronted. Why should women not *have equal economic rights as men? Women should not be seen as supplicants in a system where benefits were conferred out of the "niceness" of the hearts of those in power. Rather, women have rights, and those rights should be respected* and have the force of law.

---

3. Joint Select Parliamentary Committee, *Report on the Enquiry into the Family Law Act*, 1979, AGPS, Canberra.
4. Jocelynne A. Scutt and Di Graham, *For Richer, For Poorer – Money, Marriage and Property Rights*, 1984, Penguin Books Australia, Ringwood.

Years later, women have commented to me in Darwin, Newcastle, Morwell and elsewhere about the positive impact on them and their thinking of "Women, Housing and Patriarchy". At the time, I was aware there was a small group of dissenters in the audience.[5] This detracted not at all from logic nor passion, nor my support from conference participants. I was so strongly aware of the appreciative support the many who were present gave when I delivered the paper.

George Bernard Shaw once wrote, "Home is the girl's prison and the woman's work-house".[6] At the same time, for a man, the Anglo-Saxon (and later Anglo-Australian) approach has been that "his home is his castle":

The poorest man may in his cottage bid defiance to all the force of the Crown. It may be frail, its roof may shake; the wind may blow through it; the storms may enter, the rain may enter, but the King of England cannot enter; all his forces dare not cross the threshold of the ruined tenement![7]

Faced with this grand gender discrepancy, brave critics like Mrs MacStiger of Dicken's *Dombey and Son* fame have demanded "whether an Englishwoman's house is her castle or not".

For centuries, the home was legally, socially and politically a domain different in kind for a woman and a man, whether the woman lived there as the man's wife, sister, daughter, mother or maiden aunt. For wives, the difference was most profoundly described in court cases:

Under the old common law as it existed [until the 1880s a married woman] had no rights at all apart from those of her husband. She was treated by the law more like a piece of his furniture than anything else ... He could bundle his furniture out into the street, and so he could his wife. The law did not say him nay ... If her husband turned her out, she had to go and find lodgings elsewhere, pledging his credit for the rent, that is, if she could find anyone to trust his credit ... Even if the husband did not turn her out, nevertheless when he ceased to be entitled for any reason to the house she would have to leave it: for she had no right of her own to stay there.[8]

Problems for women arose because, in a society whose legal and political structure was based in the private ownership of property, women had no right to own land, no right to independent ownership of wealth, and no right to ownership of income. If a

---

5. Several years later one woman spoke to me of this; my paper was delivered before the lunch break, and she ate with the small group of dissenters, although she was not in dissent. The bewilderment in her voice as she recalled her companions' reaction was palpable! Why had they dissented, she asked? Why indeed?

6. George Bernard Shaw, *Maxims for Revolutionists*, reprinted 1972, Penguin, Harmondsworth, p.1.

7. *Semayne's case* (1604) 5 Co. Rep. 91A; [1558–1774] All ER 62; 15 Digest (Repl.) 978.

8. *Tory v. Tory* (1953) 103 LJ 351; see also *Barrack v. McCulloch* (1856) 3 K&J 110; *Bashall v. Bashall* (1894) 11 TLR 152.

woman had brothers, they succeeded to any property in the family; upon betrothal, any property a woman might own became subject to the rights of her husband-to-be; on marriage, a woman's property became that of her husband.

These laws did more than affect the women of upper classes. They affected the rights of all women to economic independence and to leading autonomous lives. It is impossible to be autonomous when dependent upon a man to sign a lease for the right to live on premises; impossible to be free when required to move from place to place with a husband, living where he called home; impossible to be economically free when obliged to hand over earnings – whether high or low, regular or intermittent – to the "man of the house". Where single women attempted to live lives independent of men, it was made impossible for them to do so by way of discriminatory laws or the discriminatory application of regulations. Thus in the early nineteenth century in New South Wales, one Miss Eliza Walsh "engaged in a protracted battle with colonial and British Governments after Governor Macquarie refused her a land grant on the basis of her sex". In a letter addressed from Woolloomooloo and dated 17 January 1821, Eliza Walsh wrote to Governor Macquarie:

Sir –

I beg leave to state to your Excellency that I have made up my mind to settle a Farm in this country and that I have already purchased one, about three miles from Mr Bells at Richmond Hill where I have Horned Cattle and Stock which amount to upwards of 100 pounds. I can also command 1000 pounds more if your Excellency will be so kind as to make me a grant of Land with the usual indulgencies to Settlers according to means I can exhibit for Cultivation and rearing Cattle

I remain etc.[9]

The reply?

Madam –

I have the Honour to acknowledge the receipt of your Letter dated the 17th Instant, and in reply beg to inform you, that, I cannot comply with your request; it being contrary to late Regulations to give Grants of Land to Ladies.

I have the Honour, etc.

The regulations upon which Macquarie relied were penned by himself, with no such instruction coming from London. Commenting on the interchange, Katrina Alford concludes:

Macquarie was renowned for his egalitarian attitudes to emancipists. He was less well known for his inegalitarian attitude to colonial women.

---

9. Quoted Katrina Alford, *Production or Reproduction? An Economic History of Women in Australia, 1788–1850*, 1984, Oxford University Press, Melbourne, pp. 193–194. The immediately following quotations come from the same source.

The Macquarie response is not exceptional. It exists in the present day when women seeking loans for the purchase of land are subjected to different standards from men, or denied their request on grounds of their sex – an occurrence which today may be less blatant than in the past, but nonetheless continues to occur. It exists where women seeking rental accommodation are refused on grounds linked with sex.

In 1986 the denial of women's right to a home base – being a home in which she is an autonomous dweller – continues. A married woman may believe that in having her name registered on the title of the home in which she and her husband live, she has ensured her right to a 50 per cent share of it, during the marriage and on divorce. A woman may believe that by contributing financially to the well-being of the family – with food, clothing, items for the children – she "buys" a legitimate interest in the home-ground. A de facto wife may think that by ministering to the needs of her de facto husband and their children, she has a right of ownership in any property purchased by him, or held in their joint names. In each case, the supposition is wrong. It cannot be counted upon as a reality, nor as a right, that such a woman has any property interest. For the legally wed woman, her interest in any homeground is dependent upon a determination by the Family Court, in the case of divorce, or upon the possibility of a favourable settlement worked out between her lawyers and those of her husband. According to the High Court of Australia, there is no presumption that both parties are equal contributors – which means, in most cases, that the onus to show a valid contribution lies upon the woman.[10] In the case of the de facto wife, under common law she is obliged to seek the benevolence of the state Supreme Court, where her chances of gaining recognition of her contribution are negligible. (Even in New South Wales and Victoria where legislation has been passed to extend rights akin to those of legally wedded spouses under the *Family Law Act*, 1975 (Cth), the relationship must have been established for at least two years, whatever the woman's contribution. She is then required to establish contribution in the same way as a married woman under the *Family Law Act*.)

Patriarchal notions in property ownership are also apparent in the attitudes of police and their behaviour in so-called domestics. One of the most commonly stated reasons for not investigating criminal assaults carried out on women in what they might believe to be their own homes is, say the police, that when they knock at the door, a man comes to greet them, refusing them entry. Yet if the woman of the home has called police and is joint owner or joint occupant, her right to say "enter" should equal that of her marital or de facto partner. Certainly, the statement by police that they are unable to enter a private home without the permission of the owner or occupier is wrong. The important point to be noted is that police do not talk of the request of the woman owner/occupier

---

10. *Mallett v. Mallett* (1984) 156 CLR 605. For an analysis of this case see Jocelynne A. Scutt and Di Graham, *For Richer, For Poorer*, note 4, Chapter 7, "Epilogue", p. 150.

that they intervene; they concentrate solely upon the (often illusory) gent at the door ordering them away.[11]

It is at this point that the philosophy and practice of a greater part of the woman's movement requires analysis, for it is at this point that women are confronted by patriarchal notions which too often confuse them into accepting less than a woman's right. Patriarchal notions confuse women into believing that they are "doing the best" for their sisters, when a rigorous critique reveals that the supposed best is in reality worst.

Welfare, Marx, and Marxian Welfare

In the Women's Movement, we have fallen into one of two traps, and often both of them. In our haste to alleviate the problem of homelessness faced by so many women, whether through poverty, violence, sexual abuse or a combination of these, we have failed to see the real reason for women's lack of a home base. Many women are without a place to live because a violent man is living in that place, and the woman no longer wishes to endure his violence. Our response has been to demand emergency housing, emergency funding, to provide a home for the woman (and frequently her children). It is as if we believe that the woman in fact has no home; that the home is his, and it is he alone who has a right to remain. The irony is that the woman (and children) will be forced to live, temporarily, in a women's refuge or shelter, the woman sharing a bedroom with her children and often another woman and her children, and sharing joint facilities with a number of other female-headed families. Meanwhile, the man remains in a three-bedroomed home with the support of familiar surrounds. Wife and children struggle to accommodate a new style of living, a new neighbourhood, new companions, new schools. When the temporary accommodation becomes a half-way house or other emergency accommodation, the woman and her children continue to live a half life, with little or no opportunity for long-term planning. The very nature of temporary or emergency accommodation militates against long-range thinking. Then, to the next step – which we have so often seen as the public housing solution. It is at this stage that the vulnerability of women crystallises starkly. Women, living alone with their children, are often neighbours to women living alone with their children. It is not too strong to say they are terrorised by men – some younger, some older – who believe they have a right to treat women-without-men in this way.

---

11. If the police have an honest and reasonable belief that a serious offence is occurring on private property, or that a breach of the peace will recur, they are legally entitled to enter the property, and to arrest the party they honestly and reasonably believe to have committed the offence or to be breaching the peace. In some states legislation provides that they have a duty to "protect person and property from damage", for example, the New South Wales *Police Regulation Act* 1970. See further, Jocelynne A. Scutt, *Even in the Best of Homes*, 1983, Penguin Books Australia, Ringwood, particularly Chapter 9, "The Police" pp. 216 ff. [See also Jocelynne A. Scutt, *Even in the Best of Homes*, 1990, McCulloch Publishing, Carlton, with updated material, Chapter 13, "The Politics of Violence", pp. 286 ff.]

And although women do not profit from the fact that their names may be on the joint title of a home – the home where the man continues to live, in his solitary, three-bedroomed glory, they are faced with the drawbacks. Legal aid offices may take into account the fact that the woman "owns" half a house, and therefore deny her access to legal services. Housing departments or commissions may rate the woman as a home owner, and therefore ineligible to occupy public housing. The welfare approach thus fails to address patriarchal property notions, and in failing to do so deprives the woman of the real contribution she has made to the accumulation of property, whether in the sole name of the husband or both their names. We appear to believe – or recognise – that although confronting the state is difficult, funding is limited, and demands for emergency accommodation and more public housing may not be met, it is easier to face an anonymous department or agency, than to confront the individual patriarch.

The second trap for the Women's Movement is that of attempting to prove that we are the purest of the pure in Marxist discourse, but being catapulted into a position which in fact supports individual patriarchs (and in turn, patriarchy itself). Thus, a supreme amount of energy is directed toward demanding that public housing be seen as the avenue for correcting women's homelessness. Public housing is taken to be "good"; "private" home ownership is often taken as in and of itself implying capitalist acquisitiveness and greed. Yet this juxtaposition is in itself suspect. There is a too ready dismissal of women's contribution to the acquisition of private property, that property being seen as her husband's alone. Should a woman living together with a man who is middle-class protest that she has a right to half the property which has been accumulated during the marriage, and that that half amounts to, say, several hundreds of thousands of dollars, millions of dollars, or even just thousands of dollars, the "good" marxist-feminist reaction is to deplore the capitalist tendencies of some women, and to deny that the woman (seen as a middle-class appendage) has any right to feminist support.

There are two fallacies here. First, notions of equal distribution of property will not become a part of our reality until mechanisms are put into effect which can properly lead to redistribution of all the property. Thus the principle that in marriage, women and men's rights to property must be acknowledged as equal, should be supported as effectively leading to redistribution of property between spouses which in turn will lead to general redistribution. The so-called marxian response to this proposition is that granting the wife of a middle-class male an equal right to share in his wealth extends private property ownership when we should be fighting for communal property access. Surely, a first principle in breaking down the hold some individuals have on home ownership and the ownership of wealth generally, to the exclusion of others, must be to divide property holdings. Secondly, if we do not expend any energy in having the principle of equal rights to marital assets applied universally, we deny to women for whom half a share in assets worth $50, or $100, or $500 is of direct and palpable importance, the right to that share.[12] Furthermore, we place those women who have

---

12. On equal rights to marital assets, see Jocelynne A. Scutt and Di Graham, *For Richer, For Poorer – Money, Marriage and Property Rights*, 1984, Penguin Books Australia, Ringwood.

contributed significantly (that is, equally) to substantial assets in competition with women who do not have marital assets of the same degree. All women are shunted into the public housing, refuge/shelter and emergency housing area, while the men whom they have worked together with in accumulating assets, including housing, too often remain in the private housing sector. Thus the place of women in the poverty sector is intensified.

As women and as feminists we have to rethink our notions of equality, equal rights, and the right to a homeground. Just as the Aboriginal or Black Australian movement has recognised that individually and collectively Black Australians have a right to a homeground, the women's movement must acknowledge women's right to space. Just as Virginia Woolf recognised that without a room of her own, a woman is unable to function as an autonomous being in at least certain parts of her life, we now have to come to grips with the reality that without personal space, the right to maintain such space, and the right not to be removed from it, no woman is free to put together a life in which her right to an autonomous existence is capable of becoming a reality.

Conclusion

There is no doubt that the existence of women's refuges, women's shelters and women's emergency housing has served a real need and will continue to serve such a need in our patriarchal society. However, women's salvation can lie only in a philosophy and practice which moves beyond the short-term response to women's present-day reality. We play into the hands of those seeking to keep in men's hands the determination of economic policies, each time we fail to recognise the real contribution women make to the acquisition of private property. It will be little comfort to us, and little assistance to the movement toward greater equality between women and men, women and women, and men and men, if we require our sisters to take a purist approach, divesting themselves of any right to asset-recognition of their work efforts. This is not to support any policy which would promote amongst women acquisitiveness as it has been, and is, practiced in capitalist patriarchal terms. It is to demand that all women be given the right to work toward the acquisition of a personal homeground that they can class "theirs". There is no reason for believing that once women gain a clear recognition of their right to private home ownership, they should simultaneously adopt selfishness as their mode of living. It would be extraordinary to believe that public housing policies of governments would be more likely to succeed in promoting sharing philosophies amongst home-dwellers than principles of sisterhood devised amongst women who have autonomous property rights in relation to their home space.

At the federal level and in some states in the 1980s, policies were developed to make it easier for low income earners to enter home buyer programmes. It is to the advantage of all women if we work to ensure that the women who might be in a position to gain access to these programmes, rental assistance programmes and co-operative schemes for those women (and men) who are in no position to finance home purchase. It is equally to the advantage of all women if we work to ensure that the contributions made by women to the acquisition of property, too often seen as the property of their husbands (or sometimes fathers or brothers, or de facto husbands), are recognised in real property terms.

But the promulgation of the view that women are an emergency to be dealt with by emergency measures, which in and of their very nature are temporary, one-off, susceptible to changes of policy by governments according to who is in power, is fraught with danger. The danger is that, rather than being recognised as 51 per cent of the population, in relation to whom real, lasting policies must be implemented, women remain in an extraordinary category, limping along from year to year, never able to participate in the real world of economic planning and distribution, because the questions confronting women are: how long can I remain in this bed? how long can my children and I live under this roof? where is the next emergency shelter coming from? when will governments and their housing policies change, so that I may be unable to pay the rent? when will I revert to the homeless sector, to join all the other emergencies?

14

ACHIEVING THE 'IMPOSSIBLE':
Women, Girls and Equal Rights in Education

KEYNOTE SPEECH TO THE 1986 WOMEN IN EDUCATION CONFERENCE
"Social Issues Confronting Women: Implications for Educators"
Perth, Western Australia
26–27 August 1986

Whenever reform of the tertiary education sector is raised, the predictable cry from the Committee of Vice Chancellors is that this is a threat to academic freedom. As women and disadvantaged minorities well know, "academic freedom" is the term given to practices and procedures which ensure that those who have a "right" to power and privileges within the university sector retain their *power, and* their *privileges. "Academic freedom" is the expression that always enters the arena as soon as questions of equal opportunity for women and disadvantaged minorities and affirmative action are raised, both in relation to entry to university and appointment to academic posts. This is particularly so when professorships, associate professorships, and readerships are under discussion. When tutorships are in question, there is less concern – for, after all, how can it be "bad" in the overall scheme of things if women with PhDs are "allowed" into the lowest rungs of the academic hierarchy? (They can't be kept out entirely – that would be too blatant, and too difficult a position to maintain.) Women are, as everyone knows, so ready to work harder for less pay, and to take on large workloads. Having such creatures working at tutorship level means those higher in the echelons (men) will be free to research, write and publish – and gain even further accolades. Promotions. Sabbaticals. Trips abroad. Consultancies. L-a-r-g-e fees (on top of their regular professorial salaries). Invitations to present learned papers ... And once appointed at tutorship level, it will be difficult for the women to make their way up to the "top" positions in the university hierarchy: who ever heard of a tutor being appointed professor or associate professor. Too quantum a leap, indeed.*[1]

---

1. On the ability of those in academic positions to "tolerate" women so long as they remain tutors, see Greta Bird, "Growing Up in Law School" in *Breaking Through – Women, Work and Careers*, Jocelynne A. Scutt (ed.), 1992, Artemis Publishing, Melbourne, p. 101. In the footnotes, square brackets [...] indicate new material added for this edition.

Affirmative action of the type men decry – allowing "in" persons who are less qualified in any sense of the word – is, ironically, what has enabled men to take the highest administrative positions in the primary and secondary sectors of education. Male students graduating from secondary school with marks far inferior to those of women entering teachers colleges were granted entry to the teaching profession to ensure that the profession would not only comprise women.

I was pleased to be asked to deliver the keynote address to the Women in Education Conference held in Perth in August 1986. The education sector harbours so many excellent teachers who are women and, after all, so many women have gone into teaching. It is wrong that women should be directed into particular professions (such as teaching) as "suitable for a woman", and on that basis alone. Women and girls are entitled to equal opportunity in career choices, and to have open as many career choices as are open to men and boys. Yet it is nonsensical to turn away from supporting women in teaching, with a notion that women in "non-traditional" trades and professions are worthy of more support, or to infer that women should turn away from teaching to "more challenging" or "interesting" or "demanding" jobs. How much more "challenging" or "demanding" than to teach – particularly where those set to learn are children and young people? Why should anyone who wants to teach, to "be a teacher", be shamed out of it by the notion that she has chosen an "uninteresting" profession? How can teaching – if this is what a woman wants to do – be uninteresting?!

I applaud all women who have gone into teaching and remain there, bringing new ideas to their students, and so often simply doing the slog that is required of those who teach in primary and secondary schools. I applaud, too, those women who, having initially gone into teaching, later moved to other fields of learning and have since made their way in arenas away from the schoolroom.[2] Learning to be, and being, a teacher has equipped many women for their chosen career – whether it be remaining as a teacher, going into politics, entering the legal profession and becoming a magistrate or judge ...

---

2. Numerous women have done this, including Janine Haines who, after a career she enjoyed in teaching, went into federal politics and became leader of the Australian Democrats; Fran Bladel who (after working in pubs, doing secretarial and administrative work, and many other jobs) became, after a stint in teaching which she found exhilarating, a member of the Legislative Assembly in the Tasmanian Parliament; Jennifer Coate who, after teaching for some years (her family's monetary circumstances meant that she had no other choice), went back to university to study law, graduated, ran her own law firm for some seven years then, after a "break" which included working as a locum for the Victorian Legal Aid Commission and in a position with the Victorian Department of Attorney-General, was appointed the fifteenth woman magistrate in Victoria. See Janine Haines, "A Sort of Crusade" in *Breaking Through*, note 1, p. 64; Jennifer Coate, "Slipping Through the Net" in *Breaking Through*, note 1, p. 161; and Fran Bladel, "The 'Third Eye' of Feminism" in *Glorious Age – Growing Older Gloriously*, Jocelynne A. Scutt (ed.), 1993, Artemis Publishing, Melbourne, p. 171.

In August 1993 I was in Perth once again, this time to deliver the keynote address to the 1993 Women in Education Conference, "Managing the Future".[3] A comparison of the titles given to the conferences, seven years apart, indicates that thinking has changed over the years, and that "management" has become a significant issue in teaching, just as it has been accepted as such in other spheres. As well, it was a measure of the changes that can occur in lives and careers that at the 1986 conference I met women (and a male teacher, now at the top of the administration) I had not spoken with since school or university. At the 1993 conference it was almost an entirely different group of teachers participating. Some had never been to a women's conference before. And I reflected that the 1986 conference was the last public function I attended as Deputy Chairperson of the Law Reform Commission, Victoria: the following Monday, I commenced reading for the Bar, becoming a lawyer in private practice. At the 1993 conference, I had been in practice for seven years. In the year 2000 – who knows?

Introduction

The education system has often been seen as the "front line", whether the observer be "pro" women's rights or "anti" them. Back in 1906, following the inaugural lecture of Marie Curie as professor of the Sorbonne, in Paris, an anonymous commentator wrote:

If a woman is allowed to teach advanced studies to both sexes, where afterward will be the pretended superiority of man? I tell you, the time is near when women will become human beings.[4]

In May 1776, one hundred and thirty years earlier, Samuel Johnson similarly acknowledged the central place (lack of) education has in the oppression of women. In *Boswell's Life* he wrote, "Where there is no education ... men will have the upper hand of women."[5]

Some twenty years later, Hannah More spoke out angrily against the way in which the withholding of access to education kept women in a subordinate position. Born in 1745, died 1833, in *Strictures on the Modern System of Female Education*, published in 1799, she said:

Till women shall be more reasonably educated, and till the native growth of their mind shall cease to be stinted and cramped, we have no juster ground for pronouncing that their understanding has already reached its highest attainable point, than the Chinese would have for

---

3. Jocelynne A. Scutt, *Out of the Past and Present – Into the Future*, Keynote address delivered to the 1993 Women in Education Conference, 26–27 August 1993, Ministry of Education, Murdoch University, Western Australia.

4. Quoted in R. Reid, *Marie Curie*, 1978, Chapter 13, Paladin Books, London, p. 133.

5. Samuel Johnson, *Boswell's Life*, chapter XI, quoted Simon James, *A Dictionary of Sexist Quotations*, 1984, Harvester Press, Sussex, p. 35

affirming that their women have attained the greatest possible perfection in walking, while their first care is, during their infancy, to cripple their feet.[6]

The debate about women's right to education, the form and nature of girls' and women's education, is not new; nor is it dead, despite the acceptance in Australia of compulsory schooling up to the age of 14, 15 or 16 years and increasing numbers of women undertaking tertiary level education. Past statements about women's education reveal too well a real fear on the part of some men that, being educated, women would invariably excel; some women, sadly, appear to have been convinced that if education were made open to females, women would lose whatever power they possessed – however unreal that power might be. In *Select Conversations with an Uncle*, published in 1895, H. G. Wells protested: "Higher education has eliminated the witty woman."[7] (Can one be blamed for opining that a woman had recently failed to laugh at an H. G. Wells "joke"?) More than a century before, Hannah Cowley, playwright, considered uneducated women wielded significant power which was all but destroyed by literacy. In 1779 she declared:

The charms of women were never more powerful – never inspired such achievements, as in those immortal periods when [women] could neither read nor write.[8]

Present day attitudes also reveal a certain fear, or selfishness, or both, too frequently where male attitudes to girls' and women's education are concerned. During the federal parliamentary debate on affirmative action, a Liberal Party member from a New South Wales suburban electorate railed against allegedly new procedures implemented in universities in Australia which, he contended, meant that inadequate and inferior women were gaining academic positions at the expense of men. Fortunately this was countered by an article written by Anne Suskind and appearing in the *Sydney Morning Herald* of 19 April 1986, citing statements from a senior male academic (with similar coverage in *The Australian*, 23 April 1986):

"FEMINIST" STAFF BIAS DENIED BY UNIVERSITY

Accusations that the University of Sydney was making "notorious feminist" appointments were mistaken and misleading, the University's Deputy Vice-Chancellor Professor Michael Taylor said yesterday.

Professor Taylor, who presides over the committee responsible for academic appointments, said: "Feminism or anything else is irrelevant to academic judgment. We don't ask what a person's religion is, or what their private connections are. Appointments are made on merit only." Appointments to lectureships and senior lectureships had strict guidelines and took account of teaching ability, research achievement and capacity, as well as administrative experience and skill, Professor Taylor said.[9]

---

6. Hannah More, Strictures on the Modern System of Female Education, 1799; quoted Dale Spender, *Women of Ideas – and What Men Have Done to Them*, 1982, Routledge, London.
7. H. G. Wells, *Select Conversations with an Uncle*, 1895, quoted Simon James, note 5, p. 36.
8. Hannah Crowley, *Who's the Dupe*, 1779, Act I; quoted Dale Spender, note 6.
9. At p. 4.

This will be welcome news to all those women with good teaching skills and abilities who in the past have been overlooked whilst men have been appointed because they are men.

In recent years universities have sometimes been criticised for providing places for women who, the critics assert, have decided to attend university only because they have nothing better to do and no other way of filling in time. This type of criticism has been made against tertiary institutions such as Macquarie University in New South Wales, where the arrangement of class times has made it a little less difficult for women with family responsibilities (and no partner, or no responsible partner) to attend and gain a tertiary education. In similar vein, a female academic from LaTrobe University in Victoria has reported being accosted by male members of the academic staff "... all this affirmative action business means that a generation of young men will go down the drain" because women will be accepted into positions which the men might otherwise have filled.[10] This, she observed, is asserted with various shakings of heads, and a complete refusal to acknowledge that generations of young women, and older women, any women might have "gone down the drain" through a refusal to acknowledge women's right to equal access to education and to teaching and administrative positions within the education system. [11]

Keeping Women Out – But Losing (Eventually)

Universities in Britain were established by donations of funds from the aristocracy. Not infrequently the donors were women of so-called high breeding. They gave grants to establish (male) colleges in universities such as Cambridge University and Oxford University. Unfortunately, their views on the rights of women (or lack of such rights) to attend the universities are not recorded. Some universities were established even more clearly on the donations of women. In France the brothel at Toulouse was financed jointly by the City of Toulouse and the University of Toulouse; this arrangement began in 1201 and continued until 1389. In 1389 a riot interfered with the Toulouse brothel trade, and the King issued a royal order prohibiting the destruction of the brothel buildings by the rioting mob. The order was attached to the building by the King's Seal.[12] And when the convents were taken over by the state in the Tudor period in England, many were turned into male colleges of higher education. The United States feminist scholar Janice Raymond in *A Passion for Friends* instances the nunnery of St Radegend's which was converted to Jesus College, Cambridge University in England

---

10. Personal communication.
11. Women's talents and abilities have always been utilised; the world would not function as it does without women's expertise. At the same time it is important that women not be deprived from developing different talents and abilities, or expanding on those already present, because of sexist ideology and lack of equal opportunity. [Further on this issue, see Chapter 15, "Women and the Power to Change", this volume.]
12. Jess Wells, *A History of Prostitution in Western Europe*, 1982, Shameless Hussy Press, Berkeley.

– a college which, like other colleges at Cambridge and Oxford Universities, only recently acceded to catering for women students. We do not know whether the various female benefactors of universities might have wished some women, at least, to have access to the learning which was being dispensed through their largesse.[13]

In the last half of the nineteenth century women began demanding a right to enter the universities, to participate in tertiary education to enable them to become doctors or lawyers or enter other professions, or simply to broaden their knowledge. In the 1860s one Sophia Jex Blake and six other women fought this battle for the right to study at Edinburgh University in Scotland. Sophia Jex Blake had earlier been admitted to study, the authorities not finding any legitimate reason to keep her out. However, the male students took her presence badly. They harassed and tormented her, even going so far one day as to bring into the lecture theatre a goat with a directly insulting message written on a card attached to its neck. The authorities then refused her further admittance, together with other women seeking to be students. All applied to the court to have it settled that they had a right to enter the university and join in the classes as regular students. The law which was in question was interpreted by the court as meaning that women were not persons for the purpose of the legislation. The court held, therefore, that Sophia Jex Blake, her colleagues and any other women who might apply, would rightly be refused a place. One of the judges said:

It is a belief, widely entertained, that there is a great difference in the mental constitution of the two sexes, just as there is in their physical conformation. The powers and susceptibilities of women are as noble as those of men; but they are thought to be different, and, in particular, it is considered that they have not the same power of intense labour as men are endowed with ... To some extent, I share this view, and should regret to see our young females subjected to the severe and incessant work which my own observation and experience have taught me to consider as indispensable to any high attainment ... A disregard of such an inequality would be fatal to any course of instruction ...

Add to this the special acquirement and accomplishments at which women must aim, but from which men may easily remain exempt. Much time must, or ought to be, given by women to the acquisition of a knowledge of household affairs and family duties, as well as to those ornamental parts of education which tend so much to social refinement and domestic happiness and the study necessary for mastering these must always form a serious distraction from severe pursuits.[14]

Similarly, sexist ideology found its place in Australia to prevent women from participating in tertiary education together with men, although sometimes the sexism was more understated. At the primary level, universal education was more readily accepted

---

13. It is difficult to believe that all women donating to academic institutions, or providing foundation funds, were "male identified". More than a few must surely have been cognisant of the right of women to have access to education, and no doubt intended the monies to be used fairly, rather than solely for men.

14. Per Neaves, L. J. in *Jex Blake v. Senatus of the University of Edinburgh* (1873) 11 McPherson 784–794.

in Australia than in Britain. This acceptance may have come about because the alternative was to have children brought up solely by their parents, many of whom were (initially at least) convicts or ex-convicts. Between 1872 and 1895 all Australian colonies established public primary educational institutions. This egalitarian approach differed from that advanced by authorities in England, where "conservative opinion ... agreed wholeheartedly" with the Bishop of London's conviction that it was "safest for both the Government and the religion of the country to let the lower classes remain in that state of ignorance in which nature originally placed them ..." Nonetheless, inequality existed in the Australian primary education system because girls and boys did not have equal opportunities to study all subjects on the curriculum. Girls were taught reading and writing, but not arithmetic. Sewing and needlework instruction were regarded as essential for girls. The few secondary schools catered in the main for boys. From Western Australia, Paige Porter reports that where girls' secondary schools were built, they mostly concentrated on the "feminine arts", so conformed to the views of the British court in refusing women the right to attend university.[15] Plato's admonition that girls "must be trained in precisely the same way [as boys], and I say this without any reservations about whether horse riding or athletics are suitable for males but not females" took second place to the dictum of Rousseau in *Emile* in 1762:

Once it is shown that men and women neither are nor ought to be constituted alike either in character or in temperament, it follows that they ought not to receive the same education.[16]

As for the Australian universities, women fought similar battles to those in Britain. From 1851 to 1882 the University of Sydney in effect refused admission to women, and from 1854 to 1881 the University of Melbourne similarly kept them out. Women were not admitted to matriculation until 1881 and 1882 respectively in Victoria and New South Wales, and for the other states similar problems arose for women. Without matriculation, no one could study at university without special dispensation. Although it is often said that women's treatment is "special", it takes little imagination to recognise that in this case, women would not have gained classification in the list as "special". In 1879 William Manning, at the time Chancellor of the University of Sydney, addressed the issue by acknowledging that the question of women's right to enter the university had been raised. He acknowledged that women might well excel in fields such as chemistry, botany, vegetable physiology, mineralogy and geology. However, despite this, he thought it would:

... be better to let the question stand over till our School of Science has been exchanged ... The best course to be taken by the advocates of advanced education for women, would be to found some sort of affiliated college for them in the vicinity of the University ... The suggested

---

15. Paige Porter, "Social Policy, Education and Women" in Bettina Cass and Cora Baldock, (eds.), *Women, Social Welfare and the State*, 1983, Allen and Unwin, Sydney, p. 246.
16. J. Rousseau, *Emile*, 1762, Book V, part 1, quoted Simon James, note 5, p. 35.

College would come within the spirit, though probably not within the letter, of our Affiliated Colleges Act ... There should be no difficulty in adopting some temporary arrangements to commence with, if there really be a widespread wish on the part of young women and their friends for a higher education under or "within" the University ...[17]

There was no acknowledgement of women's right to education: women were supposed to be satisfied with "temporary arrangements", "some sort of affiliated college", and being in the extraordinary situation of "not within the letter, but within the spirit (perhaps) of the law"!

But, as in Britain and the United States, women struggled for the right to gain education through universities and other tertiary institutions – and attained the goal. Yet even then, quota systems were set in various faculties – particularly medicine and law – to keep women out, in any great numbers, or numbers equivalent to their abilities. In education faculties, the opposite approach was taken – quotas were set which prevented women being too greatly in the majority, and men were admitted to teaching courses to overcome a perceived problem – that the teaching profession was far too greatly dominated by women, allegedly to the detriment of the children being taught. Thus, men who were not as intelligent as the women students were given special treatment and allowed in to courses leading to teacher qualifications.

Once the battle had been won acknowledging women's and girls' equal right of access to education at all levels – primary, secondary and tertiary – a battle had to be fought to ensure that women teachers had equal right of access to teaching posts, to promotions, to administrative positions, and to equal pay. This battle began early in Britain and Australia.

On 19 January 1923, *Time and Tide*, the feminist journal published in England, reported:

Mr Fisher continues to advise teachers in *The Teacher's World*. Last week he discoursed upon "EQUAL PAY". He was disturbed lest any one should suppose that he thought it the duty of the teacher to be occupied with political or financial questions. "The best teachers," he explained, "have better things to think about than salaries or trades union policy. They do not care about the politics of the profession ... They are in fact the salt of the earth." Unfortunately, the best grocers and butchers still continue to take an active interest in prices. Mr Fisher, however, has a soul above such mundane considerations. He is entirely opposed to equal pay; he admits that the "demand has an obvious foundation in reason. The women teachers are as well qualified as the men, and they work as long hours," but he declares that "while it is on public grounds desirable that the male teacher in our elementary school should marry early, it is desirable that the female teacher should for some years remain unmarried" (a statement which by itself is worth some consideration), and he appears to have some hazy notion that paying a woman less will somehow prevent her marrying; although why it should do so in a profession which in any case almost always dismisses her when she does marry is not very easy to see. In any case, Mr Fisher is perfectly clear as to his practical views on equal pay. To bring the women's pay up to

---

17. Quoted Jocelynne A. Scutt, *Growing Up Feminist*, 1985, Angus and Robertson, Sydney, p. 7.

the men's would cost, so he tells us, seven millions, and at present he does not think we have the money to spend. But if we had (and he does not press for fresh money) he would not dream of spending it on removing this admitted injustice – no, he would "spend it on the children". He has not the imagination to realise that to allow the majority of the teachers to suffer from a rankling sense of injustice is exceedingly bad for the children.[18]

In Australia various women's organisations – including the National Council of Women, the Union of Australian Women, the United Associations of Women, the Karrakatta Club, the League of Women Voters and various others – demanded equal rights for women in all spheres, at least from the turn of the century. Women established and joined unions when the union movement grew in Australia in the last half of the nineteenth century – setting up tailoresses unions and laundresses unions amongst others. Demands for equal pay and equal opportunities included demands for the right to stand for various public offices, including parliament and local government; the right to vote in all public elections; appointment of women as Justices of the Peace, without any limitations on their standing; and women representatives on all government boards, royal commissions and select committees. On 20 January 1926, the National Council of Women of Western Australia requested that "in the appointment of the new Physicians and Surgeons on the Perth Public Hospital there should always be equal consideration given to women, especially in the matter of gynaecological and surgical work". Councils of Action for Equal Pay were founded and worked through the years. The Western Australian organisation was disbanded in the mid-1970s but, in 1984 in Melbourne, the Council of Action for Equal Pay was revived and renewed, to fight the battle for equal pay for work of equal value, or "comparable worth".[19]

Where appointments and promotions were concerned, women again put their energies into demanding women's rights. Just as women of the nineteenth and early twentieth centuries acknowledged the need for women's work in teaching to be recognised as equal to that of men in teaching through equal pay, these women and their successors saw that it is essential for women to be in positions of power in the administration of education. In Victoria, the story of Julia Flynn's fight to be recognised as an equally appropriate, equally worthy, candidate for the post of Chief Inspector of the Education Department, as the man who had held it in the late 1920s is firm evidence of this.[20] It shows also the collective energy women devoted to supporting other women.

---

18. Extracted Dale Spender, *Time and Tide Wait for No Man*, 1984, Pandora Press, London, pp. 191–192.
19. See Kate McNeill, Sue Jackson and Pat Morrigan, "The Equal Pay Campaign – Into the '80s" (1985) 20 *Scarlet Woman* (Spring) 16. [The Australian Conciliation and Arbitration Commission is now the Australian Industrial Relations Commission – *Industrial Relations Act* 1988 (Cth).]
20. Judith Biddington, "Woman at the Top" in *Double Time*, Marilyn Lake and Farley Kelly (eds.), 1985, Penguin Books Australia, Ringwood, p. 233. The following quotations re Julia Flynn's case come from the same source. [See further on the Julia Flynn case, Chapter 4, pp. 66–67.]

Learning from the Past to Gain the Future

The social issues confronting women today have their origins in the past. Learning about the past, in order to change the future, is vital. The energetic memory of our great-grandmothers, grandmothers, mothers (and a very few of our great-grandfathers, grandfathers and fathers overcoming some of their sexist conditioning) should not be forgotten when we map out our plans for gaining the so-called impossible – equal rights for girls and women, alongside boys and men, in education as in other spheres of life. We can learn from the strategies and tactics of the past. It is important that the lessons are not lost, and that they should be recovered so that we do not begin in a vacuum, believing that actions by women have never been taken before; that the issues confronting women now, have never confronted women of the past; or that women have never won before; or that we are building on nothing, no past.

It is important not to romanticise the past. Simultaneously, we must never forget we are a part of a strong and vital tradition, and our lives are important for ourselves, and at the same time are important also because we are building on what our forebears, our sisters of the past, have built, often against tremendous odds. That building will provide an even stronger base for the girls and women following us, as they inevitably will. The odds may seem as severe today for us, as they were then. Similarly, those following us will face severe odds. But without the past, the starting point would be even less defined.

That the odds are significant today, and parallel in some ways the odds facing earlier generations of women, is revealed in current struggles for women's and girl's rights. Today, in New South Wales, a young woman named Melinda Leves is fighting through the Equal Opportunity Tribunal for the right to study the same subjects as her brother in secondary school. She and her brother are twins. He attends an all boys government school, she an all girls government school. His school provides subjects such as computer management and technical drawing. She has subjects such as domestic science. She wants the opportunity to study computer management, but cannot because there are insufficient computers in the school. His school has sufficient computers for the subject to be adequately taught, a prominent part of the school curriculum. Students at his school daily have access to the computers. The Minister for Education has acknowledged by letter to Melinda Leves' parents that their daughter is not in a position to gain equal training and education as their son. However, the problem is stated to be that providing similar subjects would be "too expensive". Thus Melinda Leves is forced to seek her rights to an equal education through the Equal Opportunity Tribunal which, ironically, was established under legislation passed by the government to provide for equal opportunities in education, employment and other areas of life – the *Anti Discrimination Act* 1977. Indeed, that government has done more in the equal rights and affirmative action field than any other government to date in Australia.[21] Yet the

---

21. For example, affirmative action being provided for throughout the public service by legislation since about 1980; tertiary educational institutions being required to establish some bona fides in relation to equal opportunities for women, and so on. [The *Melinda Leves case* is now reported: *Leves v. Haines* (1986) EOC 92–167. She won.]

same government refuses to acknowledge Melinda Leves' right to equal access to education and is vigorously defending its stand in the very Equal Opportunity Tribunal it established to provide those discriminated against with a forum.

In tertiary education, it is salutary that the experience of Sophia Jex Blake in having to compete, in the minds of men students, with a female goat, is not so far removed from the present. In Queensland, a young woman named Emel Corley fought for the right to study mechanics at a Brisbane technical college. She wrote, at the age of twenty in 1984:

I applied to the prevocational trade-based course which teaches basic principles in most trades – fitting and turning, bricklaying, carpentry, mechanics, electrics, sheet metal work – and counts as credit towards an apprenticeship.

She went on:

I was the only woman in the company of 150 adolescent boys. They had done between two to four years of woodwork, metal work and technical drawing at school. I had done two years of typing and shorthand. When the boys realised I was good at my work and didn't rely on them to carry things for me or favour me with their chivalry, they began to make life difficult. Boys constantly tripped me up and down stairs, threw food and soft drinks at me and put gum in my locker so I couldn't get my books out (making me late for classes). They smashed my carpentry and bricklaying. Then on the way to the train station, they'd throw stones at me. School was horrific.[22]

Next, think back to the excuse handed out by Mr Fisher when he wrote, as reported in *Time and Tide* in the 1920s, that even if it were seen as appropriate to pay women teachers equally with men teachers, it would cost so much that it could not be contemplated – and any extra money, anyway, should go "to the children". These words have an unfortunately modern day ring to them. In the 1983 *National Wage Case* the Women's Electoral Lobby argued that to overcome the avoidance of the equal pay decisions of 1972 and 1974, the Australian Conciliation and Arbitration Commission should establish within its ranks a special panel to deal with equal pay for work of equal value claims by trade unions representing women's claims. WEL's claim was refused by the Commission on the basis that if any such plan were implemented, then the claims which would have to be met to bring women's wages up to parity with men's wages would be so great as to be impossible to fulfil, at least in present economic times.[23] This is simply to acknowledge that women are underpaid, and to hold that women should continue to be underpaid and industry profit from that failure to recognise women's rightful claims. Apparently the economy will not be able to survive any recognition of wage justice for women. It couldn't allegedly in 1923 and the position had not changed in 1983.

---

22. Emel Corley, "Contribution" in Jocelynne A. Scutt, note 17, pp. 59, 60.
23. Paige Porter, "Social Policy, Education and Women", note 15; *National Wage Case* (1983) 291 CAR 3.

Although each of these illustrations is daunting, none of us believes that therefore we should give up, and the world we want, need and demand will never be gained. On the one hand, that it is possible to show past action by women against injustices in the same or very similar spheres, and along the same or very similar lines, could lead to a debilitated feeling of "what's the point". However, the way women fought in the past can also lead to our devising new methods of fighting, or learning new ways of looking at present social issues confronting women and educators. Two crucial areas are those of science and economics. Science is seen by many as vital to numerous aspects of present day living, and is becoming more so in an economic sense. Present day governments appear to be orientated towards viewing scientific "advances" as having a potential for providing Australia with economic growth through "sunrise" industries. A major problem is that governments are not asking ethical questions. They are not demanding that scientists and technocrats assess their own ethics in the "great march forward" of science. The sale of biotechnology, so well illustrated in the setting-up by Monash University of a semi-private company to sell reproductive technology overseas, is an area of concern – yet governments are, apparently, encouraging this as "economically valuable".[24] Is it "good" that girls and women are being encouraged to enter science, when so much of what science represents and is, is antithetical to human well-being, and particularly to the well-being of women?[25] Could it be that women have, in large numbers, foresworn science in the past because it is imbued with an anti-human ethos?

Within the Women's Movement, attitudes toward science generally take either the approach that science is "masculine" and can never be reorientated along feminist lines; or that women's voices must be heard in science, so that the orientation of science can occur along feminist lines. A third position is that *feminist science* has been forgotten, or overlooked, and must be recovered from the past. In feminist literature it is generally acknowledged that women played a significant part in the development of agricultural inventions, inventions in spinning and weaving, writing treatises on mathematics, physics and medicine, and devising theories of the universe. The use of fire to cook, the sowing of crops, the devising of cooking pots and gardening implements are all attributable to women. In more recent times, women have been pre-eminent in other developments. In the early eighteenth century, for

---

24. Philip McIntosh and Calvin Miller, "University Council Approves Sale of IVF Technology", *Age* 19 March 1985, p. 3; Philip McIntosh, "America to Market our IVF Technology Overseas", *Age* 2 July 1985. [See further Ramona Koval, "The Commercialisation of Reproductive Technology" in *The Baby Machine – The Commercialisation of Motherhood*, Jocelynne A. Scutt (ed.), 1988, McCulloch Publishing, Carlton, p. 108.]

25. See for example the work of Renate Klein and Robyn Rowland in relation to in vitro fertilisation (IVF) and other new reproductive technologies: Rita Arditti, Renate Duelli Klein and Shelley Minden, *Test-Tube Women. What Future for Motherhood*, 1984, Pandora Press, London. [See further Gena Corea et al., *Man-Made Women – How New Reproductive Technologies Affect Women*, 1985, Hutchinson, London, and 1987, Indiana University Press, Bloomington.]

example, Lady Mary Wortley Montagu introduced the smallpox vaccine to England, having observed its use in Turkey when she lived there at the British Embassy. In the early nineteenth century, chemistry became "increasingly popular among women and the lecture halls of Paris had to be enlarged to accommodate the crowds".[26]

There is a need to take care, as educators, that a tendency to laud "progress" because it *is* defined as *progress* by the dominant group, or to laud aspects of science because women were or are involved, does not interfere with an ability to assess critically the value of "advances". Just because the lack of scientific knowledge and expertise have deprived women and girls of access to particular fields does not mean that we must without critical analysis embrace a change in educational policy, which now sets to encouraging girls to enter science. Surely we should ask what science is taught, how it is taught, and what science *is not* taught; how does the dominant society frame its notions of science?

In 1982 Robin Morgan wrote in *The Anatomy of Freedom*:

Women have always been technologists. To buy into Man's lie that we have not is to consign ourselves not only to an ignorance of our own past but an alienation from our own present – and possibly an exile from our own future. It's a human tendency to dismiss what one doesn't understand – dismiss it with awe if it seems involved with power and dismiss it with contempt if it seems involved with powerlessness. Since modern technology is involved with (men's) power and with (women's) powerlessness, most women have tended to dismiss it as doubly unapproachable ... Yet how does a simplistic back-to-nature attitude differ from sexual, political, or any other kind of fundamentalist thinking. *Technological fundamentalism*, whether of the worshipful tech-fix variety or the scornful antitech strain, won't clarify the confusion, won't solve the problem, and certainly won't make technology "go away".[27]

Fortunately in Australia we have had the continuing benefit of a strong debate in science and technology, where women's voices are increasingly heard. Renate Klein and Robyn Rowland have been pre-eminent in this, and the Women in Science Network (WISENET) has also played a strong role, not the least in disseminating information and ensuring that women are not working unsupported whilst a scientific critique is developing. There is certainly no "knee jerk reaction" against science and technology in the Australian Women's Movement. A critique strongly centred in research, knowledge and understanding of women's position as "test-sites" or "living laboratories"[28] is central to women's understanding of science, and to the question whether the entry of

---

26. Margaret Alic, *Hypatia's Heritage*, 1986, The Women's Press, London, p. 98. [Today, there is a newly developing feminist critique of innoculation and injections, particularly in relation to babies and young children. Dr Robyn Rowland has commenced research in this area.]

27. Robin Morgan, *The Anatomy of Freedom*, 1982, Anchor Press/Doubleday, Garden City, New York, p. 263.

28. "Test-sites" is the expression coined by Renate Klein and Robyn Rowland. "Living laboratories" is the expression coined by Robyn Rowland. [In 1992 Robyn Rowland published a book using the expression in the title: Robyn Rowland, *Living Laboratories*, 1992, Oxford University Press, Melbourne.]

girls into scientific education will bring changes to that discipline and positive opportunities for women in the professions. It is vital that women take part in the debate, for it is clear that *masculine* science and technological developments have been detrimental to the well-being of humans, the animal and plant world, and to the world in general.[29]

In economics, similar problems arise. One of the first economists was Harriet Martineau, born 1802, died 1876. She wrote *Illustrations of Political Economy*, a series which sold ten thousand copies a month in 1834. (The feminist writer and researcher Dale Spender contrasts this with John Stuart Mill's *Principles of Political Economy* which sold three thousand copies in four years.) Her work was described as "derivative" by male commentators of the day and subsequently, although from whence outside her own intelligence, and properly taking into account relevant developments in other fields, Harriet Martineau could have "derived" her ground-breaking work is difficult to fathom. As Spender says:

At this stage there was no formal training available in economics, no degree course or institution devoted to its study, ... [so] it remains a mystery ... how one could have become an economist by any means other than those used by Harriet Martineau. What claim to fame did these other "economists" have, John Stuart Mill included, that Harriet did not, apart from their sex? Because they are male they are economists; because she is a female, "the derivative sex", she is but a publiciser of their ideas.

What Harriet Martineau was doing, what the men were not – and I think it is most significant – was trying to make much of this new and powerful knowledge generated by men, which until that time had been kept within the confines of a small privileged circle, to invest it with her own "original" refinement, and to make it available to all who could read. She got rid of the "trimmings" ... and made her own contribution to the social sciences in the process. But ... little respect is given to those who do not play the "mystifying" game and who instead insist on the *knowledgeability* of all human beings and who attempt to make knowledge accessible to them.[30]

It is possible to argue that economics is an anti-woman discipline, that it ignores the realities of humanity, and that its concerns are not ours: economics talks in terms of "economically rational man", a being who concentrates upon "economic" growth to the exclusion of almost all else, and who fails to take into account human well-being at all, or considers that human well-being is measured in accordance with free market forces or other theoretical constructs which ignore the "human" part of humanity. But there is no good reason why economics should be constructed in this way. Isn't it

---

29. Examples of male science as "deadly progress" are too numerous to mention. The development of the atomic bomb is the most obvious. [In the 1990s another example of male science interfering with women's health was discovered by Renate Klein in co-operation with Lynette Dumble – Creutzfeldt-Jakob disease (CJD) has killed a number of women who were given hPG by doctors as an "antidote" to infertility. On this, see Lynette J. Dumble and Renate Klein, "Creutzfeldt-Jakob Legacy for Australian Women Treated with Human Pituitary Gland Hormone for Infertility", in (1993) 340 *The Lancet* 847–848; Renate Klein and Lynette J. Dumble, "Transmission of Creutzfeldt-Jakob Disease by Blood Transfusion" (1993) 341 *The Lancet* 768.]
30. Spender, note 6, p. 128.

possible to construct economic theories which take into account, fully, the ideals and realities of human beings; isn't is possible to construct an economic world which recognises people as intrinsically valuable, and does not see the philosophy of "every man for himself" as necessarily, nor rightly, ruling the world?

The problem confronting women is the fear that if we move into areas which are so clearly (although some might say erroneously) labelled "male", and so fully imbued with the masculine ethic, we may be caught up in the ethos therein expressed and acted out; our way of regarding the world through those disciplines might be lost. Sometimes we are so close to the issues that we fail to see that it doesn't have to be an "either/or"; we don't have to demand of ourselves that we be "right" because otherwise we will be "wrong".

In reflecting on the present, it is important to remember that the Women's Movement is centuries old. Our most recent efforts – the efforts of those of us who became caught up in the late 1960s, whatever our age, our origins, our past – are measurable in terms of years of solid action to gain women's rights. Over the period we have all been actively involved in the Women's Movement, the feminist movement, the Women's Liberation Movement – it goes under so many headings – many tactics and strategies have been used. Many gains have been won. As well, we have all – individually and collectively met with some of what we label "failures" or "not enough". Nonetheless, even in situations rightly labelled "horrific", women have fought back, and continue to do so. Emel Corley, who found trade school boys grossly interfered with her right to study and to move freely about the school and environs, fought back – together with other women. She says:

I'm sure I would have abandoned the course if not for collective action taken against boys. Women friends decided to see how brave males were when faced with a group of women instead of me alone. About thirty women met the train from college. We grabbed the worst offenders, pushed them around, and questioned them about their continued harassment of me. They were terrified and tried to scramble across the platform to their next train. There was no attempt to fight us as a group. It was every man for himself. After their defeat, they made up stories exaggerating our toughness: they were confronted by a bikie gang arriving with crowbars and chains. This about a group of women – teachers, students, social workers, my mother, public servants and unemployed.[31]

That women were required to use their energies in this way is sad. But they saw the need for collective action and took it. Collective and individual action can be effective. Women's collective action can be strong, and we have learned this over the years. We have spent the years raising the issues, re-emphasising those which our sisters before us raised, making noise about women's rights, rediscovering the gains of early action, individual and collective action. It is vital to define the issues and to raise the consciousness of as many as we can, including ourselves, about them. But it is equally

---

31. Emel Corley, in Scutt, note 17, p. 60.

vital that we learn to think the issues through in the context of strategies and tactics.

Here, at this Women in Education Conference, as with every conference we attend, we must make a vow that every time we confer, we come with a view that the issues to be addressed should be aired in the context of what strategies will be useful to achieve our demands, what tactics we can use to gain our rights, and those of all women and girls. What are we seeking to achieve? What are our goals? What mechanisms, tactics, strategies can we use to achieve those goals? Some might say that the fact that it's all been done before, in terms of fighting for equal pay, appointments, promotions, the right to take particular subjects, the right to attend particular classes and institutions, means that the tactics and strategies of the past haven't worked. However, this is a false picture, downgrading the work of those going before us as well as ourselves. Many of the strategies and tactics women used in the past *have* worked, at minimum to give us a sense of our own value, because they knew, too, that what they were struggling for was *important*.

Women must learn to recognise our success and the successes of others fighting for women's rights. We must learn to revive or re-utilise the tactics and strategies that have worked, or reframe them to suit our needs. Where tactics and strategies have seemed to go awry, or goals have been won – then suddenly, in the new light of day, seem empty of value, it is important to sit down calmly, or stand calmly ready to go again, to consider: did parts of the strategy work, other parts not? Were some of the tactics useful, others not? How will those strategies and tactics work with new aims, or new considerations? Does the fact that some goals have been achieved mean that some strategies and tactics will work with new aims, or new considerations? Does the reality that some goals have been achieved mean that some strategies and tactics may be different, or slightly different now, because the base from which we are beginning – or rather, to which we are adding – is different?

To get where we want and need to go from here, we must first identify the issue, relatively explicitly. In the context of broader demands, isolate some demands which are a part of the broader picture, but which are manageable. We can't change all the world in one go, any one of us or any group of us. Say we want to have women's studies courses introduced into all tertiary institutions. Let some of us concentrate upon one institution, aiming at having the courses introduced there. Join with the women on campus – students, administrative staff, teaching staff who would be likely to support the goal. Who is the relevant Minister? What can other women's organisations do to positively support the proposal? Women's Advisory Council? Make certain that possible support is not ignored, or is not considered to be ineffectual because of preconceptions. Determine what philosophy is to underlie the goal. As Dale Spender has written:

None of us is free from the disposition to assume that our experience is the experience, and that what we know represents the limits of the knowable. None of us has a true analysis, a correct line, a monopoly on the right meanings. And if we want to see the end of one group defining the world of another group, on the grounds that this constitutes oppression, then all of us have a responsibility to strive to extend our horizons, to encompass and validate women's experience that is different from our own. All of us have to be vigilant about what we are leaving out of our explanations – and why![32]

Others may determine as their goal having women's studies incorporated into every subject, rather than being a subject in its own right. They should get together, determine their strategies and tactics, concentrate on one subject for a start – say history, or science, literature, economics. Work on finding out who within the particular discipline might be sympathetic. Work on them and with them to ensure that that discipline may begin to broaden out to recognise the world as it really is, rather than continue along a narrow path, taking into account only 48 per cent of the population's experience (if that!)

Here it is important to learn to listen to those who have experience – and not to define "experience" in hierarchical terms. And it is equally important to recognise that there is not just one way to achieve a goal. We must learn to use the multiplicity of talents that are available among us, and when a tactic or strategy demands experience or expertise that is not there, we must go out to find it, or develop it ourselves. Again, Dale Spender is relevant:

Feminism is not ... value-free liberalism which "tolerates" each and every view (the implication of "tolerance" is that other views are permitted to exist without meeting with or modifying one's own). Feminism is based on values, on values of self-identity, responsibility, autonomy, equality and the absence of dominance, coercion and oppression. Understandings which do not respect these values, no matter from whom they emanate, are not tolerated. And yet it is not so simple as it sounds, for within each of us is (at least) the propensity to insist on our own terms at the expense of someone else's self-identity, responsibility, autonomy, at the risk of structuring inequality and of paving the way for a form of dominance ... we must be concerned to change ourselves as we try to change the world. Feminism is about "double vision", about focusing on "in here" as well as "out there".[33]

Although it is easier at some stages to work in smaller groups, not all aiming at the same immediate result (although overall the goal is the same), larger working groups, conferences, continue to have a real place. It is important for us to meet in larger groups to review progress. The group working on getting women's studies into tertiary institution "X" should meet together with the group working on getting women's studies into institution "Y" – as well as with the groups working on getting women's studies into history, into science, mathematics, literature, economics. In this way, women working on specific issues have an opportunity to review tactics and strategies together – did this tactic work/not work for this group? that strategy for that group? More than simply sharing the issues, we need to train ourselves to share the strategies and tactics, the methods and mechanisms we have devised for changing the issues, for

---

32. Dale Spender, *For the Record*, 1985, The Women's Press, London, p. 202.
33. Spender, note 32, p. 203.

making the issues become a part of everyone's reality. Was there opposition? How was it overcome? What pitfalls arose? How were they traversed? Sharing the strategies means we all don't have to make the same mistakes, or mistakes begun can be corrected more quickly, more satisfactorily, with the experience of others who have already been "caught".

And the sharing will not just be about obstacles, ways to get around, ways to leap over, disappointments and the inevitable despair. It will be about the successes, too. Always, we must train ourselves to acknowledge the successes, our wins. For feminists, there is a fine line to be drawn between blaming the victim, and the recognition of the power of disadvantaged or oppressed groups. We must learn to recognise the extent of our power to change, and see the wins for what they are – true victories worthy of recognition. One of the problems for the Women's Movement is that, through being orientated (and rightly so) to opposing most of what occurs through powerful institutions – because most is indeed not for the benefit of women or humanity as a whole – we fail to see, sometimes, that our efforts can on occasion achieve positive ends. In Australia, the sheer persistence of the feminist movement, the Women's Liberation Movement, or a combination of two, has led to sex discrimination and the disadvantage of women and girls being a part of public debate which must be given notice on the political agenda. It is from this achievement that other feminist and women's liberation gains will be won. Recognising our achievements and those of our sisters gives us and our sisters the strength to carry on, to move on to those future successes. If we never accept we have successes, then we make it harder to believe that the rights we demand will ever be won.

Conclusion

Why the title, "Achieving the Impossible"? In the nineteenth century it was seen as impossible for women to gain access to tertiary institutions, to learn in classes together with men, to study subjects that were studied by men and boys. Yet women had gained access to places of learning prior to that time, and in other countries women were admitted to institutions of learning. Women also taught themselves, and acquired valuable knowledge in many fields because they were thinking human beings. But women's oppression was systematically organised through various facets of the dominant culture, and particularly through a design for education which was to keep women ignorant, and to make women believe that the knowledge they possessed and often strived for against the odds, was inferior, or not worthy of being termed "knowledge" at all. Today these practices continue in different forms – downgrading within the scheme of things; in the class room as students or in subjects; undervaluing or valuing not at all, areas where women might be seen to excel – ignoring our knowledge where women and men learn together; dismissing our knowledge where we learn it alone.

Kate Millett said in *Sexual Politics* in 1970, "If knowledge is power, power is also knowledge, and a large factor in [women's] subordination is the fairly systematic ignorance patriarchy imposes on women."[34] But that is not the only message women should remember. The words of Elizabeth Janeway are also significant: "Knowledge is power if it can be implemented."[35]

In the field of education, however little power we possess overall, we possess a great deal in feminist terms. We can continue to implement the knowledge we possess, as handed to us by women of earlier women's movements. We are in a position to do this, due to the painstaking research many women have carried out in past years, and particularly in the last ten to fifteen years. Research has formed the basis of books, theses, conference papers, lectures in tertiary institutions, lessons in primary and secondary schools. Simultaneously we have to change that knowledge which is taught from a patriarchal perspective. Gaining equal rights for women and girls in education does not mean we should strive solely to be admitted to courses devised by men, for men, even if ostensibly understood, now, to include women as students or even subjects. Women and girls have a right to have the knowledge we understand to be important, that *is* important, our own reality, become a part of the curriculum.

The *Feminist Dictionary* defines the law of inertia as meaning: "Bodies in power tend to stay in power, unless external forces disturb them."[36]

The Women's Movement might be seen as "external forces", and this is a correct assessment when we talk of moving from power those bodies already there. But women are also part of internal forces working to reorientate the nature of power and the exercise of power. In the education system, women work within and without, and the storm which has been building up through the years of women's agitation for change and full appreciation of women's reality commits me, in my moods of optimism, to the view that we are achieving the "impossible", by making equal rights for women and girls in education no longer so impossible.

34. Kate Millett, *Sexual Politics*, 1970, Doubleday, New York, p. 66.
35. Elizabeth Janeway, *Powers of the Weak*, 1981, Narrow Quill Paperbacks, New York, p. 19.
36. Catharine Stimpson, in Cheris Kramerae and Paula Treichler (eds.), *Feminist Dictionary*, 1985, Pandora Press, London, p. 71.

15

WOMEN AND THE POWER TO CHANGE: Recognising and Advancing Practical Economic Strategies

ADDRESS TO ZONTA CLUB OF ALICE SPRINGS, AREA 6 WORKSHOP
"Women – What Now?"
3 May 1987

It is always good to be provided with an opportunity to speak on a theme that has been an abiding concern. The Zonta Club of Alice Springs gave me that opportunity when the Club invited me to address the "Women – What Now?" workshop in early 1987. Soroptomists provided me with a chance to expand on the issues further when I was invited to give the keynote speech to the Soroptomists Conference at Wagga Wagga some six months later.[1]

Equal opportunity and affirmative action are positive moves directed toward ensuring that women are not confined to selected fields of work, which may well not suit all women. Indeed, why should they? On the other hand, we know we cannot assume that the world will change just because women move en masse into fields traditionally classed as male. The "tipping effect" is well documented in the United States: the way in which status, remuneration and reward decline as soon as women reach a "critical mass" in an area of work – whether in the professions or trades.[2]

I taught myself to touch-type when I was at school: in fourth and fifth years I was fortunate to have some free periods and spent part of the time in the typing room. A school friend from the secretarial stream showed me how to place the guard over the keyboard, so that the learner could not cheat by peeping at the keys, and set me off on my first lesson by giving me a learn-to-type primer. Throughout my career as a university student, particularly when doing postgraduate work at the University of Sydney

---

1. The Wagga Wagga Conference of Soroptomists was held on 7 November 1987. In the footnotes, square brackets […] indicate new material added for this edition.
2. Helen Remick (ed.), *Comparable Worth and Wage Discrimination: Technical Possibilities and Political Realities*, 1984, Temple Press, Philadelphia; and see generally Carol O'Donnell and Phillipa Hall, *Getting Equal*, 1988, George Allen and Unwin, Sydney.

and overseas, I was grateful to that friend, and for the self-imposed discipline of my schooldays! Today, I am well aware that I could not complete work as quickly as I am able, had I not the ability to type. (I have now progressed to a wordprocessor.)

Knowing how to type oneself makes a person far more aware of the expertise that is inherent in keyboard skills. It is far more than simply manipulating a keyboard. Setting out the material, using the various commands of a wordprocessing package, typing at x words per minute involve a particular ability. Too often, executives and others who have secretaries and assistants to do the wordprocessing they require do not appreciate the time and talent involved.

Similarly with librarianship, teaching, nursing and home economics. It is time to celebrate the traditional work of women – and to ensure that it receives proper recognition – in status, through industrial conditions, and in monetary terms. We cannot change the status of "women's work" alone, or overnight. But let's raise our own awareness of the valuable contribution made by women in traditional fields. Our recognition of the real value of traditional work of women is surely a necessity. If we don't recognise it, why would anyone else?

In the 1985 Boyer Lectures, Professor Helen Hughes of the Australian National University in Canberra painted a somewhat depressing picture of modern Australia. She pointed out that Australia is not among the world's leaders in reducing infant mortality; that our life expectancy at birth is 74 years, contrasted with 77 in Japan and Sweden, and 79 years of age in Switzerland.[3] She looked at our record in research and development: although it appears that on the research side, we fare relatively well, our record is poor in putting that research to work.

On the positive side, Hughes said:

Australia's land to population ratio makes for easy access to the countryside. Housing space is relatively large. Over 70 per cent of Australians own their own dwelling, and this is one of the highest rates of home ownership in the world. In other industrial countries, the ratio is 50 to 60 per cent. Most Australians live in an unusually pleasant climate, with low heating and cooling costs. Our distribution of income is among the most equitable in the world. Wealth is also relatively more equitably shared that in other countries although one per cent of the population owns about 25 per cent of wealth.[4]

---

3. Infant mortality rates of Aboriginal children are far higher than those of non-Aborigines, and life expectancy rates of non-Aboriginal Australians are far in excess of Australian Aborigines. See for example Gracelyn Smallwood, "Demanding More than a Great Vocabulary" in *Breaking Through – Women, Work and Careers*, Jocelynne A. Scutt (ed.), 1992, Artemis Publishing, Melbourne, p. 71.

4. Helen Hughes, *1985 Boyer Lectures – Australia and the Developing World*, 1985, Australian Broadcasting Corporation, Sydney, Australia. The immediately following quotation is from the same source. See also Helen Hughes, "Australia and the World Environment – The Dynamics of International Competition and Wealth Creation" in Jocelynne A. Scutt, *Poor Nation of the Pacific – Australia's Future?* 1985, Allen and Unwin, Sydney.

In summary, she says, Australians "do enjoy a higher relative standard of living than mere income per head figures imply". Yet on the negative side:

… concern with standards of living depends on how rich you are. There is a limit to the number of television sets or cars that rich people can use, the holidays abroad they can enjoy, or restaurant meals they can eat. To them, a relative decline in living standards is not important. For poor families, for whom a television might be the main piece of furniture, who live without cars in the sprawling suburbs barely reached by public transport, and whose children have little access to tertiary education, the answers are likely to be different. These families contribute disproportionately to statistics of infant mortality and low expectation of life. The lack of creches and afterschool childcare keep low income, particularly one-parent, families poor. A high proportion of these families are headed by women who were not encouraged in their youth to think of themselves as needing a career. Today, a lack of facilities makes it difficult for them to train for jobs once they have children. Their children suffer undue hardship. The deficiencies of Australia's care for disadvantaged children can cause acute difficulties even for middle income families. The plight of the poor, old people is well known.

Listening to this dissertation, it would hardly be surprising if listeners became depressed, seeking refuge in the thought – or words – "what can I possibly do to change it?" However, research of Australian attitudes shows that there is a great deal of compassion and caring in the Australian community. The "I'm alright Jack" – or Meg, or Mary – mentality is not borne out as an Australian reality.

For women who have grown up in a world where governments now, on a relatively major scale, acknowledge discriminatory patterns and practices, at initial glance it would be easy to assume that women would be first to say despairingly: "What can I do about it?" It is equally likely, at first glance, that women would be classed as, in the main, concerned, compassionate and caring about mortality rates, families in poverty, a dearth of childcare of good quality outside the traditional home-sphere, a lack of good educational opportunities and training avenues for children and young people, and for those seeking a career change at an older age.

It would be wrong to assume that both these "first glance" reactions are correct. The latter is true, but the first is quite wrong. Women are unlikely to say, in the real world: "What can I possibly do about it?" Or it may be that in the very act of saying it, women's actions belie the words. All around us, we find women working positively to ameliorate the economic ills and human relations breakdowns which seem to be a part of contemporary life. The problem has been that we are too likely to pass over our own actions and those of other women, because those actions are so much a part of what women have always done, and seem determined to continue to do.

In 1987, the federal government had in train a project calling for women around Australia to "tell us what you want": "fill out the form and give us your directions for the future, for future action."[5] Yet women have spent years doing precisely this –

5. The *Women's Plan of Action*, 1980, AGPS, Canberra, was drawn up for the 1980 United Nations mid-Decade Conference in Copenhagen, Denmark, as a blueprint for Australia's future efforts in raising

cont. next page

whilst simultaneously getting on with charting and plotting our directions for the future, from our own front door steps; from the local kindergarten committee; from the parents and citizens association; from the various clubs and organisations run by women; from the businesses run by women or run only because women are there to share the load, provide the support, give the direction, keep on working in the absence of "the boss"; from the schools which, whoever nominally heads the administration, are dominated by the presence of women teachers, women support staff; from the libraries and other institutions where women are in the majority. What we need is a reversal of the current approach – a recognition of the power of women in the community, and of the need for government to actually come out into the community to see what women are doing about human wants and needs, which in the end must be what the economy is all about.

Reassessing and Reworking Traditional Roles of Women

Today a move is on for women and girls to enter non-traditional areas – areas of paid employment in which women have not previously found a place, have been deliberately excluded, or have entered in proportionately small numbers. Campaigns for girls to enter apprenticeships in plumbing and as electricians or mechanics gain some governmental backing, and strong backing within the Women's Movement. These efforts are laudable. But at the same time as urging girls (and women) to find careers which will develop their expertise and gain for all women satisfaction and appropriate remuneration and reward, we must ensure that equal attention is paid to those areas in which women have traditionally worked, and in which they remain in great numbers. Rather than assuming women remain there because we suffer from "false consciousness" or because we simply don't know any better, we have to look at why even in the traditional areas women remain in lower-level positions, why hierarchical models predominate, and what can be done to reorientate society's view of what women do in these jobs, and of the hierarchical structure of work. It is not only society's *view* of women's (traditional) work that has to be reorientated. It is society's *recognition* of that work in remuneration and reward.

With affirmative action firmly on the agenda of most governments around Australia, and finding its place within the private sector, a justification for this "new" approach is often put forward: "Businesses and public service are 'missing out' on the talent of half the population." Another popular statement is: "Businesses and public service will

---

5. *cont. from previous page*
    the status of women and eliminating discrimination against women. In 1985 the United Nations End of the Decade Conference resulted in a programme being put forward by participating countries, for improvements to women's position the world over. In response to the 1985 Plan, the federal government commenced an Australia-wide consultation process, designed to "give women a voice". The Office of the Status of Women in the Department of Prime Minister and Cabinet had the carriage of the consultations.

improve their economic status by using the talents of women." What these statements fail to recognise is that business and public service are already utilising the capabilities and talents of "half the population". Sometimes they are not utilising these capabilities and talents in the most productive way, but most often it is the case that business and public service uses the talents and capabilities without recognising these abilities by adequate and appropriate remuneration and reward. At random, four areas illustrating these propositions are librarianship, the secretarial role, nursing, and the teaching of home economics.

Librarianship

Stereotypical views of librarians are not new. Before the 1870s the prevailing assumption was that the librarian was "grim, grouchy, eccentric, and *male*". But in the late nineteenth and early twentieth century, when unmarried women "began to flood into the profession", they were accepted on the basis that librarianship "appeared similar to the work of the home, functioned as a cultural activity, required no great skill or physical strength and brought little contact with the rougher portions of society". It was, therefore, deemed "suitable" for a woman. One much-cited important library figure in 1877 summed up prevailing attitudes toward women, when in his address to the conference of British and American librarians he said:

In American libraries we set a high value on women's work. They soften our atmosphere, they lighten our labor, they are equal to our work, and for the money they cost – if we must gauge such labor by such rules – they are infinitely better than equivalent salaries will produce of the other sex.[6]

Librarianship has been seen almost solely as a serving role, and one which need not be well paid.

Yet this image of the librarian distorts the reality of librarianship and what it can be. The librarian's role need not be solely to serve, and indeed many librarians do not see their job in this light. Rather, they take the initiative in hunting out research materials for users working in various areas. They provoke intellectual development and stimulate positive change in myriad areas. Parliamentary librarians, for example, do not just take down from the shelves volumes requested by members of parliament. They take up a subject matter about which a member or committee has approached them, and ferret out other materials, of varying views and ideological persuasions. Their work can effect change in the minds of politicians which can in turn lead to change in governmental policies, formulation of legislation or amendments to legislation, and ongoing change from these beginnings.

---

6. Jody Neumyer, "The Image Problem of the Librarian – Femininity and Social Control" (1976) 11 (No. 1) *Journal of Library History, Philosophy and Comparative Librarianship* 44.

Librarians' expert abilities might well not be "being tapped" as much as they should be, but what is true is that librarians' abilities are being put to work and always have been. The work that they do is what is not being recognised, and the lack of recognition results in their being ill paid and downgraded in importance.

Secretaries

Secretaries are often described as "a man's second wife". (This, of course, ignores all those secretaries working for other women, and the few male secretaries who exist.) This way of describing secretaries is accepted as downgrading secretarial work, placing it in the realm of cooking, washing and cleaning. Now, whatever one may think of the latter tasks – and that view leaves room for an entire debate in itself, the truth of the matter is that women working as secretaries have talents and capabilities which are being tapped, and made full use of. What is not a part of the equation is the need to recognise that expertise in remunerative terms.

The work of secretaries includes organising meeting agendas; organising the meetings themselves; arranging travel schedules locally, interstate and overseas, with arrangements that can be complex and difficult; keyboard work on machines ranging from the relatively straightforward to the more complex; care of various machines including wordprocessors, typewriters, dictating machines, photocopy machines and the like; executive skills of varying types and degree; standing-in for the boss in his or her absence; running the office in the absence of the boss. Thus, although the secretary's job is complex and multifaceted, and in many respects may mirror that of her boss, the lack of recognition comes in that, despite her talents and work, she is not rewarded or remunerated at a level with that employer. Like librarians, secretaries are seen as acting in a service role. But what is ignored is their initiating and controlling role, a role which is powerful in itself.

Nursing

Nursing is another field where women as service providers predominate. Currently wage battles are fought on the ground that the work done by nurses has become more demanding with the introduction of new technologies.[7] Yet although it is true that new technologies are changing various aspects of nursing, just as they are changing various aspects of other trades and professions, it is equally true that to fight for increases in nurses' wages solely on this ground is wrong-headed, because it ignores reality. The reality is that nursing work has always been more complex, responsible and technologically demanding than has been recognised by dominant community attitudes, and by rewards and remuneration. It is not that nurses have suddenly found talents and capabilities which they did not previously exhibit. What is true is that nurses are today taking a more universally assertive approach to the recognition of their always existing talents and abilities.

---

7. See 1986 *Nurses Case* (*In the Matter of Applications by RANF and HEF*) (1986) 300 CAR 185.

Nurses do not "just serve". Rather, they direct treatment for patients in the absence of doctors. Doctors float in and out of wards, spending relatively little time with "their" patients. Nurses play an ongoing role, and a vital one, in the care of patients and do not solely act as supports to the work of doctors; rather they do the work which needs to be done to keep the treatment "online". They make crucial decisions about the well-being of those in hospitals.

Home Economics Teachers
Research studies have shown that those who have cooking and general housewifely (or homemaking) skills are more likely to survive if lost in lands away from "civilisation", or if captured by others who are unfriendly towards them. These skills can be self-taught. But those who have developed their abilities in this regard are making a significant contribution, and it is wrong to say that their contribution is "untapped". Society operates on the skills of those who have home economics training, or who have developed their talents through self-taught methods.

It would be foolish to laud an everyday ability to vacuum, launder, iron and sew. But it is equally foolish to say that those who work in home economics are not contributing, or are being prevented from doing so. Again, the crucial issue is that the work they are doing is not gaining remuneration set in accordance with contribution made. The withdrawing of this labour would result in less efficiency, less economical use of time and money in cooking, cleaning, keeping the economy "ticking over". Certainly, in the absence of home economics teachers and those who have taught themselves these skills, the world would continue operating. But it is wrong to assume that these skills are unnecessary in the operation of the economy, or that the women exercising the skills are not having their expertise tapped. True, they may have additional abilities waiting to be discovered. But the point is that those they have developed are not gaining appropriate recognition nor appropriate payment for work done.

Traditional Roles and Remuneration

This is not to say women should simply continue in traditional roles, satisfied with the utilisation of our talents and not seeking to develop new ones. But it is to say that there is little point in demanding that women change our areas of work in the hope of being paid more in accordance with the demands of that work, and in the trust that our capabilities and talents will thereby be recognised. In 1983 the Australian Conciliation and Arbitration Commission in the *National Wage Case* clearly acknowledged the reality that women's work is vital to the economy and is not paid in accordance with its equal value to the work of men. At the same time, the Commission refused to introduce any system whereby women's work could be upgraded in remuneration, because the Commission said the economy would not be able to cope with the upgrading.[8] That is, women should continue to work at rates below their efforts,

---

8. *National Wage Case* (1983) 291 CAR 3. See also Jocelynne A. Scutt, *Growing Up Feminist – The New Generation of Australian Women*, 1985, Angus and Robertson, Sydney. [Extracts from the
cont. next page

subjugating their right to appropriate reward to the continuation of an economy which requires women's work, but which fails to to recognise it.

The debate is not just about money, although this is an important aspect which has to be addressed. Rather, the debate is about how women's work should be recognised in attitudinal terms and in reward terms by society as a whole, and by women ourselves. Too often it is we who, believing that the work we do is not "as important" or "talented" or "capable" as that of our confreres, fail to see the importance of the contribution. This failure brings with it a narrowness of vision. Believing our work is not "as important" interferes with our ability to see that because it *is* as important – perhaps more so – strategies can be devised to ensure that this reality is accepted by the dominant culture. If we do not believe we are as "talented" or "capable" in the work we do, we are less able to recognise that what we do does have a potential for improving the lot of ourselves and others. If we regard our abilities and expertise as inferior, then that notion must surely permeate everything we do. If we adopt strategies for change, or work out ways to enhance our skills and abilities, how can we recognise that our strategies have been successful, or the plans we have made reach a successful fruition, if we don't believe in our capabilities? Every effort is tainted by our lack of belief in ourselves. To recognise that our strategies for effecting change have succeeded, or are at least "on the way" to success, we have to have faith in our ability to strategise. If we wish to effect positive change, then we have to acknowledge that our expertise is practical and valuable and can enhance community well-being, and in turn lead to greater change. It is only then that we can acknowledge that our actions can effectively increase future possibilities.

Rejecting the "Welfare" Approach

There is little doubt that any country today needs a well-administered compassionate social security system. But it is equally true that limitations on our seeing have sometimes intruded on our ability to seek other ways of dealing with what superficially might be termed "welfare" problems, to be dealt with through the social security system or some other welfarist perspective. To illustrate, at the First National Women's Housing Conference, held in Adelaide in 1985, a worker from a women's shelter spoke in despair of a resident of the shelter who had escaped from a violent marriage. The divorce property settlement had resulted in a share of the family assets being settled upon the wife, in the amount of $50,000. "Because of that $50,000 I can't get the woman's name to the top of the public housing list," despaired the refuge worker. "Can anyone tell me how to get 'them' to see that she needs housing badly and has a right to 'jump the queue?'" No one can doubt the sincerity and concern of the shelter worker who was

---

8.   *cont. from previous page*
     Women's Electoral Lobby (WEL) submission to the 1983 *National Wage Case* and from the National Pay Equity Coalition (NPEC) submission to the 1988 *National Wage Case* are printed in Jocelynne A. Scutt, *Women and the Law*, 1990, Law Book Co., Sydney, Chapter 3, "Affirmative Action and Equal Pay", particularly pp. 93–105.]

fighting for the well-being of the resident. Yet why the seemingly automatic assumption that a woman, despite having $50,000, should take priority on a public housing list? Why the assumption that she should be *anywhere* on the public housing list?

Instead of considering that the appropriate way to deal with "women's issues" or "women's problems" is to seek welfare assistance, we should be evaluating the problem on the basis of what is most practical for the woman concerned, and what is the preferable outcome from her point of view and that of the community as a whole. What of all the other women in women's refuges who do not have a $50,000 property settlement, and no chance of ever having one? Rather than attempt to jump this queue, we need to make available in women's shelters and refuges, and other community-based organisations and agencies designed to help women, and those purportedly designed to help both women and men, financial consultants who are able to assist the woman with a $50,000 property settlement, giving her guidance as to ways to use that money to its best end. Why not consider low-interest housing loans, which are now available through government programmes? Undoubtedly there are too few of these low interest loans. But it would be better to be on the priority list for such a loan, than fighting to get to the head of a list designed to serve those who are less well financially placed.

Discrimination exists against women in the housing field. A survey by the Women's Housing Finance Inquiry in New South Wales, reported in the *Sydney Morning Herald* of 7 March 1987, showed that although the theory might be that when it comes "to renting or buying a house, women are on equal footing with men", women are "not ... taken seriously by some lending institutions in terms of understanding financial matters and the repayment of loans". A person cannot qualify for a loan unless her income is set at a certain level. Even then, lending institutions are reported as being wary of women applicants, fearing that they may leave their jobs through pregnancy, for example. With the government schemes, there can be no excuse for discriminatory practices, and we must therefore turn energies to ensuring equal treatment in the allocation of low-interest loans, so that women have an equal chance of entering the private housing market. With private schemes, discriminatory practices are outlawed at federal level and in most states, and it is preferable to utilise energies ensuring that the spirit and letter of the law is adhered to, rather than attempting to ensure that every woman who comes through a women's refuge or shelter fights for a position "at the top of the queue" at the Housing Commission or Department of Housing.[9] Equally, energies have to be spent on ensuring that where marriages break down, property settlements are favourable to

---

9. The *Sex Discrimination Act* 1984 (Cth) outlaws discrimination on the ground of sex in the provision of goods and services (including loans and other financial dealings). Most states also have legislation outlawing this discrimination (as well as on grounds of ethnicity, race and so on) – for example, *Equal Opportunity Act* 1984 (Vic.), *Anti Discrimination Act* 1977 (NSW), *Equal Opportunity Act* 1984 (SA), *Equal Opportunity Act* 1984 (WA). [In 1991 the Queensland Parliament passed the *Anti Discrimination Act* outlawing (amongst other grounds) sex discrimination in provision of goods and services; the Australian Capital Territory passed the *Equal Opportunity Act* in the same year, with similar provisions. Tasmania has yet to introduce equal opportunity or anti-discrimination legislation.]

the interests of *both* parties, so that women, like their husbands, have the opportunity of using any property settlement for purchase of their own home, rather than going into rental or public housing.

With paidwork, one area of greatest exploitation of women is that of women's work in the home, particularly where women work as "outworkers" for factories or other businesses. Yet one of the major reasons for women's exploitation is a lack of entrepreneurial skills on the part of women ourselves. Women need to be able to eliminate the "middleman" or better, to establish themselves in small businesses, even collectively run businesses with like-minded women, so that the money received for the work they do is under their control, rather than being paid disproportionately out of the sums gained by the middlemen, or by the factories purchasing their work.

It is not useful to romanticise women's home-grown skills or professional or trade training, but women who want to utilise their skills or training by going into business for themselves need desperately to have access to information about loans available from the government bank for the establishment of small businesses, entrepreneurial training, or even bookkeeping. So many women, when their husbands are starting out in business, do keep the books; despite the popular view of women being less than adept with figures, many women are the mainstay of the family business. Neighbourhood centres and learning centres need to have attached to them advisors who can direct women to concrete information about starting up in business.

In hierarchical organisations, women are at the bottom rungs. Often in business women are subject to discriminatory practices, including sexual harassment and sexist harassment. Where they do "outwork" or "piece-work", they are similarly subject to exploitation through hierarchies and discrimination. Beginning their own ventures means that they are able to exercise more control over their sphere of work, and this can lead to positive changes in other areas of their lives. Control in one area leads to greater feelings of security and well-being in other parts of one's life; and it leads to a reality of security and well-being.

There are many brave, daring, risk-taking women in the community. Those women who set up in small business despite the odds; those who persist in traditional areas of women's work, recognising that that work is not granted its appropriate recognition, but fighting to have due reward granted, rather than deserting; those who go into non-traditional areas, often alone – or now, fortunately, more often with a (very) few female colleagues – having to contend with being rarities and working out ways of working without any blueprints for action; those confronting racist as well as sexist discrimination, who fight on.

One of the most practical strategies for a woman working to gain recognition for all women in a world where, too often, the fact of that world's crucial dependence upon women's work has been passed over, is to reassess her own contribution. We can too readily ignore our own contribution. In 1979, a New South Wales Catholic women's group invited me to speak at what they described as their "coffee afternoon". Arriving, I was greeted by the member of the group who had been delegated to that task. Another had organised childcare (all the women in the group were full-time housewives and mothers of small children). Afternoon tea had been arranged by one woman, asking other members of the group to bring particular items. A further member had made her home available. To them all, it was a "coffee afternoon", but in reality, it was a monthly seminar, with catering, childcare and guest speaker organised. Thus, rather than return to the paid workforce when their children were older, saying when asked what they had done with their time out, "I was only a housewife", we agreed each could validly state on her curriculum vitae that she had participated in the organisation of monthly seminars.

It is enough that this is an important change in women's sense of their own abilities and organising capability. But an additional bonus is the way that their children can be brought to understand the importance of the seminar programme in their mothers' lives: the sense that can be conveyed of the need to adhere to a timetable, and the need for the children to understand that their mother is a person with demands on her time, where timing is crucial, and where intellectual and recreational stimulation are vital.

Going Beyond the Broader World

But for women it cannot stop here. We must confront the reality of living in a nation which is part of the global economy, and which has an important role to play in the Asian region. For those who are members of women's organisations, who have worked within the Women's Movement, or who have identified with the work of the Women's Movement or feminist movement, it is important to recognise what we have learnt within those organisations and movements. Being a part of these groups is fulfilling and rewarding in itself and simultaneously can lead to our participation in other groups and organisations with similar or allied aims. For too long areas such as taxation, fiscal policy, and the formal directing of the economy has been left in the hands of men. Women have played an informal role as actors in the economy, sometimes when close to men who play a key role in directing the economy. A few women have played a more direct role, but the pulse of the economy has not been held by the hand that "rocks the cradle". There is no logical reason why this should be so.

Just as Zonta has played a real role on the international scene in the developing economies of countries such as Sri Lanka and Colombia, other women's organisations can expand their horizons into the world outside Australia. At the same time, the lessons learned through these international projects can be applied in determining upon strategies designed to ensure that we have a greater say in tax, fiscal and economic debates. Beyond debates, we want to ensure that we gain a foothold in these areas in terms of decision-making itself.

One of the problems for women is that global or national economic issues are often portrayed as being "foreign" to our sphere. Yet the national economy is a sum of all its households and businesses. The work that women have traditionally carried out has often put women in a position to have a greater oversight of linkages between household and business, business and business, than has men's experience. That is, the woman plays a key role in the household economy. Although she may not control the overall finances of the household, she has opportunities for being more acutely aware of changes in inflationary levels as measured in everyday goods; she is often in a better position to get a sense of the policies being pursued by education departments and local government, for example; and because she is likely to be the first to know of changes in policy, she is in a prime position to begin devising strategies for taking action to change or to support those policy changes.

Indeed, many social movements have been begun by women's action; the environmental movement has been dominated at various times by women being concerned about the effect of building developments or road-building on the local environment, and the destruction of parks and other similar areas. This experience has led to further political action by women, in various areas. And it is again when women take political action that we must remember not to downgrade the efforts made. There can be a tendency to believe that because there are major changes we want to see, and for which we are striving, small changes we have effected are of no importance, or "don't count". Women must learn to recognise "wins", and not to believe that we have not won, if we don't achieve 100 per cent of a particular aim at first "go". The steps forward cannot be taken without the steps behind. Women of the future will be building on what we, the women of today, have fought for, achieved, won. If we fail to recognise the strategies we adopt as being capable of achieving some, at least, of our aims, we cannot blame our male confreres for not granting us recognition. Nor can we absolve ourselves from the responsibility of creating a world where the women coming to follow us believe that what they are seeking to achieve has never been sought before. In working towards positive goals for personal achievement and collective well-being, for changes in the world that will advantage both women and men – though some of the latter may not recognise the benefit in the short term – in the midst of our humility we have to also accept it is right to adopt, at times, a suitably congratulatory stance. Without our foremothers we would not be here, our very presence being evidence of the power of women. Without us, our daughters and their daughters, and our great-granddaughters and their daughters, would have to begin alone, at the beginning.

16

WOMEN '88

PRESENTED AT THE WOMEN '88 AWARD PRESENTATION
Melbourne Hilton, Victoria
September 1988

It was good to be asked to say "thank you" on behalf of the women who received Women '88 awards in 1988. The year itself was not free from controversy. There were, however, some great days: the phenomenal march on 26 January 1988 in Sydney: Australia Day, Invasion Day. A day when Aboriginal people marched in thousands along Sydney streets. And when throngs of non-Aboriginal people marched alongside. As Jackie Huggins writes in "But You Couldn't Possibly ...!":

A magical highlight of my life was participating in the Aboriginal march in Sydney, January 1988 ... We marched that day for our ancestors and for the generations to come. When we turned the corner into Belmore Park, a huge sea of non-Aboriginal, white, Asian and South American faces were ready to take the baton and march with us. We marched proudly in solidarity in the colours of black, yellow and red, never before realising the number of our supporters ...[1]

Looking back at where women stood in 1988, it is possible to see that the women are still going forward. In 1988 there were no woman Governors. By 1993 there were two – one in South Australia, the other in Queensland, and the names of women predominated in debate about the next Governor-General and the first President of Australia. And women now sit on supreme courts in New South Wales, the Northern Territory, Queensland and South Australia, whereas in 1988 only one woman sat as a Supreme Court judge, in New South Wales. In 1993 the number of women Federal Court judges increased by 100 per cent from the year before, with the appointment of a second

---

1. Jackie Huggins, "But You Couldn't Possibly ...!" in *Breaking Through – Women, Work and Careers*, Jocelynne A. Scutt (ed.), 1992, Artemis Publishing, Melbourne, p. 124.
2. Is it too much to hope that every increase of women judges on the Federal Court will be by 100 per cent?!

woman.[2] In 1993 Victoria saw its second female County Court judge appointed, while most other states have appointed or added to the number of women judges in their District Courts, so that now the grand figure of half-a-score at that level has been reached. The federal Attorney-General, Michael Lavarch, presided over the drawing-up of a Discussion Paper canvassing ways of increasing the diversity of appointments to Australian courts, with a particular emphasis on women, persons of ethnic origin other than anglo-Australian, and Australian Aborigines.[3] Women's groups, concerned members of the community, and the media responsibly canvassed the nature of entrenched sexism within the Australian judiciary. Every year the numbers of women marching to Reclaim the Night have swelled, and more cities and towns, including regional centres such as Geelong, have joined in. The Aboriginal women of the Centre gained their long-struggled-for birthing centre, and Aboriginal children are now born there, in surroundings conducive to their and their mothers' well-being. And in 1993 Melbourne was gearing up for the Sixth International Feminist Book Fair to fill the spaces in the Exhibition Building in July 1994: a feminist follow-on to the Judy Chicago Dinner Party of 1988.

At the same time, there have been backward steps: in 1993 only one woman (the Hon. Rosemary Follett) holds the post of leader of a government – in the Australian Capital Territory – whereas in the interim, after 1988 and before 1993, there were woman premiers in Victoria and Western Australia (the Hon. Joan Kirner and the Hon. Carmen Lawrence) in addition to the Chief Minister of the ACT. In late 1992 a directive circulated through one Victorian government department ordered that "chairman" be reinstated and "chairperson" no longer be used, despite the latter title being incorporated into a number of statues, and non-sexist titles having cross-party support.[4] June 1993 saw vocal opposition from some at the Second National Conference on Violence, deploring women marching in protest against violence against women (although this would hardly deter women from protesting, nor from marching, nor from celebrating and mourning simultaneously at Reclaim the Night). Crimes of violence against women and children have not decreased. The mortality rates of Aboriginal infants have not improved. The longevity of Aboriginal adults has not increased. Technological "medicine" continues to receive inordinate amounts of money whilst preventative medicine, Aboriginal health care and Aboriginal housing receive comparatively little.

---

3. Department of Attorney-General, *Judicial Appointments – Procedure and Criteria*, 1993, AGPS, Canberra.
4. In 1984 the Victorian Parliamentary Legal and Constitutional Committee, comprising six members of the Upper House, six from the Legislative Assembly, and even numbers of government and opposition, unanimously supported a recommendation that all titles for government and statutory office should be non-sexist. This policy was adopted by the (then) Labor government. See Legal and Constitutional Committee, *Report on the Interpretation of Legislation Bill 1983*, 1984, Government Printer, Melbourne. The departmental directive was dated 9 December 1992.

Still, many people are beginning to look toward the year 2000 as an opportunity for harnessing the goodwill that a new century presages. But we know, too, that the years between now and then should not be simply frittered away ...

For 60,000 and 200 years there has been a Women's Movement in Australia. For 60,000 and 200 years women have placed Women's Business on the Agenda. For 60,000 and 200 years Australian women have been proud, outspoken, brave, courageous, shrewd, shrewish, loud, noisy, gentle, patient, resourceful, militant and persistent. This year, 1988, we celebrate 200 years and 60,000 years of Aboriginal culture, Australian culture and Women's Business as a part of this culture.

For the Women's Movement, the Bicentenary has been problematic. Many women chose deliberately not to participate in events. They foreswore funding from the Bicentennial Authority, refusing even to submit proposals. A feminist conference in Albury-Wodonga in early 1988 concluded with a rousing debate on the pros and cons of accepting monies or joining in "celebrations" of the 200th year of Australian colonisation. The "cons" were loudest heard.

It was in 1988 that Senator Susan Ryan, member of the Hawke Labor government and of the Cabinet, resigned from Parliament after some fourteen years to take up publishing as head of Penguin Books, and then moved into her own consultancy business. It was the year that Judge Lynne Shiften (as she then was), the first woman ever appointed to the judiciary in Victoria, and member of a very small band Australia-wide, resigned and took on an executive position in private industry. It was in 1988 that Prue (Sibree) Leggoe resigned from the Victorian Parliamentary Liberal team to enter the world of the corporate lawyer. (For none of them a government sinecure. For each a productive job gained in her own right.)

It was in 1988 that women around Australia once more joined nationally (and this time, internationally – New Zealand was in it too) to hold "Reclaim the Night" rallies and march exultantly through Canberra, Sydney, Melbourne and elsewhere ... to demand and to celebrate women's assertion that the streets are ours, too, to walk in, to live in, to dance, skip, run in, not to be raped and harassed in, or abused and derided.

It was in 1988 that Aboriginal women continued to die, alongside their children and their mates, at a rate and at an age against which any nation should cry out. And do more than cry out – pour funding and resources and attention and love and consideration and respect and concern into preventing those deaths, by such simple, human and humane means: running water, availability of nutritious food and drink, basic housing and more – comfortable housing, grants to neighbourhood houses and womanspace. (In Tennant Creek, Topsy Napparula Nelson and the women of the Centre are fighting on for a space of their own, space taken from them with the imposition of white male culture upon their traditional women's culture and beliefs.)

The Bicentenary year saw the numbers of women beaten, bashed, abused, raped in their own homes and on the street grow, not lessen. (And, at last, the acknowledgement by government that women's greatest fear of brutality is centred upon the violence in our homes, rather than on the street.) The pornography debate limped on in simplistic homilies about Non-Violent Erotica (what is violent erotica, for Goddess sake?!). It saw the sexism-in-language debate rise yet again, with attention from columnists and feature writers directed at dealing with their own contradictory notions: that women's desire to be recognised in language is too trivial to require consideration; and that efforts to meet this desire are too serious to let pass. (And yes, it was the year writer and feminist Dale Spender declared that manholes are the perfect place for men and that there should be more of them.)

In 1988 Lilla Watson, Aboriginal writer, academic and poet, was visiting scholar from the University of Queensland to Phillip Institute in Victoria. It was the year Professor Diane Bell went from Professor of Australian Studies at Deakin University in Geelong to Professor of Social Justice in Massachusetts, USA. Elizabeth Reid was restored to contributing prominently to the well-being of Australia and Australians at federal government level once more, as consultant to the National Advisory Council on AIDS. It was the year the number of women Ministers of the Crown rose to four in Western Australia and three (perhaps four) in Victoria, with the first woman appointed as Government Whip in the Victorian Parliament.

In 1988 South Australian universities saw the value of women chancellors, and their wisdom, in for the first time electing Sister Deidre Jordan as Chancellor of Flinders University and re-electing (the former Justice) Roma Mitchell as Chancellor, once more, of Adelaide University. In Tasmania Anne O'Byrne was appointed convenor of the National Women's Consultative Council, comprising twenty members from all states and territories. Tasmania appointed two women as conservators to travel to Antarctica to assess the conservation potential of the original huts in long-ago settlements at the South Pole.

It was the year that Linsey Howie and others organised for Judy Chicago's artwork *The Dinner Party* to be exhibited in Australia, and the Exhibition Building in Melbourne was filled with 1200 women celebrating a real Australian dinner party in strength and in spirit with Chicago's work. The Spoleto Festival in Melbourne had more women writers and speakers visibly contributing to the festa than ever before.

It was the year the first woman Lord Mayor of Melbourne, Councillor Leckie Ord, was followed by the second woman Lord Mayor of Melbourne, Councillor Winsome McCaughey, and they joined women mayors in Brisbane, Alice Springs, Warrnambool, and many other cities and towns throughout Australia.

The Bicentenary year saw the first Australian Feminist Research Conference at Deakin University produce the Waurn Ponds Manifesto (some called it the Geelong Declaration) demanding 52 per cent of the total national research budget be granted to projects designed and proposed by women scholars and researchers, and that all research be attuned to goals of social and economic justice, the real concerns for the humanity of women and men.

The twenty recipients of Women '88 awards and commendations are sincere in our appreciation of your appreciation. We too give our thanks to Libby Darlinson and Robyn Hobbs for their cool, calm collectedness, their efficiency, their enthusiasm and their support. The artists' creativity presented in remembrance of this occasion and their beautiful work demands commendation and celebration: we thank Sandra Black, Liz Williamson, Margaret Ainscow, Jan Ervine, Yolanda Cholmondelay-Smith, Helen Rechter, Vicki Torr, Bronwyn Kemp, Fran Clark, Pauline Griffin, Carolyn Delzoppo, Sue Wright, Miriam Porter, Jeanni Keefer Bell, Diane Appleby, Denise Oates, Fiona Murphy, Kerrie Lester, Robyn Gordon, Jenny Orchard. Anne Deveson's words in her keynote address highlighted the triumphs of Women's Business writ large in the national arena and in the everyday lives of us all. Judi Connelli's glorious irreverence, verve and voice bring home to us the versatility of women and special women's talents, her talents. And our thanks go to Margaret Whitlam, Ita Buttrose, Edith Hall and Alex Pucci in the evening's presentations for their kindnesses, their energy, their persistence and grace. All are admirable women.

We can stand here honoured by the support of you all, only because in the past and in the present each one of us has been and is supported by other women, and some by special men, many of us by the women here together with us. This is a representative recognition, a recognition extending to all Australian women who have fought and continue to fight for women's recognition within this, our Australian culture, our Australian country, in a world that too little has recognised women and women's achievements. But more often today this world is able to see and to understand, to appreciate and applaud, the power, the strength, the contribution, the celebration of women.

As the feminist writer and thinker Adrienne Rich has said:

If I could have one wish for my own sons, it is that they should have the courage of women. I mean by this something very concrete and precise; the courage I have seen in women who, in their private and public lives, both in the interior world of their dreaming, thinking, and creating, and the outer world of patriarchy, are taking greater and greater risks, both psychic and physical, in the evolution of a new vision.[5]

That new vision has been with us all for a long time. It is the work and the power and the support of all women that will make – is making – that vision real.

---

5. Adrienne Rich, *Of Woman Born*, 1976, W. W. Norton and Co. Inc.; quoted Carol McPhee and Ann Fitzgerald (compilers), *Feminist Quotations – Voices of Rebels, Reformers and Visionaries*, 1979, Thomas Y. Cromwell, New York, p. 241.

17

CELEBRATING WOMEN'S STUDIES

PRESENTED AT THE CELEBRATION TO COMMEMORATE
10 YEARS OF WOMEN'S STUDIES AT VICTORIA COLLEGE
27 October 1989

Women's Studies came onto the university scene in the 1970s. Courses were established at Flinders University in South Australia, the Australian National University, Rusden College and Deakin University in Victoria, Murdoch in Western Australia, the University of New South Wales, Griffith University in Queensland and, eventually, at most tertiary institutions. Women's Studies was, for some years, a subject in the High School Certifi-cate (HSC) in Victoria, but was phased into Australian Studies when the HSC became the Victorian Certificate of Education (VCE).

I was pleased to celebrate ten years of Women's Studies with teachers and students of the Rusden College course. My pleasure was more so, because Rusden had (wisely) adhered to its original charter: keeping alive Women's Studies as an essential discipline.

The 1980s saw a strange twist of language occur, from which Rusden remained (and still, in the 1990s, remains) immune. "Gender" became the substitute word for "sex" and, somewhat paradoxically, for both "women" and "anti-woman". Instead of "sex bias" or "sexual prejudice" (meaning anti-woman bias or plain misogyny), (some) people began referring to "gender bias". In other institutions, instead of Women's Studies, (some) people began to speak of "Gender Studies". This language is more palatable to those who would prefer not to address the realities of anti-woman preju-dice. To those in power, or who wish to benefit from male power, it is less confronting, after all, to accept that bias in disciplines such as history, law, medicine affects women and men equally. Aren't men (sometimes) cut out of history? Aren't men (sometimes) dealt with unfairly by the law? Aren't men (sometimes) treated inappropriately by doctors? Don't men (sometimes) miss out on optimal health care?

No one – women least of all – denies the endemic problem of class, race and ethnic-based prejudice. No one – women least of all – denies that men may be unfairly treated by social and political institutions. Patriarchal society, built on hierarchy and notions of "male right", by its very nature is bound to disadvantage some men, some where, some time. But there is nothing more calculated to divert clear thinking into unprofitable paths than the notion that "gender" is the problem.

A pregnant woman is not discriminated against because pregnancy is ascribed to her. She is discriminated against because she is a woman – and a pregnant one at that. Women are not discriminated against because female characteristics are ascribed to us. We are discriminated against because we possess *characteristics that are labelled "female". We are discriminated against* because we are women, *not because we are ascribed some notion of "womanhood".*

Women's Studies is an essential discipline, because it names women as the central focus. Women's Studies is not designed to canvass discriminations against men. It is designed to reinstate the herstory of women, to take the realities of women's lives as the significant measure, to acknowledge and to celebrate the fact that women have lived, contributed, written books, plays and poetry, sung and painted, sculpted and danced. Women's Studies exists so that the pain of women can be articulated clearly, and understood, and mourned – without being downgraded or denied by the cries of others. Women's Studies has been founded so that women's work in factories, shops and houses, women's toil as charwomen and skivvies, as housekeepers and childcarers, as unpaid drudges and housewives, can gain acknowledgement as WORK. Women's Studies is vital to the recognition that the population is made up of not just 48 per cent, but of 100 per cent, and Women's Studies concentrates on the larger "half".

Women's Studies is central to the understanding of society, culture, the world. Women's Studies is about burrowing through the layers of deceit and obfuscation that cloud reality. It is about dispensing with language games, and facing up to the truth: a world that is biased against women and women's interests is a world that is anti-woman.

In 1992, Victoria College, including the Rusden Campus, amalgamated with Deakin University. A Graduate Diploma and Master of Arts in Women's Studies is now being taught, by coursework, on and off campus. Women's Studies remains strong.

In 1979 the first accredited Women's Studies course at Victoria College began classes. Ten years on, we are able to celebrate the beginning, a re-accreditation in 1984, and confidently look forward to a second accreditation this year.

In 1979 the course began with some twenty-five students, all women. The proposal was put forward to the college "powers that be" in 1978, by Rae Walker, Marilyn Poole, Julie Mulvaney, Joan Walsh, and Geulah Solomon. Rae Walker has since moved on to La Trobe University, Julie Mulvaney to Swinburne Institute, Marilyn Poole remains at the helm, and Joan Walsh and Geulah Solomon have retired from formal teaching, but no doubt continue their role of forward thinkers: teachers can never really retire, particularly those who are feminist.

The 1960s and 1970s had seen, not a "new wave" of feminists or feminism, but a world more ready to acknowledge the demands of women for equal rights; just recognition of women's past achievements, present capacities and capabilities; and the reality that women had something to say for ourselves, that that something was important, and that the world must listen. The 1960s and 1970s were full of noisy women, just as the years before had throbbed and thronged with women asserting the right of women to be recognised as valuable contributors to the world.

In the 1960s and 1970s, however, our voices were more often heard. Those in positions of traditional power could not resist, at least to some degree, the truth of women's voices and the value of noisy women.

The noisy women at Rusden (shortly after to become Victoria College) solidly succeeded in having their voices heard. In approaching what might have been a thorny field of accreditation, the proponents of Women's Studies – Walker, Poole, Mulvaney, Walsh and Solomon – caught up in the new and exciting ferment surrounding the feminist movement, moved so smoothly and surely that the proposal for the course went through in relative calm.

The idea of Women's Studies was at the time so new, that many in positions of authority were not quite sure of what precisely it was, and if they were not, did not quite like to ask. The notion that Women's Studies is a powerful force for change; that it can operate to subvert traditional and authoritarian modes of operating, styles of teaching; and that it can work to excise the cultural dominance of traditional ideas was not readily appreciated.

That first year, courses available in the newly introduced Women's Studies included "Changing Sex Roles", "The Women's Movement", "Women and History", "Sex Roles in Education", "Women and Work", "Health and Life Cycle Issues" and "Communications Skills". Every year since then, twenty to twenty-five students have come fresh to the course. There have been massive disputes relating to differences in ideology and modes of teaching and learning. Opinionated women – the students – questioned how the courses should be gone about, what was to be done, or should be done, who should do what. Students often adopted stroppy poses. The course acted as a catalyst for change in women's lives. Sometimes, it made teaching in the course as bumpy a ride as learning in any tertiary institution can be.

At the 1984 accreditation, there was an assumption that Women's Studies might be seen as relevant to students for a further five years, but that its interest and usefulness might then surely wane. Five years on, in 1989, this notion appears to have dropped by the wayside. The value and relevance of Women's Studies remains; its interest to current and potential students is not questioned.

That the course remains solidly defined as Women's Studies is vital. And it is significant. Elsewhere a disturbing trend is emerging, for Women's Studies to be bypassed in favour of what is projected as the "new" discipline: Gender Studies. This discipline is classed by some as superior to Women's Studies, the notion being that Women's Studies is a mode or mechanism for "ghettoising" "women's concerns" or "women's issues". We should, runs the theory of "Gender Studies", be talking of teaching about "people issues"; concerns of all people, gender, not women.

There can be little doubt that the more that traditional courses – engineering, business studies, plumbing, law, medicine, architecture, motor-mechanics – are taught from a feminist perspective, the better. This means that traditional courses must be infused with feminist perspectives. "Women's Studies" notions must infiltrate into the bastions which fail to acknowledge the relevance of "women's concerns" or "women's issues".

Who can question the need for traditional concerns of women to be infused into architecture, engineering or plumbing? How many design failures can be laid directly at the feet of those who have refused to acknowledge the need for proper and appropriate planning and design in the building of houses, whilst women have acute sensitivity to family and individual needs? How many businesses and educational and other institutions operate in buildings constructed without regard to human needs, with spaces for childcare and shops readily available? What negative debating points could be marshalled against the proposition that professions such as law and medicine need huge doses of full-frontal feminism, in theory and in practice, to ensure that the workers trained in those disciplines are able properly to function as real professionals, aware of real community and individual needs?

Examples of the inadequacies of medicine and law are not difficult to find. Women's writing is replete with them. Di Graham writes of an observation she made in 1939 of the (male) medical profession and its attitude toward women:

English newspapers contained similar evidence of male arrogance and insensitivity to women's rights as in Australia. One morning newspaper reported findings of a medical committee enquiring into whether or not women should be permitted some form of pain relief at childbirth. By a majority decision the male members of the committee decided that women should not have relief, as pain may be necessary to establish a mother's love for her child. The two women on the committee recorded a minority finding in favour of pain relief during childbirth.[1]

Time has not worked dramatic change in the medical profession. In the 1970s, a similar disregard for women as human is described by Elsa Atkin:

One strikingly memorable event of 1972 was [my] suffering a very painful (both emotionally and physically) miscarriage. During the stay in hospital the doctor interacted almost solely with my husband. There I was in pain, it was my body, but the doctor really only discussed matters with my husband, with me in the room being of no more use than a bystander in an event of some significance.[2]

---

1. Di Graham, "Through Life in Pursuit of Equality" in Jocelynne A. Scutt (ed.), *Different Lives – Reflections on the Women's Movement and Visions of its Future*, 1987, Penguin Books Australia, Ringwood, p. 180.
2. Elsa Atkin, "In Retrospect" in Jocelynne A. Scutt, note 1, p. 95.

She goes on to add that she and her husband refused to pay the doctor's bill for "professional" services, hearing nothing more from him!

Not only do these "professional" attitudes (and the behaviours arising out of them) persist over time; they span different cultures. Gillian Bouras discovered this when, married to a Greek-Australian and living in Greece she attended the local clinic:

We made an appointment with a Kalamata obstetrician now practising elsewhere in Greece ... The gentleman had an extremely brusque manner. When he discovered that English was my native language, he grunted and said, "I speak German". Without even looking at me, he enquired of George, "Does she want to have it? She needn't." Had I not been so outraged, perhaps I could have seen the funny side of one male virtually offering an abortion to another. But nothing was funny that day ..."[3]

Law and those who work within it exhibit like problems. Spanning the years of law school in the mid and late 1960s it is said:

In 1965 when I enrolled at the University of Western Australia and on-campus agitation against the war in Vietnam was gradually being voiced, at law school endless arguments raged about law students' dress: "All students should wear dark suit, white shirt, tie and academic gown." One student, Higgins, persisted in coming tieless, in shorts, without academic gown – and thonged, ignoring regular censure motions against him and his dress. Women's dress was never mentioned. Women weren't "seen", or simply didn't count.[4]

In the 1970s, significant change had not come about. Vera Levin attended the University of New South Wales, first graduating in Arts, then Law:

When I entered the faculty of law, my youngest child was attending university with me. I had pleasant expectations of what lay ahead. My home responsibilities had lessened and I had visions of savouring and analysing and learning the law ... my only recollection of the first semester is shock. My fellow students were also graduates, but none of the thirty who started with me (and the numbers quickly dwindled) was prepared for the work ... all teachers were men. With minor exceptions, they regarded women students whimsically, and mature women like myself as some sort of special curiosity. If I spoke to my teachers for any reason, almost without exception the question would creep in: "Why are you studying law?"[5]

Her answer was always, "Why does anybody study law?" The response? That despite Vera Levin's academic achievements, taking into account her age, there would be nowhere for her to practise upon graduation. Yet just as so many women have shown through their persistence, hanging on and doing well, showing the chauvinistic pessimists to be wrong, Vera Levin became a lawyer. One of the first in her graduating year to be employed, she practised with the New South Wales Legal Services Commission

---

3. Gillian Bouras, *A Foreign Wife*, 1989, McPhee Gribble/Penguin Books Australia, Ringwood, p. 143.
4. Jocelynne A. Scutt, note 1, p. 195.
5. Vera Levin, "You'll be Fifty Anyway" in Jocelynne A. Scutt, note 1, pp. 122–123.

for some time. She then moved to Melbourne to reunite disparate parts of her family, and has since become head of the Assignments Division in the Victorian Legal Aid Commission. As she says: "I should perhaps, be grateful to [those] teachers, for it was probably an innate, stubborn reaction to their kindly advice that made me persevere."

At the same time as engaging with non-traditional courses and "straight" professions and trades, we urgently need to continue our development of Women's Studies as a discipline. The subjects now taught here and in other states, other institutions, are sometimes the same as those taught in the original Victoria College Women's Studies course – "Women and History", "Women and Work". New courses, or new developments in original courses, also take their place in Women's Studies courses around Australia – such as the developments in medical technology, and other new, although failed, reproductive technologies, in particular, IVF; new debates about cohabitation rules in social security determinations; developing feminist perspectives on the economy and taxation. It is imperative that these courses be developed in the context of Women's Studies. The issues can then be transposed back into traditional courses, whilst Women's Studies continuing alongside, as a distinct discipline. It is only in this way that the traditional and dominant courses and ideology can be affected, and it is only in this way that "gender" courses can be continually required to live up to their liberated promise, rather than to degenerate into more of the same. Women's Studies must maintain its own very real character and integrity. Women's Studies must not be sidestreamed into "gender studies", just as the fight for women's rights should not be placed as secondary to the demand for human rights. Too often when the broader term is used – whether "gender" or "human" – the tendency is to forget that 52 per cent of the category is female, and that many within that category are from varying cultural, ethnic and racial backgrounds.

The high profile given to women as students and women as teachers within tertiary institutions through the 1970s and 1980s, and particularly with the introduction of Women's Studies, led to many women taking up tertiary studies, though never before would it have seemed possible. It also meant women became increasingly likely to study in male dominated areas, where before women may have been "frightened off" or simply reluctant to do so.

Patricia Boero, born in Lima, Peru, in 1952, of Uruguayan/Cuban parents, emigrated to Australia in 1973. Escaping a violent marriage and moving from Tasmania to New South Wales, she (despite her fluency in five languages) progressed through factory jobs to support herself in her "new" country. She worked, later, amongst migrant groups. Then:

My decision to study law in 1983, the thirty-first year of my life, felt tentative. I was optimistic and enthusiastic, but had doubts about my suitability. I was longing to understand fully our legal system, but the pomp and arrogance of it made me apprehensive. I wanted, in a very Aussie sense, to "give it a go".[6]

---

6. Patricia Boero, "The Double Burden – A Woman and a Wog" in Jocelynne A. Scutt, note 1, p. 65.

Just as Patricia Boero overcame discouragement and some feelings of reluctance, so too did Vera Levin. Married young, moving from place to place, country to country, with husband and small children, and required to follow her husband's career rather than her own, in her late forties Vera Levin decided to apply for university. With the abolition of fees by the Whitlam Labor government, there was a real opportunity. Without matriculation or a Higher School Certificate (HSC), she was "talked into" taking the mature-age entrance exam. (Her daughter did the "talking into".) "Dozens of times", she says:

I began writing, as many times deciding this was foolishness. Such cold fear overcame me that were it not for the nagging and being put to shame by my daughter, I would never have finished the [entrance] essay or sent it off. I was convinced my essay was not university standard; the essay would never be accepted; that I was a fool at my age to harbour such a remote hope as a university education.[7]

Then – shock! horror – Vera Levin proved her daughter right, her qualms wrong:

On arrival of my letter of acceptance from university no one was more surprised than I. At first I was afraid someone had made a mistake. Then I was afraid they hadn't and that I could never have the nerve to attend full-time university studies, going to lectures and tutorials with students the age of my own children. I revealed my fears to my family, giving every excuse – we couldn't afford to lose my salary [as a secretary], the two younger ones could not be left alone if I had evening lectures. My husband and all three children stood together as a wall, until wearily I said: "If I do an Arts degree, by the time I graduate I'll be fifty years old." A friend of my daughter, another university student, took part in the conversation. He said: "You'll be fifty whether you graduate or not."

Deciding it was preferable to be fifty with a degree than fifty without, Vera Levin went. Just as she was encouraged to believe in herself and her abilities, so too with Pat Eatock:

When a friend first suggested I go to university, I laughed. I laughed again when Liz Reid suggested it in 1972. After dropping out for a year in 1975, I completed my degree in 1977 at the age of forty.[8]

As we go into the 1990s, standing here on the verge of a new decade, it is important to give full recognition to the work of women in the centuries before us: women in Australia, providing us now with a positive and real tradition of separatism, within the context of a fully functioning society. Within the Aboriginal culture there has always been a recognition of the value and importance of separatism, and no notion that women's separatism is contrary to the interests of women, nor to the interests of

---

7. Vera Levin, note 5, p. 121. The immediately following quotation comes from the same source.
8. Pat Eatock, "There's a Snake in my Caravan" in Jocelynne A. Scutt, note 1, p. 25.

society as a whole. Women fill Australia, providing us, through their own lives, past and present, and through their teaching, with solid and substantial examples of how battles to gain women equal private and public rights, civil rights and human rights were won, against significant odds: the right to vote; the right to stand for, and sit in, parliaments, local councils and other public bodies; the right to own property; the right to earn and own our own wages; the right of custody, care and guardianship of children we have borne; the formal right not to be raped in marriage; the right to speak out against, and be heard on, violence against women in its many guises – whether against women on the streets, or criminal assault, rape and exploitation at home. And women fill Australia, providing us with examples of how women can establish and maintain courses directed at women learning the background to those earlier and present battles, the way the battles were won and will in the future be won, and feminist perspectives on every aspect of human life and living.

In 1963 the United States' feminist Betty Friedan, in her book *The Feminine Mystique*, wrote: "You do have to say 'no' to the old ways before you can begin to find the new 'yes' you need."[9]

Women's Studies courses are exemplified by the Women's Studies course celebrating its ten years at Victoria College. It is saying "no" to the idea that women's concerns and interests should be downgraded or denied relevance in the tertiary curriculum. It says "no" to the proposition that women do not want to learn about women and women's activism. It says "no" to the proposition that women have nothing to teach each other. It simultaneously says "no" to the notion that women alone are concerned to learn of women's history, women's activism, women's achievements, women's politicism. It says "yes" to the proposition that we can and we will find new answers in learning of women and women's actions of the past, and concentrating upon current concerns and activities of women. It says "yes" to the reality: that feminism is alive and well, and living, from the centuries before, the now of ten years of Women's Studies at Victoria College.

The black American feminist Beverly Smith says:

To be courageous means to be afraid but to go a little step forward, anyway. If you say: "I'm not afraid of anything," that's white boy bullshit.[10]

Setting up the Women's Studies course at Rusden, and keeping it at Victoria College, was a step of mammoth proportions, in keeping with the ethic of courage of which Beverly Smith speaks.

It took the courage of the women who established the course to persist and insist that it should be a part of the tertiary curriculum. It has taken the courage of the women who

---

9. Betty Friedan, "Epilogue" in *The Feminine Mystique*, 1963, W. W. Norton and Co., New York.
10. Beverly Smith, quoted Jill Clark, "Becoming Visible – Black Lesbian Conference in New York City" (1981) *Off Our Backs* (March), p. 14.

have taught in the course to maintain the course, and ensure its continuing accreditation. And it has taken courage for those who have studied in the course, to acknowledge its importance and to trust in the good sense of themselves and their teachers. Courage is, of course, a quality well known to women. It is a woman's quality, to be encouraged and recognised.

In the years leading up to the achievement of the vote in the United Kingdom, to a young woman discouraged in the battle, another older woman, said: "Trust in God, my dear, she will help you."[11]

Women's Studies has had an important role to play in creating a real trust amongst and between women; in our ability to study together, to appreciate one another's views; in our acknowledgement of the value and achievements of women who have gone before us. We put our trust in them, and in the growing recognition of women of our own time, in achieving changes to curricula and the learning processes which feminists of the past might never have dreamt possible.

To – decades more success for Women's Studies.

---

11. Mrs O. H. P. Belmont, quoted in Doris Stevens, *Jailed for Freedom*, 1920, Boni and Liveright, New York.

18

The Personal is Political:
Power, Autonomy and Peace

ORIGINAL VERSION PRESENTED TO WOMEN FOR PEACE CONFERENCE
Baha'i Peace Exposition, International Year of Peace
5 April 1986, Sydney

More than seven years after "The Personal is Political" was written,[1] *in May and June 1993 the* Age, *a Melbourne morning newspaper, ran a series of articles under the title "The War Against Women". Appearing on a daily basis, the articles covered rape, criminal assault at home and other forms of domestic violence – the whole gamut of violence against women on the street and in the home. The writers dealt also with the inadequacies of the justice system in addressing these crimes. The apparent inability of people in power at all levels of the system, and in all (male dominated) institutions, to acknowledge violence against women as criminal was recorded. Whilst a rape by a stranger may in theory be seen as a crime, this avails women little, when most women are raped by men whom they know. And even if theoretically rape by a stranger is accepted as criminal, when the case comes into the courtroom, lawyers make their living out of turning stranger-rape into consensual sex.*[2]

---

1. "The Personal is Political" was revised for the Geelong Women's Week of Action Against Violence Against Women, and presented on 25 September 1990, and was published in three parts in the *Age Monthly Review*: "The Personal is Political" (August 1986), "Hypocritical Peace" (October 1986) and "Public and Private Silence" (November 1986). In the footnotes, square brackets [...] indicate new material added for this edition.
2. See the examples given in Real Rape Coalition, *No Real Justice*, 1992, Real Rape Coalition, Melbourne, Australia; Jane Lloyd and Nanette Rogers, "Crossing the Last Frontier – Problems Facing Aboriginal Women Victims of Rape in Central Australia" in *Without Consent – Confronting Adult Sexual Violence*, Patricia Easteal (ed.), Australian Institute of Criminology, Canberra, p. 149; Donna Stuart, "No Real Harm Done – Sexual Assault and the Criminal Justice System" in *Without Consent*, Patricia Easteal (ed.), p. 95; Jocelynne A. Scutt, "The Voice of the Rapist", 1993, Paper delivered to the Second National Conference on Violence, 16 June 1993.

The public response to the series was, generally, to accept the truth of the expose – after all, women have known for years that women are too often victims of male violence; and men have known for years that women are victimised and abused by men – after all, a large number of men are engaged in the violence: being responsible for it, they surely must (and do) know they are.

This was not, however, the only response. There was another. It was not new. It was the response of denial or exculpation that has so often arisen when women have spoken out against violence against women. The contortions engaged in to exculpate men from responsibility were, often, risible. The vehemence of the denial was almost overwhelming.

The question of whether or not there is a "war against women" arose at the Second National Conference on Violence, held in Canberra, ACT, from 14–18 June 1993. "There is no war against women," declared some of the speakers. "There is no epidemic of violence against women," they said, meaning that violence against women was not a concern for all women, and that violence by men against women is relatively minor in the grand scale of things; that "epidemic" is a gross exaggeration. It was said, too, that women who march in Reclaim the Night rallies are themselves to blame, effectively, for violence against women: if women weren't in the streets, they wouldn't be targets for victimisation, ran the rationale. Women supporting Reclaim the Night were told, by those who should know better, that to support and promote Reclaim the Night is to encourage women to place themselves in danger! And the demon drink reared its head more than once as a "reason" for male violence against women. The grand exculpation of the bottle is again being erected, although what the teetotaller basher is to make of this it is difficult to see. And equally importantly, what of the woman who is beaten, bashed, raped and abused by a non-drinker husband? Where does his violence, her torment, fit into the equation? If there's no drink, is the bashing, then, her imagination? Or is this violence simply to be ignored as not fitting into the "drink 'n' bash" "theory" that we all thought had been dispensed with years ago?[3]

In response, a number of conference participants published a Statement of Concern, addressing some of these issues and pointing out, amongst other matters:

- *all women have a right to walk safely in any street at any time, anywhere, any place, any how, and Reclaim the Night marches are an appropriate affirmation of this right;*
- *all women have a right to be in their homes without fear of violation;*
- *all men, women and children will benefit if violence can be significantly alleviated and we must all co-operate to achieve this goal;*
- *overwhelmingly the perpetrators of violence against women, children and men are men ...;*
- *it is not accurate to speak of an epidemic of violence against women, only because "epidemic" relates to one given period in time; male violence has been endemic throughout time;*

---

3. See further Chapter 7 this volume, "The Alcoholic Imperative", p. 119.

- *cultural notions of men as being masculine only where they are dominant and aggressive underpins the practice of violence in our society against women, children and men;*
- *abuse of alcohol and situational factors aggravate violence but are not core causal factors of violence;*
- *so long as persons in authority within the justice system continue to exculpate men from the crimes of violence they commit against women and children, those men and their fellows will be supported in their practice of violence;*
- *until the justice system listens to the voices of women and, in particular, survivors of violent crimes perpetrated by men, it will not dispense justice to women or men;*
- *until there is true economic, social and political equality between women and men, violence against women, children and men by men will continue unabated.*[4]

For a few who responded to the Age series, and for some at the Second National Conference on Violence, the "answer" to the problem of violence against women seemed to be to declare "women are violent, too". As the Statement of Concern noted, "women are both recipients of and participants in the dominant culture. A feminist analysis of violence does not preclude acknowledgement that some women are also violent". Nor, indeed, does an acknowledgement that some women are violent answer at all the reality that many men are violent, and that women and children are so often the targets of this violence. How could it?

Another response put forward as, apparently, an answer was: "But I don't bash my wife." "I'm not violent to women ... and none of my friends bash their wives." "None of my friends is violent to women." As if this ends the matter! Women do not have to be beaten, raped and abused to recognise the importance of ending crimes of violence against women, and women work endlessly to do so. Why then do men think they need do nothing, that they have no responsibility, just because they (as they say) do not engage in violence?

No war against women?

When a woman walking home at night hears pounding steps behind her and turns, in that very instant realising that no, he's not intending to run past her. And his left arm circles her upper chest and throat, dragging her back. And his right hand slaps itself right over her face, so that his thumb is digging deep into her right jaw, and his fourth finger is gouging deep into her left jaw. And his whole hand is over her face so she can't breathe and her nose starts bleeding from the force of the blow and blood pours down her chin and she feels the blood dripping onto her hands as she reaches up to drag away his hand and she can't. And she's flung forward into the driveway and falls on her hands and knees and elbow and arm.

---

4. The Statement of Concern is printed in its entirety in Lou Doherty, "Report on Second National Conference on Violence – Canberra June 1993" (1993) *Waratah Magazine* (Winter) 24. Contact persons were Karen Struthers, Director of the Domestic Violence Resource Centre in Brisbane, Queensland and Ron Frey, Lecturer at Queensland University of Technology.

She knows – there's a war against women.

And when she fights back, and she twists and turns and tries to punch him, but what difference do her fists do. And she bites his finger and he gouges at the inside of her cheek and he pulls her tooth right out of her jaw. But she continues fighting. And – she survives.

She knows she's survived a war against women. This time.

When a woman in her bedroom at night is punched in the chest and the stomach and the upper parts of her thighs because, he says, they won't see the bruises that way. And when she's shoved up against the walls and her head pounded against the wainscoting, and he kicks her when she's down. Then he yells at her to get up, and flings her on the bed. And he rapes her.

She knows – there's a war against women.

And when she fights back, by thinking she can reserve some small part inside her for herself that he can't invade. But she can't. He does. So she fights back, by leaving. And survives.

She knows she's survived a war against women. This time.

And when she says all *men must take responsibility, she knows that the man in the street is not every man. And when she says* all *men are responsible, she knows that the man in the bedroom is not every man.*

But she knows, too, sure as hell, that this war against women won't stop – until all *men take action to stop it.*

Yes. There is a war against women.[5]

And in the 1990s, as in 1986, the war against women continues not only on our domesticated streets, in our peacetime homes. The war against women takes place in male battlefields, in civilian cities and towns ravaged by men's wars. An Amnesty International report has listed the atrocities committed in Somalia. In Mogadishu and Baidoa, women are raped by twenty or thirty men; women are bayoneted in the vagina; pregnant women have their stomachs slit open.[6] Women are raped in Bosnia and Herzogovnia. In the most recent conflict, a conservative figure of 20,000 is set as the number of Muslim women who have been raped repeatedly by Croats and Serbs in the Balkans. The women are raped as objects in a deadly game of war played out between generals and other officers who use common men as their weapons, too. The raping of women is a special kind of "ethnic cleansing": if Muslim women are impregnated with the sperm of the dominant ethnic group, then they are "preserved" from the "unclean" sperm of their own countrymen and cultural group.

And it is not only in the theatres of war having prominence on the international news and current affairs networks that women are maltreated, mistreated, used,

---

5. The text commencing "No war against women?" was published as a Letter to the Editor (by the writer), *Age* 19 June 1993.
6. See for example Dorian Wild, "Cry, Somalia" *Ita*, April 1993, p. 17. See also Catharine A. MacKinnon, "Turning Rape into Pornography – Postmodern Genocide", *Ms. Magazine* July/August 1993, p. 24.

abused, raped and killed by men of war. Whether wars involve powers invading from outside, or battles for supremacy in internal jockeying for power, women bear the brunt. And where are the women's voices heard? In the United Nations? Around the war-tables? Around the peace-tables? In the media?

"Anyone here been raped and speak English?"

We keep striving for peace. We know that no war can make peace.

Men fight for – peace? They think war can make a difference. That's the difference.

People see peace as a destination but it is not. It is a way of travelling.

Stella Cornelius[7]

When the women's liberation movement took as its slogan "the personal is political", it was saying in shorthand to the world at large that it is time to give up the fragmented view of reality which has persisted in accordance with dominant views. The women's liberation movement was putting down a statement of the need to cease viewing reality as a jigsaw where the pieces never fit. It demanded that reality be reintegrated; that the world view become one wherein individual lives are seen as part of a whole, instead of being isolated away from general events. It articulated a need to recognise that what happens to each one of us, in our private lives, directly affects and is affected by what happens to all of us in the public sphere. The need is to see that the private lives of citizens are a part of the public world, of the standards set in the public world, and the events occurring "out there".

"The personal is political" has a direct relevance to calls for peace and ecological compassion. Accepting or subscribing to standards of violence, exploitation and abuse in the private world makes a mockery of any calls for peace and environmental care in the public arena. In Australia, the calls for peace and an end to the pillaging of the earth are drowned out, in the ears of those who are open to them, by the cries of women and children who are beaten, abused and raped in their own homes. Demands for peace and environment are drowned in the debasement of everyone living in a world where class and race violence are everyday events.

The violence of war and ravaging of the earth are too often replicated in the personal lives of ordinary, everyday Australians – and those who would not describe themselves as "ordinary" but are, nonetheless, in their acceptance of home-based violence as the norm. And the violence against women and Black Australians, class-based violence and ethnic-based violence experienced on a personal level by many in Australia is replicated on the world stage when international differences are fought out in the wartime arena. Calls for an end to war, for an end to exploitation of the earth, for peace, will

---

7. Stella Cornelius, quoted Deborah Wood, "Tribal Elder of Peace Seeks Security for All" *Australian* 3 April 1986, p. 3.

always be uttered from hypocritical lips and therefore never result in fulfilment, as long as violence on a personal level is not seen as closely aligned with, indeed inseparably a part of, the political violence of war and environmental degradation.

Violence Against Women

Indisputably the major violence taking place the world over is violence exercised against women and girls. This violence takes place on a global scale. Every country is involved. All of our countrymen are involved, so long as they condone that violence by letting it go on.

Since the first feminist refuges and rape crisis centres were set up in 1974 and 1975 in New South Wales and Western Australia, the women's shelter movement has burgeoned, so that around Australia today there are more than 190 women's refuges. But women and children are often turned away from these sanctuaries because the numbers are beyond the level with which the shelters can cope. Long before, women's voices were raised on behalf of women suffering from violence at home. Louisa Lawson at the end of the last century published impassioned pleas against criminal assault at home, furious in her anger at the brutality to which women and children were subjected.[8] Her ire was matched by that of other women, and by the less passionate, but no less felt, calls for changes to divorce laws so that bashed, beaten and abused women could be freed from their brutal mates.

But the violence – and recognition of the violence – does not end there. Rape is common within the family, and more common where the aggressor knows his victim than where he does not. As a crime against daughters, and less often sons, rape and sexual exploitation at home is euphemistically called incest, which implies there are two consenting parties. More realistically, the Women's Movement is now achieving the right to label the event in accordance with the girls' (and boys') reality.[9] The reality is:

- between 90 and 97 per cent of offenders in all cases are male;
- in over 87 per cent of cases, the assaulted is female;
- sexual assault of children is coercive, and often but not always violent; coercion exists within the structural positions of the offender and the assaulted;
- the assaulted suffers emotional trauma; the longer the behaviour has been going on, the deeper the trauma is likely to be;
- incestuous assault, like other forms of violence against women, is steeped in myths about seductiveness, and consequently the blameworthiness, of the assaulted;
- the incidence is grossly underestimated.[10]

---

8. Louisa Lawson spoke out in *The Dawn*, the feminist newspaper she established in the latter part of the nineteenth century and published from Sydney, Australia. [Excerpts from *The Dawn* have now been published in Olive Lawson, *The First Voice of Australian Feminism – Excerpts from Louisa Lawson's The Dawn 1888–1895*, 1990, Simon and Schuster, Brookvale.]
9. See for example Elizabeth (Biff) Ward, *Father Daughter Rape*, 1984, The Women's Press, London.
10. Elizabeth A. Stanko, *Intimate Intrusions – Women's Experience of Male Violence*, 1985, Routledge and Kegan Paul, London, p. 24.

Arising out of the evidence, Strauss has said: "Although there may be exceptions, such as the police or the army in time of war ... the family is the most violent institution, group, or setting that a typical citizen is likely to encounter."[11]

Ironically, the truth is that the army in time of war lives out not a new form of violence, but the old violence learned on the home front.

In the 1970s small groups of women took to the streets to mourn for all women raped in all wars. They chose Anzac Day to do this, in defiance of the bellows of indignation from self-appointed spokesmen who claimed the day was reserved for returned service-persons. The rape of women had nothing to do with war, they proclaimed. The women were not deterred. Each year, on 25 April, women went back out to march. The numbers swelled. The opposition did not cease. Representatives of the Returned Servicepersons League (RSL) attested they were affronted for all service personnel. The notion that home-grown, Aussie soldiers might be implicated in rape of women, any women, was absurd, they claimed. It was a slur on every man who fought for his country. It was a slur on every man who died for his country. The women ought to be ashamed of them-selves and their perfidy, it was said. They were an insult to Anzac Day and to Australia.

The women sought only to have the truth spoken. They wished only that their presence should be seen and their voices heard in mourning for women ignored in remembrances of the dead and injured: "There is no acknowledgement of them in casualty lists."[12]

Women demanded a right to mourn their sisters who not only met death as war spoils, or lived on after rape, but were forgotten by the dominant culture at the same time.

> Lest they forget the countless children
> burned alive in napalm's fire
> Lest they forget the dead civilians lying
> tangled in the wire
> And the faces of the women raped and
> shattered to the core
> It's not only men in uniform who pay the
> price of war.[13]

---

11. Murray Strauss, "Stress and Assault in a National Sample of American Families" in *Colloquium on Stress and Crime*, 1978, National Institute of Law Enforcement and Criminal Justice – MITRE Corporation, Washington DC.

12. Rayner Hoff, sculptor of three female figures supporting on their shoulders a corpse upon a shield, at the Hall of Memory in Sydney's War Memorial, Hyde Park, circa. 1934. [Now that (some) women raped in war are being remembered, and governments are purporting to take some responsibility for the rape, the grand euphemism "comfort women" has been invented. Whose "comfort" was in issue, when women were used and abused as objects to be raped and ravaged by soldiers in wartime, with the imprimatur of governments? Certainly not the comfort of the women, who should rightly be named survivors of rape, survivors of war, survivors of rape-in-war. See Martin Daly and David Porter, "Allies had to protect brothels: academic", *Age* 24 September 1993, p. 7; Martin Daly and Dugald Jellie, "Diggers raped Japanese women: academic", *Age* 23 September 1993, p. 1.]

13. Judy Small, "Lest We Forget" (song).

Class and Race Violence

The violence of war and its depiction in the popular mind as extreme, extraordinary, the result of unusual circumstances, shades the reality of violence in the domestic sphere – on the homeground and in the national arena. Violence against women covers the field: no woman is immune, whatever her race, her class or class origins, her ethnic background. But women and men suffer added burdens of violence and exploitation by reason of class or ethnic background, or race. In Australia, as elsewhere, the major group filling prisons is from the lower socio-economic strata. The violence of prison is simultaneously notorious and hidden.

Violence occurring in prison was graphically recounted by Justice Nagle in the Royal Commission into New South Wales gaols, writing of conditions existing there in the late 1970s:

Until May, 1976 – the Royal Commission's first day of formal hearings was 14th April, 1976 – there can be little doubt about that: "... upon first admission to the gaol, intractable prisoners were the subject of a 'reception biff', which consisted of a physical beating of the prisoner about the back, buttocks, shoulders, legs and arms by two or three officers using rubber batons." These are the words of an admission made by the prison officers serving at Grafton and endorsed by the union – the Public Services Association, Prison Officers' Vocational Branch.

This admission added an account of the routine practised in Grafton Gaol should a prisoner breach any of the Rules either written or unwritten ...[14]

The Royal Commission considered that a "mere reciting" of the admissions "tends to conceal the enormity of the conduct involved". A witness, whose evidence was fully accepted by the Commission, spoke of his arrival at Grafton as a prisoner, and of the Deputy Superintendent explaining to him "the somewhat extraordinary rule that prisoners were not to look prison officers in the face": "Look at the ground. Don't look at us mongrel."

The witness then described to the Commission how, after being ordered to strip, he was seized by the hair and dragged naked into a cell, where he was beaten by a number of officers who:

... did not say anything at all to me during the beatings. They were talking to each other saying such things as: "We'll fix this bastard up ... We'll teach him to hit one of our mates." They hit me about the back, shoulders, buttocks and back of the neck and head. This bashing went on for about five minutes and during this time I remained upright in the corner trying to protect my head and private parts.

---

14. *Report of Royal Commission into NSW Prisons* Vol. 1, Parliament of New South Wales, 1976–1977, 1978, Government Printer, Sydney, pp. 14–15. The immediately following quotations are taken from the same source.

This mechanism for obtaining compliance with the "written and unwritten rules" was described to the Commission by a one-time superintendent at Grafton as "using a little psychology". This meant two or three officers hitting prisoners "... around the buttocks with batons. If they sought to cover or to protect themselves or to retaliate they would get hit on their back or on their legs as well."

Justice Nagle concluded:

The prison officers have claimed that the routine at Grafton was "departmental practice". Although some of their members had taken part in what they now describe as "indefensible conduct", it was said that they were not to blame because they were acting in accordance with the practice under superior orders. The Commission would not wish to under-estimate the difficult circumstances facing ordinary custodial officers in the execution of their duty but such a defence is redolent of other debates concerning more sinister and more notorious happenings ...[15]

Justice Nagle went on to point out that there could be little doubt, from evidence before the Commission, that such practices "had been in vogue in Grafton for at least thirty years". He added, "... brutality practised on prisoners by departmental officers was not confined to Grafton."

These conditions are replicated in prisons around the world, and although it would be preferable to believe they pertained no longer to prisons in New South Wales or to any other Australian prison, evidence of brutality in prisons or in police lock-ups remains available.[16] Stories surface with some frequency in Australian states of violence said to be meted out on people in custody – most often Black Australians.[17] Women – particularly women working as prostitutes – are also at risk, and the violence comes not only from those in authority.[18] It comes from fellow inmates. In the United States, although the Constitution forbids "cruel and unusual punishment", it is reported that the overwhelming majority of judges, attorneys, police officers and gaolers "have long known about the vicious sexual assaults among male as well as female inmates of jails and prisons throughout the country". Writing in the journal *Victimology*, Tom Cahill points out that instead of trying to stop this brutality, "makers and enforcers of

---

15. *Report of the Royal Commission*, note 14, p. 15. The two immediately following quotations come from the same source.
16. Work of the Australian Institute of Criminology and the Human Rights Commission shows a number of these allegations being made in various states. [On 10 December 1986 the Human Rights Commission became the Human Rights and Equal Opportunity Commission, under the *Human Rights and Equal Opportunity Commission Act* 1986 (assented to 6 December 1986).]
17. See for example "Black Died Naturally – Coroner", *Age* 4 April 1986, p. 5. [Subsequent to the writing of this paper, the federal government set up the Royal Commission into Aboriginal Deaths in Custody, as a consequence of longtime agitation and intense lobbying over many years by Aboriginal Australians (and some supporters), so that there could be a (possibility of a) proper enquiry into the inordinate number of deaths of Aboriginal people whilst in custody – whether in police lockups or in gaol.]
18. See generally *Report of the Inquiry into Prostitution in Victoria* 1985, Government Printer, Melbourne. Information also received in personal communication from the St Kilda Legal Service, St Kilda, Victoria, Australia.

the law have consistently turned a deaf ear to inmate rape". Loretta Tofani of the *Washington Post*, who won the Pulitzer Prize in April 1983 for her series exposing rape and violence in the American prison system, reported one judge as saying "you shut your mind to it".[19]

Sexual violence is not confined to United States prisons. In New South Wales in 1978 a series of vicious gang and individual rapes in New South Wales prisons gained the headlines for a short time. Over the years, stories continue to be related by those involved in prison activism, fighting for the rights of the imprisoned not to be raped by fellow inmates. In Victoria in mid-1986 similar tales reached the public through the news media. Dormitory living arrangements were scheduled to be replaced by individual accommodation as a result of this exposé.[20]

Yet the irony for women (who may be raped or sexually harassed in prison also) is that women live in a world where rape and sexual harassment are everyday events. Women do not have to go to prison to be bashed, abused and sexually assaulted. For too many, this exploitation and brutalisation occurs too often in their own homes. In their own homes, there are "written and unwritten" rules; failure to conform with the rules results in violence inflicted upon them, not infrequently of the magnitude meted out on the men in Grafton prison and other gaols. Unwritten rules consist of "opening the cornflakes packet from the wrong end" (what is the "right" end?); "squeezing the toothpaste tube from the middle"; not cooking to the satisfaction of "the master of the house". "I felt like a slave in prison", wrote one woman of her thirteen years of intolerable violence, abuse and damaging psychological battering.[21]

The violence is not always overt. It takes more subtle or psychological forms, as described by Elizabeth Williams, Koori activist, who experienced the negative effects of racism in a New South Wales country town:

In December 1981 I was appointed by the Minister for Health as director on the Queanbeyan Hospital Board. My experience in community work and being Aboriginal helped. The following

---

19. Quoted Tom Cahill, "Cruel and Unusual Punishment – Rape in Prison" (1984) 9 (1) *Victimology* 8.
20. Press Release, Attorney-General of Victoria, Melbourne, Australia, July 1986. [In 1993 it was mooted that Fairlea, the women's prison in Victoria, be closed and prisoners transferred to Pentridge Prison. The proposal was that women should be held in Jika Jika, the top security wing of the prison. Its equivalent in New South Wales (Katingal) had been called an "electronic zoo" when it was closed in the 1980s. Women from Fairlea lodged a complaint with the Commissioner for Equal Opportunity, Moira Rayner, detailing sex discrimination in the decision. Two of the matters raised were that the majority of women in prison "are survivors of various forms of abuse, i.e. domestic violence, incest, sexual assault from men, and being placed in a male prison would be detrimental to their recovery" and "women in male prisons are more exposed to incidents of sexual and verbal harassment": Exhibit MB1 in the matter of *Michelle Bonello v. State of Victoria/Department of Justice, Victoria, Correctional Services Division*, July 1993, in the Equal Opportunity Board, Melbourne, Victoria; see also *Draft Proposal to Relocate Women Prisoners from Fairlea and Barwon to Metropolitan Reception Prison*, developed by the Policy Implementation Committee for Women in Corrections, July 1993, Victorian Government.]
21. See Jocelynne A. Scutt, *Even in the Best of Homes – Violence in the Family*, 1983, Penguin Books Australia, Ringwood. [Reprinted with updated chapter, 1990, McCulloch Publishing, Carlton.]

year, in December, I was nominated as chairperson by two other women directors, and was elected by majority. I had no idea of the flak in store for me. My election upset a few people – some on the board. At that December meeting tension was high. I was stunned. This was the first time I had experienced such strong feelings against me ... People I thought would be happy with my new appointment now presented a complete turn about. Some showed outright rudeness, ignoring me. Some were disgusted I would even consider myself capable of performing the duties of chairperson. Others urged me to resign. To avoid further abuse I found myself walking the back streets and staying home. Just when I thought calm had arrived, I received a letter from my predecessor. My first reaction on reading it was shock. I read it many times before the words sank in. Before the letter arrived, I was under tremendous pressure to resign. Now I was angry. This man has such a nerve to send me what was an awful letter. Little did he realise his words would have the opposite effect of what he intended. I would now do the job and do it well, in fact better than any of my white male predecessors ...[22]

Violence of War

During wartime, race, sex and class violence are meted out on a grand scale, although that grand scale does not begin to match the violence meted out along sex, race and class lines the world over. During the war in Viet Nam, women were raped and beaten and killed as "kikes" or "goons", words depicting them as less than human. Chris Domingo writes:

> an ex-marine
> who had been to
> Vietnam
> raped me.
> He saw
> my small
> dark female body
> in the woods.
> He had learned to rape.
> He had learned to kill.
> He pointed his
> rifle
> at my head
> He had learned this
> somewhere
> maybe
> on tv.
>
> Maybe
> over there
> in a country

---

22. Elizabeth Williams, "Aboriginal First, Woman Second" in *Different Lives – Reflections on the Women's Movement and Visions of Its Future*, Jocelynne A. Scutt (ed.), 1987, Penguin Books Australia, Ringwood, p.70.

of small dark
people.
He had learned to rape.
He had learned to kill.

At a slide show
about violent pornography
i see the photographs
that some men use
to ejaculate by.
Among the slides
of nude wimmin
bound by ropes,
in a meat grinder,
misrepresented, degraded,
demeaned
in various ways
was an actual photo
from Vietnam
of a small dark
womin's
dead body
under a tree,
taken from a series
of such photos
in a popular porn magazine.
i affirmed aloud
THAT COULD
HAVE BEEN ME.[23]

But where did he learn it? The violence of bashing, raping, killing; the violence against women, against those of another race, or another class: in Viet Nam, at war, or at home – in so-called peace?

To be trained for war, men learn domination, control, and violence. Or they build on the learning that has already been done through socialisation in the broader world. To learn to kill, one must learn to despise the killed, to debase them as a group, to downgrade them from human beings to less than human. Violence is an issue for the military not only on the battle field, but in their own homes. Lillian Tetzlaff, a trained psychological counsellor and wife of an American airforce officer, tells of the reception she received from the "powers-that-be" on a United States airforce base in England, when she sought to find out simply whether there was a sufficiently high incidence of wife-battering to justify a shelter on the base:

---

23. Published in *Anzac Day – Thinking About the Future – A Forum for Women*, papers from a Forum for Women, 25 August 1984, YWCA, Melbourne, p. 11.

I had hoped to present the problems, then get some sort of figures so far as the numbers of women [the chaplain] might be seeing each month, compile them with those figures of other organisations on base, such as medical, Security Police, etc. I was hoping to present those figures along with other emerging evidence, to the Wing Commander, thereby convincing him of the base's need for a shelter ... A Chief Master Sergeant informed me most emphatically that if the military wanted the men to have a wife, it would issue them one. In the meantime, the military was an instrument for fighting wars, and a wife's role – if any – was incidental only ... I think that the most ignorant and unenlightened person I have encountered has been the Fundamentalist military chaplain. He was one of the first persons I approached about setting up a shelter, and I think that he hit me the hardest ... He pointed out that "after all, this is the way that some couples communicate with each other. They simply batter as a sign of affection ..."
... The women's group that I spoke with were unusually warm and responsive, often coming forward and offering their help and support. Mainly, the argument against having a shelter at Mildenhall (the USAF base) is that there is one at Lakenheath (five miles from the base) ... but the one at Lakenheath is very small ... and therefore often filled, especially at weekends ... Also when a woman is running for her life ... dragging small children with her, five miles is a long way to run, especially in the middle of the night ... I am about to give up.[24]

A lack of violence, covert or overt, does not exist for many during the time governments label "peace". "Peace" has little real meaning during so-called peacetime, at least for those who are downtrodden, oppressed or demeaned by those in dominant positions – who in Australia are, in the main, white, middle-class, anglo-Australian men.

"Peace" can be positively frightening during war, although its currency is debased in "peace" time too. In the United States during the war in Viet Nam, Seymour Hirsch writes of differences between Secretary of State Kissinger and President Nixon on the value of preaching peace. In 1979 a deal was arranged between Hanoi and Washington, Kissinger officiating, which was described as a "truce". Kissinger leaked the news to the media, having "his version of the peace treaty splashed all over the *New York Times'* front page".[25] One of the aims was apparently to "neutralise" George McGovern, Nixon's opposing candidate for presidency. On learning of the leak:

Nixon was so mad his teeth clenched ... He was furious. The President complained later ... that I suppose now everybody's going to say that Kissinger won the election. The men at the top in the White House ... were ... bickering over who would get the credit ...

Later, however, Nixon consulted with the pollsters: where did peace stand in the popularity stakes? When Kissinger announced "Peace is at hand", the Republican pollsters were furious. One said:

---

24. Lillian Tetzlaff, in correspondence, October 1982, quoted Cynthia Enloe, *Does Khaki Become You? – The Militarisation of Women's Lives*, 1983, Pluto Press, London, pp. 88–89.
25. Seymour M. Hersh, *Kissinger – The Price of Power – Henry Kissinger in the Nixon White House*, 1983, Summit Books/Simon and Schuster, New York, pp. 605–606. The immediately following quotations are from the same source.

You've just elected McGovern. My God. There are seventeen million Democrats who will vote for Nixon because he's tough and a crook. All the polls have Nixon so far ahead that these fellows will now vote straight Democratic.

The view was, "You've made a mistake talking peace. You've lost the election." An hour later, reports Hirsch, Nixon telephoned to ask his pollsters, "What would be the public reaction if we bombed Hanoi?" The pollsters agreed to research the issue.

The Dominance of Silence

Writing in 1978 in *A World of Men: The Private Sources of American Foreign Policy*, Lloyd S. Etheridge says:

That international politics is a "world of men" is a central and probably consequential fact; one that may illuminate the underlying sexual dynamics, and one that is important to the strength, power, activity, dominance, competitive achievement: such qualities make them more fearful to others and more predisposed to unleash violence.[26]

He questions whether hope for cessation of hostilities and international warring "is a realistic stance":

Men may have the capacity to be rational, generous, and mutually cooperative, but as we face a world in which nuclear weapons and conventional armaments proliferate, it is sobering to know that the world in which they proliferate is a world of men.

Unfortunately, that world of men rules the world of women. When that world destroys itself, it destroys the world of women too: even separatists cannot escape the consequences of man-made war.

As long as those ruling the world continue to ignore the violence endemic in the everyday lives of the ruled, and as long as those in power see "peace" and environment as narrow political issues to be used for personal political gain, peace and a cared-for and caring environment will never be "at hand". Rather, the hypocrisy that currently goes for "peace" and ecological concern will continue. And in its continuing, women will continue to be raped, bashed and beaten by those whom they (thought they) loved and who (they thought) loved them. Those of minority racial and ethnic background will continue to be scorned, attacked, verbally demeaned by the bully boys. The state will continue to imprison, in intolerable conditions of violence and despair, women who defraud social security in order to feed themselves and their children, or who "go on the game" of prostitution for the same purpose. And men who grow up in a violent milieu, being taught to believe that their only design for living is a replication of the

---

26. Quoted Brian Easlea, *Fathering the Unthinkable – Masculinity, Scientists and the Nuclear Arms Race*, 1983, Pluto Press, London. The immediately following quotation comes from the same source.

violence meted out against them by an unfriendly world, will continue to fill prisons and police lock-ups. For these men, their problem (in dominant-ethic terms) is that they are unable to exploit and abuse their physical strength or brains in "respectable" middle-class ways – such as engaging in extortionary activity on the stock exchange and the ultimately debilitating competition so often applauded in the financial pages of newspapers by pundits who should know better.

Where the violence of men's world has penetrated the world of women, women have been trained to be silent about it. And where women have been permitted to enter into the violent world of men, women have similarly been frightened into maintaining that same silence. Cynthia Enloe talks of the militarisation of women's lives, noting that the armed forces "get nervous" when nurses start telling their stories of wartime, because "they reveal so much about the nature of the war itself". In *Does Khaki Become You?* Enloe points out that it is not only the military gender structure that is protected by the silence of military nurses, but "the basic legitimacy of the military as a pillar of civilised society is being protected ..." A nurse who talks of war as seen from a military hospital or a Mobile Army Surgical Hospital (MASH) unit is, writes Cynthia Enloe, "a dangerous woman".[27]

And where women are raped, or children are sexually abused and exploited, they are ordered by their attackers to maintain silence. The fear of shame and humiliation, or guilt that they are "responsible" for the attack, "wanted" it, or "led him on", compounds this silencing. Where they do speak out, women's voices, women's truths, are barely listened to, or are dismissed as fiction, sham or bitter lies.

But men too maintain the silence. Writing in *The Sexuality of Men*, a contributor recalls a discussion amongst a group of men who had begun to think about their need to reassess their dominant attitudes:

One of us distributed copies of an article from the American radical journal *Mother Jones*, which reported the story of the rape and mutilation of Mary Bell Jones, a teenage girl attacked while hitch-hiking in California. We didn't know how to begin talking about it and found ourselves avoiding each other's eyes. When our reactions came they varied from "I can't bear to read this", and "we cannot be expected to take responsibility for these atrocities simply because we are men", to "we have to accept that at the bottom this is what men are about." It soon became clear that any notion of responsibility was meaningless unless we started from our own violence and our experiences both as perpetrators and victims, as a way to some understanding of how men acquire such a capacity for brutality. We found it was essential to develop a political analysis which looked toward possibilities for change, and a concept of personal responsibility not based on guilt but on positive challenge to destructive aspects of masculinity.[28]

One can start such a challenge, he writes, by asking what lies behind men's silence.

Men's violence has been meted out against women while a vast silence prevails.

27. Cynthia Enloe, note 14, p. 113.
28. Tony Eardley, "Violence and Sexuality" in *The Sexuality of Men*, Andy Metcalfe and Martin Humphries (eds.), 1985, Pluto Press, London, p. 88.

Where women have spoken out, our voices have often been swamped in that male silence. Men have been silent too about class and race violence, or speak out in numbers which falter against the silences of many.

Rightly it is said that it is doubtful whether the power to demand or force sexual services from women "has led to any widespread sexual satisfaction or happiness amongst men".[29] Similarly it is doubtful whether the power to demand or force services from black men or women, or others racially or ethnically in the minority, has led to any widespread satisfaction or happiness amongst those who perpetrate the oppression. Yet the silences about this violence remain. But within the peace movement, if the full force of the demand for peace is to be maintained and realised, it would be well for all within it to end the silences about this violence which is endemic in our society and which founds the very nature of war. That so-called personal violence is inseparable from the violence of war. Without concern for the environment of the hearth, there can be no concern at all. Without peace on the home front, there can be no peace at all.

Power, Autonomy and Peace

There is another vision of the world, a vision that can be reached if the personal is recognised as political and the political in turn acknowledged as personal responsibility and trust. What is needed to make peace a reality, to put an end to the earth's ravishment, an end to all war, is a recognition of what goes on in our own lives as crucial to the question of what goes on in the world. Our lives are a part of the world. Women have recognised that truth, probably for millennia, sometimes in greater numbers, sometimes in less. Talking about women's position, in *The Powers of the Weak*, Elizabeth Janeway has said:

... the timing isn't up to them, it's up to us. We can affect the lives we lead in major, public ways. The problems that have marched into woman's place and upset our lives are overall human disruptions, and we know more about them than anyone else in the world. We know we need a new map and a new, adjusted society to match it; and each will influence the other. We can never forget the obscure half of existence, the emotional female sphere, and so we shall not be caught in the foolishness of trying to solve difficulties without reference to the questions – the future of the family, gender identities, building communities, creating new urban settings, adolescent violence, exploitive pornography, and all the too-familiar topics for high-level, one week conferences – it will never deceive us. If you live with such crises you grow expert in telling lip-service from constructive efforts at change.

Distrust, the first power of the weak, is already ours ...[30]

---

29. Tony Eardley, note 28, p. 89.
30. Elizabeth Janeway, *Powers of the Weak*, 1980, Alfred A. Knopf, New York, p. 318. The immediately following quotation comes from the same source, p. 292.

To talk about distrust, as if it is positive, is frightening at first. We have been taught that trust is one of the most important emotions we can express. And we are right, but the pity is we have been taught to trust those who have no right to our trust, those whom we should distrust. The potential for peace is subverted for as long as we trust those who are in positions of power, who abuse the power and move us so surely down the road to disaster, their "little" violences strewing the way. We must learn to think more clearly about the value of our emotions and refuse to debase them as we are expected to do. Thus will it become more easy for us to progress toward autonomy and peace. This takes courage:

There is a kind of courage that's very familiar to the weak; endurance, patience, stamina, the ability to repeat everyday tasks every day, these are the forms of courage that have allowed generations of the governed to survive without losing ultimate hope. The knowledge of one's own vulnerability, the choice of restraint in the face of provocation, the ability to hear oneself described as unworthy without accepting the stigma as final – that takes courage of a high order. We do not want to lose it, for it's still a source of strength when the time comes to be patient no longer, when direct confrontation with the powerful for independent aims must be risked if not sought.

Many people may be driven to say: why raise issues of violence on the homeground, when nuclear war and depletion of the ozone layer stare us in the face? In response I say, so long as violence in our everyday lives goes unchecked, unremarked, left alone or ignored, then repeating "peace" and environment as a litany will never prevent any expression of war, whether national or international, "contained" or of holocaust proportions. The status of women is crucial to the way what we say, and what we demand, is perceived. So long as women's claims are denied *because we are women*, our status *as* women is used against us. Our standing is valued less than the standing of men. Race, class and ethnic discrimination play an important role, too, in depriving many women of full status. Our determination to have women recognised as human is central to the claims we make for all women. Not being recognised as fully human means that those great male silences will never be penetrated. Women's power to refuse to accept a downgrading of our opinions, our rights, our demands, is the beginning of a fundamental change in the way we are seen and the way the world operates. We need the courage to continue to speak out loudly again and again against violence and aggression in whatever form it takes. The importance of any peace and environmental movement is its recognition of the value of working for peace at various levels. It is also its recognition that isolating forms of violence is precisely what is needed to de-politicise and downgrade the origins of violence as a way of life. Peace too has its origins in a way of life:

Peace is not a destination. It's a way of travelling.

List of Abbreviations of Law Reports and Law Journals

A. Atlantic Reporter

Ala Alabama Reporter

ALJ Australian Law Journal

ALJR Australian Law Journal Reports

All ER All England Reports

Am. Jrn. Crim. Law American Journal of Criminal Law

Ariz. Arizona Reporter

ATC Australian Tax Cases

Brit. Jrn Criminol. or *Brit. Jrn Criminology* British Journal of Criminology

CAR Conciliation and Arbitration Reports

Car. & P. Carrington and Payne (see also reprints in ER)

CLR Commonwealth Law Reports

Columbia Law Review University of Columbia Law Review

Co. Rep. Cook Reports (see also reprints in ER)

Cox CC Cox Criminal Cases (see also reprints in ER)

Cr. App. R. Criminal Appeal Reports

Crim. Justice and Behavior Journal of Criminal Justice and Behavior

Crim. Law Bulletin Criminal Law Bulletin

Crim. Law Quart. Criminal Law Quarterly

Dowl Dowling (see also reprints in ER)

ER English Reports

F. & F. Foster and Finlayson (see also reprints in ER)

F. Supp. Federal Supplement (USA reporter)

Iowa Iowa Reporter

JP Justice of the Peace Reports

Keb. Keble (see also reprints in ER)

KB Kings Bench Reports

K&J Kay and Johnson (see also reprints in ER

LJ Law Journal Reports

LR (NSW) Law Reports (New South Wales)

LT Law Times Reports

McPherson McPherson Reports (see also reprints in ER)

Min. Law Rev. Minnesota University Law Review

Mon. Law Review Monash University Law Review

NW North Western Reporter

NY New York Reporter

P. Pacific Reporter

QB Queens Bench Reports

QCR Queensland Criminal Reports

Qd R Queensland Reports

QSR Queensland State Reports

SASR South Australian State Reports

SCR (NSW) State Criminal Reports (New South Wales)

So. Southern Reporter

Stanford Law Review or *Stan. Law Review* Stanford University Law Review

State Tr. State Trials Reports

Stra. Strange (see also reprints in ER)

Tas. SR Tasmanian State Reports

TLR Times Law Reports

UNSWLJ University of New South Wales Law Journal

US United States Reporter

UWA Law Rev. University of Western Australia Law Review

VLR Victorian Law Reports

WAR Western Australian Reports

Wis. Law Review Wisconsin University Law Review

Yale Law Journal Yale University Law Journal

Index

7